Perilous Commitments

The Battle for Greece and Crete
1940–1941

PERILOUS COMMITMENTS

THE BATTLE FOR GREECE AND CRETE 1940–1941

by

Matthew Willingham

SPELLMOUNT
Staplehurst

British Library Cataloguing in Publication Data:
A catalogue record for this book is available
from the British Library

Copyright © Matthew Willingham 2005
Maps © Matthew Willingham 2005
All photographs in plate section © War History Collection,
Alexander Turnbull Library, Wellington, New Zealand

ISBN 1-86227-236-0

First published in Great Britain in 2005
by
Spellmount Limited
The Village Centre
Staplehurst
Kent TN12 0BJ

Tel: 01580 893730
Fax: 01580 893731
E-mail: enquiries@spellmount.com
Website: www.spellmount.com

1 3 5 7 9 8 6 4 2

The right of Matthew Willingham to be identified
as the author of this work has been asserted by him
in accordance with the Copyright, Designs
and Patents Act 1988

Typeset in Palatino by MATS, Southend-on-Sea, Essex
Printed in Great Britain by
T.J. International Ltd
Padstow, Cornwall

Contents

List of Maps

Preface

The conflicts in Greece and Crete during the Second World War are inexorably linked; both events are equally significant for differing reasons. The Battle of Crete has attracted many writers, which has understandably drawn the limelight away from Greece. The conflict in Crete was a dynamic and fiercely contested battle that captured the imagination of the world. Crete heralded the first operational use of ULTRA signals intelligence by the British, and produced the first airborne invasion the world had witnessed. Contrastingly the conflict in Greece was dominated by politics and diplomacy.

In 1940 Greece resisted the Axis powers at a time when Hitler looked to achieve complete domination of Europe and the British war effort was stretched to breaking point. Britain's unlikely collaborator placed Churchill in an intriguing dilemma; would he stand by and allow yet another small ally to be overwhelmed? Or could the British military afford the loss of further precious resources in a campaign doomed to failure? What followed was a classic example of military considerations being sacrificed for political gain, a subject matter which is just as pertinent in contemporary world politics. The decision to send a British expeditionary force to Greece soon provoked an inevitable response from Germany. In just three weeks German forces drove Britain and her allies from the Greek mainland to the island of Crete where they would make a courageous stand against elite German paratroops. It is the aim of this book to provide a comprehensive evaluation of events leading to the conflict in Greece and a vivid account of the subsequent battle for Crete.

This work has drawn on many published works, but owes a great debt to the New Zealand National Library. Thank you to the Oral History Centre in the Alexander Turnbull Library and the British Library for allowing me access to superb oral history interviews; thanks also to the Nathan family for permission to use Ned Nathan's account. I am especially grateful to Megan Hutching and her team who have assisted me greatly. I would like to thank my family for tolerating and supporting me throughout the research and writing. Special thanks go to my Mother and

Father; my Brother Andrew, who drafted the maps and my Grandfather, George, a veteran of the battle for Crete, who provided inspiration along with a good single malt.

Matthew Willingham
April 2005

PART ONE

The Greek Decision

I am not protesting against the conduct of the war, but against the political errors and insincerities for which the fighting men are being sacrificed.

Siegfried Sassoon
July 1917

CHAPTER I
Perilous Commitments

On 19 April 1939, before the outbreak of the Second World War, Britain gave a guarantee to uphold the independence of Greece in the event of war. This led to Britain's involvement in an ill-fated campaign in Greece and one of the bloodiest, most innovative, battles of the Second World War in Crete.

During the late 1930s, Britain faced the unviable prospect of withstanding hostility from three different areas: Germany, Japan and Italy. The British government were aware of the Nazis' aggressive intentions, but they lagged way behind Germany in the arms race, and therefore found it impossible to restrain Hitler. Lack of resources meant that diplomacy, rather than military intervention, was key to the fortunes of Britain and the security of Europe. Via a policy of 'collective security', Britain issued various guarantees to countries threatened by Germany, which implied an open-ended commitment, the like of which Britain had shown reluctance to become involved in – most notably in 1938 when Germany invaded Czechoslovakia.

Despite accurate intelligence reports from MI6, Britain's Prime Minister, Neville Chamberlain, was taken by surprise by the German invasion of Czechoslovakia. Chamberlain's initial reaction was to play down the significance of the event, as Britain had no intention of honouring the guarantee they had given to Prague. Following the German invasion, Hitler ordered the Slovak Prime Minister to declare Slovakia independent from the Czech state. This gave Chamberlain a pretext for breaking his pledge to Czechoslovakia on the grounds that the country no longer existed. When addressing the Commons on the matter, Chamberlain merely stated that Czechoslovakia had become 'disintegrated'.[1]

With Romania and Poland coming under threat, Chamberlain realised that he would have to seek support from Balkan and eastern European countries if further German aggression was to be resisted. In March 1939 Britain sought to guarantee the independence of Poland against German aggression in the hope that Hitler might rethink a strike against them. The guarantee was intended to give Britain leverage in forcing Poland to come to terms with Hitler and his claim to Danzig and the Polish Corridor.

Britain's commitment to Poland was carefully worded to guarantee her independence but not her borders; therefore redrawing the boundary in Germany's favour would not trigger British action. As *The Times* noted, a nice distinction was maintained between 'territorial integrity' and independence.[2] Chamberlain aimed to satisfy Hitler's demands for Danzig without forcing a wider European war; only if Germany occupied Poland would Britain be obliged to declare war on the Poles' behalf. Reinstated to his old post of First Lord of the Admiralty, Winston Churchill had observed Chamberlain's diplomacy with apprehension. Churchill warned that Britain risked becoming a pawn of the German Führer unless: 'by a supreme recovery of moral health and martial vigour, we arise again and take our stand for freedom as in the olden time'.[3] Germany's subsequent invasion of Poland made a mockery of Chamberlain's policy and the British government had little option but to go to war with Germany.

Against this background of diplomacy based on Realpolitik,[4] the British guarantee of independence to Greece evolved into the most controversial commitment offered by the Chamberlain administration. To fully appreciate the Greek debacle it is important to explain its inception, which was born from the relationship between fascist dictators, Mussolini and Hitler, and also the bravery of the Greek people.

The Tripartite Pact was formed in September 1940, and was a powerful alliance consisting of Germany, Italy and Japan. While Britain sought alliances strong enough to challenge Germany, Hitler was confident that by applying diplomatic pressure on the weaker powers of central and south-eastern Europe, he could coerce them to adhere to the Tripartite Pact. Hitler hoped that by rallying Spain, France and the Balkan states, he could present a united Europe to the world. If peace under German hegemony was achieved, Hitler could portray Britain as a warmonger whose obstinate resistance kept Europe at war. Despite his vision of a united Europe, Hitler's partner in the Rome–Berlin Axis was to shatter the idea of a short-lived war. Desperate to leave his mark on the war, the Italian leader, Mussolini, or Il Duce as he was increasingly known, pro-ceeded to embark on a disastrous campaign against Greece that proved the catalyst for British and German intervention in the area. Mussolini's exploits would break the illusion of a 'continent at peace' and expose Italy as the weak link of the Axis.

The invasion of Greece by Italy in October 1940 was essentially the culmination of Mussolini's ego and frustrated aspirations of Italian grandeur. When the Duce rose to power in 1922 he had no clear foreign policy, his intention was simply to make Italy 'respected and feared'.[5] Britain's control of the Mediterranean and the French African Empire made Mussolini intensely jealous, a trait that would reappear and cloud his ability to act rationally. Like Hitler, Mussolini condemned the peace

4

settlement at the conclusion of the First World War. Despite having fought alongside the Allies, Italy felt aggrieved that Britain and France had monopolised the spoils of the Central Powers' defeat. Germany, the principal defeated nation, naturally resented the territorial losses and reparations imposed by the Treaty of Versailles. Italy, one of the victors, found its territorial gains derisory, insufficient either to offset the cost of the war or to satisfy its ambition. Mussolini considered it a great injustice that France and Great Britain could increase their colonisation, while Italy received only minor gains for her sacrifice.

After the First World War it was clear that any actions of a resurgent Italy would have to be sanctioned by Britain and France. The Duce proceeded to put constant diplomatic pressure on the dominant powers to test where they would yield. Thus Italian foreign policy under Mussolini was erratic, alternating between aggression and conciliation where it suited. The first instance of aggression against Greece came in August 1923, when an international commission was setting the frontier between Greece and Albania. While on Greek soil the chief Italian delegate was murdered along with four members of his staff. Quick to seize the initiative, Mussolini held the Greek government responsible for their deaths and demanded 50 million lire compensation with an official apology. When the Greeks refused, Mussolini ordered the naval bombardment of Corfu, which was swiftly followed by its occupation, clearly his original intention. After pressure from the League of Nations, and Britain in particular, Italy was forced to withdraw on 27 September. The Greeks paid the 50 million lire compensation, albeit without an official apology. The Duce had revealed his insatiable appetite for swift glory that could be cheaply bought. Mussolini had learned an important lesson about frontier incidents, which was to be applied again in 1940. Greece had experienced what it meant to be small and without allies in the postwar period.

Italy recovered her respectability in Europe by signing the Locarno Pact along with Britain and France. In July 1934 Mussolini gained further esteem from Britain for his tough stance against Germany who threatened an armed annexation (*Anschluss*) of Austria. After Nazi operatives assassinated the Austrian chancellor, Englebert Dollfus, Mussolini dispatched Italian troops to the Austrian border. Despite standing alone against Germany, Mussolini secured Austria's independence and thwarted Hitler's aggressive intentions. Success in Austria served to bolster the prestige and diplomatic importance of Italy among the European powers, which in turn fuelled Mussolini's desire to realise his dream of a new Roman Empire. Britain viewed Italy as a pivotal ally and an important factor in restraining Hitler. After the incident in Austria, an alliance between Germany and Italy seemed unlikely. Mussolini had described Hitler as 'muddle headed', and after the Dollfus assassination called him a 'horrible sexual degenerate'.[6] Relations deteriorated further after Mussolini joined the Stressa Front with Britain and France, which condemned German rearmament.

The amiable relationship between Mussolini and Britain did not last, and praise for Italy was promptly replaced by an international embargo. The isolation of Italy began with the invasion and annexation of Abyssinia (modern day Ethiopia), which again illustrated Mussolini's desire for expansion. Plans for the conquest of Abyssinia had long been under way when Mussolini used a convenient incident on the Somaliland frontier for the pretext of an invasion of Abyssinia. On 3 October 1935 Marshal Rodolfo Graziani and the newly mechanised Italian forces swept across the Abyssinian border from Italian Somaliland and Eritrea. Despite being a slave-trading autocracy, Abyssinia was a member of the League of Nations, therefore she was entitled to the protection of fellow members. This gave the British government a major dilemma. Britain was forced to make a moral judgement either to uphold the principles of international law and lose a potential ally in restraining Hitler, or side with Mussolini and discredit the League of Nations.

Mussolini's invasion of Abyssinia culminated in the ill-fated Hoare-Laval Pact of December 1935, in which Britain and France advocated a settlement that conceded a substantial part of Abyssinia to Italy. The pact was retracted after a public outcry, but the incident revealed that Britain and France were desperate to avoid making fascist Italy an enemy. 'These men are not made of the same stuff as the Francis Drakes,' concluded Mussolini of Chamberlain and his colleagues: 'these are the tired sons of a long line of rich men and they will lose their Empire.'[7] Dynamic and contemptuous of material comforts, Mussolini found he had more in common with Germany's nationalist dictatorship than with corrupt, antiquated parliamentary democracies. From 1936 Mussolini was more inclined to look upon Germany as a potential ally. Chamberlain's strenuous attempts to appease the Duce only served to fortify Mussolini's opinion. Mussolini's perception of Britain had been made popular in 1933 when undergraduates at the Oxford Union famously stated that under no circumstances would they fight for 'King and country'.[8]

The invasion of Abyssinia and Italian support for fascists in the Spanish Civil War (1936–9) blacklisted Italy from the western powers and the League of Nations, which forced a closer relationship with Nazi Germany. Mussolini's Spanish venture demonstrated conclusively the expansionist direction of his foreign policy. The Duce had realised that the League of Nations did not have the backbone to stop Italy or Germany. Mussolini described the newly formed alliance between Rome and Berlin as an Axis, around which all other European countries would revolve. The Rome–Berlin Axis was further strengthened in 1937, when Italy joined Germany and Japan in the Anti-Comintern pact. Despite strong relations between

Mussolini and Hitler, the German leader would soon dominate the Axis.

Mussolini saw his standing with Hitler diminish in the late 1930s; after a visit to Germany in 1937, the Duce was said to have been in awe of German military strength. Hitler's domineering persona was in evidence in 1938 when Mussolini reversed his original support for Austria, and endorsed a German invasion to 'restore order'. Despite Mussolini's support, Hitler proceeded to carry out the operation without consulting the Duce. Although the lack of consultation appeared an impertinent act, the annexation of Austria only served to bolster Mussolini's respect for Nazi dynamism. The invasion of Austria signalled the beginning of Hitler forcing the pace between the two dictators. At the Munich Conference in October 1938, Mussolini attempted to pose as the arbiter of Europe, but he was visibly a peripheral figure. Germany's annexation of Austria was followed by the destruction of Czechoslovakia and the success of Hitler's aggressive foreign policy motivated Mussolini into a blatant act of emulation.

In February 1939 the Italian dictator made his most candid analysis of his foreign policy before his Grand Council. Mussolini described Italy as a semi-independent state; he believed that Italy's path to the ocean through the Suez Canal could be easily blocked and the Gibraltar Straits were: 'dominated by the cannons of Great Britain'. Mussolini went on to say: 'Greece, Turkey, Egypt have been ready to form a chain with Great Britain and to complete the politico-military encirclement of Italy.'[9] Despite draining campaigns in Africa and Spain, detailed plans were drawn up to invade, and formally annex Albania. Mussolini used past debts to justify the annexation and sent his foreign minister, Count Ciano, to present a list of impossible demands to the Albanian king. Predictably the demands could not be met and two divisions of Italian troops invaded. Albanian resistance was weak and sporadic; by 16 April the Italian King Victor Emmanuel III united the crown of Albania to that of Italy and the Abyssinian Empire.

After Italy annexed Albania, it was widely believed that Greece would be her next target. There were already Italian bases in the vicinity with installations on the Dodecanese Islands, and the Greeks were well aware that Italy would soon install bases in Albania. Churchill was furious that Britain had failed to constrain Italian aggression. Harold Macmillan recalled in his memoirs that, while lunching at Chartwell, Churchill had sought the whereabouts of the British fleet, and after a vigorous investigation, he was furious to find the fleet scattered throughout the Mediterranean. Churchill stated that the British fleet should have prevented 'the rape of Albania'. On 9 April 1939 Churchill wrote to Chamberlain stating: 'Hours now count . . . to recover the initiative in diplomacy'.[10] He went on to suggest the immediate British Naval occupation of the Greek island of Corfu.[11] Churchill stressed that if Corfu was not taken by Britain, Italy would capture the island and would make its recapture impossible. He also stated that if Britain reached Crete and Corfu first, it would confront Mussolini with the prospect of beginning a war of aggression with England.

Italy's resources had been ravaged by the campaigns in Africa and the Spanish Civil War and they were not adequately prepared for war. Churchill explained that early action against Mussolini's ambitions in Greece would give the 'best chance' to 'forces in Italy that are opposed to war with England.'[12] Churchill furthered this argument stating: if Greece continued to be: 'exposed to German and Italian pressure' while Britain appeared 'incapable of action' they would be forced to 'make the best possible terms with Berlin and Rome. How forlorn then will our position become!'[13] Churchill strongly advocated that the: 'Mediterranean Fleet should be sent to Corfu and Crete' which would 'decide the action to be taken by Greece.'[14] Churchill went on to explain that if the Balkan countries were forced to make peace with Germany, they would have lost the opportunity to form a 'large alliance' with Balkan countries that 'might spell salvation'.[15] Churchill's idea of promoting a Balkan alliance was to feature heavily in his future policy towards Crete.

On 19 April 1939, in an attempt to curb German, as well as Italian expansion, Paris and London furnished Greece the same guarantee previously given to Poland. Greece was assured that any aggression against them would be met with all the military help possible. The Mediterranean was seen as an essential link in uniting the British Empire and the Suez Canal, the loss of which would be catastrophic. Keeping the Suez Canal open was paramount for British interests as traffic ran through it from both India and Australasia.

In the House of Commons, Churchill not only spoke of approval of the guarantee to Greece, but also urged Chamberlain to make more effective arrangements with Turkey. After the announcement that Britain had also guaranteed Turkey and Romania, Churchill declared: 'we have committed ourselves in every direction, rightly in my opinion.'[16] It was generally agreed by the British government that the Balkans could not come under the sphere of influence of either Italy or Germany. Churchill seemed particularly enthusiastic about the prospect of devoting less attention to the inaccessible Poland and negotiating prospective alliances with Turkey, Greece and Yugoslavia. The Balkans was certainly favourable for strategic counter-attacking positions and securing Britain's position in the Mediterranean.

Mussolini was pleased with his success in Albania, but he was infuriated by the British and French guarantee of independence given to Greece. To Mussolini, the guarantee was an aggressive move against legitimate Italian interests. Greece had been considered within the sphere of Italian influence; a point Mussolini intended to emphasise with the Corfu incident as early as 1923. An extract from Ciano's diary revealed that the Duce was considering a forceful gesture, because he had an: 'account to settle since 1923 . . . the Greeks are deceiving themselves if they imagine he has wiped the slate clean.'[17]

Prior to the guarantee to Greece, Chamberlain had been under increasing pressure to become involved in the Balkans. Greece, a potential ally, was positioned between Italy, Albania and Bulgaria, all of whom were sympathetic to Nazism. The Greek dictator, Metaxas, had been deported from Britain for his Germanophile tendencies during the First World War and was rumoured to have made Greece the most Germanised state in south-eastern Europe. Greek security was based heavily on the SS and the Gestapo. At Athens police headquarters, pictures of Hitler and Goebbels were openly displayed. *Mein Kampf* was widely read and became a major influence behind the organisation of youth. The Italian foreign minister had noted that the sympathy for Nazi ideology shown by Metaxas had 'caused the British and French to intrigue against his regime'.[18] The Greek dictator's distrust of Britain was heightened when Italy was allowed to invade Albania. Metaxas's suspicions were not without foundation; in 1938 the British government had actively encouraged the Greek king to dispose of him. Churchill stressed to Chamberlain: 'Metaxas is on the verge of joining the Rome–Berlin Axis . . . they [pro-British sources] believe that General Metaxas is wavering [and they] are extremely perturbed.'[19]

In retrospect, the threat of Greece joining the Axis powers seems less conceivable. Despite maintaining precarious neutrality under the right-wing dictatorship of General Metaxas, Greece was financially and strategically bound to Britain. The Greek royal family maintained close British connections. Also, Churchill's concerns over Greece joining the Axis failed to take into account the overriding ideology of Metaxas, which placed Greek nationalism above all other considerations, and set Greece apart from other Balkan nations sympathetic to Nazism. Germany failed to gain from the Greek people the sort of collaboration received from puppet regimes such as Hungary, Croatia, Romania and Bulgaria. Hungary and Bulgaria, like Greece, were ideologically sympathetic to Nazism, but unlike Greece, they lacked the Hellenic drive that made Metaxas and the Greek people primarily nationalistic, and prevented them becoming a puppet state of the Axis powers.

Italy's occupation of Albania had made Greece anxious, particularly over Corfu and Crete, which naturally drove them further towards Britain for protection. German and Italian pressure on Greece saw the restoration of King George II, which was designed to stabilise the Greek government and also to promote a regime that was favourable to their traditional ally, Great Britain. The dependence on Britain was accentuated by the fact that Greek finances were to a large extent in British hands, thus automatically determining the negative attitude of influential Greek circles towards the Axis powers.

Following the invasion of Albania, Mussolini strengthened his relations with Hitler on May 1939, when he committed Italy to the Pact of Steel with Germany. The pact committed both Germany and Italy to each other in the event of war. On the advice of his foreign secretary, Ciano, Mussolini wrote to Hitler stating that, although there was no doubt about the willingness of Italy to go war, they would need three years in order to rearm fully. Hitler ignored the appeal and did not reply. Mussolini had been deceived by Hitler's timetable; he assumed that Germany would not be ready to fight a war before 1943. When Germany invaded Poland in September 1939, Mussolini was severely embarrassed by Italy's total inadequacy to meet the required commitments of the Pact of Steel. Italy's resources had been stretched by the attack on Albania, thus Mussolini could not contemplate conflict with France and Britain. Ciano was forced to submit a plea to Berlin for a list of vital materials required by Italy. Germany responded with only a small quantity of supplies and Mussolini was forced to ask for a release from the military obligations dictated by the pact. It was announced that Italy would be a 'non-belligerent', to the relief of the majority of Italians. This state of affairs invariably damaged Mussolini's ego and forced the Italians into a humiliating situation that was to be reversed at the earliest opportunity.

Throughout the winter of 1939, Mussolini, who had prided himself on dynamism, could not decide what policy to pursue. In August 1939, when Mussolini learned of Hitler's aggressive intentions in Poland, he had seriously considered breaking the alliance with Hitler. After the capitulation of Poland, Mussolini counselled Hitler to make peace. Ciano wrote: 'the idea of Hitler waging war, and worse still, winning it, is altogether unbearable.' Ciano concluded: 'He [Mussolini] would be greatly pleased if Hitler were slowed down.'[20] Mussolini even went as far as warning the Dutch and Belgian ambassadors of Hitler's intention to invade the Low Countries. Hitler blamed the Italian king, Victor Emmanuel, for the breach of confidence, but thereafter Germany's intentions were not relayed to Mussolini.

As late as 2 May 1940, eight days before the German invasion of western Europe, Count Ciano told the British minister in Rome that: 'the Allies need not expect Italy to take action if things went well for them.' However, if Germany had more military successes then: 'he could promise nothing.'[21] Historian Chester Wilmot eloquently described the nature of Italy's promiscuous approach to entering the war: 'Mussolini found himself ousted from the driving seat in the Axis chariot.' Wilmot likened the Italian dictator to a 'bewildered footman . . . tempted to leap off and risk lacerations when he feared it was heading for disaster.' But: 'clinging more firmly and leaning over to urge the driver on when prospects of quick and easy booty stretched ahead.'[22]

Mussolini believed it was his duty to ally Italy with Hitler, as he thought that Britain and France were already defeated. On 16 May Churchill appealed to Mussolini in a letter stating that the joint heirs of Latin and Christian civilisations must not be 'ranged against one another in mortal strife'. Mussolini replied with reference to the British guarantee made to Poland, stating that if it was to 'honour your signature' that Britain declared war on Germany, the same sense of honour applied in the 'Italian–German Treaty [which] guides Italy today and tomorrow'.[23] The German people still had memories of Italian betrayal fresh in their minds from the First World War; Mussolini felt compelled to show that Italy was a worthy ally. Although he shared an alliance with Mussolini, Hitler did not need Italy as an ally; he cared little for the Italian people, and less for Italy's proposed entry into the war. In contrast to Hitler, an ally represented a lifeline for Churchill and the isolated British forces. Hitler believed that Britain's hopes lay with Russia and America who had yet to enter the war. 'If Russia drops out of the picture, America too is lost for Britain.'[24]

Italy's neutrality, announced by Mussolini on 3 September 1939, came to an end on 10 June 1940. From the balcony of the Palazzo Venezia, the Duce formally declared war on Britain and France. Italy was unprepared for war, but Mussolini was desperate to show that he was equal to Hitler. Hitler's *Blitzkrieg* in Europe had already crushed Poland and brought the collapse of Norway, Holland and Belgium. Mussolini felt that he would not be committing Italy to a prolonged battle, France was on the verge of defeat and it was only a matter of time before Britain fell. If Italy remained neutral, she would be faced with the prospect of a Europe dominated by Germany, who would be angry at Italy's refusal to honour her treaty obligations. By entering the war, Mussolini could reverse the humiliating memory of 'non-belligerence' and join the Axis as an equal partner, which would result in a peace settlement where Italy could receive the equal spoils of a victorious power. However, Mussolini's expectations were not instantly fulfilled.

Italian troops made painfully slow progress during the Alpine war, resulting in only a few square miles of territory gained, before Germany had crushed France. The main disappointment for Mussolini was that Hitler was not prepared to hand French North African colonies to Italy, preferring to leave them, and the French Mediterranean Fleet, under the Vichy French to ensure their collaboration. Despite declaring war on Britain and France, there remained the danger that Italy would remain the subordinate nation in the Axis partnership unless Mussolini could regain the initiative. This inspired Mussolini to embark on a campaign designed to develop an Italian sphere of influence in the Balkans and North Africa, leaving Germany to dominate northern Europe. After the fall of France, Mussolini immediately thought of Greece and Yugoslavia as possible conquests. In the summer of 1940, Italian troops concentrated on the

Yugoslav border and sought German and Hungarian consent for possible action against Yugoslavia. Hitler vetoed the plan fearing that if Yugoslavia were attacked: 'England and Russia' would 'discover a community of interest'[25] which would bring turmoil to the area. Lack of resources meant that the Italians were not in a position to carry out the attack without German logistical support; therefore Hitler was in a strong position to counter Mussolini's aggressive intentions. Germany's establishment of the 'new order' seemed to preclude the possibility of serious Italian military action.

From the outbreak of war, Hitler had consistently stated that Germany had no territorial ambitions in the Balkans. Germany relied on the Balkan countries for a variety of vital raw materials, not least Romanian oil from the wells at Plöesti, which supplied the Reich with 1.2 million tons a year, and accounted for over half its total annual oil imports. Among the network of unstable Balkan states, Germany endeavoured to keep the peace, and ironically Hitler appeased Bulgaria and Hungary in the area by casually conceding large areas of Romania. When a map representing the new frontier was shown to the Romanian foreign minister, he collapsed on the conference table and had to be revived by smelling salts. The government in Bucharest disintegrated. King Carol, along with his mistress Magda Lupescu, and her ninety-eight suitcases, fled on a train filled with riches to Switzerland. Germany guaranteed what remained of Romania, and a large military 'training session' was dispatched to Bucharest, with the secret objective of protecting the oilfields from the Russians. On the arrival of German troops, British oil engineers were given twenty-four hours to leave the country.

The guarantee to Romania meant that Germany was committed as far as Russia's southern flank, which had caused dismay and suspicion in the Soviet foreign minister, Molotov, who had called for an immediate consultation with Germany. While Hitler had accepted that war with Russia was inevitable, he believed it was vital that it was instigated at a time of his choosing and not as the result of a marginal Balkan dispute. Hitler resolved that Russia should be given no reason to suspect his intentions and that no further disturbances should be allowed in the Balkans until further consultations with the Russian government.

In August 1940 Hitler announced to Mussolini what Ciano described as 'a complete order to halt, all along the line'. Mussolini replied in a letter that the Italian military presence on the Greek and Yugoslav border was taken as a: 'precautionary character' against states poised to 'strike a dagger into the back of the Axis.'[26] Mussolini was furious that he might not accomplish a successful campaign against an enfeebled enemy, and prove Italy was a nation of 'iron men'. He told Ciano: 'It is humiliating to remain with our hands folded while others write History'.[27] It was not surprising that in seeking an easy, bloodless victory, Mussolini turned his attention to Greece, despite the fact that Italy had offered Greece a guarantee in June 1940.

It was against this background that Mussolini and Hitler met at the Brenner Pass on 4 October. According to Ciano, during these meetings Mussolini 'resented the fact that Hitler did all of the talking'. But on this occasion Mussolini failed to show his frustration at Italy's inactivity. Ciano wrote: 'Rarely have I seen the Duce in such good humour.'[28] However, an omission from Hitler's summary of current affairs was to trigger a series of significant events. Among the topics Hitler discussed were issues concerning Britain, France, Spain and Russia, but crucially, he failed to mention that he had mobilised German troops to occupy Romania. This unilateral decision was to have a profound effect on Mussolini. When the Duce heard that German troops had arrived in Romania he was furious. 'I will pay him back in his own coin,' he told Ciano. 'He [Hitler] will find out from the papers that I have occupied Greece. In this way the equilibrium will be re-established.'[29] Mussolini's anger was fuelled by the fact that only weeks earlier Hitler had called a halt to Italian operations; furthermore Italy and Germany had jointly enforced a frontier settlement upon Romania during a dispute with Hungary. Hitler may have thought it prudent not to notify Mussolini of German military movements in the light of previous security leaks, but he remained highly suspicious of the Italian royal family and the Vatican. Speculation still surrounds Hitler's decision not to inform Mussolini, but there is little doubt that the omission was deliberate.

On 14 October Mussolini astonished the chief of the General Staff, Marshal Pietro Badoglio, and his deputy, Mario Roatta, by demanding the occupation of Greece. On 22 October Mussolini sent a letter to Hitler officially informing him of the imminent action against Greece. Mussolini backdated the letter to 19 October, and was careful not to mention a specific date or the form of the attack. Hitler, who was still in France at the time, was informed of the contents of the letter on 24 October and immediately requested a conference. In his reply to Hitler, Mussolini casually suggested that 28 October would be the most convenient date for a meeting. On 28 October, as the Italian troops advanced on Greece, Mussolini received Hitler from his train in Florence proclaiming: 'Führer, we are marching! This morning a victorious Italian army has crossed the Greek border!'[30] Mussolini proceeded to outline plans for simultaneous offensives to be carried out on the Greek and Egyptian fronts. A successful invasion of Greece, combined with the seizure of Crete, would serve as strategic outposts for the Italian advance on the Suez Canal, and allow the Axis to dominate the eastern Mediterranean. In his letter of 25 October, Mussolini emphasised that an Italian attack on Greece would preclude British aggression against Italian positions; the Duce likened Italian operations in Greece to that of German *Blitzkriegs* in Europe. Mussolini described Greece as a 'Mediterranean Norway' that 'must not escape the same fate'.[31]

Historians have traditionally stated that Mussolini's invasion of Greece was strongly opposed by Hitler. More recent studies have shown that Hitler's initial reaction was to offer assistance to Mussolini in operations against Greece and 'especially for the protection of Crete against occupation by the English'.[32] Martin Van Creveld, in his study of German foreign policy, has revealed that Germany actively encouraged Mussolini to take action against Greece. The German High Command (OKH) studied the possibility of a joint German–Italian offensive in the eastern Mediterranean. The German Naval Command stated that Hitler had given Italy 'a free hand in Greece'[33] in the event that it became necessary to block a British initiative. The German navy had been enthusiastic about an assault on Greece and Crete to assist in the capture of Egypt. Hitler was well aware of Mussolini's intentions, but he failed to veto the invasion of Greece as he had done in Yugoslavia. The fact that Hitler ignored Mussolini's intentions is explained by the convictions of German strategy, which attributed greater strategic and economic importance to Yugoslavia than to Greece. The Yugoslav government under the regent, Prince Paul, had shown signs of succumbing to increasing pressure from Hitler to sign the Tripartite Pact. Hitler, therefore, had no objections to an Italian attack on Greece, provided it was swift, decisive and coordinated with the advance on Suez.

Hitler later complained that he had done his best to prevent the Italian attack on Greece, and described it as an act of 'criminal folly'. It appears that the Führer had attempted to distance himself from the campaign after it later descended into farce. Hitler's failure to reveal his disapproval from the outset may be explained by the fact that he himself had established the practice of acting without consultation and therefore felt he could not reprimand Mussolini for doing the same thing. Furthermore, there seems little doubt that Hitler shared Mussolini's confidence in a swift, inexpensive conquest of Greece. This appraisal of Greek defensive capabilities seemed logical. Greece was a poor country with only eight million inhabitants, over half of whom were peasants, and whose economy was dominated by primitive agriculture. Van Creveld wrote: 'Nobody, least of all the Greeks themselves, expected her to hold out for as much as two weeks'.[34]

The capitulation of France meant that Greece had no assurance Britain would honour the guarantee that was given as a joint Anglo–French agreement. The regime of the Greek dictator, General Ioánnis Metaxas, was acutely aware of the threat from the Italian army since their occupation of Albania in April 1939. Metaxas endeavoured to maintain good relations with the Axis powers while not discouraging Britain from their tenuous agreement. This ambiguous policy provoked criticism from the majority of the Greek military who demanded closer co-operation with Germany, while politicians accused Metaxas of drifting toward the 'Axis'. The Greek population were conscious that such ambiguity risked jeopardising Greek national interests.

Prior to the Italian invasion, the Greek government endured a series of provocations including the sinking by an Italian submarine of their cruiser *Helle*, which was acting as a ceremonial guardship during religious celebrations on the island of Tinos. Despite the widespread public anger caused by this incident, Metaxas refused to give Mussolini any excuse for war. Such moderation was to prove futile. It was clear that Mussolini was building a case to justify an attack on Greece. Italy's aggressive intentions became obvious on 26 October as border provocations were intensified by Ciano's order. In a blatant act of aggression, Italian aircraft flying over Greek territory had dropped three bombs between Thebes and Levadia. The incident was quickly silenced by Greek censorship. Despite the transparency of Italian intentions, Metaxas maintained that the pressure exerted by Italy was a prelude to political demands, and would not result in war. The limited amount of Italian troops in Albania and with winter approaching, the prospects of immediate aggression seemed to decline.

The Greek theatrical season started that year with Giacomo Puccini's *Madam Butterfly*; ironically after the show a party was given in the Italian embassy dedicated to friendship between Greece and Italy. The tables were decorated with intertwined Greek and Italian flags with the words 'Long Live Greece' written on a cake. In accordance with Greek custom, the guests gathered until late. While they were talking in the legation rooms, long telegrams in cipher started arriving from Rome. An uneasy air of nervousness communicated itself through legation staff as secretaries began to decipher the text. The Italian ambassador, Grazzi, was presented with the transcript and was tasked with delivering it to Metaxas. During his role as ambassador, Grazzi did all in his power to establish friendly relations with Metaxas who liked him personally. Mario Cervi described Grazzi as 'a man of good sense and an excellent diplomatist'.[35] Despite Metaxas's personal liking of Grazzi, he was under no illusions that he was a faithful servant of Rome under the orders of Mussolini.

Metaxas was a small, plump man with a thick moustache; he wore civilian clothes and lived modestly. He was not bloodthirsty by nature, but imposed a hard regime on his country in which press censorship was severe and the atmosphere oppressive. Metaxas lived in a two-storey villa in Kifisia, an exclusive part of Athens that exuded an air of prosperity. It was peaceful, surrounded by pine trees and fresh air, a marked contrast to other areas of the hot, noisy Greek capital. The area surrounding the villa was floodlit at night and patrolled by guards. Grazzi arrived at the villa at 02:45 in the car of the Italian military attaché, Luigi Mondini. Mondini described it as a mild, clear night and the sky was 'dotted with a myriad of stars that make the sky of Attica so marvellous'.[36] The guard commander was asked to wake the Greek dictator. Metaxas had lived for months in expectation of what he was about to receive; the pressure had taken its toll on him physically, although mentally he remained alert. As a statesman Metaxas was modest and approachable, he had assumed none of the titles that distinguished other dictators, such as Duce, or Führer. Metaxas met Grazzi in the most unpretentious manner; he put on a pair of slippers and a dark dressing gown, and made his way downstairs to the door himself. After Metaxas had taken Grazzi into a small room on the ground floor, Grazzi announced in French that his government had charged him with handing over an urgent note. As Metaxas slowly read the document he shook his head, visibly shaken by the contents.

Grazzi had delivered an ultimatum from Mussolini that accused Greece of collaborating with the British and demanded the Italian occupation of Greek strategic positions for the duration of the conflict with Great Britain. The occupation of these strategic points was seen as a guarantee of Greek neutrality. As Count Ciano boasted, it was a document that left no way out for Greece: 'either she accepts the occupation or she will be attacked.'[37] When Metaxas enquired which strategic positions were to be seized, the Italian ambassador was forced to admit that he did not know. Grazzi was also shaken; he was well aware of the injustice of the cause he was compelled to deliver. Grazzi informed Metaxas that the Italian army were massed on the Greek border and were under orders from Ciano to enter Greece at 06:00, regardless of his decision. This was Ciano's ploy of allowing Greece 'no way out'. Metaxas claimed that Italy had not left a chance for negotiations as they had only given him three hours to make a decision. Metaxas told the Italian ambassador: 'I could not set my own house in order – much less surrender my country – in three hours. The answer is no.'[38] Metaxas wrote in his diary: 'I shall place the problem of Greek dignity over and above everything else. I shall not bow my head to the Italians.'[39]

Before the Italian ambassador had left Metaxas's house at 03:15, the Greek premier had started to issue directives and orders by phone. Metaxas talked to the King of Greece and Britain's ambassador, Michael Palairet, to ask for aid; he also summoned the government for a meeting. At the subsequent cabinet meeting, a close colleague of Metaxas said that he saw the Greek dictator: 'When I entered the office, I found him [Metaxas] seated in an armchair.' He described Metaxas as a man from whose back an enormous 'burden had been lifted: a man who felt he had done his duty to his country and to himself.'[40]

Just before dawn on 28 October Italian troops crossed the Albanian frontier. Shortly afterwards the air-raid sirens began to wail in Athens and the Greek population awoke to find their country at war. All the Greek newspapers published the order for a general mobilisation and Metaxas addressed the Greek people in a radio broadcast with the call to fight. Metaxas described the fanaticism of the Greek people as 'beyond description'. Leaflets were dropped in the streets of Athens, buildings were decorated with national flags and propaganda posters; the whole city was agitated. After hostilities began, Italian officials in Greece, including Grazzi, had traumatic experiences. Italian aggression was met with Greek indignation, which erupted into violence. Many Italians were arrested and Italian offices and schools were attacked. Italians in Athens were extremely worried about the forthcoming war; many had Italian passports, but by birth and education they were predominantly Greek, their friends and interests were all based in Greece, and their future was now very uncertain. Police had to protect the Italian embassy from angry crowds who demonstrated outside. On the Greek island of Crete the outburst of patriotism also led to unrest. The Italian view of Greek apathy towards their invasion was severely misguided. In the patriotic fervour, anti-monarchist liberals overlooked the crimes of Metaxas's royalist dictatorship, which had brutally suppressed all opposition and per-petrated various breaches of the constitution. The mobilisation for war was the first movement for many years that found the Greek people and their government united. Soldiers fired their weapons wildly in the air as they crammed on to trains travelling to meet the Italian advance. Motor transports were scarce in the Greek army and many troops made their way on foot through the rugged terrain of the Pindus mountains; women and children generously offered pack animals to carry ammunition and supplies.

When Grazzi reached the safety of Italy, he was met by Ciano, who was in an arrogant mood. When Grazzi enquired about the situation on the Greek–Albanian border, Ciano confidently told him that in 'two weeks it will all be over'.[41] Grazzi maintained deep respect for Metaxas and distaste for the odious role given to him. No doubt Metaxas would have preferred to pursue his policy of neutrality but Mussolini's action left him with only two options, to fight or capitulate. Legend has refined Metaxas's reply to the Italian ultimatum to one word, 'No!' Known as 'Ohi' day, Metaxas's response to Grazzi is commemorated in Greece with a national holiday each year on 28 October. History should not forget that in 1940 Greece was the only country to join the war against the Axis when Britain and her Empire stood alone.

NOTES

1   Chamberlain to the Commons, 15 March 1939, cited in Stewart, G, *Burying Caesar*, London: Weidenfeld & Nicolson, 1999, p. 353.
2   Smart, N, *The National Government 1931–40*, London: Macmillan, 1999, p. 196.
3   Churchill to the Commons, 15 March 1939, in Stewart, op. cit., p. 330.
4   A harshly realistic national policy.
5   Lee, S J, *European Dictatorships 1918–1945*, London: Routledge, 1987, p. 115.
6   Stewart, op. cit., p. 350.
7   Ibid, p. 200.
8   Ibid.
9   Robson, Mark, *Italy, Liberalism and Fascism 1870–1945*, London: Hodder & Stoughton, 1992, p. 126.
10 Churchill to Chamberlain, Premier Papers, NA (formerly PRO), Kew (hereafter PREM PAPERS), 1/323, 9 April 1939.
11 Corfu had been a British protectorate from 1815 until 1863, when it was united with Greece.
12 Churchill to Chamberlain, PREM PAPERS, op. cit.
13 Ibid.
14 Churchill to Mediterranean, PREM PAPERS.
15 Churchill to Chamberlain, PREM PAPERS, op. cit.
16 Ibid.
17 Cervi, Mario, *The Hollow Legions. Mussolini's Blunder in Greece 1940–41*, London: Chatto & Windus, 1972, p. xii.
18 Ciano to Grazzi, DDI Viii, XII No. 35, in Cervi, op. cit.
19 Churchill to Chamberlain, PREM PAPERS, op. cit.
20 Wilmot, Chester, *The Struggle for Europe*, Wordsworth, 1997 edn, p. 63.
21 Lukacs, J, *The Duel*, Yale University Press, 2001, p. 75.
22 Wilmot, op. cit., p. 62.
23 Lukacs, op. cit., p. 75.
24 Wilmot, op. cit., p. 56.
25 Documents on German Foreign Policy, series D, vol. X, Washington DC, 1957, p. 54.
26 Wilmot, op. cit., p. 58.
27 Ibid, p. 63.
28 Ibid.
29 Ibid.
30 Van Creveld, M, *Hitler's Strategy 1940–41. The Balkan Clue*, London: CUP, 1973, p. 49.
31 Ibid, p. 45.
32 Documents, op. cit., p. 54.
33 Van Creveld, op. cit., p. 49.
34 Ibid, p. 51.
35 Cervi, op. cit., p. 2.
36 Ibid, p. 114.
37 Muggeridge, Malcolm (ed.), *Ciano's Diary 1939–1943*, London, 1947, p. 300.
38 Kiriakopoulos, G C, *Ten Days to Destiny: The Battle for Crete*, New York, 1985, p. 13.
39 Cervi, op. cit., p. 54.
40 Ibid, p. 118.
41 Ibid, p. 123.

CHAPTER II

Through the mud: The Greco–Italian war

The text of Mussolini's ultimatum to Greece read: 'Greek neutrality has become more and more a pretence. The responsibility for this falls primarily on Great Britain.'[1] The reply from Metaxas was swift, stating that the Greek government had 'observed the strictest of neutrality towards all' and that Italy's demands for the occupation of Greek territory had infringed the nation's right 'to live as free Greeks' therefore he urged his countrymen: 'Fight for your country, for your wives and children and for our sacred traditions.'[2]

The accusations levelled at the Metaxas regime by Italy were ill-founded. The Italian foreign minister, Grazzi, wrote: 'the real decisions are made by Metaxas alone, and it is certain that personally [he is] anything but pro-British.' Grazzi concluded: 'If in all Greece there was a single man who really had a feeling of affection for Italy, that man was Metaxas.'[3] There was undoubtedly an affinity between the Greek and Italian regimes. Greece had adopted the Roman salute, which nationalistically was renamed the Greek salute. Metaxas was an enthusiastic soldier who admired Germany, and had previously trained in German military academies. Spiritually and politically, Metaxas felt closer to Mussolini or Hitler than to the British. However, Metaxas fully appreciated that the threat to Greek security came from Berlin and Rome, and not their traditional allies in London.

In 1935 the Republic was overthrown and the monarchy re-established with King George II. General Ioánnis Metaxas established his dictatorship as a result of a coup d'état and soon reduced the king to a decorative puppet. Metaxas put an end to party politics with his decree on 4 August 1936 taking advantage of the ruthless efficiency of his loyal supporter, Maniadakis, the Minister of National Security. With the help of Maniadakis, Metaxas was able to establish a repressive regime that banished and suppressed all opponents of his dictatorship.

Although faced with the fundamental problem of the division between a self-absorbed capital and impoverished countryside, Greek politics was preoccupied with disputes over the constitution. Greece was bitterly divided for years between Monarchists and Republicans, a division that the Metaxas dictatorship had not sought to resolve. However, despite being socially and politically divided, Greek society united around a higher goal, the defence of Greek independence and sovereignty. The war united all factions in resistance to Italy; even political exiles returned to fight. One exile explained: 'I loathe the Metaxas regime. I think the man is a bastard – but, by Christ, he's a good soldier.'[4] Detractors from the Metaxas regime have often found it difficult to reconcile their criticisms of him as a Fascist and Germanophile, with the fact that he so effectively prepared his country for war. The Italian attack on Greece was an open secret – the whole world was talking about it. After the fall of France, and the declaration of war from Italy, there seemed little doubt about Greek involvement in the war. Metaxas, along with his Chief of General Staff, General Papagos, hastened the modernisation of the armed forces and put plans in place for mobilisation.

Only a few days before Germany embarked on the conquest of Poland, Italy began to concentrate troops on the Greek border. Thus more than a year before war broke out, Greece was put on her guard and she made intelligent use of this advantage and the order of a partial mobilisation. Despite being carried out in confusion, it served as a valuable experience for the Greeks. Papagos had set in place a system of persistent, but unobtrusive, mobilisation that included the development of a signals network, improvements to air defences and strengthening of the army by training reservists. By using a unique system of numbers, the Greek government was able mobilise troops discreetly, thus avoiding the impression of large-scale operations; even individual troops were un-aware of the significance of their allotted number. Therefore, when newspapers or the radio announced a call up, the great mass of the population and foreigners alike had no clue as to the nature or size of the call up. The transparency of Mussolini's intentions had ensured that the Greeks were well prepared for the Italian offensive. The representative of the Albanian higher council, Nebil Dino, had ominously written to the Italian governor-general of Albania, Francesco Jacomoni: 'I do not think it opportune to give warning to and anger a people whom it is proposed to conquer.'[5]

The nature of the Italian campaign in Greece was epitomised by the way it was technically bungled and improvised from the outset. Operations commenced in the worst season of the year, against an enemy who had been primed for an Italian invasion. Motivated only by the puerile actions of Mussolini, Italian divisions moved against Greece without conviction; they fought with archaic arms and equipment, and were led by incompetent generals who were divided by professional resentment and individual antagonism. The unfounded optimism that deluded the Italian government is illustrated in a dispatch to Ciano from Jacomoni, who proclaimed: 'the Greek population as a whole does not seem inclined to fight.' Jacomoni went on to explain that in the event of an Italian attack there would be a 'show of initial resistance' to show 'the world that Greece tried to resist the aggression of authoritarian states.' Jacomoni stated that the Greek 'government is hated by many. The King is neither esteemed nor loved.'[6] This assessment of the situation in Greece could not have been more misinformed. Greek military preparations were intense and ready to repulse an aggressor. Moreover, Metaxas, for the first time, enjoyed wide support from the Greek people. Jacomoni's notion of an ideological stand by Greece to demonstrate resistance against an 'authoritarian' state was absurd; the Metaxas regime had itself shown all the characteristics of such an authoritarian state.

Historian Mario Cervi wrote that Mussolini and the Italian government prepared for war 'jealously, almost as if they feared someone might rob them of it'.[7] Mussolini's desire for war in Greece was evident in his preparation which was hopelessly improvised. A considered evaluation of the situation in Greece was neither sought nor undertaken. Grazzi had done his best to advise the Italian government and he warned Ciano that Greece had the majority of 250,000 men deployed at the frontiers. According to Grazzi, Metaxas had 'adopted the attitude of defending Greek territorial integrity and neutrality to the limit'. Grazzi was also certain of the will of the people stating: 'never has Prime Minister Metaxas had such total unanimity behind him.'[8] Grazzi's pragmatic approach to the situation in Greece was largely ignored by Mussolini, who preferred to listen to the bogus rhetoric of his other ministers, Jacomoni and Ciano, who fuelled his illusion of a rapid victory. Cervi described Grazzi's assessment of the situation as 'an example of honest and able diplomacy in service of arrogant and reckless political masters'.[9]

Visconti Prasca, who was to lead the Italian attack, lent ill-founded enthusiasm to Italian troops in the disconsolate Albanian countryside. Prasca arrogantly declared that the Greeks were a 'people who did not like fighting'.[10] He stressed that the 'march' on Athens would begin with the occupation of Epirus and the port of Preveza. Prasca predicted that Italian superiority in Epirus was 70,000 to 30,000, and promised to bring about a shattering blow to the Greek army. Mussolini's response was to advise Prasca that he should not be concerned with Italian casualties. Mussolini failed to notice Prasca's sweeping generalisations and assumptions; his consciousness of such details had long been desensitised by the adulation of his followers who had been captivated by his own rhetoric.

At a meeting in Palazzo Venezia on 15 October 1940, Mussolini set out his uncomplicated objectives for the offensive in Greece. The first phase of the operation was to seize the southern Albanian coastline, leading to the occupation of Zante, Cephalonia, Corfu and Salonika. The second phase of the operation would include the entire occupation of Greece. Mussolini expected the liquidation of Epirus by 10–11 November, which would allow an extra month for sending fresh forces for the occupation of Greece.

Prasca stated that he did not want too many divisions involved in the initial offensive; he preferred that extra troops be deployed, subject to how favourably the operation developed. When the discussion turned to the occupation of Athens, Prasca believed that a group of six divisions would suffice. Mussolini could not have failed to realise that six divisions would not be sufficient to capture Greece. The aged General Badoglio had previously advised twenty divisions for the offensive, and stated that three months would be needed to implement the operation. However, the Duce could not afford to wait and ignored the advice given to him by his senior general. Mussolini's acceptance of less than twenty divisions illustrated that he was prepared to risk defeat in order to begin the operation as soon as possible. Visconti Prasca's insistence on only six divisions was motivated by his own personal ambition. Prasca realised that the commander of two army corps qualified as a commander of an army. Under Italian regulations, an officer who commanded an army during wartime would be eligible for the rank of full general, which meant that Prasca would be promoted ahead of fierce personal rivals. Therefore it was in Prasca's own interests to keep the number of divisions to a minimum and under his complete command; if the invasion force grew too large, then the command would become divided and Prasca would not obtain the rank of general.

Professional jealousy was endemic among the Italian military hierarchy and attempts were made to displace Prasca. On 25 October Mussolini wrote to him stating that he had opposed all attempts to take his command away from him on the 'eve of the operation'. Mussolini expected his loyalty to be repaid with a rapid victory that other, more prudent generals, could not promise him. Mussolini wrote: 'I believe events, and above all your actions, will justify me.' However, the Duce was quick to emphasise: 'Attack with the greatest determination and violence. The success of the operation depends above all on speed.'[11] The Duce had found a general who shared his own values; Prasca, like Mussolini, was prepared to compromise rational military preparations in order to realise his own personal glory. Professional interests and preoccupations motivated both general and dictator; Mussolini did not want to be outdone by Hitler and Prasca did not want to lose the command that might further his military career. General Badoglio remained pessimistic about the whole Greek venture; he foresaw a prolonged war, and the exhaustion of Italian resources. King Victor Emmanuel III advised Badoglio to express his opinion to Mussolini at once, but before he could relay his concerns, a rumour reached Mussolini that Badoglio would resign if the invasion of Greece went ahead. In an outburst of anger Mussolini replied that he would readily accept his resignation, and would go to Greece in person to witness the incredible shame of Italians who were afraid of the Greeks.

The German military attaché, Von Rintelen, had observed the build up of Italian forces since German troops entered Romania. Von Rintelen commented: 'Italian superiority is probably not sufficient to fulfil expectations of rapid success if the Greeks put up serious resistance.'[12] Mussolini belatedly attempted to bolster his forces by writing to King Boris of Bulgaria to request aid in the offensive against Greece. The reply from the king explained that, due to the delicate situation and 'unfavourable circumstances' that had delayed 'a sufficient rearmament of her army', Bulgaria would have to 'refrain from armed action'.[13] Mussolini vented his rage at the king's reply, describing him as a 'gutless royal'. Operating in isolation from Germany, Italy lacked the diplomatic and military support they needed to carry out a 'lightning' offensive. In Bulgaria, German influence carried much weight; if Mussolini acted with the open support of Germany, King Boris probably would have fallen into line.

Thus six divisions, plus one in reserve, were to carry out the assault over a 150-mile front, while a further two divisions were to secure the Yugoslav frontier. As the Albanian winter set in, Italian troops were without adequate mountain equipment and provisions. Supply lines had not been properly established and the units had with them a mere five-days' supply of small arms ammunition, forty days' fuel for motor vehicles, and forty days' other supplies. Altogether 87,000 men were deployed against Greece, while 12,000 were left on the Yugoslav frontier. These few men were to invade a nation that had already mobilised its army and was fully conversant with Italian intentions.

The majority of the Greek army was made up of land forces. Tank troops were virtually non-existent, heavy, anti-tank and anti-aircraft artillery was inadequate and motorisation was rare, while transportation was mostly sustained on horses, mules and oxen. General conscription provided cannon fodder and a deep social gap divided the rank and file from commanding officers, and military careers were reserved exclusively for the upper classes. The Greek army was primitive; they had far less equipment than the Italians, but they had a great sense of injustice that motivated them; they were defending their country and their families.

The Italian army was of the old type, they were well supplied only in light arms: Manlicher 6.5 and Mauser 7.92 rifles; Hotchkiss 6.5 light machine guns, Schwerzlose 7.92 machine guns, and Brandt mortars. The Italian army was deficient in tank and armoured units, while also lacking in artillery and motor transport. Italian divisions had a distinct advantage in mortars over the Greek army, but Greek forces used their limited mortars with great skill and accuracy. The typical Italian division of around 10,000 men did not have adequate anti-aircraft weaponry and motor transport consisted of twenty-four vehicles. The Italians did have a crushing superiority in aircraft over the Greeks. The Greek Air Force consisted of only 150, mostly obsolete, planes.

The nine Italian divisions that undertook the initial offensive were made up as follows: the Littoral Group, commanded by General Rivolta, included the 3rd Grenadier Regiment (3,082 men and four pieces of artillery), and the 2nd Cavalry Regiment (1,741 men) with two mule drawn batteries and 200 Albanian volunteers. The Siena Division consisted of 9,200 men and approximately fifty guns; the Ferrara Division had 12,785 men, sixty guns, and an auxiliary force of 3,500 Albanian volunteers. The Centauro Division had 163 light tanks, 4,037 men, twenty-four pieces of artillery and anti-aircraft weapons. The heart of the deployment was the strong Julia Division, which consisted of 10,800 men and twenty guns. The Parma Division had 12,000 men, 163 tanks and sixty field guns. The Piemonte Division had 9,300 men and thirty-two field guns. The Venezia Division consisted of 10,000 men, and five groups of artillery. Finally the Arezzo Division (mountain infantry) was made up of 12,000 men and thirty-two field guns.

Prasca proposed to seize two key areas in a pincer movement; the eastern arm would be provided by the highly reputed Julia Division, who were to occupy the Metsovon Pass. The western movement would be led by the Littoral group who had the objective of seizing the town and harbour of Preveza. Meanwhile, the main thrust of Prasca's troops, consisting of the Siena, Ferrara and Centauro divisions, would advance centrally (with the Julia Division and Littoral group on their east and west flanks), towards the Kalamas river and engage Greek resistance at the key area of Kalpaki, which would provide a platform to push forward in the direction of Yanina. Prasca's strategy left the entire Macedonian sector in the east to the Parma Division. The Arezzo and Venezia Divisions were required to guard the Yugoslav frontier and the Piemonte Division was kept in reserve.

Prasca's strategy reflected his pomposity over the capabilities of Italian troops, and undervalued what the Greeks could achieve. He stated in his directive for the opening offensive that in the event of 'exceptionally favourable developments' (the internal collapse of the Greek army) then the operations against Koritsa and Athens could be undertaken without 'awaiting the reinforcements that would normally be required'.[14]

In October 1940 a beautiful Mediterranean autumn ruled in Rome and Athens. But on the Greco–Albanian frontier, running through the wilderness of the Pindus mountains came Balkan winter, bringing cold, rain and snow. On the frontier that separated Greece from Italian-occupied Albania, were freezing soldiers of both sides: Greek forces preparing to defend their country, and Italian soldiers who expected a tourist march to Athens. The commander of the Aquila Battalion from the 3rd Alpine Division, Major Fatuzzo, noted in his diary on 27 October 1940: 'The war starts tomorrow. The rain is frenetic and incessant. Water gets into the tents; it's hard to sleep.'[15] On the eve of the attack on Greece, Genserico

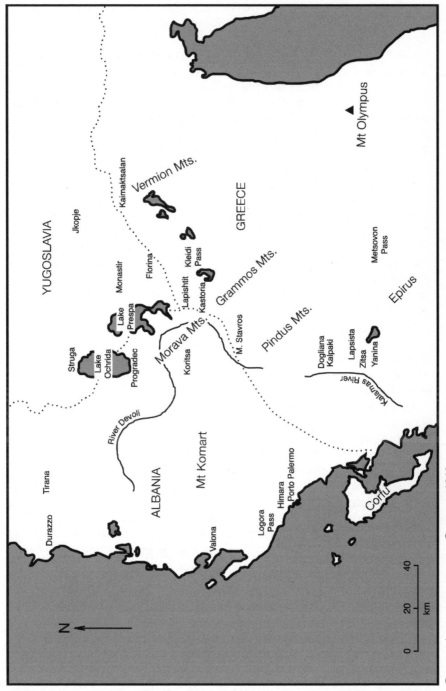

GRECO–ALBANIAN BORDER, OCTOBER 1940

Fontana, an officer of the Littoral Group noted: 'They have told us that we shall have to strike sparks, because we are only a few divisions, and the declaration of war could not be postponed.'[16] Italian troops crossed the Greek border at 05:30, half an hour before the ultimatum expired. Italian headquarters suddenly became a hive of activity as the order came to move across the frontier. The Italian governor-general of Albania, Francesco Jacomoni, had organised groups of Albanian saboteurs to infiltrate Greek territory and destroy communications, eliminate guard posts, and incite the population to rebel. However, perhaps symbolic of the battle to come, the 'saboteurs' committed no acts of sabotage, but simply took their payment and disappeared without trace.

The weather had taken an abrupt change on 26 October; torrential rain fell causing floods of water to pour into the valleys, swelling small rivers. General Francesco Rossi wanted to postpone operations, but Prasca took the view that the weather would be equally problematic to the enemy. In reality it was a greater disadvantage to the Italians, as they had to advance through the quagmire to engage Greek positions. The adverse conditions also prevented the Italians making effective use of their advantage in artillery and airpower. The Greek gunners would prove to be so skilful that the weather acted as useful cover for their advancing forces. The Italian columns pushed forward under darkness in the driving rain, their laden boots sank deep into the mud, and horse and mule transports kicked up showers of dirt as their hooves churned up the ground beneath. The rain was so intense that as the Littoral group advanced down the coast, they could barely make out the sea.

The main advance of the Centauro Division making towards the Kalamas river was slow but steady; they encountered little resistance as they progressed towards the Perati bridge at Kalpaki. An eerie silence presided over the surrounding valleys, broken only at brief intervals by bursts of fire as minor skirmishes took place. Italian troops entered Greek frontier posts with caution. The majority had been abandoned without confrontation; on the walls were photographs of Metaxas and King George, on the tables were the remains of meals and newspapers. The Greek forces had yet to show themselves. Italian units penetrated Greek territory at various points and were testing the ground; both sides were still manoeuvring. An Italian communiqué summed up an uneventful first day, stating that military targets, including docks, wharves and railway yards, had been struck by the Italian air force despite the weather conditions.

On 29 October the operation for the capture Corfu was postponed due to the adverse weather. The Kalamas river was causing problems for the Littoral and Siena Divisions. The Kalamas was badly swollen and its violent course swept away carcasses of cattle, tree trunks and wreckage of bridges that had been demolished by the Greeks. The Italians were lacking in bridging equipment and the swollen streams and rivers bogged down their advance, while tanks were simply abandoned after getting stuck in the quagmire. The fighting remained at the skirmishing stage until 31 October when the first casualties were reported to Prasca, the loss of three officers and thirty men, evidence that Greek resistance was becoming livelier.

By 1 November there was a break in the weather, which instead of signalling an Italian advance, saw the opening of a devastating Greek counter-offensive. Papagos launched an assault designed to reach the Devoli river through western Macedonia and gain control over the Morava area. Greek troops, clad in khaki uniforms and British style helmets, launched their assault at 08:00. The strong counter-offensive in the north was launched against the Parma Division and caught them unprepared. Greek forces quickly broke through the Italian defensive line and advanced towards Treni and Verniku. The Piemonte Division was brought forward to assist in a recovery but it was short lived. The news of Greek success was described in a communiqué issued on 2 November: Greek troops have 'smashed strong enemy resistance, penetrated five kilometres into Albanian territory and occupied fortified positions at the point of the bayonet'.[17] The men chiefly responsible for this victory were the kilted Evzones, who were familiar with the terrain and had stealthily scaled the heights and attacked with surprise. On 3 November the Greeks pressed once more, emerging from over the mountains and utilising their mortars to great effect in pounding Italian positions. Italian troops were bewildered at the sudden ferocity of the attack from an enemy that was not expected to resist. General Jacomoni sent one of the best Albanian units to counter-attack. After heavy fighting, the Albanians took a hill in the Lapishtit range, but a swift counter-attack from the Greeks shook the Albanian unit, which promptly disbanded and fled across the valley in disarray. When Italian troops tried to restore order they came under Albanian fire. As the Albanians fled down the valley, Greek machine-gun fire and shells from Italian tanks mercilessly cut them down. The Albanians suffered crippling casualties; out of 1,000 men only 120 remained. The panic instigated by the Albanians spread across the whole Italian line and caused them to fall back.

Advancing from western Macedonia, Greek forces proceeded to push the Italians back into Albanian territory; as a result the troops of the prized Julia Division found themselves in an extremely precarious position. Greek units advanced along the flanks of the Julia Division and cut across their rear, leaving them dangerously exposed. The Greek advance severed vital supply lines to the isolated division, who were subjected to increasingly heavy attacks from the rear by highly mobile Greek mountain cavalry, mounted on small, agile horses. While the Greeks advanced in the east, the central Italian thrust remained stranded in Greek territory by the

Kalamas river. The Siena, Ferrara and Centauro Divisions attempted to join the Julia Division, but were held up by minefields, poor leadership and the Kalamas itself, in which they lost many men in establishing a bridgehead. On 6 November the order was given for the Julia Division to retreat, but due to communication defects the order did not reach them until 7 November. The already battered division had the thankless task of fighting a retreat back through the Greek forces at their rear.

Greek generals had outwitted Prasca by enticing the Italians into deep mountainous gorges, which explained the inactivity during the opening days. The Greeks had left the entrance to the Aeos valley undefended for a week, in order to maximise the number of Italian troops lured into their trap. The Greeks steadily reinforced their troops who dominated the high ground and monitored the invader's progress in the valleys below. Then, when the moment was right, Greek troops launched their counter-attack with devastating effect. From the heights, Greek forces attacked from the rear and sides, throwing Italian columns into confusion. The Italian forces were completely overrun; in their haste to avoid being surrounded their subsequent retreat fell into disorder. Whole platoons threw away their weapons and plunged into mountain torrents that had been swollen by heavy rain; many were swept away and drowned before they could reach the opposite bank. Many more Italians sought refuge from the Greek onslaught in the mountains; days after the offensive, Greek patrols in the wooded heights came across enemy corpses that showed signs of having being mauled by mountain bears or wolves. By 10 November the counter-attack was complete, a large number of Italian prisoners were taken and useful equipment and weapons fell into Greek hands. As the Italians fell back they suffered heavily; the Greeks took around 3,500 prisoners, who, after a long trek down the mountainside, were transported to Athens by train. The Italian prisoners were a sorry sight, their uniforms were torn and covered in mud, they were tired and hungry; no longer did they look like the elite troops of Mussolini, the once proud plumes in their hats were now bedraggled and broken. One Italian prisoner of war told of the plight of his unit as they came under attack from Greek forces when half way up a ravine. He described how they were unable to return fire as: 'the Greeks had chosen their positions too well. They had left us no targets that we could see.' As more machine guns opened up on the Italians their situation was hopeless. 'It was impossible for us to advance farther; it was quite as impossible to retreat.'[18]

Ten days after the beginning of the battle, the main thrust of the Italian troops were held up on the Kalamas river and pushed back on two other fronts through Pindus and western Macedonia. The mechanised forces of Italy were cumbersome in mountainous areas where the cold was extreme and dense mist diminished Italian air superiority, and deep snowdrifts made it impossible to drag heavy guns. Given the adverse conditions, the

Italian mechanised divisions were at a disadvantage, compared with the Greeks whose transport was drawn almost entirely by horses and mules. Despite the greater mobility of the Greek army, their equipment was inadequate and Greek troops suffered bitterly from the extreme conditions. A great number of men went without blankets (this was due to a fire in Athens that had destroyed 200,000 blankets). Many of the boots worn by Greek troops had perished after weeks of marching; Arthur Merton of the *Daily Telegraph* described the conditions Greek troops had to endure. 'The covered wagons or open carts on which the drivers are huddled under pieces of canvas trying to protect themselves from the driving rain and wind, were drawn by sturdy little horses or mules.' Leland Stowe, also of the *Daily Telegraph*, declared: 'Surely this Greek army today is just about the highest-spirited army in the world.' He concluded: 'regardless of mud, rain and snow . . . day after day they march on'.[19]

Morale among the Italian troops was beginning to suffer. Captain Fernando Campione, of the Siena Division, described one of the many victims of Greek mortars in his diary on 10 November. 'Another infantryman is lying on the road. His hands contracted, a shell splinter tore open the right side of his stomach.' Campione concludes: 'the clotted blood has formed a huge dark filthy stain on his jacket.' This evening he will be buried 'probably beside the river at the foot of a small isolated mountain.'[20] Prasca described the initial losses as 'temporary difficulties' that were 'essentially due to transport and bad weather.'[21] Despite Prasca's excuses he was held responsible for the calamitous start to the Italian campaign. His tactics proved unimaginative and static and Mussolini effectively dismissed him on 11 November when he was put on permanent leave; his replacement was General Carlo Geloso.

Julia Division remained isolated, pinned down by mud and snow, and harried relentlessly by Greek forces who sensed the Italians' vulnerability. The Julia Division had fought their retreat through intense artillery and machine-gun fire, where hand-to-hand battles took place lasting up to seven hours. When the Julia Division reached the Perati bridge it was a shadow of the division that had set out on 28 October. A fifth of the division's men had been killed or captured; many of the transport animals had also perished. Those who remained were exhausted; several days' fighting in mountainous country sapped the strength and notably affected the morale of its men. The Julia Division suffered most of the opening Italian losses. Greek tactics of attacking from the rear and laying ambushes psychologically affected the Italian troops. The reckless optimism that marked the initial Italian advance was replaced by a cautious and pessimistic approach. In a speech on 18 November, Mussolini dismissed reports that the Julia Division had suffered enormous losses at the hands of the Greeks, describing the Division as:

'prouder; stronger than ever' and 'granite like'.[22] While the Duce made his speech, the Julia Division were fighting for their lives. Subjected to deadly mortar and machine-gun fire, they attempted to consolidate their position and check the Greek offensive. These men in tattered uniforms, filled with lice and heavily bearded, continued to fight for survival. A medical officer from the Julia Division wrote that at school these soldiers heard: 'it was a fine thing to die with a bullet in one's heart kissed by the rays of the sun . . . no one had thought that one might fall the other way up with one's face in the mud'. The medical officer of the Julia Division went on to describe the squalid conditions of the men in the dirt: 'there is no hope of washing; beards are long and thick with mud, and uniforms are torn to shreds'.[23]

After their initial counter-attack, the Greeks took the initiative all along the front. Greek Highland troops, who had a good knowledge of the area, worked their way along the Movora mountain range until they reached the Italians' supply base in the heights above Koritsa. With their newly acquired mountain artillery and heavy guns, Greek forces again sent the Italians on the retreat. Burning buildings illuminated the mountainside; Italian troops were seen evacuating the town in their masses. The RAF participated in the Greek raid on the Italian supply base and British pilots successfully attacked Italian transport columns and headquarters. 'We dived on them from about 20,000 feet and released our bombs dead over the column,' said one of the British pilots. 'I saw one bomb burst in the centre of one big lorry. The Italians were running like hares.'[24]

Under Air Vice Marshal D'Albiac, the RAF were quick to honour Britain's guarantee to Greece and rapidly dispatched an improvised collection of squadrons – comprising mostly Blenheims and Gladiators sent from Egypt. The first RAF operations in Greece started on 6 November with a highly successful bombing of Valona airfield in Albania. These missions were undertaken in perilous conditions and involved low-level flying through mountainous terrain with no fighter escort. On 28 November the RAF scored an impressive victory – two squadrons, one of Hurricanes, the other Gladiators, had shot down twenty-seven Italian aircraft over the Albanian front. Despite these victories, the RAF provoked some criticism from their Greek allies for not working in close support of their troops. Further British aid arrived on 16 November when an advance British convoy landed at Piraeus. It consisted mostly of non-combatants; intelligence units, bomb disposal detachments and officers with specialised knowledge of modern weapons and mountain warfare. The British were not very successful in passing on their expertise, as the Greek troops believed that mountain warfare was not suited to modern methods and had reverted to the warfare of their ancestors of more than a century earlier.

In Rome, the Duce gave the order to send two extra divisions to Albania, the Bari and Trieste Divisions. The Koritsa sector in Albania was to be organised for the consolidation of the Italian front. Papagos gave orders for a further Greek offensive against Italian forces with the ultimate objective being Koritsa. The Greeks attacked along the Macedonian front; the 9th, 10th, and 15th Divisions were in the first line of the Greek advance. At 06:30 on 14 November the 15th Division was the first to move with devastating results. Greek penetrations took place all along the front, causing confusion within Italian ranks, which was the catalyst for a general retreat. The newly arrived Bari Division was left horribly exposed with a completely open flank. Chaos prevailed at the rear as the Greek mortar rounds fell on Italian headquarters; wind driven snow added to the confusion. 'The 81mm shells caused horrible wounds; [the injured] filled hospitals [where] bandages, lint, drugs were lacking.' Operations were carried out: 'under lorry tarpaulins or in the debris of cottages'.[25] The ferocity of the Greek assault tore through the Italians, who had not prepared themselves for such defensive battles. Reinforcements immediately found themselves in the midst of battle before realising they were anywhere near the front. In the middle of heavy shelling, Italian troops disembarked from German Junker transports at Koritsa airfield and within minutes many were wounded and sent back in the same aircraft to hospitals in Italy. On the night of 19 November the Italians decided that their position had become untenable and Koritsa would have to be abandoned. Aerial reconnaissance reported that one retreating Italian column was twelve miles long. The majority of Albanian battalions had disintegrated completely.

Greek detachments entered Koritsa on 22 November to a joyous welcome from the Albanian inhabitants who received them as liberators. When Metaxas announced the capture of Koritsa in Athens, there were scenes of intense patriotic enthusiasm; crowds stood in front of the king's palace waving Greek flags, mixed with the Union flag. Through the streets military bands marched and British soldiers and airmen were carried shoulder high. The capture of Koritsa was greeted with elation in Greece and it became a symbol of the humiliation of their Axis aggressor. In Britain, Lord Halifax spoke of great admiration for the Greek victory. Meanwhile, the RAF continued to carry out operations against ports on the Italian mainland and positions in Albania. British aid was acknowledged by Metaxas after the fall of Koritsa; he expressed the nation's 'profound gratitude to the valiant Greek army' and added 'the grateful acknowledgement of the Hellenic nation to our valiant British allies' and for the 'exploits scored by their unconquerable Navy and brilliant Air Force'.[26]

Metaxas's acknowledgement of the 'unconquerable Navy' referred to the British raid on the Italian port of Taranto. On 11 November the Italians suffered another unexpected defeat, this time at sea, which further strengthened Britain's position in the Mediterranean. The Fleet Air Arm's attack off the south coast of Italy was described as one of the most daring episodes in the Second World War. Half the Italian fleet was crippled in an exhilarating raid on the port of Taranto by obsolete torpedo biplanes, launched from the aircraft carrier *Illustrious*. Shortly after 21.00 the aircraft took off and embarked on Operation JUDGEMENT; eleven aircraft were armed with torpedoes and the remainder carried flares and bombs. There was little wind and just enough cloud to offer protection from a bright three-quarter moon. By 22.50 the aircraft were approaching Taranto and a heavy barrage of anti-aircraft fire, which resembled a firework display. Red and blue tracer bullets appeared to rise slowly at first, until they were just short of the aircraft, when suddenly they would accelerate and whistle past. From 5,000 feet the torpedo planes descended to around fifty, whereupon they dropped their torpedoes and quickly rose again. After the raid, Taranto was left in chaos, two Italian battleships were sunk and a third critically damaged for the loss of only two aircraft.

On 5 December the RAF won their most decisive victory of the Greco–Italian war. Fighters had shot down a large number of Italian aircraft without loss, and bombers had successfully attacked retreating Italian troops. Only in the air were the Italians able to claim any sort of victory, the bombing of defenceless civilians on the island of Corfu; the RAF retaliated with the bombing of Italian positions in Valona and Durazzo. A communiqué issued in Athens on 23 November stated that the Italians were looting and plundering as they withdrew from Greek villages in Epirus. 'Villages present horrible scenes where the Italians are leaving traces of savagery and barbarity.'[27]

The Italian retreat stretched across the entire line from the Yugoslav frontier to the sea. Italian commanders were reduced to communicating via messengers. On 23 November the Air Chief of Staff, Francesco Pricolo, stated in a report to Mussolini that the commanders had 'many doubts about the fighting spirit of the troops who are tired, mixed up in different units and sometimes disorganised'. Pricolo stressed: 'they [Italian troops] have the feeling of having been badly used and badly supported' and particularly 'they are depressed at having suffered the humiliation of defeat at the hands of the Greeks'.[28]

Papagos hesitated to give the order for an all-out offensive, fearing that his Greek forces might fall into a similar trap that he had successfully utilised against the Italians. Papagos was not a dynamic military leader, he was a soldier from the 'old school', who favoured traditional tactics and would not advance without his rear and flanks well protected. General Tsolakoglou, who had commanded Greek troops on the right wing of western Macedonia, had suggested to Papagos that a task force of four infantry battalions, backed by an artillery unit, should assault Pogradec where the Italians had recently settled after their defeat at Koritsa. Greek troops once again seized the initiative, and Pogradec fell on 28 November after fierce fighting. After the debacle at Pogradec,

Mussolini summoned the head of military intelligence to his office and raged: 'I want the truth, because I am going to have various heads blown off by firing squad.'[29]

On 4 December Cavallero replaced Badoglio as Chief of the General Staff. Cavallero was a brilliant academic: he had a degree in pure mathematics, could speak German and English, and was promoted to general at the age of 38. Despite his academic credentials, he could not halt the slide of the Italian army. When he was handed a report describing the state of Italian resources in Albania, he discovered that arms and artillery supplies were exhausted, medical equipment was inadequate, and reserve rations had been expended. Some units were forced to withdraw from battle as they had run out of ammunition. The Albanian winter proved to be severe, and Italian troops faced it in horrifying conditions. The devastating losses to Italian divisions, accompanied by a grave shortage of mules, lorries and ammunition, meant that the Italian forces could not hold out for long. The 8th Alpini Regiment, of the Julia Division, had incurred eighty percent losses and the Bari Division had been almost entirely wiped out. Corporal Peppino Caramuta, of the Bari Division, wrote of the indescribable hardships endured and of the 'famous Greek mortars' which had 'taken the lives of thousands of young men; the sound of them continually in my ears.'[30]

'The small untidy Greek soldier had performed a miracle. What was intended to be a murder now looked like suicide.'[31] The state of the Italian assault on Greece had been so critical that the Nazi foreign minister, Ribbentrop, had issued a circular instructing how to react over the sensitive subject of Albania. Ribbentrop stressed that it was important to emphasise that Italian immobility was due to the season, and that the Italian retreat was a passing phenomenon. The Italian failure inevitably put Mussolini in an intolerable situation, as his aspirations of emulating Nazi victories lay in ruins. 'There is no more to be done. It is absurd and grotesque, but that is how it is,' Mussolini stated to Ciano on 4 December: 'We shall have to ask for a truce through Hitler.' Ciano replied: 'Impossible. The Greeks' first condition will be the Führer's personal guarantee that nothing else will be done against them.' Ciano concluded that: 'Rather than telephone Ribbentrop I shall put a bullet through my head.'[32]

In a letter to Mussolini on 20 November, Hitler claimed that the Italian attack on Greece had 'displeasing psychological consequences' and the 'military consequences' were very 'grave'.[33] Hitler complained that the Italian campaign had unsettled the political situation in the Balkans and brought British air power within range of Romania and southern Italy. After reading Hitler's rebuke, Mussolini remarked: 'He really smacked my fingers.'[34] Hitler noted that the defeats suffered by Italy were the first by an Axis power, and enabled 'Churchill to revive the courage of his countrymen which gave hope to all Anglophiles the world over.'[35]

Goebbels bitterly remarked: 'Rome has really put a spanner in the works . . . Our fascist allies are turning into a real millstone around our neck.'[36] Hitler was furious and condemned the whole Greek adventure as madness. Marshal Graziani hoped that the simultaneous launching of a second-stage offensive in Egypt to capture Mersa Matruth could prevent British intervention in Greece. But Graziani's failure in the desert accentuated Hitler's frustration. Mussolini fended off Hitler's pressing offers of help, intending to preserve his freedom of action within the Axis alliance by fighting a 'parallel war'. The offer to seize Crete by airborne troops was ignored, although Italy did not have the resources to capture the island on its own. As General Franz Halder noted bitterly on 4 November, the Italians 'do not want us'.[37] The Italian failure to capture Crete was a strategic error; British possession of the island jeopardised the Italian lines of communication to North Africa and assured Greece of a reliable supply line from Egypt. Hitler also believed that the Italian defeats led other Balkan states to view the Axis powers with 'scorn' and 'contempt'. Hitler alleged it was the Italian blunder in Greece that stiffened Yugoslavia's attitude towards Germany. Hitler made some valid points but it was convenient to magnify the consequences of the attack on Greece, in order to minimise his own mistakes.

Despite the victories won by the Greek troops, Metaxas's mood remained sober; he knew that his country's efforts, though heroic, were ultimately in vain. The Greek dictator was ill with cancer and the winter in Athens had taken its toll on him. Instead of rejoicing over Greek victories, Metaxas had privately expressed sympathy in his diary for his soldiers, noting 'who knows how my poor soldiers are suffering'. On 31 December Metaxas was deeply depressed about his situation, his life was coming to an end, and the future of Greece was uncertain, and the menace of German intervention loomed. Having noted the brilliant Greek successes, he wrote: 'I do not see a way out.'[38]

Papagos's principal strategy was aimed at the prevention of a renewed Italian offensive. Greek troops were suffering in the harsh conditions, men were covered with lice and wore long beards and tattered clothing, but they endeavoured to besiege the Julia Division with increasingly weary assaults. By January the unfortunate Julia Division had been reduced to just 1,000 men, with only fifteen machine guns and five mortars, and they had lost 153 officers. General Nasci described the condition of his troops to the newly appointed Cavallero: 'twenty cases of men frozen to death and several dozen of frostbite have impaired the last moral energies of men.' Italian troops 'slept in the open in temperatures which in the last few days have dropped to several degrees below zero'. Nasci noted that Greek troops were by contrast operating in a 'friendly environment . . . with few worries about supply . . . with a numerical preponderance of strength that enables him to continually vary his offensive patrols'.[39] Nasci went on to explain that the Greeks had received assistance from the local population, an interesting observation, as the Albanian locals were expected to be aiding the Italians. Word that the Greek troops were suffering from lack of food and the freezing conditions was spread throughout the mountain villages. Villagers hastened to help Greek troops; they carried baskets with bread and carved paths through the snow with improvised sleighs where mules could not pass. A Greek officer and historian, Angelos Terzakis, recalled 'black zigzags of their columns here and there on the white horizon' where 'black clad women forced their way through the snow.' On the slopes of the Grammos mountains 'an Italian air patrol detects one of those processions and opens fire'.[40] Terzakis witnessed eleven women cut down by the machine-gun fire, only to be promptly replaced by other women in the column.

The extent of Greek success was remarkable given that they fought with First World War weaponry, much of it taken from the Austrian army. Conditions for the Greek troops were appalling; they often went hungry relying on supplies brought to them from neighbouring villages. Ration and ammunition supply lines from Greece were unreliable as they depended almost solely on pack animals. British officers described the Greek soldiers as having 'clothing and footwear of a deplorable quality'.[41] During the march to the front, some soldiers were given civilian overcoats by pitying onlookers. Only the walking wounded stood a chance of survival. Stretcher cases proved impossible to evacuate and inevitably died in the harsh winter conditions. Lame pack animals were killed and eaten by troops desperate for food. RAF Blenheims dropped sacks of food to starving, snow-bound units, who were lacking even basic essentials such as water, as there was no fuel to melt the snow.

On 20 December the Greeks took Porto Palmero and attacked Himara on the coast. Greek troops broke through Italian ranks after a brief battle. Italian aircraft mistakenly attacked the Siena Division, which was already in a state of disarray, the repeated strafing from their own aircraft resulting in forty killed and many wounded. The Siena Division had suffered severely; long columns of tattered troops dragged themselves along in retreat. On 14 December the Siena Division's withdrawal became more desperate and disorderly. Captain Fernando Campione wrote: 'More than ninety mules are lying along the road; they collapsed from exhaustion . . . abandoned on the spot with their load.' Campione went on to describe the major in command of the Siena Division, who had been suffering from the initial stages of frostbite and was returning from a mountain position: 'His serious, emaciated, livid face betrays the tragedy of the days and nights passed in the cold and snow.' Campione noted on 17 December that there were no reserves: 'there is nothing to fall back on. Mule drivers, lorry drivers, everyone available has been thrown into the defence.' The freezing conditions proved as dangerous as the enemy:

'forty men are frozen to death daily . . . It is not the fighting that kills, but exhaustion that brings terror and humiliation.' Among this degradation Italian machine gunners had orders to fire on anyone who withdrew. Campione concluded: 'It was desired to put blame on heroic, exhausted and sick fighting men.'[42] The Siena Division, who had confidently advanced up the Kalamas river, had been practically wiped out after two months' fighting.

After days of inactivity, the Greek victory at Himara was hailed as a great success in Greece, proving that the Greeks were still capable of offensive operations. After the offensive at Himara, the front became somewhat stationary. Greek raids still besieged Italian lines but penetrations were minor; it seemed the severity of the winter had also paralysed the spirit of the Greek forces. As it began to snow in Rome, Mussolini remarked triumphantly that he approved of the snow and cold as it would 'kill off the weaklings and improve this mediocre Italian race'.[43] Italian soldiers slept in open trenches without drainage, they lived in mud and snow, lacking winter clothing, without suitable footwear or any change of clothing. Uniforms were torn and weighed heavily without providing warmth or protection. Frostbite ravaged Italian troops and claimed a total of nearly 13,000 men. Legs began to swell and feeling disappeared from the foot, flesh changed colour, to purple then black. Men who suffered the effects of frostbite endured agonising journeys to overcrowded field hospitals; they often had to be carried by their comrades due to the lack of stretchers. All along the Italian front line it was the same story: freezing conditions, uniforms that fell apart, rations that did not materialise and continual pressure from Greek raids. Those who went on patrol risked death or capture but at least it gave them a break from the front line.

In Italy, the illusion of the great Italian military expedition was shattered; the Italian public resented the humiliation suffered at the hands of the Greeks. At the height of Mussolini's arrogance he erected a giant map in a Rome square designed to depict Italian gains in the Mediterranean and North Africa. The collapse of Graziani's offensive in the desert had signalled the beginning of a series of military defeats, and Mussolini's propaganda stunt had gone horribly awry, publicly exposing their military ineptitude. Meanwhile the troops on the icy mountains of Albania grimly consumed the contents of frozen stiff food parcels that had got through the chaotic supply route to the front line.

On 21 December Air Vice Marshal D'Albiac stated that the RAF had destroyed thirty-nine Italian planes with the loss of nine and had completed a total of twenty-six raids on Durazzo and Valona. On Christmas Day British planes dropped supplies on the island of Corfu, which had suffered heavy bombing from the Italians; these gifts were well received by the inhabitants as many of the islanders had been left homeless. At the start of the New Year, Italy was coming to terms with the disastrous invasion of Greece that had seen thousands of Mussolini's finest soldiers slain, wounded or taken prisoner. Those who remained seemed doomed to an ineffectual battle against a determined Greek defensive wall.

Significant numbers of British forces had not landed in Greece, nor had the Greeks asked for such aid. Greece still thought of the war as being a Greco–Italian concern. However, the British had given considerable assistance to the Greeks in the form of 5,000 men of the RAF. Despite Greece not calling for the implementation of full British assistance, Germany was increasingly concerned about the British presence, and in the New Year Hitler was drawing up plans for the invasion of Greece.

Mussolini was desperate for some good news to report to Hitler at their meeting in Salzburg. There he had to endure a lecture by Hitler but he stopped short of humiliating the Duce. Mussolini arrived back in Rome with the single-minded objective of gaining a victory before the inter-vention of Germany. Mussolini repeatedly stated that Italy must 'attack, attack, attack'. By the end of February, Italian reinforcements had boosted their strength to twenty-five divisions, only ten of which were in a satis-factory condition. Cavallero prepared two plans, the first for an advance and another as a contingency plan in the event of another defeat. Mussolini implored Cavallero for an offensive; at a meeting with his Chief of Staff, he described the campaign in Greece as a political masterpiece that had been turned into a military failure.

As the Germans began planning the invasion of Greece, codenamed Operation MARITA, British and Greek officials started discussing the possibility of collaboration. During this period an interesting paradox occurred. Prince Erbach, the German ambassador, remained in Greece and had maintained good relations with Metaxas. The ambassador made it clear that Hitler did not share Mussolini's recklessness and Metaxas assured Erbach that Greece had no expansionist aims in Albania and asked the prince to give Hitler his good wishes for the New Year. There was a rumour that Germany had offered to mediate between the Greeks and Italians in the middle of December, but this is not substantiated by documentary evidence.

The war now entered a static phase. It was clear that Cavallero wanted to ensure that he suffered none of the catastrophes that had beset Prasca. Cavallero was still preparing for Mussolini's offensive at the end of February, when the Duce was preparing to visit the troops in Albania. Mussolini left Bari for Albania on 2 March. As he arrived at Tirana airfield, he feared a hostile reception from the troops. Cavallero greeted Mussolini with the face of optimism; Mussolini returned his greeting and quickly entered a waiting car. As he drove past infantry from the Bari Division, soldiers began to cheer loudly as they recognised the Duce. The spontaneous cheering lifted Mussolini, who was very sensitive to public applause, and he temporarily forgot about the tragedy that had befallen the Italian campaign. As the Duce was mobbed by demonstrations of mass enthusiasm, General Pricolo noticed 'a solitary individual who remained apart on the slope of the valley along the roadside and went on quietly eating'. He carried on eating but every now and then stopped as if he was dumbfounded 'by a scene that was obviously incomprehensible to him.' After the young soldier noticed Pricolo looking at him he 'began slowly backing into the bushes.'[44]

On 9 March Cavallero's offensive got under way; the Italian troops advanced slowly and suffered bloody losses. The ground they gained initially was immediately retaken by Greek counter-attacks. The battle was fiercely fought at close quarters with bayonet and hand grenade. Mussolini watched the battle unfold from an observation post on Mount Komarit. As it drew into the second day Mussolini saw that the offensive was failing and he realised that he would not inspire a victory to impress Hitler. As the assault reached its fifth day, no ground had been won despite relentless offensives from Italian forces, which struggled through the mud to attack an enemy that was dug in on high ground. The attack had cost the Italians 12,000 casualties, a very heavy price to pay for an offensive that had not ventured beyond the starting point. On 16 March Mussolini called the offensive to a halt.

Mussolini's aircraft left Albania on 21 March, it was said that the Duce was 'disgusted' with his troops efforts. There was a certain justice in the failure of the March offensive; no doubt Mussolini would have utilised a victorious offensive to 'wipe the slate clean' and erase the horrific waste of life that took place in the mountains of Albania. The Italians had expected a war of waving flags and playing bands, and had made little preparation for the realities of a bloody war and frostbite. Italian prisoners made a melancholy, pitiful spectacle; a Greek officer sarcastically remarked of a column that passed: 'There goes the second Roman Empire.'[45] The Greeks had to face the same snow and mud as their Italian enemy, they too suffered terribly from frostbite, and were equally exhausted from fighting in appalling conditions. Yet Greek troops persisted in their endless assault on little more than a crust of bread and melted snow, with no fires, shelter or equipment. Despite suffering similar hardships, there was a tangible difference in morale between the two forces. This was indicative of the contrast in motivation of the conscripts fighting a war for which they had no heart, and free men, fighting for their homes and families. The war in Greece was the result of a whim from the Italian dictator who decided to pay Hitler back in his 'own coin'. As Mussolini made his way back to Rome, the snow began to melt in Albania. From under the brilliant white layers an apocalyptic scene began to emerge, dead bodies littered the mountains along with helmets, water bottles, dead mules and blood-splattered letters.

According to the Italian Defence Ministry, the Greek campaign had cost the Italians 51,190 dead or missing and 64,476 seriously wounded or hospitalised. Greek official casualties numbered 13,408 dead and 42,485 wounded. Many others suffered mutilations as a result of frostbite. The efforts of the Greek troops had left them over-stretched and with numbers thinned, they were also in desperate need of re-equipment. The Greek armed forces needed a period of recuperation, but a worse ordeal was soon to befall them. Diplomatic developments in the winter of 1940–1 saw Britain explore the possibility of assistance to Greece, and brought Germany to the verge of intervention.

NOTES

1 Hammerton, John, *The Second Great War*, Historical Documents CXC–CXCIV, text of the Italian ultimatum to Greece, 28 October 1940, Vol. 4, London: Waverly, 1950, p. 1309.
2 Ibid.
3 Cervi, Mario, *The Hollow Legions. Mussolini's Blunder in Greece 1940–1941*, London: Chatto & Windus, 1972, p. 18.
4 'Athenian', *The Greek Miracle*, London, 1942, p. 12.
5 Cervi, op. cit., p. 54.
6 Dispatch from Jacomoni to Ciano, 24 August 1940, Italian Diplomatic Documents (hereafter IDD).
7 Cervi, op. cit., p. 121.
8 Dispatch from Grazzi to Ciano, 3 October 1940, IDD.
9 Cervi, op. cit., p. 50.
10 Ibid, p. 69.
11 Ibid, p. 74.
12 Ibid, p. 89.
13 Letter from Boris III of Bulgaria to Mussolini, 18 October 1940, IDD.
14 Cervi, op. cit., p. 100
15 Diary of Major Fatuzzo, 27 October 1940.
16 Cervi, op. cit., p. 243
17 Hammerton, op. cit., p. 1296.
18 Ibid, p. 1304.
19 Ibid, p. 1356.
20 Cervi, op. cit., p. 141.
21 Ibid, p. 246.
22 Speech by Mussolini, 18 November 1940, IDD.
23 Cervi, op. cit., p. 249.
24 Hammerton, op. cit., p. 1303.
25 Cervi, op. cit., p. 160.
26 Hammerton, op. cit., p. 1308.
27 Ibid.
28 Cervi, op. cit., p. 167.
29 Ibid, p. 169.
30 Ibid, p. 256.
31 'Athenian', op. cit., p. 127.
32 Cervi, op. cit., p. 175.
33 Letter from Hitler to Mussolini, 20 November 1940, IDD.

34 Macdonald, Callum, *The Lost Battle – Crete 1941*, London: Macmillan, 1993, p. 53.
35 Cervi, op. cit., p. xiii.
36 Macdonald, op. cit., p. 53.
37 Burdick, C and Jacobsen, H A (eds), *The Halder War Diaries 1939–1942*, London, 1988, p. 277.
38 Cervi, op. cit., p. 184.
39 Ibid, p. 187.
40 Terzakis, Angelos, www.tripod.com/Balkans/before
41 De Guingand, F, *Operation Victory*, London: Hodder & Stoughton, 1947, p. 59
42 Cervi, op. cit., p. 247.
43 Ibid, p. 193.
44 Ibid, p. 229.
45 Hammerton, op. cit., p. 1583.

CHAPTER III

The Threat from Germany

In the summer of 1940 Germany was at the pinnacle of her power as master of Europe; only Britain remained defiant. Hitler assumed that Britain would soon realise the hopelessness of her situation and begin peace negotiations, whereby Germany would be accepted as ruler of continental Europe and Britain would remain a great maritime power with its vast overseas empire intact. Hitler perceived Britain's empire to be essential for his vision of a 'new world order'; it was therefore perplexing to him when the British government rejected offers of mediation.

Hitler gave British troops a reprieve at Dunkirk, inexplicably halting the advance of German forces, as the British Expeditionary Force lay stranded. Rundstedt, the German commander at Dunkirk, stated after the war that the Führer had deliberately allowed the British to escape. The motives for Hitler's hesitation at Dunkirk are open to debate, however there is strong evidence to suggest that he hoped to come to an arrangement with Britain. On 17 May Hitler told his officers of plans to divide the world with the British. He repeated this assertion to Halder on 21 May, and on 2 June Hitler told a group of generals that he hoped Britain would accept a 'reasonable peace'.

On 10 May 1940 Churchill replaced Neville Chamberlain as Prime Minister. Churchill had opposed Chamberlain's appeasement policy and would not contemplate reaching a compromise with Germany. Hitler's aspirations of a negotiated settlement with Britain were misguided, but were by no means without foundation. Not all of Churchill's colleagues shared his determination to continue the war, or his refusal to negotiate with a detested enemy. In a letter to Roosevelt, Churchill hinted at the possibility that his government might not survive the pressure from those who hoped for an arrangement with the enemy. National Peace Council efforts were endorsed by such well-known figures as economist G D H Cole and the actor John Gielgud, but it is difficult to assess how 'real' Churchill believed the threat to be.

The objective of the Luftwaffe raids on Britain was not only intended to cripple Britain's war industry, but to demoralise the workforce and strengthen those industrialists, politicians and military leaders who wished to dispose of Churchill and end a 'senseless' war. Goering's staff convinced themselves that the industrial magnates of the Midlands were Churchill's strongest supporters and when they saw their capital investments reduced to rubble they would call for peace. According to Goering's staff, the Midlands was the homeland of the 'truly conservative, stubborn and obstinate Englishmen who are the intellectual and moral foundation of Britain's resistance and endurance'.[1] Contrary to German expectations, the Luftwaffe did not break the British people, but only strengthened Britain's will to resist and avenge the 23,000 who died in the blitz between July and December 1940.

By the winter of 1940 the Luftwaffe had failed to reach its strategic objectives; they were hampered by bad weather, which reduced the number of raids. In England there was a general feeling of relief brought on by the outcome of the Battle of Britain. Churchill was quick to use the Battle of Britain as a triumph in the face of adversity; his language immortalised the battle as it had done with Dunkirk. The saying 'the spirit of Dunkirk' became a popular, and soon overworked, cliché that became part of the mythology of the time.

The evacuation of the British army at Dunkirk liberated Britain from a war of attrition involving large land forces. This allowed Britain to enjoy the flexibility of naval and air forces that could engage the enemy at chosen strategic points. Britain had a tradition of the precise application of small, but highly skilled forces that could sustain her against greater adversaries. Churchill's refusal to yield faced Hitler with a dilemma on how best to tackle Britain, either to invade or attack her interests abroad. With the largest army in the world, Germany could not afford to hesitate; Hitler had to retain the initiative and seek a decisive outcome before the United States joined the war and the balance of power shifted against the Reich.

German foreign policy in the winter of 1940 was incoherent and confused. Hitler had stated in a letter to Mussolini that: ' War in the West is in itself won. A violent effort is still necessary to crush England.'[2] This statement was in itself contradictory and indicative of the confused nature of Hitler's thinking during this period. The situation was finally resolved at the end of 1940 when the focus of the German war effort shifted to the east. On 12 November the Soviet foreign minister, Molotov, arrived in Berlin for talks designed by Hitler to initiate Russian membership of the Tripartite Pact and turn Stalin's attention away from the Balkans. The negotiations with Molotov were the catalyst for the deterioration of relations between Russia and Germany. When it was suggested that Russia should join the Axis alliance, Molotov replied that: 'paper agreements would not suffice for the Soviet Union' and insisted on 'effective guarantees for her security'.[3] Both Hitler and the Nazi foreign minister, Ribbentrop, maintained that Britain was defeated and offered

Molotov a share in the British Empire. Hitler stated that all countries 'interested in the bankrupt estate would have to stop all controversies among themselves' and concern themselves solely with 'the partition of the British Empire'.[4] However, Molotov refused to be sidetracked from Soviet claims in north-west Europe and the Balkans. He bluntly stated that Russia wanted all of Finland and was interested in Bulgaria. The interpreters were amazed at the way in which Molotov hurled incessant questions at Hitler. Hitler's response was said to have been 'meekly polite'. To avoid further questioning, the Führer suggested they adjourned, 'otherwise we shall get caught in the air-raid warning'.[5] On the resumption of the meeting the following day, Molotov set about questioning Ribbentrop regarding German intentions in Greece, Poland and Yugoslavia. The German foreign minister complained that he was being 'interrogated too closely'. In an attempt to escape Molotov's pointed questions, Ribbentrop continually reiterated the proposed liquidation of the British Empire, but Molotov refused to be silenced by distant promises. Molotov remarked: 'If England is in fact defeated and powerless, why have we been conducting this discussion in your air raid shelter?'[6]

Two weeks later Stalin replied to Ribbentrop's offer, stating that the Soviet government was prepared to join the Tripartite Pact subject to a list of conditions, which included the withdrawal of German troops from Finland. Stalin's provisos conceded Hitler a free hand in the west in exchange for bases, and territorial rights that safeguarded the Soviet Union from a German attack. Hitler was staggered at Stalin's demands stating that the Russians had 'let the cat out of the sack. The Balkans and Finland are endangered flanks.'[7] Hitler told Raeder: 'Stalin is nothing but a cold-blooded blackmailer.'[8] On 18 December 1940 Hitler issued Directive No. 21, Operation BARBAROSSA, which ordered an attack on Soviet Russia before the defeat of Great Britain. The defeat of Russia was recognised as a vital factor in the war against Britain. Hitler informed his senior military commanders: 'The USA and Russia hold Britain erect . . . beaten Russia will permit Japan to turn all energies against the United States.'[9]

Operation BARBAROSSA had revised the strategic context in which German foreign policy viewed Greece and Crete. Hitler had prepared for the invasion of Greece as early as November 1940. The invasion of Greece (Operation MARITA) was initially aimed at aiding the Italians and securing the Plöesti oilfields against the RAF. But BARBAROSSA now dictated the objective of Operation MARITA. The failure of Mussolini's attack on Greece meant that Germany had to secure its southern flank for the forthcoming offensive against Russia. The 'psychological and military consequences' of Italy's reckless invasion of Greece, as Hitler described them, were now even more pertinent. On 13 December Hitler gave a revised directive for

Operation MARITA, which called for the occupation of Greece and the employment of airborne troops against Greek islands. Prior to the operation the Führer forced the Bulgarians to allow Germany to set up an early warning station along the frontier with Greece. Hitler ordered plans to occupy Macedonia and Thrace, where air bases could be established to counter any threat to the Romanian oilfields. In preparation for the invasion of Greece, the German garrison in Romania was strengthened and troops were sent to Bulgaria to establish infrastructure for the deployment of the invasion forces. The Soviets were alarmed by these developments, although Hitler tried to reassure Molotov that these measures were aimed solely at Britain.

The threat of German intervention changed the perspective of British aid to Greece. A successful defence of Greece against a German assault would require substantial British land forces deployed on the mainland. These were troops that Britain could scarcely afford as they were already engaged in North Africa meeting the advance of the Italians. The confusion of counsels that preceded the decision to aid Greece is surrounded by ambiguity and intrigue. Prominent figures such as Churchill, the commander of British ground forces in the Middle East General Archibald Wavell, the foreign secretary Anthony Eden and the Chief of the Imperial Staff Sir John Dill, had all shown opposition to intervention at some stage. The Greeks themselves were also reluctant to receive British assistance for fear of provoking Germany into action against them, without the strength to repel them. Previous guarantees issued by the Chamberlain administration illustrate that the decision to uphold the guarantee to Greece was by no means a foregone conclusion. What followed was a diplomatic game of 'cat and mouse'.

Chamberlain had issued the guarantees to Turkey and Greece; Churchill approved them then, but later stressed the need to ensure they could be implemented. It was possible that Churchill bore these reservations in mind when he told the War Cabinet that Britain was entitled to argue that the fall of France had rendered the guarantee to Greece invalid. Churchill explained it was a 'joint guarantee, but unhappily the Vichy government is at this moment engaged in sincere and loyal collaboration with Herr Hitler'.[10] Churchill warned that 'it would be foolish to make promises which we could not fulfil'.[11] However, Churchill did not use the fall of France as an excuse to pass responsibility, adding to his speech to the War Cabinet: 'no answer would really help if another small ally were overwhelmed.'[12]

Before the Italian invasion of Greece, on 27 May 1940, the Chiefs of Staff studied the prospect of sending aid to Greece, and sent a telegram to British headquarters in the Middle East stating: 'Owing to vital commitments elsewhere and our limited resources there can be no question of taking Greece under our protection.' However: 'we appreciate your wish to take the Greeks into our confidence ... without present resources' there would be 'no question, repeat no question of direct support by land or air'.[13]

Despite the reservations of the Chiefs of Staff, British aid was dispatched within days of the Greek request. From the onset of the Italian invasion the Greek government asked Britain to honour the commitment given by the Chamberlain administration. Churchill replied to Metaxas: 'we will give you all the help in our power'.[14] Churchill appeared positive, but he was careful not to commit Britain to any specific action. After spirited Greek resistance indicated that a prolonged battle might occur, Operation BARBARITY was dispatched. BARBARITY consisted of a small detachment of an RAF strike force with army ancillaries; it was designed only to provide air support for Greek resistance. Air Chief Marshal Sir Arthur Longmore acted on his own initiative and ordered squadrons from Africa to Greece. Churchill approved of Longmore's course of action and expressed his gratitude over the squadrons taken from the Middle East to aid Greek resistance. 'Tell Longmore that I much admire his calling in of the Southern squadrons.' Churchill stressed: 'the part played by the R.A.F. in Greek victories has been of immense military and political consequence'.[15] With the assistance of the RAF the Greeks forced the Italians back, inflicting on them severe losses in men and hardware. The events in Greece prompted mutual respect and generous acknowledgement from both countries. Metaxas declared his gratitude for the assistance of the RAF and the 'whole hearted aid rendered to our struggle'. Churchill replied to Metaxas: 'we are all inspired by this feat of Greek valour against an enemy so superior in number and equipment'.[16]

Despite the show of gratitude from both countries, the first attempts to bring British aid to Greece were not carried out in the efficacious spirit that Churchill and Metaxas expressed publicly. Disagreements quickly arose about how best to utilise the RAF. Greek commanders wanted the RAF to operate in close support of the troops on the ground, but Air-Commodore, J H D'Albiac believed that the small force of bombers would be best employed striking at the disembarkation points in Albania and at important lines of communication. Due to the heavy rainfall, D'Albiac suggested to Metaxas the immediate construction of all-weather airfields at Agrinion and Araxos. The Greek authorities agreed and D'Albiac was given assurances that these airfields would be complete by the end of January. Lack of transport and resources meant that neither of these airfields was complete by the time of the German invasion; ironically it was the Germans who made first use of them.

More controversial was the question of RAF access to Greek airfields. The German government had pointedly refrained from withdrawing their minister from Athens, who had privately assured Metaxas that Germany would not interfere in the conflict with Italy, provided British bombers were not permitted use of the northern airfields of Greece. Hitler was evidently worried about the security of the Plöesti oil installations. Metaxas subsequently complied with Germany's request and denied D'Albiac use of the northern airfields. Metaxas was prepared to use restraint, as he was desperate not to provoke German intervention that would signal the inevitable destruction of Greece. It resulted in a bizarre situation in which British airmen, who, in other theatres were engaged in a deadly struggle with Germany, lived side by side with German diplomats in Athens, who observed and took notes. The RAF advance party were the first British forces openly back on European mainland since the fall of France. The young British pilots soon settled into life in Greece; during the day they would carry out daring bombing raids on Italian positions, by night they would unwind in the night clubs of Athens, occasionally brawling with dubious German 'holiday-makers'.

Anglo–Greek relations were stretched by the increasing threat from Germany. This was illustrated in an incident when Greek authorities refused the RAF permission to visit the scene of a crashed British aircraft in Salonika. Each meeting with the British was conducted in extreme secrecy and the head of the British military mission in Greece, General Heywood, had his movements severely restricted. The British commanders in the Middle East took the view that German immobility would not last long and Greek efforts to appease Germany would ultimately be in vain. The British felt that they should be allowed a certain freedom with which to prepare the Greeks for an inevitable invasion. General Wavell foresaw German intervention in Greece as inevitable regardless of provocation. He wrote: 'I am sure Germany can not afford to see Italy defeated or even held, and must intervene.'[17]

A letter to conservative MP Leo Amery reveals that Churchill was ardent that Britain remained ambiguous on intervention, in spite of the prospect of a German invasion. In a speech, Amery made it clear that a British force should be made ready to land on Greece. Churchill began his letter to Amery: 'It was a pity that your speech dealt with strategy and military policy.' Churchill continued: 'if the Germans thought we were establishing a land front in Greece' Hitler would 'certainly be inclined to intervene against Greece. The longer we can put this off the better.'[18] Churchill's letter explains the apparent apathy shown by the Chief of Staff and the British government in preparing a sufficient land force to defend Greece.

Metaxas had not pressed the British government for further assistance despite the threat from Germany; he was a realist and was well aware of the limited resources of the British. Accordingly, the Greek dictator appealed only for naval and air support. The British Naval Fleet already commanded the eastern Mediterranean; therefore the most urgent need was for airpower as the Greek air force was of negligible value. Operation

BARBARITY was satisfactory for both countries; Britain was able to give Greece valuable support and a share in its victories against the Italians without committing large-scale forces.

The Joint Planning Staff and the Chiefs of Staff in London were careful not to go beyond the small number of aircraft they had initially committed. The Chief of Staff explained that indirect support would result from Allied success against the Italians in other theatres: 'the interests of Greece must depend upon our ability to defeat Italy' as opposed to Britain's ability 'to afford local support on the Greek mainland.' The Chief of Staff went on to say it: 'would be clearly militarily unsound to compromise the ultimate issue of war by diverting our resources from our vital objectives.' The 'vital objectives' obviously referred to the British war effort in North Africa. They also highlighted the need not to be: 'drawn into discussing the precise measures we intend to take in support of Greece' as they may constitute 'some form of direct land and air support.'[19] The Joint Planning Staff reiterated the policy of non-committal in a paper sent to the Middle East: 'our policy will be to sustain Greek resistance by all means in our power' but without 'committing in Greece forces which are vital to our security elsewhere.'[20]

Despite the lack of enthusiasm for sending forces to Greece, British military leaders were anxious that the island of Crete was denied to the Italians. Sir Andrew Cunningham, Admiral of the British Fleet, wrote to Wavell on 14 May 1940: 'Crete is so vital that I feel strongly that we should make preparations for rapidly landing a small force.'[21] On 30 October, in a paper to the Joint Planning Staff, it was recognised that there would be political ramifications if Crete were occupied without subsequent support for Greece. 'The occupation of Crete by us' and failure to support mainland Greece 'will be used by the enemy as an instance of Great Britain helping herself at the expense of her ally.'[22] Metaxas was suspicious of Britain's selfish designs on such a strategically important island, but clearly Britain was a lesser threat than the Axis powers to Greek security. A Greek Liberal statesman of the First World War had described Greece as: 'the beggar of the Great Powers'.[23] In the Second World War this was still the case.

The military hierarchy in London were in agreement that a naval base should be established in the large natural harbour of Suda Bay, despite the danger of provoking an attack from Germany. Churchill ordered that Suda Bay be turned into 'a second Scapa'.[24] On 29 October 1940 Churchill sent a telegraph to Eden in the Middle East, stating that he and the Chiefs of Staff were 'convinced an effort should be made to establish ourselves in Crete, and risks should be run for this valuable prize'. Churchill went on to say that the 'loss of Crete would be a serious aggravation of all Mediterranean difficulties', adding that Crete was 'almost equal to a successful offensive in Libya'.[25]

On 31 October, with the consent of the Greek government, British forces occupied Suda Bay, strategically the most important harbour in Crete. On 3 November a British Expeditionary Force was landed in Crete; as they came ashore local shepherds, shopkeepers and fishermen welcomed them. Gifts of wine, milk, fruit and nuts were showered on the soldiers as they made their way through the pleasant countryside of hills and fields, a distinct contrast to the desolate landscape of the desert in Egypt. The first British troops to be sent were the 2nd Battalion the York and Lancaster Regiment, who had received their orders within forty-eight hours of the Italian invasion. The 2nd Battalion of the Black Watch, and part of the 14th Infantry Brigade, followed in the next few days. The British troops landing in Crete allowed the Greek government to move the Cretan V Division to the mainland to fight the Italians. The Chiefs of Staff originally proposed that the Cretan Division remain on the island, but as Churchill pointed out, it would be 'difficult to deny the Greeks use of their own troops'.[26] The esteemed V Division distinguished themselves in battle against the Italians, but Cretans would lament their departure from the island in the following months.

The haste and conviction with which the decision was taken to occupy Crete is significant in revealing Britain's attitude towards intervention in Greece. Crete was perceived as vital for the defence of Egypt and Britain had wasted little time in occupying the island. Mainland Greece, which posed huge logistical problems and was less strategically important, received an ambiguous approach from Britain. In considering the Greek situation, Britain put the emphasis on political rhetoric and diplomacy rather than military action, as had happened in the Chamberlain years prior to the outbreak of war.

A military appraisal concerning a German attack on Greece was not made by the Chiefs of Staff, or considered by politicians, throughout November and December 1940. On 8 January the Chiefs of Staff again concluded that no effective resistance could be offered if Germany invaded Greece, therefore British resources would be wasted if deployed in this area. The Chiefs of Staff had given a military viewpoint divorced from political expediency and they concluded that there was no question of intervention in Greece with land forces.

British military leaders advocated that due to scarce resources in the Middle East, all available equipment should be sent to Crete rather than mainland Greece. It was generally believed that Greece would crumble under the Italian invasion and the British forces in Crete would neutralise the strategic and political implications of an inevitable Italian victory on the mainland. The Chief of Staff stated: 'our own ability to help them [Greece] must be dependent on their powers to resist initial attack until help comes.'[27] As a result of Italian incompetence, and their own fighting prowess, the Greeks had shown that they were worthy adversaries for their aggressors and continued to fight into the new year. Paradoxically the Greek success against the Italians placed the British government in a difficult position. Less resilient defence by the Greeks would have ended Britain's debate on honouring their guarantee as it had in Poland. However, the Greeks showed no sign of capitulation and the question of honouring the guarantee to Greece remained an important issue.

The unexpected ferocity with which the Greeks fought off their Italian aggressors won admirers across the world and added to the pressure on Britain to assist their unlikely comrades with land forces. Churchill was increasingly aware that German propaganda would relish the capitulation of another ally under British guarantee. He believed that if no effort was made in Greece, Britain's prestige in the Balkans and throughout the world might be tarnished irreversibly. The Chiefs of Staff convincingly argued that national honour alone could not withstand overwhelming numbers of tanks and aircraft. Despite these reservations, Churchill insisted that Britain could not remain 'in Egypt with ever growing forces while the Greek situation and all that hangs on it is cast away'.[28] Under the influence of Sir John Dill, the Chiefs of Staff opposed the notion of sending an expeditionary force to Greece, fearing it might produce a second 'Dunkirk'. For Churchill, military objectives were not the main priority; the main impetus for intervention in Greece was the diplomatic benefit involved. In a series of telegrams to foreign secretary Anthony Eden, Churchill argued that the collapse of Greece would have a 'deadly effect on Turkey' and that 'surely effort must be made to aid Greece indirectly even if only with token forces'.[29]

The idea of sending aid to Greece brought an immediate protest from Eden who was in the Middle East. He wrote that it would be 'unwise to employ our forces in fragments in the theatre of war where they can not be decisive'.[30] Eden was also concerned about the lack of preparation; on 2 November he wrote 'the weakness of our policy is that we never adhere to plans we make'. He concluded: 'If we ever sought to help Greece we should have long since made our plans accordingly.'[31] Churchill reiterated that aid to Greece must be 'attentively studied lest the whole Turkish position is lost through proof that England never tries to keep her guarantees'.[32] After further pressure from Churchill, Eden was forced to concede that any attempt to accelerate the rate, or increase aid 'to Greece beyond that laid down will mean serious risk to our position in Egypt'.[33] On 8 November Eden arrived back in England and informed Churchill that the proposed reinforcements to Greece would jeopardise plans for a forthcoming operation in the desert. This explained Eden's negative response to Churchill's telegrams; the Foreign Secretary had waited to tell the Prime Minister in person due to security measures.

Operation COMPASS, planned by Generals Wavell and Wilson, envisaged an attack upon General Graziani's Italian forces in North

Africa. Wavell, who was based in Cairo, wanted to keep Operation COMPASS to himself for security reasons, but pressure from Churchill, who proposed to divert resources from Egypt to aid Greece, had forced Wavell to reveal his plan to Eden. Characteristically, Churchill wished to know the precise details, and held out greater hopes for the operation than Wavell was prepared to concede. Previously, Wavell had sent a warning to Dill cautioning him 'not to encourage optimism' on the part of Churchill. When this became known to Churchill, he was shocked at Wavell's apparent pessimism, and stated that he was not 'hurling on his whole available force with furious energy.'[34] Churchill agreed that the limited air and logistical support for Greece should not be increased until the result of the offensive in North Africa was known. Churchill gave his support to the operation, but his thoughts were still on the situation in Balkans; he believed that if COMPASS was successful it might persuade both Turkey and Yugoslavia to enter the war in favour of the Allies. COMPASS was launched on 9 December 1940; General O'Connor led the attack, which brought immediate success as Sidi Barrani was taken within three days.

Churchill's enthusiasm to confront the Nazi war machine was fuelled by signals intelligence that gave valuable information about Hitler's intentions. It was a source so confidential that its very existence was not officially recognised until long after the war. Signals analysed at Bletchley Park in Buckinghamshire were responsible for cracking the German ENIGMA codes, intercepts that were codenamed ULTRA. Churchill was fascinated by secret intelligence and read ULTRA decrypts on a regular basis. On 10 January 1941 Churchill received ULTRA decrypts stating that a German build-up of forces in Romania posed a great threat to Greece. Other reports suggested that two German armoured divisions, supported by two hundred dive-bombers, would cross Bulgaria to invade Greece. A telegram sent by Churchill to Wavell stated that: 'Germans are now establishing themselves upon the Bulgarian aerodromes and making every preparation for action against Greece.'[35] Churchill subsequently ordered draft contingency plans for a British Expeditionary Force to be committed to the Greek mainland. The same day Churchill issued explicit orders to Wavell to aid Greece: 'Nothing must hamper the capture of Tobruk, thereafter, all operations in Libya are subordinated to aiding Greece.'[36] The Defence Committee agreed that in the view of a German advance through Bulgaria 'from a political point of view, we should do everything possible to send Greece the fullest support within our power'.[37]

Wavell was against furthering military commitments and he maintained that he did not have the resources to oppose a German invasion in Greece. Instead of citing this perfectly valid reason to the Prime Minister, Wavell insisted that the threat from Germany was a ploy 'designed to help

Italy by upsetting Greek nerves' and to 'stop our advance in Libya and disperse our forces'.[38] Churchill replied with severity. 'Our information contradicts [the] idea that the German concentration in Romania is merely a "move in a war of nerves."' Churchill maintained that the 'Destruction of Greece will eclipse victories you have gained in Libya, and may affect decisively [the] Turkish attitude.' Churchill concluded: 'We expect and require prompt and active compliance with our decisions, for which we bear full responsibility.'[39]

An increasingly frosty atmosphere developed between the Prime Minister and Wavell. In the face of Churchill's ranting, Wavell would remain silent, perhaps the worst possible response to a man such as Churchill. At headquarters in Cairo Wavell's silences were legendary, his customary response was 'I see', followed by no further comment. Within close circles, Wavell possessed a keen sense of humour and was outgoing. Professionally, Wavell's abrupt and detached style proved an asset in moments of crisis, but ultimately his lack of charisma in public damaged relations with his Prime Minster, which he never sought to repair. Churchill quickly became restless over Wavell's apparent lack of decisive action in the desert and his pleas for further supplies. On 13 August 1940 Churchill wrote of Wavell to Eden: 'I do not feel in him that sense of mental rigour and resolve to overcome obstacles which is indispensable to war.'[40] On 15 August 1940 their relationship deteriorated, British Somaliland was evacuated with the loss of just 260 casualties, as compared with the estimated 1,800 inflicted on the Italians; Churchill immediately demanded the resignation of the British commander responsible. Wavell replied: 'a heavy butcher's bill' was 'not necessarily evidence of good tactics.'[41] Dill noted that this incident infuriated Churchill to a level greater than anything he had previously experienced. Wavell was a Lees Knowles lecturer at the University of Cambridge. His third lecture ironically dealt with the troubled relationship between soldiers and politicians.

The most apparent friction between the Prime Minister and his generals was caused by Churchill's highly personalised, fastidious approach to military operations. It was this overzealous approach to military matters coupled with accepted 'parliamentary practices' that alienated Churchill from his generals. Wavell's biographer, John Connell, explained that Churchill had matured in an environment in which: 'it was taken for granted that one Member may . . . abuse another with unrelenting ferocity on the floor of the House' and when the session had ended 'walk out arm in arm with his opponent to a drink in the smoking room or bar.'[42] In December 1940 after midnight, Dill returned to the War Office incensed after a long meeting with Churchill: 'I cannot tell you how angry the Prime Minister has made me.' He told the Director of Military Operations. 'What he [Churchill] said about the Army tonight I can never forgive.' Dill continued: 'He complained he could get nothing done . . . he wished he had [Greek General] Papagos to run it.' Dill explained that Churchill asked him to: 'wait and have a drink with him after the meeting, but I refused and left Anthony [Eden] there by himself'.[43]

Churchill had a reputation for recklessness and he demonstrated scorn for senior officers and generals whom he thought lacked the will or vision to fight. The failed campaign in Norway exposed Churchill's enthusiasm for conflict, as it was the Prime Minister who refused to recognise that British forces were not adequately prepared. In Norway British forces were short of artillery and aircraft and within two weeks British troops succumbed to superior German airpower. Norway represented the first instance of Churchill demanding more than his generals could deliver. Churchill nicknamed Dill 'Dilly Dally' which was typical of Churchill's contempt for generals who showed caution. Wavell and Dill maintained that operations could not be launched without adequate training and logistic preparation. Wavell stated: 'Winston is always expecting rabbits to come out of empty hats.'[44] Churchill could not appreciate the dilemma that faced his generals in 1940–1; the Prime Minister found it difficult to see beyond the elusive victory that would impress the neutrals and raise morale in Britain.

The suspicion that Metaxas might find a compromise with Germany influenced British policy towards Greece. According to Metaxas: 'if Hitler and Mussolini were really fighting for the ideology they preach, they should support Greece with all their forces.'[45] Military intelligence indicated that Hitler intended to intimidate Greece, Bulgaria and Yugoslavia into the sphere of Nazi influence as a preliminary move for an advance against Turkey. These reports were coupled with rumours that Germany was attempting to mediate between Italy and Greece. Although Metaxas vehemently denied rumours of Nazi mediations, Britain remained suspicious of veiled German threats, mixed with cajoling, that could result in the loss of Britain's tenuous foothold in south-eastern Europe.

It was against this background that Churchill thought it 'politically' necessary to send further aid to sustain the Greek resistance against the Axis. The Chiefs of Staff remained doubtful about military intervention; General Dill in particular was sceptical, but he kept silent to avoid a confrontation with Churchill. Predictably, Wavell's protests were overruled and he was ordered to fly to Athens for official talks with Metaxas. On 13 January General Wavell, dressed in civilian clothes, met with Papagos and Metaxas whose ashen faces were beginning to show the strain of German pressure. The negotiations were inevitably a meeting of divergent perceptions. Wavell was the commander of a vast area of operations and therefore saw the merits of a particular theatre within a wider perspective. He viewed territorial losses and victories within a framework of defeating the Axis powers on various fronts. Greek interest in the war only went as far as defence of their country and the security of their frontiers. Britain's conflict with Germany was based on a fundamental difference in ideology. Ideologically, Metaxas was closer to the Axis powers than Britain, but it was the Greek sense of national pride that gave them the will to fight.

Metaxas opened the meeting by optimistically stating that Greece would resist a German attack with the same resolution with which they had met the Italian invasion. Papagos had already outlined his ideas for British intervention and recommended that Wavell send nine divisions with appropriate air support. The Germans would be given the impression that these nine divisions were being made ready for operations in North Africa. Technically, the Greek plan was sound, but it did not take into account that from Wavell's point of view, Greece was an important, but ultimately secondary theatre of operations. The struggle for Greece did not represent the centre of world conflict, and the state of Britain's resources could not afford excessive military equipment spent on the expedition. Wavell listened to Papagos's account with a typically preoccupied air; he polished his spectacles and replied simply: 'I see.' He then set about delivering cold hard facts about the state of British resources, concluding that all that could be offered was a single artillery regiment and 'perhaps' sixty armoured vehicles. Metaxas stated that the offer was inadequate and explained that to send an advance guard of a small artillery unit would only serve as a pretext for a German offensive. The British general reiterated his offer before departing to London. On his return, Wavell explained to Churchill that the offer was declined mainly on the grounds that 'the landing of further British forces was likely to provoke German aggression without being strong enough to check it'.[46] Papagos believed that British intervention would 'fail to produce substantial military and political results in the Balkans' and also was against 'sound principles of strategy'. The division that Britain 'proposed to withdraw from the army in Egypt to send to Greece would come in more useful in Africa'.[47] Wavell was relieved at the Greek reaction to his offer; privately Churchill and the War Cabinet knew that the offer would have proved disastrous and were said to have 'heaved a sigh of relief'.[48] The offer by Wavell was no more than a goodwill gesture to reinforce Britain's support in the face of what Churchill perceived as German coercion.

The proposal by the British was a token political offer. If the Greeks had accepted the offer, it would have served little or no military purpose other than to prompt an offensive by Germany. The Chiefs of Staff had introduced the use of token forces for political impact as early as 1934, when they produced a paper arguing the need to send forces to protect the Low Countries against possible German aggression. The paper stated that it was not the size of the force sent 'as the moral effect which their arrival would have on Belgian defence' and the knowledge that the British Empire was ready and determined to 'wage war with all its available resources in defence of the independence of the peoples whose frontier we have guaranteed'.[49] This paper illustrates the importance of fulfilling obligations in terms of the moral and political implications. Churchill believed that non-intervention in Greece would have a damaging effect on Turkey and Yugoslavia who were perceived as potential allies. Despite being eager not to repeat the events in central Norway, Churchill continued to flirt with intervention and refused to heed Wavell's warning that any aid to Greece would be a 'dangerous half measure'.[50]

NOTES

1   Kitchen, Martin, *A World in Flames*, London: Longman, 1990, p. 45.
2   Clark, Alan, *The Fall of Crete*, London: Cassell, 1962, p. 1.
3   Wilmot, Chester, *The Struggle for Europe*, Wordsworth, 1997 edn, p. 70.
4   Ibid, p. 69.
5   Ibid, p. 68.
6   Ibid, p. 70.
7   van Creveld, Martin, *Hitler's Strategy 1940–1941: The Balkan Clue*, London: CUP, 1973, p. 81.
8   Hitler, Adolf, Führer Naval Conferences, 8 January 1941.
9   Ansel, Walter, *Hitler and the Middle Sea*, Durham NC, 1972, p. 92.
10   Hammerton, John, *Churchill Speech to the House of Commons, 5 November 1940*, Historical Documents CXC–CXCIV, London: Waverly, 1950, p. 1309.
11   Churchill, Winston, 'Most Secret' CAB 127/4, 31 October 1940.
12   Hammerton, op. cit.
13   Chiefs of Staff, Middle East, Telegram No. 333, WO 201/2, 27 May 1940.
14   Hammerton, *The Second Great War*, Vol. IV, London: Waverly, 1950, p. 1295.
15   Churchill, Winston, *The Second World War*, Vol. II, London: Cassell, 1949, p. 484.
16   Hammerton, John, *The Second Great War*, Vol. IV, p. 1307.
17   Buckley, Christopher, *Greece and Crete 1941*, London: HMSO, 1952, p. 15.
18   Churchill, Winston, Churchill Papers – Personal and Secret 20/30, 3 December 1940.
19   Chiefs of Staff, Middle East, Telegram No. 333, WO 201/2, 27 May 1940.
20   Joint Planning Staff Paper No. 30, CAB 44/120, 30 October 1940.
21   To C-in-C Mediterranean from Admiralty 85, WO 201/2, 21 May 1940.
22   Joint Planning Staff Paper No. 30, CAB 44/120, 30 October 1940.
23   Beevor, Antony, *Crete: The Battle and the Resistance*, London: John Murray, 1991, p. 11.
24   PM to General Ismay, 3 November. *Crete: Official History of New Zealand in the Second World War, 1939–1945*, Wellington: War History Branch, 1953, p. 6.
25   Churchill, Winston, *The Second World War*, Vol. II, p. 473.
26   Ibid, p. 477.
27   Chiefs of Staff, CAB 79/23, 31 May 1940.
28   Churchill, Winston, *The Second World War*, Vol. II, p. 476.
29   Ibid.
30   Ibid.

31 Rhodes-James, R, *Anthony Eden*, London: Weidenfeld & Nicolson, 1986, p. 242.
32 Churchill, Winston, *The Second World War*, Vol. II, p. 474.
33 Ibid, p. 479.
34 Keegan, John (ed.), *Churchill's Generals*, London: Weidenfeld & Nicolson, 1991, p. 77.
35 Churchill, Winston, *The Second World War*, Vol. III, p. 18.
36 Ibid, p. 27.
37 Ibid, p. 14.
38 Dispatch from Wavell to GHQ Middle East, (101) COS JP (41) JPS, 'Appreciation of Allied Policy', January 1941.
39 Churchill, Winston, *The Second World War*, Vol. III, p. 27.
40 Rhodes-James, Robert, op. cit., p. 238.
41 Keegan, John, op. cit., p. 79.
42 Ibid, p. 56.
43 Ibid.
44 Ibid.
45 Tsoucalis, Constantine, *The Greek Tragedy*, London: 1969, p. 55.
46 Despatch from Wavell to GHQ Middle East, (101) COS JP (41) 23 JPS, January 1941.
47 Papagos, Alexander, *The Battle for Greece*, Athens: 1949, p. 315.
48 Beevor, op. cit., p. 14.
49 Chiefs of Staff paper, CAB 79/23.
50 Beevor, op. cit., p. 16.

CHAPTER IV
Balkan Unity

In light of the Greek refusal, Wavell was told to continue his advance in the desert while being ready to assist Greece if necessary. Operation COMPASS continued to exceed even the Prime Minister's expectations with the capture of Tobruk and Benghazi. The Italians under Marshal Graziani were lacking mobility and constantly harassed by a series of hit and run raids by General Creagh's 7th Armoured Division, soon to be nicknamed the 'Desert Rats'. Brigadier Dorman-Smith, General O'Connor's unorthodox and highly controversial staff officer, devised a plan to hit the Italians hard with their limited resources. The 7th Armoured Division cut off the Italian lines of retreat by driving towards the sea at Buq-Buq; the Desert Rats had covered 170 miles in just thirty-six hours and across difficult terrain. The 7th Royal Tank Regiment and 4th Indian Division then proceeded to attack the widely dispersed Italian positions around Sidi Barrani. By 7 February the 6th Australian Division and British 7th Armoured Division had advanced 500 miles through Cyrenaica in just two months. General Berganzoli's Italian army of over nine divisions had been destroyed with the capture of 130,000 prisoners, 400 tanks and 1,290 guns, at a cost of only 500 soldiers killed. The conquest of Cyrenaica was now complete.

The rapid progress of the British army in Cyrenaica was all the more remarkable as O'Connor was denied badly needed reinforcements, and had further units taken away from him, which were used for the building up of forces in the Balkans. The series of defeats experienced by the Italian army left the British with a clear passage through the Aghelia bottleneck to Tripoli. There appeared to be nothing to check a British advance; the few Italian troops that remained were panic-stricken, and were expecting British tanks to appear at any moment. O'Connor longed to press on to Tripoli, even though his troops were exhausted and the supply lines inadequate. While Wavell's forces were advancing through the desert, Churchill remained focused on the Balkans. Britain's ability to intervene in Greece, even with token forces, was facilitated by Italy's failure in North Africa. Wavell's success in the desert allowed aid to Greece to go beyond air support and resources. Churchill instructed Wavell that

Cyrenaica was to be held with the smallest force possible as a secure flank for Egypt. The advance on Tripoli was to be delayed, and the largest force possible was to be made ready to send to Greece. Churchill stated: 'your major effort now must be to aid Greece. This rules out any serious effort against Tripoli.'[1] On 12 February, crucially it was the German commander Rommel, not O'Connor, who advanced on Tripoli.

General Metaxas died of mouth cancer on 29 January 1941; German propaganda was as crude as ever and claimed that he had been poisoned. Rather than being remembered for his repressive regime, the victories won in Albania made the Greek dictator's name synonymous with one of the finest hours in modern Greek history. Metaxas had an air of prestige and authority that served his country well during the crisis; most notably when he had refused to be drawn by Britain's token offer of assistance. As he died, he confided in his diary: 'Tired . . . I have done my duty . . . If the British only had available five divisions with substantial armour . . . but they have nothing.'[2] Metaxas' successor was Alexandros Koryzis, who was not a politician, but a banker by profession. Koryzis reiterated his predecessor's pledge to fight Germany, but compared to Metaxas, he proved to be a weak figure in power, and relied heavily on advice from the king, who was known to be pro-British. Lacking the force of personality of the former dictator, Koryzis was eager to share the responsibility of his nation's plight and indicated that he would accept British assistance in any quantity.

Inspired by the sudden acquiescence of the Greek government, Churchill was keen to initiate diplomatic efforts to bind Britain and Greece with the promise of military aid. Churchill hoped that a firm British commitment to Greece would create a catalyst for other countries to join them in a Balkan alliance united against Germany. Churchill stated: 'throughout this phase of ever extending war was an organised plan of uniting the forces of Yugoslavia, Greece and Turkey'.[3] Eden believed that the total number of divisions could reach seventy, including Greek, Yugoslav and Turkish forces. This would be matched against the typical German advance that had 'no more than thirty in the theatre'.[4]

Seventy divisions appeared impressive in terms of manpower, but did not take into account their military effectiveness against highly mechanised German divisions. A successful Balkan front against Hitler was unrealistic, as the primitive armies of the Balkans had no power to withstand Germany's modernised tanks and air force. From the outset a Balkan alliance looked unlikely, Turkey vowed to remain neutral and Yugoslavia under Prince Paul looked increasingly susceptible to German diplomatic pressure. All three countries, Greece, Yugoslavia and Turkey, were vital to the security of each other – Yugoslavia to protect the northern flank, the Turks in the east and Greece in the centre. Persistence in this policy may have been strengthened by the fact that in 1934 Turkey, Greece and Yugoslavia had signed a pact stating that in the event of Italian aggression they would form a united front. Realistically, none of the prospective members were prepared to place unqualified reliance on such an agreement in the face of an invasion by Germany.

It is unlikely that Churchill failed to notice the misgivings of the proposed Balkan alliance. However, his Balkan policy was to some extent motivated by the desire to favourably influence the attitude of the United States. Throughout this period the American President, Roosevelt, had supported Britain's presence in the Balkans and he was anxious to halt the Nazi advance. On 7 January Roosevelt sent his personal emissary, 'Wild Bill' Donovan, on a tour of the Balkans designed to stimulate Nazi resistance in the area. Donovan attempted to convince the Balkan nations that the US would not allow Germany to win the war and that the proposed Lend-Lease Act would mobilise American industrial resources against the Axis. However, the leaders of the Balkan nations were not convinced, as Donovan could not pledge US intervention or modern military equipment.

In December 1940 Roosevelt was informed that Britain could no longer pay for American supplies. His solution was the Lend-Lease Act, which was designed to defeat the Nazis through aiding Britain. Roosevelt urged the American public to make the United States 'the great arsenal of democracy'.[5] Roosevelt had pledged to help Britain, but Churchill had to justify the President's decision by appearing to resist Germany. Donovan, whose opinion Churchill respected, had advised the British Prime Minister that if Britain stood by and watched Hitler overrun the Balkans, it would undermine the moral appeal of Britain's cause in the United States. The Lend-Lease Act was to be put before Congress for debate during February 1941. Therefore, it is no coincidence that during this month Churchill was inspired into positive action to aid Greece, by diverting resources from North Africa and promoting a Balkan alliance. The Lend-Lease Act was passed by Congress on 8 February and Churchill had taken another step towards forging a much greater alliance than the one he was attempting in the Balkans.

On 8 February Koryzis stated that he was willing to accept British assistance and suggested that the 'size and composition of the proposed force should be determined'.[6] Eden and General Dill were promptly dispatched to Cairo to co-ordinate British diplomatic efforts in Greece alongside Wavell. With the presence of the British Foreign Secretary, the emphasis of the mission became political and diplomatic rather than military. A conference led exclusively by military personnel would have inevitably ended in the conclusion that an expeditionary force was impractical.

On hearing of the visit, General Wavell resigned himself to a heavy commitment in Greece. Dill's token opposition to intervention in Greece was insignificant; when Dill raised his objections with the Prime Minister he was subjected to a 'Churchillian rage' and was quickly silenced. Churchill ranted: 'What you need out there is a Court Martial and a firing squad. Wavell has 300,000 men etc etc.'[7] Paradoxically, in a letter informing Wavell of the mission, Churchill concluded on a rather sobering note: if it proved 'impossible to reach any good agreement with the Greeks and to work out a practical military plan' then 'we must try to save as much from the wreck as possible.' He stressed, Crete must be kept 'at all costs' and 'any Greek islands which are of use as air bases.' But he also warned that 'these will only be consolation prizes after the classic race has been lost'.[8] On 16 February the first encounters in the desert took place between British and German forces in North Africa. It was four days later that Churchill acknowledged the danger of dispersing his forces in Africa, signalling to Eden, Dill and Wavell: 'Do not consider yourselves obligated to a Greek enterprise if in your hearts you feel it would be only another Norwegian fiasco.'[9] Churchill was both a visionary and a realist; initial extravagant plans would often be curtailed by a pang of pragmatism. Although Churchill must have known that intervention was now inevitable, Eden was bound to dominate proceedings in Greece. The Foreign Secretary shared Churchill's vision of a Balkan alliance and was driven by the prospect of impressing the world with a diplomatic coup.

On his arrival at Wavell's headquarters in Cairo, Eden chaired a staff briefing prior to their meeting in Athens, which was also attended by Dill, Admiral Cunningham and Longmore. Wavell remained pessimistic: 'I can never see much prospect of the Balkans becoming an offensive military front from our point of view.' He went on to point out that 'our forces available are very limited and it is doubtful whether they can arrive in time'.[10] However, Wavell did point out that from an offensive perspective Greek airbases could be used effectively. Wavell's reservations seemed to bypass Eden, who proceeded to convince those present that an attempt to help the Greeks should be sought. The rest of the meeting was spent deciding tactics for the defence of Greece. In accordance with the proposed Balkan alliance, Wavell targeted Salonika as the critical position that Turkish and Yugoslav fronts would hinge on. Privately he felt that it would be impossible for the Greek army to defend a line as far advanced as the Macedonian passes, and that the operation might fall apart. Cunningham reflected after the war that 'though politically we were correct, I had grave uncertainty of its military expedience'. Dill himself had doubts, and commented to Cunningham after the meeting: 'well, we've taken the decision. I'm not at all sure it's the right one.'[11]

The tepid acceptance of intervention by those present at the meeting was met with enthusiasm by Eden who immediately cabled Churchill stating that he thought there was a: 'fair chance that we can hold a line in Greece', although he recognised that limited naval and air forces 'make it doubtful whether we can hold a line covering Salonika, which General Wavell is prepared to contemplate'.[12] The following day, after further contemplation, Eden again contacted Churchill, and conceded that the Greek venture was a 'gamble', but thought it was better to 'suffer' with the Greeks than to make no attempt to help them. Eden explained that if Britain failed to help Greece, 'there is no hope of action by Yugoslavia, and the future of Turkey may be easily compromised'. He concluded: 'we believe that this attempt to help Greece should be made.'[13]

On 22 February Eden, Wavell, Longmore and Dill flew to Athens to confer with the Greek government. Eden wanted an immediate conference, but the Greeks insisted on taking them to the Royal Palace at Tatoi. It resembled a country house rather than a palace and was surrounded by a magnificent wood. Eden, enthusiastic as ever about the prospect of a Balkan alliance, promised the Greeks embellished figures from that provided in the staff briefing. The figures quoted by Eden included three infantry divisions and one, possibly two, armoured divisions. It was decided that Wavell was to send to Greece, as early as possible, 100,000 men, 700 guns and 142 tanks. These resources would be made up of Australian I Army Corps, the British 1st Armoured Brigade, and a Brigade of Polish Infantry. It is worth noting that the figure for 'guns' included anti-tank rifles, and less than a third of that quoted by Eden was actually sent. Even with the deceptive figures, the Greeks were not convinced and took a great deal of persuading. In the early hours of the morning, the Greeks finally accepted the British offer of intervention; de Guingand, of the Middle East Joint Planning Staff, commented: 'Eden preened himself in front of the fire while his subordinates congratulated him on a diplomatic triumph.'[14]

But the most difficult part of Eden's diplomatic mission was yet to come. If the alliance was to stand any hope of success the Foreign Minister would have to convince the Yugoslavs and Turks to 'get off the fence'. After the meeting Eden was asked to meet the new Greek Prime Minister. Koryzis stated that he hoped Eden would clear up the uncertainty surrounding the ultimate intentions of Turkey and Yugoslavia. Favourable Yugoslav intervention meant that Salonika could be held, which would be invaluable for landing British reinforcements. Prince Paul was wavering between pro-British demonstrations and promises to the Germans, causing increasing perplexity in both camps. Eden and Papagos agreed that failing Yugoslav intervention, Salonika would have to be abandoned. Papagos apparently agreed that the bulk of Greek forces were to be withdrawn from the Metaxas Line in Albania to form a defensive line along the Aliakmon river.

Eden believed that British intervention in Greece could help resist Germany's offensive long enough to inspire the Turks into positive action. But he had little success in his negotiations with Turkey who, like Metaxas before them, considered the units offered by Britain insufficient. Wavell recognised the difficulty of forming a Balkan Front, commenting: 'Greek and Turkish hesitations and Yugoslav timidity have made our task very difficult.'[15] Churchill stated his fear that Balkan countries would 'fool away their chances of combined resistance, as was done in the Low Countries'.[16] Eden remained convinced that the Greeks would defend their country with or without assistance, therefore: 'His Majesty's Government have no alternative but to back them. While recognising the risks we must accept them.' After bringing the matter before the War Cabinet Churchill stated: 'while being under no illusions, we all send you the order full steam ahead.'[17]

On 1 March German divisions crossed the Danube and entered Bulgaria. Dill and Eden returned to Athens on 2 March and were horrified to learn that the withdrawal from the Metaxas Line in Albania had not taken place. In the absence of any clear indication of the Yugoslavs' intentions, Papagos was insisting on defending a forward line in Macedonia, which was originally advocated by Wavell. Without assurance of Yugoslav collaboration, the Greek divisions in eastern Macedonia were dangerously exposed and the security of the defensive line's left flank was in doubt. Papagos refused to move his troops, insisting that he had inadequate transport and he was awaiting British intelligence on the position of Yugoslavia. The need to withdraw to the Aliakmon Line was not in doubt, but the controversy lies in the timing of the withdrawal. Was the withdrawal to begin immediately? Or was the withdrawal to be postponed until the British had determined the attitude of Yugoslavia? The British maintained the former and the Greeks the latter. The confusion lay in Eden's instructions to Papagos. Eden told the Greek general that 'preparations should at once be made and put into execution',[18] for the withdrawal of Greek troops. Both parties laid emphasis on contrasting parts of Eden's ambiguous sentence. The British stressed 'execution' of the withdrawal, while Papagos emphasised 'preparation' for the withdrawal. Papagos's failure to move the Greek divisions probably owed more to a reluctance to relinquish hard fought positions to the despised Italians.

At a subsequent meeting, the Greek general proposed that it was logical to send British units to the Metaxas Line, as his troops would not withdraw to the Aliakmon Line until the Yugoslav issue was resolved. The British immediately dismissed the idea as folly and sought a compromise. A British colonel described the meeting as a 'drama as intense as any played on a classical Greek stage . . . I knew the plot, the author and the players'. Eden likened the negotiations to the 'haggling of an Oriental Bazaar'.[19] It soon became clear that the British military had over-estimated the size of Greek forces and it was decided that the three Greek divisions on the Metaxas Line were to stay in their defensive positions, while three impromptu Greek divisions were to join the British on the Aliakmon Line for the decisive battle against the Germans. The British saw this as an unwelcome compromise created by the obstinacy of Papagos, but in the circumstances it was their only option.

Despite these unfavourable developments, Eden remained defiant and sent Churchill text of the agreement. On receipt of Eden's note, the reality of the situation began to register with the Prime Minister, who began to panic. American emissary Harry Hopkins summed up Churchill's attitude: 'he [Churchill] thinks Greece is lost – although he is now reinforcing the Greeks and weakening his African army.' Hopkins stated that Churchill was 'preparing for the attack which must bring its inevitable result', and that the Prime Minister believed 'the debacle in Greece would be overcome in part by the sure defeat of the Italians in Africa'.[20] In a telegram to Eden on 6 March, Churchill further illustrated his anxiety: 'we must be careful not to urge Greece against her better judgement into a hopeless resistance alone.' Churchill concluded on an ominous note: 'we have only a handful of troops to reach the scene in time.' He predicted that the 'German advance will probably prevent any appreciable British forces from being engaged'.[21] This insight by Churchill reflected an accurate assessment of how events would unfold in Greece. After reading Churchill's telegram the British ambassador in Athens, Michael Palairet, replied: 'How can we possibly abandon the king of Greece after the assurances we have given him?' He stated: 'we shall be pilloried by the Greeks and the world in general as going back on our word.'[22] Michael Palairet is argued to have been a significant factor in influencing Eden's positive stance on intervention.

Faced with the destruction of the Expeditionary Force Churchill began to reconsider the whole prospect of intervention in Greece. The language used by Churchill in a telegraph to General Smuts is indicative of his apprehension; he described the decision as: 'grave' and 'hazardous ... It must not be said, that, having so little to give, we dragged them by over persuasion.'[23] Field Marshal Smuts arrived in Cairo on 7 March where he attended a conference orchestrated by Eden. Smuts was of the opinion that to pull out at such a late stage would be politically unthinkable. Churchill valued Smuts' opinion and Eden was relieved to have his support.

Churchill's negative attitude towards intervention was in distinct contrast to his earlier decision to halt the advance on Tripoli and concentrate resources on Greece. The Prime Minister may have been trying to distance himself from the responsibility of intervention in Greece. Churchill later stated that he had given Eden full powers 'in all matters diplomatic and military'.[24] Ironically, Churchill and the Chiefs of Staff had also maintained that they did 'not see any reason for success, except that of course we attach great weight to the opinions of Dill and Wavell'.[25] Churchill pointed out that the opinion of Wavell was significant as he was inclined to underestimate what he could achieve. Wavell seemed to take Churchill's initial positive rhetoric literally and concluded that the Prime Minister was fully committed to intervention. Given Wavell's previous encounters with Churchill, it was understandable that he did not express his military objections and assumed that he was unable to alter a politically predetermined decision. Australian Prime Minister Robert Menzies stated that Churchill was not a good listener and disliked opposition: 'Most people in his cabinet were wary of crossing him.' Menzies described Churchill's personality as 'almost tangible; you felt it like a physical blow'.[26] Historian Callum MacDonald wrote that Wavell looked a 'tired man who acted as if he knew that any military objections to the Greek expedition would be overruled'.[27]

Despite being opposed to operations in Greece, Wavell was resigned to intervention by the fact that the decision lay in the hands of politicians. Many officers found it hard to forgive Wavell for not speaking out against the project. Major-General Sir Francis De Guingand believed there was a 'grave risk of losing our whole position in the Middle East as well as suffering a major disaster in Greece'.[28] Wavell was quoted as saying that the situation in Greece was 'not that different from Egypt', and compared Greek mountain ranges with the Qattara Depression. Wavell's judgement was certainly contrary to his previous opinion that listed operations in Egypt and East Africa above that in Greece. He went on to state that it was not 'really relevant to ask how many divisions are needed, since only a certain number can be deployed'.[29] Wavell's strategic analysis of holding an advanced line in Salonika was a complete departure from his previous thinking; it appeared to be an improvised strategy that was based on the premise that Yugoslavia would resist a German advance. Given Wavell's lack of resources he could ill afford to leave military planning to the chance of favourable political events. The optimism shown by Wavell was made in an effort to salvage a small amount of merit from a venture that Britain was politically obligated to uphold.

If Wavell's true convictions seem missing in the decision to aid Greece, his presence was of value. In belatedly securing troops from the governments of Australia and New Zealand, Churchill had been eager for Eden to emphasise that the decision to aid Greece was made by military commanders. Churchill stressed to Eden that the New Zealand and Australian governments must be told that the decision was undertaken 'not because of any commitment entered into by a British Cabinet Minister' but 'because Dill, Wavell, and other Commanders in Chief are convinced there is a reasonable fighting chance'. Churchill concluded: 'Grave Imperial issues are raised by committing New Zealand and Australian troops.'[30] Over eighty percent of the troops deployed in the Expeditionary Force consisted of Australians or New Zealanders. Neither the Australian commander, Lieutenant General Blamey, nor New

Zealand's Major General Freyberg were consulted or included in the discussion that preceded their dispatch. The failure to consult the military leaders of New Zealand and Australia illustrates the confusion surrounding intervention in Greece, which was plagued by the contrasting dictates of diplomatic necessity and military practicality.

Operation LUSTRE was the codename for sending British forces to Greece and the first convoy sailed from Alexandria to Piraeus on 7 March. The German military attaché observed the convoy arrive while idly chatting to British officers about his fox hunting exploits. Dressed in a tweed suit and with a convincing accent, the officers had mistaken him for an exiled country gentleman. Therefore, Field Marshal von List, who was to command German operations against Greece, had excellent intelligence on the British forces landed. General Henry Maitland Wilson, who was to command British and Dominion forces in Greece, arrived wearing civilian clothes and using the alias 'Mr Watt'. The Greeks were still concerned about provoking the Germans and insisted that the British commander arrive incognito.

'Jumbo' Wilson was a good-natured man; he was heavily built, bald, with a round face and a moustache. Wilson was a prominent figure in operations in North Africa, but now he was removed from that vital theatre of operations and committed to a military venture that he considered pure folly. Despite his jolly disposition, Wilson was under no illusions about the gravity of the task that faced him. After listening to Michael Palairet's rousing speech about British expectations for the battle, Wilson was quoted as saying: 'Well, I don't know about that. I've already ordered my maps of the Peloponnese.'[31] Unknown to Wilson, the Joint Planning Staff in the Middle East had indeed started planning the evacuation details.

Germany had exerted pressure on the Italian Navy to intercept and destroy British convoys on route to Greece. This led to the first engagement of Operation LUSTRE. Admiral Cunningham was tasked with securing the munitions line for Operation LUSTRE. On 25 March ULTRA decrypts indicated the presence of the Italian fleet in the Eastern Mediterranean, and Cunningham had forewarned British shipping in the area. A northbound convoy from Alexandria was turned back, and a southbound ship from Piraeus was stopped from sailing. On 27 March an RAF reconnaissance plane sighted three Italian cruisers heading in the direction of Crete. The British Battle Fleet slipped their moorings in Alexandria and headed to intercept the Italians that evening. Cunningham had at his disposal a force of destroyers, his flagship *Warspite,* and sister vessels, the *Valiant* and *Barham*, accompanied by the aircraft carrier, *Formidable.* South of Crete, Vice-Admiral Pridham-Wippell commanded a light force consisting of his flagship the *Orion* and supported by the cruisers *Ajax, Perth* and *Gloucester.* At 08.00 Pridham-Wippell and the *Orion* made first contact with the Italian fleet off Cape

Matapan, after coming under fire from the cruiser *Vittorio Veneto*. The *Orion* escaped from the incident unscathed. Shortly afterwards, Cunningham, who was still some eighty miles away from the action, ordered 826 Squadron to assist Pridham-Wippell with six Albacore torpedo bombers launched from *Formidable*. The attack from the torpedo bombers failed to land a single hit on the Italian fleet, but after their losses at Taranto, the presence of torpedo bombers was enough for the Italians to turn for home. After failing to catch up with the Italians, Cunningham launched a second air attack the following day. At 15.00 three Albacores sighted the *Vittorio Veneto* and started their attack. Supported by two Fulmar fighters, the Albacores relentlessly strafed the battleship. In the course of the attack the *Vittorio Veneto* suffered a direct hit to her stern from an air-dropped torpedo, and thick plumes of smoke could be seen billowing from the mid-ship section. The *Vittorio Veneto* began to take on water and was reduced to a speed of fifteen knots as she headed for Italy.

After receiving a reconnaissance report on the position of the *Vittorio Veneto*, Cunningham ordered a further torpedo attack. This involved six Albacores and two Swordfish from the *Formidable*, supported by a further two Swordfish from 815 squadron on Crete. In his dispatch after the battle Cunningham mentioned Lieutenant Torrens-Spence, who had gone to great lengths to take part in the attack. Torrens-Spence flew the only available aircraft across Crete from Eleusis to Maleme, and then arranged his own reconnaissance, before flying a second aircraft to join the assault. During the attack it was Torrens-Spence who scored a direct hit with a torpedo on the Italian cruiser *Pola*. The torpedo struck the *Pola's* engine room, disabling her turrets and leaving her helpless in the water. After the second air attack, Cunningham signalled to Pridham-Wippell to advance on the Italian fleet, although at this point unknown to the British, the *Vittorio Veneto* had already escaped.

Pridham-Wippell reported a large stopped vessel approximately ten miles away. Fearing it might be the *Vittorio Veneto*, he waited for the heavy guns of Cunningham's approaching Battle Fleet. At 22.00 HMS *Valiant* received a radar report of the stopped vessel four and a half miles off her port bow. Simultaneously, Cunningham had visual confirmation of a number of enemy vessels. Cunningham prepared his fleet for action. The large stopped vessel in question was the *Pola*, which was still immobilised from the previous air attack; the other Italian destroyers present in the area had been sent to assist the *Pola*.

The Italian vessels were taken completely by surprise as they were not equipped with radar, and did not expect the British Battle Fleet to be in the area. As the British Fleet approached, they were either not seen in the darkness or were mistaken for Italian vessels. Italian guns were trained fore and aft as they were not expecting any action. The Italian ships did not have time to train their turrets before they were overwhelmed by salvoes from the fifteen-inch guns of the British cruisers. HMS *Greyhound* switched her searchlight, the firing bell sounded, and her fifteen-inch guns opened fire. HMS *Barham* and *Valiant* joined *Warspite* and inflicted heavy damage at close range to the Italian cruisers *Fiume* and *Zara*. Gunnery control officer, Alex Dennis, described the destruction of the *Fiume*: 'The enemy ship virtually disintegrated in an appalling series of explosions, flinging one of her turrets high in the air.'[32] The same three British cruisers then took evasive action to avoid a torpedo attack, before opening a rapid salvo of six-inch gun fire that sank a further three Italian cruisers, the *Vincenzo Gioberti, Maestrale* and *Alfieri*. The latter vessel had the whole of her stern, guns and steering gear destroyed, which inflicted heavy casualties. Out of control the *Alfieri* reeled in circles, before a second salvo blew the bridge to pieces and she sank by the stern. Attention was then turned towards the disabled *Pola*. As HMS *Jarvis* approached the *Pola*, a white sheet was displayed from her quarter-deck rail; the *Jarvis* received the order from the flagship to finish her off. *Jarvis* drew alongside the *Pola* and took onboard twenty Italian officers and 236 ratings before torpedoing her.

After the battle was won, British ships managed to save nearly 1,000 Italians from the water before German dive-bombers appeared and forced the British Fleet to withdraw, leaving approximately 400 Italians stranded. Admiral Cunningham duly sent a message to the Italians advising them of the position of the men left in the water, and recommended that a hospital ship should be sent. The Italian Commander-in-Chief replied, thanking Cunningham and stated that the Italian hospital ship, *Gradista*, was en route.

Approximately 2,400 Italians perished in the battle without loss to the British Navy. Two torpedo planes were missing with one Italian and two German planes shot down. Although *Vittorio Veneto* escaped, Cunningham was praised for continuing the pursuit at night, against the advice of his staff. There was no doubt the Italians lacked an admiral of a similar calibre. By mid 1940 the Italian navy had outnumbered Cunningham's fleet, but after the losses at Taranto and the defeat at Cape Matapan its morale and resources were at a new low. Chastened by their defeat, the Italian navy did not intervene in operations around Greece and Crete, which, in the circumstances, could have wreaked havoc. Churchill stated that the naval victory was the greatest since Trafalgar. However, the taste of victory would be short lived as German troops prepared for their assault on Greece.

NOTES

1   Churchill, Winston, *The Second World War*, Vol. II, London: Cassell, 1949, p. 58.
2   Cervi, Mario, *The Hollow Legions. Mussolini's Blunder in Greece, 1940–1941*, London: Chatto & Windus, 1972, p. 217.
3   Churchill, op. cit., p. 33.
4   Ibid, p. 59.
5   Wilmot, Chester, *The Struggle for Europe*, Wordsworth, 1997 edn, p. 74.
6   Clark, Alan, *The Fall of Crete*, London: Cassell, 1962, p. 13.
7   MacDonald, Callum, *The Lost Battle – Crete 1941*, London: Macmillan, 1993, p. 103.
8   Churchill, op. cit., p. 149.
9   Ibid, p. 63.
10   Clark, op. cit., p. 15.
11   Ibid.
12   Telegram Eden to Churchill, Cabinet Papers 65/2, 20 February 1941.
13   Churchill, op. cit., p. 65.
14   Beevor, Antony, *Crete – The Battle and the Resistance*, London: John Murray, 1991, p. 18.
15   Churchill, op. cit., p. 33
16   Ibid, p. 58.
17   Ibid, p. 68.
18   Carlton, D, *Anthony Eden*, London: Allen Lane, 1972, pp. 175–6.
19   Beevor, op. cit., p. 20.
20   Sherwood, R E (ed.), *The White House Papers of Harry Hopkins 1939–1942*, London: Eyre & Spottiswoode, 1948, p. 240.
21   Defence Committee, Churchill to Eden, Cabinet Papers 69/2, 6 March 1941.
22   Churchill, op. cit. p. 91.
23   Beevor, op. cit., p. 17.
24   Churchill, op. cit., p. 91.
25   Beevor, op. cit., p. 19.
26   MacDonald, op. cit., p. 105.
27   Ibid, p.106.
28   Churchill, op. cit., pp. 85–92.
29   Clark, op. cit., p. 17.
30   MacDonald, op. cit., p. 107.
31   De Guingand, Sir Francis, *Generals at War*, London: Hodder & Stoughton, 1964, p. 33.
32   Somerville, Christopher, *Our War. How the British Commonwealth Fought the Second World War*, London: Weidenfeld & Nicolson, 1998, p. 70.

CHAPTER V
Hitler Strikes

Throughout March, Hitler had strengthened his position in the Balkans and Greece was effectively isolated, though Turkey and Yugoslavia still anxiously guarded their neutrality. All the other countries in the region had joined the Three-Power Pact, and signed trade agreements that enabled Germany to secure adequate supplies of vital materials. In the course of the month, fourteen German divisions arrived in Bulgaria and were stationed along the Greek border. Yugoslavia was surrounded by German satellite states; six out of seven countries that bordered Yugoslavia were linked to Germany: Italy, Austria, Hungary, Romania, Bulgaria and Albania. Prince Paul, whom Churchill dubbed as 'Prince Palsy', was under increasing pressure from Germany to join the Tripartite Pact. In spite of German assurances to the contrary, it was clear that Germany wanted to exploit the Yugoslav railway to attack Greece.

During March, British diplomats made one last, almost half-hearted, failed attempt to bring Yugoslavia into their Balkan alliance against Germany. Prince Paul was originally pro-British, but he compromised his views in order to protect his country from war. On 25 March Yugoslavia finally gave way to German pressure and signed a pact of loyalty to the Axis. The pact did not commit Yugoslavia to direct intervention on the side of Germany, or allow the passage of Axis troops through their country. Ribbentrop assured Yugoslavia that Germany 'would not make demands on Yugoslavia to allow them passage or transit of German troops'.[1] However, the pact did contain clauses stating that Yugoslavia would be asked to allow Germany passage of war material and medical supplies in sealed trains. Although the pact seemed placid, its implications were obvious. It was naïve to think that the sealed trains would not accommodate German troops.

When details were leaked of a secret meeting between Prince Paul and Hitler, four cabinet ministers resigned. There were public demonstrations against the government in the streets of Belgrade and the German ambassador was attacked by an angry mob, which thumped and spat at his car. Less than forty-eight hours after the signing of the pact, a group of Serbian officers mounted a coup and deposed Prince Paul's regime in a widespread revolt. King Peter assumed power in place of Prince Paul, and the new government was established under the leader of the coup, General Simovich. Simovich's new government did not renounce the Three-Power Pact, but clearly distanced itself from Germany. When Hitler was informed of the coup on 27 March he was speechless with anger. In a rage, he summoned Goering, Jodl, Keitel and Ribbentrop to discuss preparations for the destruction of Yugoslavia. Hitler was angry at the arrest of the Yugoslav signatories of the Three-Power Pact, and suspected the British had masterminded the coup. Indeed Britain had been encouraging the revolt for some time with the help of Colonel Donavan.

Although it was obviously an anti-German putsch, Serbian resentment at the pro-Croatian policies of the Cvetkovic government was an important factor for the revolt. Yugoslavia was split by ethnic tension between Serbs and Croats. Hoping to play the Croats against the Serbs, Ribbentrop promised the Croatian politician, Macek, that Germany would make Croatia an independent state. Macek refused this offer, and accepted the role of vice-president in Simovich's government in an attempt to unite the country. Simovich tried to convince Hitler that he wished to remain on close terms with Germany and had no intention of rejecting the Three-Power Pact, but Hitler remained convinced that the Yugoslavs were playing for time and were preparing the ground for an anti-German Balkan alliance.

Hitler was eager to restore the prestige of the Reich and silence Churchill, who was 'crowing' with delight. After the coup, Churchill stated that 'Yugoslavia had found her soul.'[2] The *coup d'état* in Yugoslavia revived Britain's aspiration of forming a Balkan Front. On 3 April Russia signed a non-aggression pact with Yugoslavia, in order to deter Hitler. Churchill, inspired by new information from ULTRA decrypts, hoped that he could also persuade Russia to openly challenge Germany. Churchill was so eager to gain the allegiance of Stalin, that he instructed the British ambassador in Russia to disclose highly confidential information derived from ULTRA as evidence of the proposed German attack on the Soviet Union. Churchill was later furious when he learned that the information had not been delivered to Stalin before Hitler invaded Greece and Yugoslavia.

The Yugoslavian coup gave Hitler the perfect excuse for immediate action; he was now determined to destroy Yugoslavia without further diplomatic enquiries. German troops were well placed for the invasion that was to take place simultaneously with the invasion of Greece. At this stage the Greeks had not given Wilson a free hand in Greece and were still desperate not to provoke Germany. Greek negotiations with Germany were ongoing. Secret attempts were made by Greek officials to assure the Germans that their only quarrel was with the Italians. It was reported that a senior military commander in the Greek army, Colonel Petinis, had met with the German consul at Salonika and discussed the possibility of 'a cessation of hostilities on the Albanian front, if the place of Italian troops were taken by German troops'. Other terms were that 'the Italians were excluded from negotiations between Greece and Germany on Albanian territorial questions'.[3] However, Hitler was so concerned with the possible threat to the southern flank of Operation BARBAROSSA, that the situation in Greece and Yugoslavia could no longer be tolerated. Victory in Greece would secure the exposed southern flank for the attack on the Soviet Union, and drive Britain from continental Europe. The German minister in Athens, Erbach, stated that the general view was that, if Germany attacked, Greek resistance would be 'hopeless but necessary for reasons of national honour'.[4]

Sir John Dill flew to Belgrade for discussions with Yugoslav leaders on 1 April. Dill got the impression from the Yugoslav ministers that they did not understand the imminence of their peril. Yugoslav political leaders repeatedly stated that they were determined not to take any steps that might provoke a German armed attack. Wilson and Papagos met with General Yankovitch, the Yugoslav Chief of Staff. It transpired that the Yugoslavs had made no preparations for the forthcoming German invasion and had an exaggerated impression of British forces.

At 05.45 on Sunday 6 April German forces simultaneously thrust across the Yugoslav and Greek frontiers. Germany had afforded thirty-two divisions to the Balkan campaign, twenty-one of which were directly committed to battle. Von Weichs of the Second Army was instructed to invade Yugoslavia from the north and north-west. Von List commanded the Twelfth Army and attacked Greece from the east.

The Yugoslav government declared Belgrade an open city to prevent its destruction by the Luftwaffe. Berlin ignored the plea and stated that Belgrade possessed legitimate military targets that could not be spared. The people of Belgrade paid dearly for their open support of the coup ten days previously. German bombers mercilessly attacked Belgrade in an operation that was code-named RETRIBUTION, with reference to the recent coup. Churchill knew of the intended attack on Belgrade from ULTRA decrypts and duly warned the Yugoslav government, without avail. The Yugoslav people could not have prepared themselves for the horror they were about to face.

On Sunday morning as church bells rang, Belgrade was subjected to a ruthless and callous bombardment from the air. Some 150 bombers and dive-bombers with a heavy fighter escort appeared over Belgrade. Indiscriminate bombing of hospitals, churches, schools and cultural institutions took place in broad daylight. A mixture of incendiary and explosive bombs tore through homes and gutted the city. The weak Yugoslav air defences and inadequate aircraft were rapidly destroyed,

71

allowing dive-bombers to operate unchallenged at rooftop level. Throughout the streets bodies of all ages were scattered, and German aircraft were witnessed machine-gunning civilians fleeing their homes. It is unclear how many perished in the bombardment, but some estimates are as high as 17,000 casualties. Communications from Yugoslav high command were quickly severed and the operational centres of the government and military were destroyed. The savage bombardment of Belgrade forced the government to retreat southward to Uzice under constant air attack.

As the bombs fell on Belgrade the Yugoslav authorities were in the midst of mobilising their forces; as a result, the positions of their troops were wholly inadequate. The Yugoslav army was almost a million strong, but it was unwisely stretched along the length of their frontier. From twenty-eight Yugoslav infantry divisions and three cavalry divisions, only five infantry divisions and one cavalry division were involved in decisive action against the Germans. The Germans had thirty-three divisions, including six armoured and four mechanised divisions. The Yugoslav campaign was destined to repeat the disparity of the Blitzkrieg in Poland that saw mechanised divisions against ox-carts. Combat in these circumstances made the art of battle strategy largely irrelevant.

Yugoslav military authorities predicted that the main German offensive would be delivered from the north via Hungary. Therefore the main body of the Yugoslav forces were grouped in the northern provinces, with elaborate defences such as tank traps. In fact the main thrust of the German attack came from von List, in a highly successful three-pronged assault upon Nis, Skopje and Monastir in southern Serbia. A break-through was also made at the Strumitsa Pass in the south of Yugoslavia that paved the way for an assault on Salonika. German troops at Skopje met some tough resistance, but German tanks crushed their enemy and captured the town less than thirty-six hours after hostilities began. A Greek report read that the Yugoslav army in the south had 'been obliged under pressure to withdraw to consolidate its positions, leaving the Greek flank uncovered'.[5] German forces pushed through to link up with the Italians in Albania, thus driving a wedge between Yugoslav forces north of Skopje and their Greek and British allies. At 11.00 on 9 April General von Kleist's army captured Nish. In southern Serbia 20,000 prisoners were taken, together with large numbers of guns and equipment. In southern Serbia the remnants of the Yugoslav Third Army had been destroyed in Krivolak. With Monastir, Nish and Skopje all captured, the Germans were in control of the lines of communication in southern Yugoslavia.

The hardest fighting took place in the Kacanik Pass, where the Germans lost a number of tanks and were held up for some days. This allowed Yugoslav units time to disband and withdraw. The resistance at the Kacanik Pass seemed an isolated incident, and German forces met with little resistance elsewhere. On 10 April Croatia claimed itself an independent state with Hitler's blessing. Croat political leaders promptly absconded from the national government in Belgrade and returned to Zagreb. Zagreb fell almost without any defensive action after being invaded by German tanks. In some instances, Croat troops had deserted their positions. They refused to fight the Germans whom they considered liberators from Serbian oppression. Open hostilities broke out between Serb and Croatian factions at Dalmatia, where German planes were diverted to blast Serb troop concentrations. Monastir was captured on 10 April, and the Germans drove through to attack the Greek positions at Florina.

On 16 April the Germans claimed Sarajevo where Serbian forces laid down their arms en masse, and 50,000 prisoners were taken. Berlin radio claimed: 'The roads present a picture of a complete military rout. They are strewn with abandoned and broken down tanks, as well as rifles and machine guns.'[6] In twelve days Yugoslavia had been crushed. General Simovich had described the German invasion as a 'terrible onslaught of an enemy superior both in number and technical equipment . . . Steel and technics were stronger than warriors and heroes.'[7] On 17 April Yugoslavia officially surrendered.

The Germans took 254,000 prisoners, excluding a number of Croat, German, Hungarian and Bulgarian nationals, who had been drafted into the Yugoslav army, and were released after screening. The 146,000 Hungarian troops who had joined the invasion of Yugoslavia behaved in a brutal manner, committing numerous atrocities against Jews, Serbs and even Germans. The Wehrmacht acted with extreme brutality against the Serbs who, unlike the Croats, were believed to be strongly opposed to the Germans. The savage persecution of the Serbs strengthened their determination to resist, and thousands joined the partisan movements. The losses on both sides were relatively slight, and many of the Yugoslav troops fled into the mountains to fight another day as guerrillas under the command of General Mihailovitch, and Marshal Tito. Throughout the whole campaign the Yugoslavs only managed to kill 151 German troops.

The German campaign in Greece opened in devastating fashion. On 6 April the Germans launched an evening bombing raid on the Greek port of Piraeus. During the raid the SS *Clan Fraser*, a 12,000-ton ship that was weighed down with munitions was hit by a bomb. Two soldiers who went on board to inspect the blaze left just in time as the ship exploded in the early hours of the morning. The explosion shook the port of Piraeus, destroying the main harbour and shattering the town. Surrounding vessels in the harbour were sunk and an ammunition barge and train were destroyed. The force of the blast was felt seven miles away in Athens where windows were shattered and blown in. A Royal Engineer company remained in Piraeus to clear the debris. Apart from the loss of the cargo, the effect of the powerful blast served only to enhance the myth of Germany's Blitzkrieg offensive.

As Piraeus burned, an American aid worker, Laird Archer, noted in his diary: 'The whole sky flamed over Piraeus.' He and his wife were left 'shaken, speechless a sense of the world's end.' He went on to say that no Hollywood film could 'match the crashing thunder, the crackling individual blasts under the great roar, the howl of dogs and human shrieks'. Archer concluded that it was a stroke of good fortune for Hitler: 'as it has given a terrific impression of German power and the awfulness of German-waged war.'[8] This incident coincided with the intense bombing of Belgrade which aroused panic among the population of Athens who believed their annihilation was imminent. The Piraeus bombing set a precedent for the pattern of the war. As Commonwealth troops landed at the port, they saw large numbers of refugees searching for a passage away from the island. According to Geoffrey Cox, a young New Zealand officer, there was a 'ruin of smashed quaysides and burnt-out dock buildings [and the] unmistakable stench of coming defeat was in the air'.[9]

The Expeditionary Force under Wilson was known as W Force and consisted mostly of New Zealand and Australian troops from the Middle East. British commanders were disappointed to receive 2,000 untrained Greek mechanics to fortify the Aliakmon Line, instead of the battle-hardened troops from eastern Macedonia that they had hoped for. The Greek troops from the 19th Motorised Division had no real prospect of fighting effectively as a mobile force; their equipment consisted of only a few Bren carriers, motorcycles, and captured Italian lorries and tanks. The 19th Motorised Division was to occupy the coastal sector with the New Zealand Division holding the Servia Pass and the 6th Australian Division to their left. The 12th and 20th Greek Divisions were allotted to the defence of Edessa Pass on the left flank. The British 1st Armoured Brigade was positioned in the Vardar Plain, to act as a screen, forward of the main positions. The Greek 19th Motorised Division were eventually moved to the plains to counter parachute landings, which meant that the New Zealand Division had to cover an impossible area of 23,000 square yards.

As the troops made their way through the mountains they were met with a warm reception from Greek villagers. One officer wrote that he felt more 'like a bridegroom than a soldier with my truck decorated with sprigs of peach blossom and my buttonhole with violets'.[10] For many it was hard to believe that they were going to battle in such idyllic scenery; they were surrounded by wild flowers and lush green valleys. At the officers' mess, dinner consisted of lamb and wine, which was bought locally and on Sundays after a service was held in the village church. British officers attempted to recall ancient Greek from their school days to communicate with their Greek colleagues, while their soldiers traded rations for fresh farm produce.

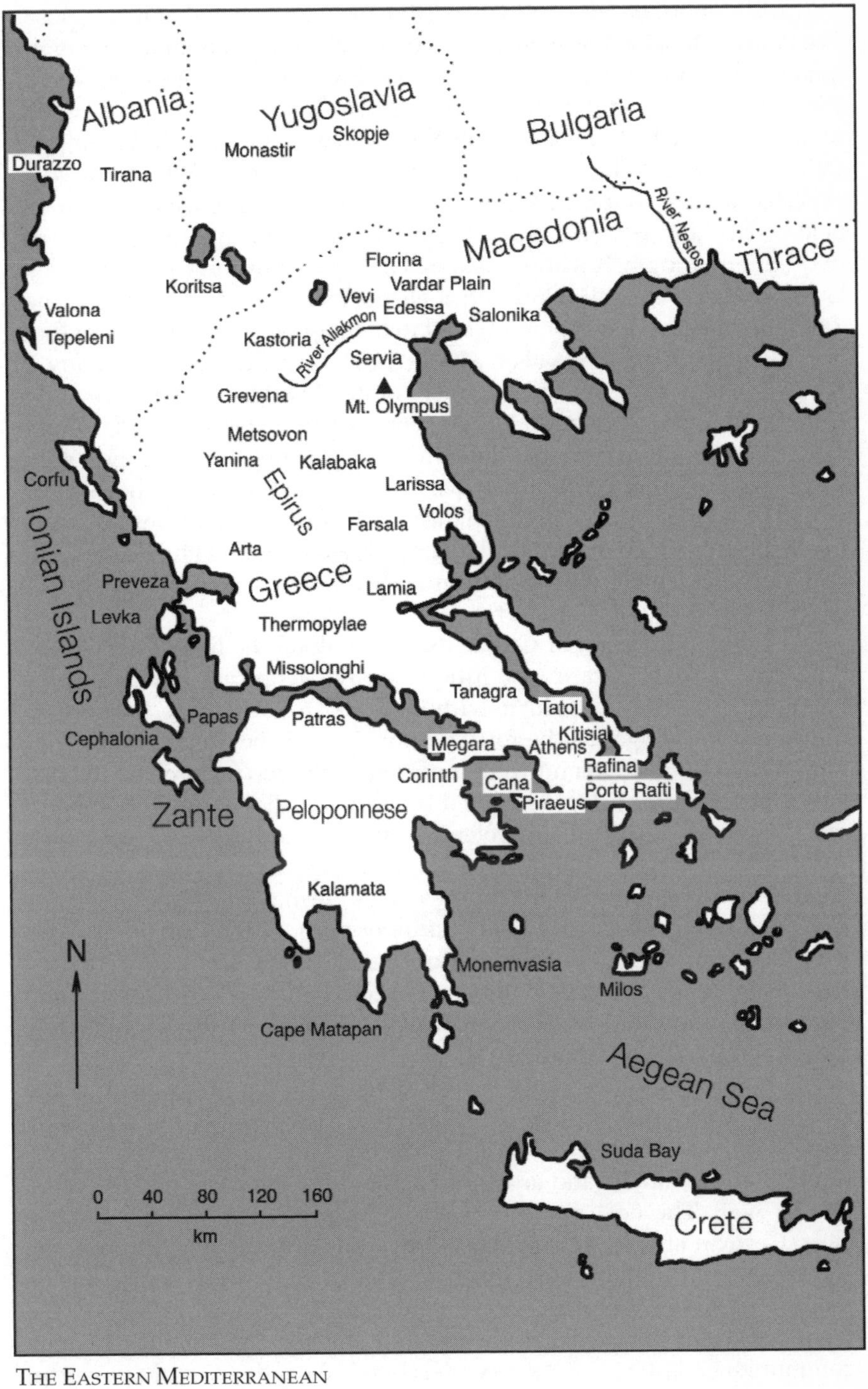
Albania
Yugoslavia
Bulgaria
Monastir
Skopje
Durazzo
Tirana
River Nestos
Macedonia
Thrace
Florina
Koritsa
Vevi
Vardar Plain
Edessa
Salonika
Valona
Tepeleni
Kastoria
River Aliakmon
Servia
Grevena
Mt. Olympus
Metsovon
Yanina
Kalabaka
Corfu
Epirus
Larissa
Volos
Farsala
Ionian Islands
Arta
Preveza
Greece
Lamia
Levka
Thermopylae
Missolonghi
Tanagra
Tatoi
Papas
Patras
Kitisia
Cephalonia
Megara
Athens
Rafina
Corinth
Cana
Porto Rafti
Piraeus
Zante
Peloponnese
Kalamata
N
Monemvasia
Milos
Cape Matapan
Aegean Sea
Suda Bay
0
40
80
120
160
km
Crete

THE EASTERN MEDITERRANEAN

In addition to the SS Adolf Hitler Division, von List had at his disposal five Panzer Divisions, as well as two motorised, three mountain and eight infantry divisions. Germany had nineteen divisions in Bulgaria, eleven of which were grouped directly opposite three Greek divisions holding the Metaxas Line, which ran along the Nestos river in the east, and along the Bulgarian border as far as Yugoslavia. Six or seven German divisions were expected to carry out the assault on the Aliakmon Line, which was to be held by two improvised Greek divisions of negligible fighting value, and two under-strength British divisions. On the eve of the German attack, Greek troops were still taking up their positions on the Aliakmon Line. The 1st Armoured Division remained in their advanced position that they had taken up on their arrival on 21 March. The 4th Hussars, a company of Rangers, a battery of the 2nd Regiment of the Royal Horse Artillery and a battery of Northumberland Hussars were positioned in the Vardar Plain. Their mission was to carry out demolitions and to delay the advance of the enemy to the main positions. It was clear from the outset that Britain would be heavily outnumbered in the air. The British squadrons in Greece totalled eight, which included Gladiators, Blenheims and Hurricanes. The RAF could assemble only eighty aircraft to combat approximately 800 German and 300 Italian aircraft.

The German invasion of Greece extended along the line of the Greco–Bulgarian border. Thrace saw little offensive action, as it was not the intention of Greece to hold it without Turkish assistance. As German troops advanced against the fortified positions of the Metaxas Line they met spirited opposition and were repulsed. Only two forts fell on the first day, and only after being destroyed by heavy artillery and air bombardment. German assault teams relentlessly advanced against Greek forts with flame-throwers, hand-grenades and explosive charges in fierce hand-to-hand fighting. For the first two days the majority of the Greek line along the Bulgarian border held fast; only parts of the Rupel Pass area were overrun. The main forts at Rupel and Ussita repulsed perpetual assaults by tanks and dive-bombers. Forts at Perithori and Dassavli had been briefly captured by German troops but were almost immediately recaptured by Greek counter-attacks.

The heroic resistance of the Greek defenders was of no avail as the Germans were penetrating the Strumitsa Pass where the Yugoslav opposition was weak. On 7 April a German armoured division broke through at the Vardar and advanced across the Greek frontier at Doiran and Gevgeli. The next day the extent of Yugoslav capitulation became clear. German armoured units now drove towards Salonika through the Vardar corridor, where only token resistance came from a ramshackle medley of Greek vehicles. An unequal battle ensued in which the Germans swept the Greeks aside and took the port of Salonika. A Greek communiqué, issued in Athens, described the advance of 'powerful

German forces equipped with most modern war machines, supported by tanks, abundant heavy artillery and numerous aircraft'.[11] The Yugoslav collapse had opened a route through the Monastir Gap, and exposed the left flank of the Aliakmon Line. The Greek army in Albania now faced a fatal German attack to their rear.

Following the fall of Salonika, Greek forces, numbering a mere three divisions, were cut off from their comrades west of the Vardar. However, the German 5th Mountain Division, which later formed part of the invasion force in Crete, was still repulsed in the Rupel Pass. It was the 6th Mountain Division who managed to cross a mountain range 2,000 feet high, which the Greeks considered impassable, and were able to break the Greek line. One Greek division fought so bravely that the Germans allowed officers to retain their side arms and saluted them.

After the opening days of the conflict the main British force stood firm and unopposed on the Aliakmon Line. The majority of the British detachments found themselves carrying out demolitions and destroying bridges to forestall the German advance. In Salonika, oil reserves were destroyed before German troops occupied the city the following day. In eastern Macedonia Greeks still held firm while the withdrawal of units from the Metaxas Line had begun from the ports on the Aegean coast.

During the night of 9 April snow fell and Allied troops suffered from the bitterly cold conditions. Cover from the elements was provided only by a tent-fly, which sagged under the weight of the snow. Brigadier George Clifton recalled how they had been issued with 'tropical kit of Bombay bloomers [shorts] and Bombay Bowlers [pith helmets] and shirts ... as practical kit for fighting in a Greek spring'. Clifton concluded: 'the bowler was an unmitigated bloody nuisance. I threw mine into a snow drift on Mount Olympus.'[12] The conditions were described by an Australian war correspondent, as the temperature dropped ten degrees below freezing. The troops were 'fighting in the snow sleeping huddled together, wrapped in one or two blankets which they were able to carry'. Allied troops were living in starkly contrasting conditions from what they had experienced in the desert. 'Libya was like a billiard table compared with the terrifying ranges and yawning ravines [of Greece].'[13] Some units were living on the edge of snow clad ridges, their only protection against the cold being: 'shelters which they erect in stony hollows with the aid of ground sheets'.[14] The majority of bomber and fighter missions were hampered by the adverse weather conditions. But the RAF won their first victories as twelve Hurricanes had engaged thirty ME 109s and shot down five enemy aircraft without loss.

On 9 April General Wilson arranged a conference with his fellow commanders at New Zealand divisional headquarters. As he travelled to join them he was met by a tide of Greek and Yugoslav refugees, both military and civilian. The bulk of the refugees were on foot, others travelled on donkeys, ox-carts and antiquated vehicles, with various belongings strapped to the roofs. The Allies had no means of organising or policing this exodus. After Wilson arrived at the headquarters, he met with Blamey and Freyberg. In light of the German advance through Monastir and Florina, it was established that the line could not be held. The New Zealand Division was holding a front of sixteen miles, which it was agreed, was far too much for a single division. Despite the work carried out on the Aliakmon Line, it remained inadequate to repulse a powerful German strike. There was a general feeling of disappointment that so much material used to reinforce the line would be wasted. It was decided to disband forces along the Aliakmon river and withdraw to the Olympus-Servia-Mountains west of the Kozani-Amyntaion valley. After the battle, Freyberg wrote that if his forces had stayed to fight on the Aliakmon Line 'we should all have been rounded up in the first phase of the campaign.'[15] A composite force from the British 1st Armoured Brigade and 16th Australian Brigade were sent to defend the area south of Florina. The redeployment of the New Zealand Division to the Olympus Passes was complete by 10 and 11 April, under considerable German air activity. The foothills of Mount Olympus began abruptly and rose rapidly. The lower slopes were covered in scrub where it had been deforested; next came a belt of a variety of trees with fairly thick undergrowth; above this was a forest of mixed oak and beech with open undergrowth of fern and wild pear trees. Winding through the valley were deep gorges surrounded by trees that reached high into the sky.

On the morning of 10 April German columns were spotted approaching Vevi and the Rangers were sent forward to destroy roads to hinder German progress. As the Germans came into range, British and Australian gunners opened fire, putting a German tank out of action and inflicting some casualties. An ULTRA intercept read that German troops reported that they were meeting 'violent resistance'. During the night German raiding parties scaled the slopes held by 2/8 Australian Battalion and the Rangers, capturing ten prisoners in the process. Under the cover of darkness, German troops had managed to deceive their enemy by hailing them in English. To avoid further infiltrations the commanding officer of 2/8th Australian Battalion gave orders that between 21.00 and 05.00 hours, all troops were to remain in their rifle pits and fire upon any movements. The order concluded: 'you may be tired. You may be uncomfortable [but] you will continue to do that job unless otherwise ordered.'[16]

On the afternoon of 11 April German machine-gun and mortar fire opened up from Vevi village. Allied movement between posts became restricted and Australian anti-tank gunners began to take casualties. The Rangers managed to suppress some German machine-gun positions with small arms fire, but the Allied line of defence was woefully thin. Later that day reports of German tanks attacking Greek positions were received, and the 3rd Royal Tank Regiment was moved from Amyntaion to Pandeleimon. This exposed the weakness of the Allied armour. Six cruisers were put permanently out of action by a combination of broken tracks and mechanical failures. Tracks designed for the desert regularly broke on the difficult terrain. Tank repair facilities were lacking and spare parts were in short supply, moreover there was scarcely time for repairs. Damaged tanks had to be simply abandoned where they lay and set on fire.

On the morning of 12 April the SS Adolf Hitler Division launched a frontal assault on the Vevi position supported by heavy artillery. In the face of this new onslaught with superior fire-power, Australian battalions on the flanks were ordered to gradually pull back, leaving the Rangers to hold a rearguard action. The Rangers and 2/8 Australians began to take increasing casualties as the Germans rained in artillery, mortar and machine-gun fire on their positions. The Rangers returned artillery fire and inflicted considerable damage on advancing German infantry before dispersing. The 2/8 Australians became totally severed from the Rangers by late afternoon and were in danger of being isolated. The 2/8 Australians headed for Sotir in a desperate attempt to escape, and weary survivors discarded equipment and arms as they went. At 09.00 the following day 200 exhausted men arrived at Sotir, many of whom bore no arms whatsoever. During the night these men were transported to Servia by lorry.

In the early hours of 15 April, at the Servia pass, the 9th Panzer Division engaged the 4th New Zealand Division. A group of German infantry crossed the Aliakmon river during the night and were progressing towards New Zealand positions. Initially they were mistaken for Greeks and were allowed to pass some New Zealand advanced posts, but the German patrol was soon discovered and they were destroyed by mortar and machine-gun fire. A further infantry assault was repulsed in the late afternoon in which the New Zealanders were able to take 200 German prisoners. During the action, German losses amounted to approximately 400 killed in contrast to the New Zealanders' two killed and six wounded.

Along the Allied defences, Wilson found that his hands were tied. He did not have sufficient troops to carry out any movements as the line was too thinly held; in many places there were few or no reserves. Given the impossible circumstances of insufficient men and equipment, the Allies achieved all that could have been expected at Vevi. They inflicted casualties on the Germans, but at a considerable cost in equipment; three Allied infantry battalions had lost valuable arms and equipment. There was a loss in heavy equipment also; the Australian field regiment abandoned two guns and many other vehicles, including tanks, and ten guns were lost after a road demolition accidentally cut off a troop of Northumberland Hussars.

The 1st Armoured Brigade were given orders to hold the German pursuit as long as possible, enabling the Greek 12th and 20th Divisions to reorganise in their new positions. The withdrawal of Greek forces from Albania was imperative for the security of the western flank of British forces. As German tanks made for Komanos close to the 1st Armoured Brigade's headquarters, a group of Northumberland Hussars led by Lieutenant A W Trippier engaged German armour with anti-tank guns. A spirited resistance ensued, eight German tanks were destroyed and the Germans were forced to withdraw after expending their ammunition and nearly all their fuel.

In the early hours of the morning of 14 April, the 1st Armoured Division reached Grevena. The 3rd Royal Tank Regiment had lost numerous Cruiser tanks, not from enemy action, but from broken tracks. The high mileage of the vehicles was beginning to tell; the tanks had already covered nearly 500 miles of bad roads to reach their original positions. The Northumberland Hussars lost six anti-tank guns at Komanos and the Rangers, who were reduced to half of their original fighting strength, were short of equipment and weapons. The 2nd Royal Horse Artillery had fought for three days running and had expended 3,100 rounds of ammunition. They reported only two men wounded, with the loss of four vehicles abandoned in the retreat. Observers noted that Allied forces equipped themselves professionally in arduous circumstances. In each instance, when the Allies were forced to retreat, they did so in an orderly and controlled manner. By contrast, when the Greek 12th and 20th Divisions pulled back from the Vevria–Edessa heights, they were reported to have disintegrated. What happened to the bulk of these forces is unclear due to a breakdown of communication between Greek and British commanders; the lack of sufficient transport would have undoubtedly been a factor causing chaos in the narrow and tortuous mountain roads. The withdrawal of Greek armies in Albania, as predicted by Papagos, was fatal to Greek morale. It was optimistic to expect Greek troops to maintain their fighting spirit after a long campaign against the Italians. Greek troops had suffered unimaginable hardships and they were now ordered to retreat along some of the most unforgiving terrain in Europe, swamped by refugees and under unrelenting air attack.

Demolition work was carried out at the entrance to the Olympus Pass where New Zealand sappers completed the destruction of roads and tunnels. It was reported that along the coastal road the New Zealanders were defending the advance of some eighty tanks and 150 other vehicles. Attempts to collapse the Platamon Tunnel failed. After a number of explosions, only the brick lining of the tunnel had been destroyed. Throughout the night the rumble of heavy vehicles could be heard and it seemed inevitable that a heavy assault would ensue at daybreak. The battle opened with an exchange of artillery fire. New Zealand positions provided an excellent vantage point for observing enemy movements. It

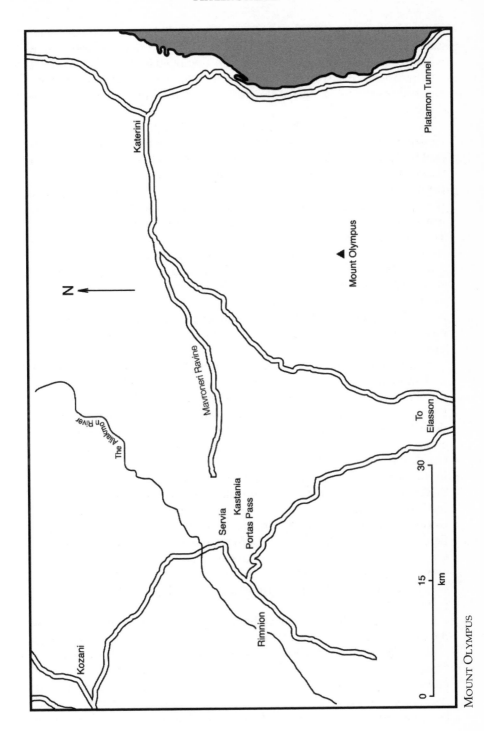

MOUNT OLYMPUS

was estimated that 150 tanks with infantry would be used in the German assault. Despite the great weight of the German offensive, the terrain worked against them. German units were deployed in long columns along narrow roads that severely restricted their movement; if a single tank were knocked out or broke down it would disrupt the movement of others.

On 16 April heavy fighting occurred at the Platamon Tunnel. After resisting for three hours, the 21st New Zealand Battalion were forced to pull back to a reserve position south of the tunnel. They eventually moved back towards the Pinios river, demolishing the road as they went. Fire from Bren gun carriers pinned down German infantry while a further withdrawal was carried out. The New Zealanders successfully retreated to a gorge where the Pinios river emerged from the mountains into the sea. The New Zealanders were forced to transport their light vehicles across the river by a barge operated by hand ropes. Artillery was driven across a railway bridge nearby. A flock of sheep and goats accompanied by shepherds were the last to cross the barge and railway bridge, before extensive demolitions were carried out. The German attempt to crush the New Zealanders at the Platamon Tunnel failed. The Allied force had escaped in good order and they had lost only one officer and thirty-five men.

At the Olympus Pass, mist and rain covered the mountain top. German tanks and infantry had taken advantage of the poor visibility and attacked the 22nd and 28th New Zealand Battalions. The Maoris of the 28th Battalion launched a counter-attack, which left many Germans dead for the loss of four Maoris killed and eighteen missing. Although the counter-attack forced the Germans back, orders were given to withdraw the battalions to the top of the pass. Repeated air attacks from the Luftwaffe in support of the infantry failed to make an impression on the New Zealand defenders. New Zealand field guns, supported by British medium batteries, hindered the enemy artillery fire and prevented German engineers from bridging the Aliakmon. On the extreme right flank of Olympus, the 23rd Battalion were forced to climb 2,000 feet through deep mud and snow. As they climbed they pushed trucks and anti-tank guns over the ravines, and ammunition and other equipment was blown up. Despite the German advances, the New Zealanders still held the pass.

The successful defence of the Olympus position was overshadowed by the developments on the Greek front to the west, where Greek armies in central Macedonia and Thrace ceased to exist. Greek divisions north of Grevena had also dispersed and were scattered throughout the mountains; only General Tsolakoglou's force remained in Epirus, and they were running short of ammunition and water. The Greek troops had been cut off from the bulk of Allied forces since the loss of Salonika.

General Bakopoulos surrendered on behalf of the Greek army in Macedonia. The three Greek divisions lost in the Metaxas Line were some of the finest troops in the Greek army. British commanders were frustrated that they were not in an area where they could be better utilised.

The Anglo–Greek front now extended from the Albanian frontier to Mount Olympus. In light of the Greek capitulation, General Wilson began to have grave doubts whether his forces could hold out against a concentrated German attack. ULTRA signal intelligence warned Wilson of German attempts to encircle forces on Mount Olympus from the west, therefore orders were given to withdraw to the Thermopylae Line running south of Lamia, over a hundred miles from their position at Olympus. If German forces broke through the mountains on to the plains before the Allies retreated fully from Olympus, the entire Anglo–Greek army faced annihilation.

At daybreak on 16 April the 1st Armoured Brigade started their march from Venetikos to Kalabaka. The damage inflicted by the Luftwaffe slowed the pace considerably; it was imperative that the New Zealanders held the passes to allow the rest of the Allied forces time to head out of the mountains. Fortunately, heavy rain and low clouds meant that the 1st Armoured Brigade would not be an easy target for the Luftwaffe. After his failure to break through the passes, von List decided on a different angle of attack, and pursued the 1st Armoured Brigade through the Thessalian plain to Kalabaka. The 5th Panzer Division were given the task to pursue the 1st Armoured Brigade, but they made slow progress initially as they had to endure the damage created by the Luftwaffe coupled with British demolitions. It took the 5th Panzer Division three days to cover forty miles from Grevena to Kalabaka. By the time the Germans reached the plains, British forces had nearly reached their destination at Thermopylae over a hundred miles away.

On 19 April Wavell arrived in Athens to discuss the possibility of an evacuation with General Wilson. In light of the situation in North Africa, Wavell and Wilson decided that it was certain that no further assistance could be sent to Greece. It was agreed that the 7th Australian Division and the Polish Brigade, which were originally destined for Greece, were better deployed in the Western Desert where Rommel was rapidly advancing on Tobruk having won back El Agheila, Benghazi and Derna. Also, if the battle was prolonged, there was the humanitarian problem of feeding the Greek population. The devastating raid on the port of Piraeus had left it inoperable, and after the withdrawal at Volos, a secondary port could not be found; therefore the whole country was isolated from European sources of supply. With all hope of reinforcements relinquished, General Wilson concluded that preparations should be made for a general withdrawal. The series of delaying tactics and rearguard actions performed by

British Commonwealth troops had finally culminated in an inevitable general retreat, which was now in full progress.

NOTES

1   Hammerton, John, *The Second Great War*, Vol. IV, London: Waverly, 1950, p. 1613.
2   Ibid.
3   Cervi, Mario, *The Hollow Legions. Mussolini's Blunder in Greece 1940–1941*, London: Chatto & Windus, 1972, p. 265.
4   Ibid, p. 264.
5   Hammerton, op. cit., p. 1619.
6   Ibid, p. 1622.
7   Ibid.
8   Archer, Laird, *Balkan Journal: An Unofficial Observer in Greece*, New York, 1944, p. 165.
9   MacDonald, Callum, *The Lost Battle – Crete 1941*, London: Macmillan, 1991, p. 109.
10 Beevor, Antony, *Crete – The Battle and the Resistance*, London: John Murray, 1991, p. 31.
11 Hammerton, op. cit., p. 1623.
12 Flower, Desmond and Reeves, James (eds), *The War 1939–1945*, London: Cassell, 1960, pp. 182–3.
13 Buckley, Christopher, *Greece and Crete 1941*, London: HMSO, 1952, p. 54.
14 Ibid.
15 Freyberg, Paul, *Bernard Freyberg VC – Soldier of Two Nations*, London: Hodder & Stoughton, 1991, p. 250.
16 Buckley, op. cit., p. 54.

CHAPTER VI

Run, Rabbit, Run

During 16 and 17 April pessimistic rumours emanated that the British line had been fatally broken at the Olympus front, and that the Australians were cut to pieces at the Larissa Plain. In reality, successful delaying tactics were holding the Germans and the retreat was going to plan. However, Athens was badly shaken by these rumours. The tension grew in the capital as armed police roamed the streets to prevent a pro-German coup and frantic Greek civilians tore down anti-Nazi posters. Pictures of Goebbels and Hitler began to appear on the desk-top of the Athens police chief. Greek civilians were shocked by the sudden change of their plight. Within a few days the Greeks had experienced the elation of the victories won against Italy, and imminent defeat by Germany. The nation was suddenly gripped by a feeling of defeatism.

The Greek minister for war, Papademis, issued a declaration stating that further resistance was futile. He gave his generals the go ahead to act on their own judgement and suspended the call up of reservists. Further defeatism came from the Greek minister for communications, Oeconomou, who had called for the grounding of Greek aircraft and the destruction of petrol reserves at Tatoi and Elevsis, to prevent unnecessary loss of life. However, the Greek king revoked the order after being informed by the British military mission. Many of the Greek hierarchy favoured an honourable surrender and believed that prolonging the fight would lead to the destruction of their country.

On 15 April German aircraft attacked British airfields on the Thessalian Plain. The observation system set up in conjunction with the Greeks had failed, the anti-aircraft defence was inadequate, and the aircraft were poorly camouflaged. This resulted in disaster for the RAF. Sixteen Blenheims and fourteen Hurricanes were destroyed on the ground. D'Albiac, who was present at Larissa at the time of the attack, subsequently ordered all RAF units to be transferred to the vicinity of Athens. Therefore air support was no longer possible for Allied troops, unless in withdrawn positions near to the airfield in Athens.

Allied troops retreating through the dangerous bottle-neck of Larissa were subjected to heavy air attacks as the Luftwaffe now dominated the skies. Vehicles were congested in narrow roads and could not move beyond fifteen miles per hour. German dive bombers would circle above their prey then swoop on their target. On their descent their sirens wailed in a crescendo of noise, punctuated by ineffectual small arms fire from the ground, followed by a deep thud as the bombers' ordnance hit. As the snow and rain cleared, air attacks increased from clear blue skies. General Wilson observed that his men were becoming 'bomb-happy'. Wilson stated that soldiers would abandon their vehicles at the first sight of aircraft. On one occasion a retreating soldier looked skywards and saw what he thought was a Stuka poised to strike against the clear cobalt sky. He threw himself under a truck before glancing back, when he saw the same menacing form flap its wings. He noted: 'a hawk at two hundred feet looked just like a Stuka at two thousand.'[1]

Bombing raids were followed by a group of fighters that would strafe columns of soldiers with a hail of machine-gun fire. Tom Somerville, with the 5th Field Unit of Artillery, recalled: 'we'd never run . . . the pilots got great sport out of a running target.' Despite these terrifying attacks, Somerville described morale as: 'good' although 'everybody would be very shaken . . . some would be cursing and shaking their fists . . . others would be taking it calmly.'[2] Greek civilians were unequivocal in their hatred of the Luftwaffe. The commander of a signals squadron, Gerry de Winton, recalled seeing a German pilot bail out from his aircraft and land just outside a village. As he went forward to take the pilot prisoner, de Winton was stopped by a group of civilian mechanics brandishing heavy spanners. They told him: 'You stay out. We'll settle this.'[3]

On the retreat to the Thermopylae position, Sidney Raggett, of the Australian artillery, commented in his diary that daylight hours were 'filled with bombing and machine-gunning and the nights with constant shelling. To survive is a matter of luck.' Raggett noted that German dominance of the air was having an effect on the troops. 'We were ready to move again at mid-day and were bombed non-stop for three hours. Where is the bloody R.A.F?' Shaken by the continuous air attacks Raggett stated that it was a new experience for the troops and was 'not only outside their experience but outside their training'.[4] An Australian correspondent for *The Times* observed that: 'The Germans are using a fantastic amount of aircraft.' He noted that Stukas attacked his party for two days and destroyed three cars and one truck. German airpower was being utilised to an intensity not previously experienced by the Commonwealth troops; the Luftwaffe were: 'bombing every nook and cranny, hamlet, village and town in its path'.[5] German propaganda predictably capitalised on the London musical hit 'Run, Rabbit, Run'. It was probably a fair analogy.

With Allied airpower nullified, the Luftwaffe bombarded Larissa without retribution. Larissa was in the unfortunate position of being the focal point of a network of roads that the British were forced to retreat along. While passing through the barricaded streets of Larissa, the retreating troops witnessed the devastation caused by unopposed air power. The town had previously been damaged by an earthquake, and was in ruins. Soldiers and civilians were lying under sacks or blankets and bullet-ridden trucks were piled on the side of the road. Just outside the town was the bizarre sight of numerous dead horses, cows and sheep that were slaughtered by the Lufwaffe en route to the safety of the hills.

The 1st Armoured Division had taken sixteen hours to reach their new position south of Gevera. They were forced to travel along a narrow gorge where the Luftwaffe had previously raided, and where bombs had blasted away huge sections of the shale-covered hillside to create large gaps. They were delayed by assorted debris, including dead horses, broken carts and an endless stream of Greek and Yugoslav refugees. Engineers worked tirelessly to clear roads improvising with what materials they could muster; on one occasion a crater twenty yards wide was filled with dead mules and riveted with discarded Greek rifles.

German bombing proved to be indiscriminate and lacking in direction. In the course of the retreat from Larissa, none of the major bridges had been destroyed; the nearest incident of a direct hit on a bridge occurred when an ammunition truck was struck by a bomb when approaching a bridge north of Pharsala. The explosion from the truck badly damaged the bridge and caused a four-hour delay. The Luftwaffe also failed to target leading vehicles in convoys moving along narrow passes, which was a sure tactic to slow the progress of vehicles. Wrecked vehicles were pushed aside and detours were taken where possible. Most convoys tried to move through the night to reduce the risk of aerial attack. Increased accidents were caused by fatigue; drivers would often fall asleep at the wheel, some falling into such a deep sleep that the officers who sat behind often fired their revolver past the cab window to rouse them. On 18 April Allied forces began to arrive at the Thermopylae position where some of the exhausted men rested their aching limbs by bathing in the warm sulphur springs. Brief respite was given to the men at Thermaopylae as the Italians had not followed up the Greek collapse and were progressing across the Albanian border with extreme caution. Wavell hoped that they could hold on to their position at Thermopylae to buy time to organise the defence of Crete and Egypt.

On 18 April Papagos presented a report to the king about the progress of Greek troops. From the report it was patently obvious that troops in Albania were withdrawn too late. Von List was successful in driving a wedge between Greek and Yugoslav forces within the opening days of the campaign. British and Greek troops were hopelessly separated, and the Germans were preparing an advance on Yannia to destroy the Greek army. Koryzis was overawed by the immense national disaster that faced his country. The Greek premier was under pressure from members of his cabinet to end the war and halt the destruction of Greece, and he became increasingly desperate over what course of action to take. After returning from a cabinet meeting he locked himself in his bedroom took his revolver and shot himself in the head; nobody in Athens believed the story of 'heart-failure.'[6] Koryzis was replaced by another banker named Tsuderos.

With the knowledge that the Greek will was broken, and having already decided to withdraw his forces, Wavell gave the king assurance that British forces would fight alongside the Greeks as long as they were willing to resist. Predictably Papagos had no reason for optimism and suggested that the British forces leave before the further destruction of his country. The British ambassador, Sir Michael Palairet, went to great lengths to stress that the Greek king and government gave their un-equivocal approval for the evacuation of Commonwealth forces. Even now it seemed that politics were still not divorced from military decisions. The Nazi Propaganda Minister, Dr Goebbels, sensed that a British evacuation was imminent and proceeded to capitalise on Churchill's failure in Greece. German propaganda pre-empted a British evacuation and claimed that Churchill had incited a small nation to fight his battles and was now prepared to leave them to their fate without protection from righteous German wrath.

The SS Adolf Hitler Division had been assigned the task of pushing through to Yanina and cutting off the Greek withdrawal. Greek troops encountered a German motorised division and fought with characteristic courage, but were unable to prevent the Germans from reaching Yanina. On 21 April British HQ in Athens sent a message to Yanina asking about the situation there. A reply came back in German: 'Hier is das Deutsche heer.'[7] On 20 April General Tsolakoglu surrendered the army of Epirus on his own initiative. Two days later the Greek High Command stated: 'the Italian forces had not succeeded in entering Greek territory, but were held by our troops on Albanian territory.'[8] The Greeks stressed that they had not given ground to the Italians, but were forced to surrender when faced with the threat of a German attack to their rear. As requested by the Greeks, Field Marshal von List was prepared to exclude the Italians from the settlement. Typically ungallant, Mussolini argued that Greece belonged to the Italian sphere of influence and Hitler insisted that his Fascist ally must be involved. Therefore the Italian General, Ferrero, was permitted to take the formal surrender alongside General Jodl.

The disintegration of Greek armies in Epirus and Macedonia had forced the king and the government to leave Athens for Crete. Before leaving for Crete, the Greek government sent a message to the British minister in Athens expressing their gratitude to the British government and the 'gallant Imperial troops for the aid which they had extended to Greece in her defence against the aggressor'.[9] On hearing the news of the Greek surrender in Epirus, Wavell decided to bring the date of the evacuation forward. The Germans were seemingly conscious of the forthcoming evacuation and concentrated the efforts of the Luftwaffe on railways to the rear of British positions. Shipping in the area also reported increasing attacks.

On 22 April the evacuation orders were made known to the Commonwealth troops. The wounded and nursing personnel would be the first to embark. Only light weapons that could be carried by hand would be taken and all heavy equipment was to be destroyed. The method used to destroy guns was to place a shell, nose first, into the barrel and then fire another round, thus destroying the barrel of the gun. Greek children were encouraged by the troops to help destroy their equipment. Motor vehicles were also to be rendered useless; sand was put in the oil intake, radiators were drained and stones were placed on the accelerators until the engines seized. Sledgehammers were used to smash engines, radiators and batteries; all fires and explosions were avoided. Horses were shot and mules given to the Greeks. More elaborate destruction took place on the Greek railways where locomotives were rammed into one another. The retreating troops aimed to destroy anything of use to the German war effort, which meant that Greek civilians would also suffer. As sappers went to the RAF base to destroy 30,000 tons of petrol, a valuable prize for the Luftwaffe, they were met by armed Greek guards who forced them to withdraw without completing their mission. These tasks were reluctantly carried out in a melancholy atmosphere. The Brigade Major of the 1st Armoured Brigade, Dick Hobson, took little pleasure in the destruction 'as I sat in front of the wireless about to give the order for the demolitions'. He wrote: 'I remember reflecting what a foul thing I was about to perpetrate. The Greeks had been wonderfully kind to us.' Hobson concluded: 'we were about to lay waste to their countryside and ruin their livelihood; and run away apparently without a fight.'[10]

In Athens there were chaotic scenes as 'lorries were being hurriedly packed ... suitcases were lying open with their contents scattered around'.[11] The British civilians in Athens crowded outside the British embassy, demanding details of their evacuation. As confidential papers were hurriedly destroyed, the stench of burnt paper filled the British Legation at the Hotel Grande Bretagne. At the Tatoi Palace, instructions came from the king to distribute the contents of the wine cellars, two bottles for each officer and one each for the soldiers. Troops would be initially evacuated to Crete for later transfer to Egypt. Lack of air cover remained a fundamental problem in Greece. John White, personal assistant to General Freyberg, recalled that it was 'remarkable how much the air force had been endeavouring to cover us [and] help us when we were being attacked by German bombers. But only a couple of Hurricanes would appear.'[12]

The writer Roald Dahl, then a young Hurricane pilot, was among those who made the futile trip across the Mediterranean to Greece. With the high casualties and insurmountable airpower of the Luftwaffe, Dahl described the morale within the squadron as poor: 'No real friendships existed . . . each man was wrapped up in a cocoon of his own problems.' He wrote: 'the sheer effort of trying to stay alive was concentrating the minds of everyone around me.'[13] The RAF made their last major effort against the Luftwaffe on 20 April, Easter Day. Fifteen Hurricanes (the remnants of three Hurricane squadrons) fought an air battle against an estimated 120 to 200 German aircraft. Dahl recalled that the sky was 'so full of aircraft that half my time was spent trying to avoid collision'.[14] Pilots, who went by names such as, 'Timber' Woods, 'Scruffy' Dowding and 'Dixie' Dean, fought bravely destroying twenty-two enemy aircraft for the loss of five of their own and four pilots.

D'Albiac highlighted the problems faced by the RAF. He argued that if the aircraft were brought within range to provide protection to British forces, the Luftwaffe would certainly destroy them. With the evacuation imminent, D'Albiac withdrew his remaining aircraft to the small airfield of Argos, which was still in range to provide cover for British forces. Almost inevitably the Luftwaffe obliterated the remaining Hurricanes. Dahl described the attack as a 'leisurely performance, occupying some forty minutes'.[15] Thirteen Hurricanes were destroyed on the ground and one in the air. This ended any hope of air cover for the evacuation; the remaining seven fighters finally withdrew to Crete the following day. In view of the absence of airpower, it was decided that the evacuation should be carried out in the ports of the Peloponnese, rather than the beaches of Attica, which were exposed and offered less defence against air attack.

The Germans made their move on Thermopylae at dawn on 24 April; a New Zealand patrol had discovered German engineers repairing the bridges over the Sperkhios river. German dive-bombers fiercely attacked Allied positions and tanks were spotted advancing near the Thermopylae cliff face. However, the advance of German armour was checked by British and New Zealand gunners who knocked out fifteen German tanks with heavy shell fire from 25-pounders. The Allied gunners were not concerned with expending ammunition as they were trying to use up their reserves before the evacuation. By 25 April the majority of the troops were withdrawn to Athens; only remnants of 4th New Zealand Brigade and 1st Armoured Brigade were north of Athens fighting a rearguard action protecting two of the principal routes to the capital. German troops entered Thermopylae to find it deserted. The main road to Athens had been so badly cratered and damaged by Allied sappers that German tanks had to be diverted to treacherous mountain tracks. The German advance on Athens was slow and cautious. It seemed that German intelligence had over-estimated the number of Commonwealth troops in the Thebes area,

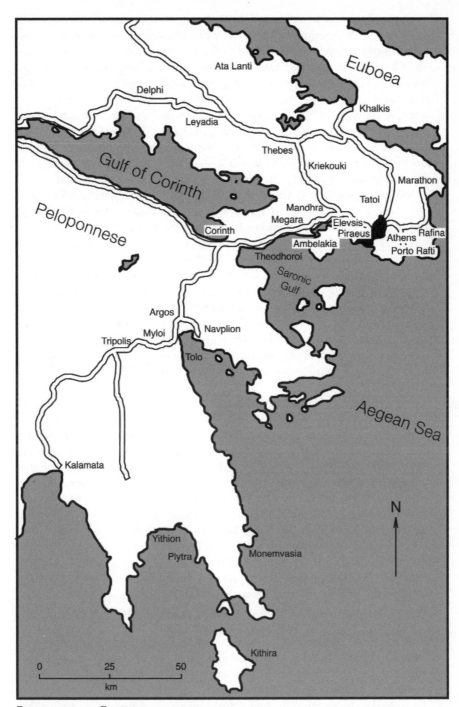

BEACHES IN THE PELOPONNESE

protecting the road to Athens. On 25 April Wilson and his party were driven to the Peloponnese in a convoy of cars, one of which was Prince Paul's limousine, which he had abandoned after leaving Yugoslavia in exile. General Blamey was taken to Egypt and Major-General Freyberg, who insisted on staying, was placed in command of troops evacuating the Peloponnese.

On 26 April von List opened an airborne assault that had been threatened throughout the campaign in Greece. At 06.00 there was an intense aerial bombardment aimed at silencing British anti-aircraft guns around Corinth. The bombardment lasted for about half an hour and consisted of around thirty dive-bombers supported by eighty ME 110s. Men on the ground sat helpless in their slit trenches or searched for what cover they could find. What the dive-bombers missed, fighters strafed with deadly machine-gun fire, until all the gun positions were silenced. Then Ju 52 transport aircraft emerged from a thick haze that masked their approach in formations of three. As the lumbering aircraft moved ominously across the sky at 200 feet, parachutists began to emerge. Assigned to the mission were two battalions of the 2nd Parachute Rifle Regiment, an engineer platoon, artillery, and one medical company, approximately 800 men in total. Their objective was to secure the canal area and seize the Corinth bridge. Capture of the bridge would give German troops swift access to the Commonwealth troops' embarkation points in the Peloponnese, and prevent further troops from being evacuated.

The 19th New Zealand Battalion met the bulk of the German assault. Many parachutists perished in the air, while others fell into the canal itself. The defenders inflicted numerous casualties on their enemy but began to suffer losses as the paratroops numbers grew and became organised. After chaotic fighting over the canal, the bridge was rapidly seized by the Germans. German engineers immediately set about disarming explosive charges set on the bridge by British demolition teams. South of the bridge, two young British officers, Captain J F Phillips and Lieutenant J T Tyson, took cover in a position 200 yards from the bridge. Despite being under fire, one of the officers took his rifle and aimed at the explosive charge; his first shot missed, but the second 'detonated the charge with a violent explosion'. The bridge was destroyed as a dozen Germans were crossing to engage the young officers. 'Down crashed the bridge, the hundred and fifty feet into the waters of the canal, taking the Germans with it.'[16] The two officers eventually reached Navplion where they were evacuated. Historians have subsequently dismissed their feat as impossible, and it is widely accepted that a stray British anti-aircraft shell caused the detonation of the charges. However, both Phillips and Tyson were awarded the Military Cross after the war.

Despite the destruction of the bridge, German paratroops had won the battle for Corinth after only two hours. Outside Corinth, in Isthmus, the 4th Hussars had been overwhelmed before they could get their tanks into battle. German engineers quickly set about building another bridge across the canal, but no attempt was made to advance on British embarkation points in the Peloponnese. The German strategy seemed to be to cut the British off to the north of Corinth rather than attack those who had moved south towards the Peloponnese. Fortunately for the Commonwealth troops, the majority had already crossed the bridge and were waiting in the Peloponnese for evacuation. Despite the spectacular German victory at Corinth, they had failed to cut off the Commonwealth troops' evacuation; the remainder of troops were on beaches in eastern Attica. However, the Germans inflicted a significant loss on Commonwealth forces, claiming over 900 prisoners with the loss of only 237 paratroopers killed.

After the defeat at Corinth, Freyberg signalled via radio for the remnants of Commonwealth forces north of Corinth to head for Porto Rafti. The 4th New Zealand Brigade formed a defensive perimeter at Porto Rafti and Rafina under perfect spring skies. At nightfall the majority of the troops made their way to the beach, where they waited in the gloom for salvation. Requisitioned merchant ships and destroyers endeavoured to ferry the evacuees out to the cruisers. The Royal Navy captains faced an anxious wait as this process was carried out. They knew that if they were not well clear of the dangerous waters before first light, they would be subjected to the horrors of the Luftwaffe. Vessels hired and requisitioned by Commonwealth troops were excluded to Greek troops, which included the Cretan V Division, who were desperate to return home. Lieutenant Bert Dyson recalled an incident as they boarded their evacuation ship at Porto Rafti: 'It was essential not to make any noise [and] to do as you were told . . . there was no problem embarking except for one soldier down at the beach was drunk, making a terrible noise . . . he was shot because he was putting lives at risk. He was putting a warship at risk.'[17] At Porto Rafti 5,200 men were taken aboard HMS *Calcutta* and SS *Glengyle*.

A further 4,700 had been embarked at beaches in Megara where the ships had put to sea by 03.00 in order to be sufficiently out to sea by daybreak. The 1st Armoured Brigade and the rearguard troops were the last to arrive at Rafina. After painstakingly slow embarkation by rowing boat, around 1,000 troops were left stranded. The beachmaster suggested to Brigadier Charrington that he could get on board in front of the other men. Charrington bellowed with anger: 'Who do you take me for?'[18] Charrington and his men withdrew to the cover of the woods where they rested and resigned themselves to the fate of German prison camps. However, Charrington's men were woken at around 01.00 and were told that HMS *Havoc* had appeared offshore to evacuate them. The destroyer had been sent up the coast by the remnants of the 4th New Zealand

Brigade at Porto Rafti. Some 15,000 troops had embarked during the first night and the evacuation was going to plan, with a quarter of the troops at sea and the vast remainder ready for embarkation at various beaches. Blenheim aircraft ran a constant shuttle service to Crete with passengers crammed into bomb-bays and turrets. It was reported that a Sunderland flying-boat managed to take off with eighty-four men on board, nearly three times the permitted limit on the civilian equivalent.

At Nauplia, the SS *Slamat* continued to take evacuees until 04.00, despite warnings that she would be unable to clear the danger area of the Antikithera channel before daylight. The *Slamat* was caught by dive-bombers at 07.00 and was badly damaged. She sent out a distress signal that was heeded by *Diamond* and *Wryneck* who recovered the survivors, but after a relentless pursuit by dive-bombers both the *Diamond* and *Wryneck* were sunk in the afternoon. The destroyer *Griffin* arrived to picked up around fifty survivors, but over 700 men had perished from the three ships.

In the evacuation a total of twenty-six vessels were sunk, including two hospital ships. One of the worst incidents occurred when the ferry *Hellas* was hit, killing virtually all of the civilians and wounded Greek soldiers below deck who were burnt to death. The Luftwaffe pilots seemed detached from the horror and savagery of their attacks. One pilot wrote of the destruction of the *Hellas,* that the passenger liner at anchor was a 'fascinating sight' and offered a 'unique target'. After the bombs had hit, the pilot recalled feeling 'relief after maximum tension, pride that a junior crew had been successful'.[19]

Captain Michael Forrester left Greece from Monemvasia in a sailing boat full of civilians and soldiers. As a Messerschmitt approached to strafe them, Forrester's quick thinking saved those on board. He moved all the soldiers below deck and asked the women to sit at the front of the boat and wave. The German aircraft swooped over the masthead, taking a close look, before turning back for a second run. The women continued to wave as hard as they could, as the plane approached for a second time. Seemingly satisfied, the pilot waved back and set off for other prey.

For many troops the evacuation voyage from Greece was more harrowing than the battle itself. Planes appeared overhead, flipped over on their side, and then dropped vertically, nose first, screaming towards their target. The deafening crackle of rifle fire added to the din as troops on the deck took pot shots at the offending aircraft. Each near miss would send a huge column of seawater spiralling into the air, the whole vessel reverberated with a metallic clang as the shock-wave hit the side, and seaweed and other debris littered the deck. Some of the crew, who were determined to make the most of their situation, put nets over the side to catch fish floating on the surface that had been killed by the blast.

By the end of 27 April over 17,300 men had been evacuated from Greece.

Those who had been cut off from the embarkation points made their way through the Greek capital where they were met with compassion and assistance. Greek civilians made the 'thumbs up' sign, which was widely believed to be the customary form of British greeting. Some New Zealand troops, who found themselves stranded at Megara, took a bus into Athens and then a taxi to Rafina. This was an unorthodox method of retreat, but was typical of the stories of stragglers who were desperate to reach the embarkation points. On his retreat through a town named Markopoulon, a New Zealander recalled that the town square was crowded with Greek civilians of all ages. 'They knew we were leaving them to darkness and oppression but there were no reproaches.' Instead 'they gave the men oranges and water, showered flowers on them and cried ... "Come back again New Zealand."'[20]

On 27 April German motorcyclists drove into Athens followed by armoured divisions and infantry. An announcement from Berlin stated that 'an advance German armoured column entered Athens at 09.25 ... The swastika flag flies over the Acropolis.'[21] By the morning of 28 April the German advance guard attacked at Navplion, where a handful of troops escaped in small boats. At Monemvasia the destroyers *Isis*, *Hotspur* and *Griffin* successfully evacuated 4,000 troops, mainly consisting of the 6th New Zealand Brigade. Admiral Baillie-Grohman decided to risk an hour past the normal hour of departure of 03.00 to accommodate as many men as possible. This proved a well judged gamble and all 4,000 men were evacuated without loss. At Kalamata a total of around 10,000 men remained awaiting evacuation, including 2,000 Yugoslav soldiers and Greek civilians. During the day the demoralised troops lay in the shelter of olive trees outside the town to avoid the attention of the Luftwaffe.

On 28 April German infantry, backed by armoured cars and self propelled guns, broke through a weakly held line of 4th Hussars at Kalamata and raced for the quayside. It was reported that seven destroyers, two cruisers and three merchant ships waited off the harbour to evacuate the men. Torches were used to signal to the ships that attempts were being made to secure the quay. New Zealand Sergeant J D Hinton led a counter-attack to clear the evacuation area. Under fire, Hinton charged a German gun position and destroyed it by hurling two grenades at close range. Then, with bayonets fixed, Hinton proceeded to lead a group of New Zealanders to attack further gun positions. Faced with a bayonet charge, German gunners abandoned their positions and fled into nearby houses. Hinton and his group smashed through windows and doors, eliminating their enemy at the point of the bayonet. Small groups of men throughout the Kalamata area followed Hinton's lead, and fought similar actions against their attackers. After some spirited fighting, Kalamata was secured with the capture of around 150 German prisoners. The time won by the counter-attack proved to be in vain; after giving the waiting ships offshore the all clear signal, a message came back stating that all ships must rejoin the main fleet immediately. The urgency of the fleet's premature departure was due to reported sightings of the Italian Fleet approaching. This order effectively condemned those at Kalamata to captivity; the tragedy was that the reported sighting of the Italian Fleet later turned out to be false. Only around 400 men were able to embark before the fleet sailed. When the troops were aboard they were greeted with cocoa, bully beef sandwiches and blankets. The gratitude of the retreating forces to the Navy was well deserved; Cunningham had committed nineteen destroyers and six cruisers to the operation.

Soon fighting broke out once more in the northern outskirts of Kalamata. Sergeant Hinton was again in the thick of the action and was subsequently wounded in the abdomen and captured. While in a German prisoner of war camp a few months later, Hinton learned that he had been awarded the Victoria Cross. Brigadier Parrington had assessed the situation with his senior officers and decided that the shortage of ammunition and food meant that Kalamata would not be held for long. Eventually, with the aid of a captured English-speaking German officer, Parrington informed the Germans that no further resistance would be offered after 05.30.

On the morning of 29 April British resistance in Greece officially came to an end. The Germans had taken around 7,000 prisoners at Kalamata. For weeks after the campaign in Greece, men continued to arrive on the islands of the eastern Aegean. It was estimated that around 1,400 were evacuated after the close of official operations in Greece. Because of the various methods used to escape from Greece, it is difficult to put a precise figure on the numbers who were evacuated. Revised official figures suggested approximately 50,732 evacuated out of 62,500 men deployed, and casualties at approximately 3,000 killed and missing. Many of the missing counted in the losses were still on the run in the hills of Greece. German losses amounted to 5,000 officers and men. The Germans had taken captive 344,000 Yugoslavs, 218,000 Greeks and 9,000 British and Commonwealth troops.

The loss of equipment during the evacuation was by no means on the scale of Dunkirk, but was sufficient to cause problems for Wavell. The losses in heavy equipment, artillery and transports were disastrous. Approximately 8,000 vehicles were left behind in Greece, along with 104 tanks, forty anti-aircraft guns, 192 field guns, 164 anti-tank guns, 209 aircraft and 1,812 machine guns. Unsurprisingly, the troops who returned from Greece were short of arms, ammunition and basic equipment. The navy insisted during the evacuation that no items of significant bulk or weight could be carried on board. Gunner Raggett recounted that men were allowed to carry 'only one haversack containing our most personal possessions'.[22]

The defeat in Greece had been coupled with a series of setbacks in the desert. On 24 March a small German contingent under Rommel launched an offensive and succeeded in capturing Benghazi and Egypt; only Tobruk remained under British control. The decision to concentrate on Greece and not to advance on Tripoli was widely perceived as a grave strategic error. Many believe that British and Commonwealth forces employed in Greece should have been used to augment forces in North Africa. The German General Warlimont revealed that he could not understand why the British did not take Tripoli. Major-General de Guingand has argued that Wavell should have advanced on Tripoli when the Italian forces were incapable of offensive action and the Germans had only just arrived. According to de Guingand, the Joint Planning Staff were 'convinced' that Tripoli could be captured before spring.[23] But one must take into account that Wavell's force contained a few battle-worthy divisions and only a limited force could be pushed forward quickly to occupy Tripoli and holding the position would have posed further problems. However, German victories in North Africa might have been significantly reduced if the men sent to Greece had been available in the desert.

Wavell described the Greek venture as a 'gamble with the dice loaded against us'.[24] The British were well aware of the dangers of intervention in Greece; they recognised that they could not compete with German airpower, and without effective resistance from Yugoslavia they would struggle to establish a solid line of defence. Co-operation between Anglo–Greek forces proved difficult and, in spite of the obvious goodwill shown by both sides, the language barrier proved a problem that was never overcome. The breakdown in communication was illustrated by the fact that three of the best Greek divisions remained isolated in the Metaxas forts, when they were expected to augment the Aliakmon Line. The Aliakmon Line was always open to attack from the Monastir Gap and had no depth in defence. The Greeks under General Wilson were ill-equipped and lacking in artillery; all that could be expected was a series of delaying actions. Even if resources were available to augment troops in Greece, without corresponding airpower their presence would have made no difference to the outcome. The series of rearguards actions that often matched artillery against German armour brought a considerable amount of success. Many of the losses inflicted on Commonwealth troops were a result of German airpower. In his speech on 30 April, Churchill gave his appraisal of the campaign; he stated that the conduct of the Common-wealth troops merited the 'highest praise' and he commended the troops' discipline under prolonged aerial bombardment. He went on to highlight that on more than one occasion the Germans were fought to a standstill by one-fifth of their number.

Wavell had been included in the ULTRA intelligence loop in 13 March and helped prevent a greater tragedy in Greece. Due to the tight security, sharing the information with the Greeks was prohibited. Although the signals were never received in time to lay traps for the enemy, historian Anthony Beevor stated that ULTRA decrypts of German radio signals 'certainly helped British and Dominion forces from disaster'.[25] ULTRA signals intelligence offered Britain a unique opportunity to fulfil the guarantee to Greece with minimal losses.

British intervention in Greece was largely, if not wholly, motivated by the political implications of not doing so. In a broadcast to the nation on 27 April, Churchill stated: 'the action of the United States will be dictated not by methodical calculations of profit and loss but by moral sentiment'.[26] In contrast Metaxas once stated: 'Few realise how easy and how dangerous it is to mix sentiment with strategy.'[27] It is difficult to assess the political impact of British intervention in Greece. Limitations in land fighting and another evacuation could not have been calculated to impress neutrals. However, President Roosevelt stated to Churchill: 'You have done not only heroic but very useful work in Greece . . . you have fought a wholly justified delaying action.'[28] Roosevelt described the campaign in Greece as the 'heroic struggle of the Hellenic people to defend their liberties and their homes against the aggression of Germany'. After thwarting the Italian invasion, Roosevelt noted the Greeks had 'stirred the hearts and aroused sympathy [among] the whole American people'.[29]

Military historian Liddell-Hart described the guarantee to Greece as 'Chamberlain's folly', although he believed Churchill's judgement was 'hot-headed and impulsive' instead of the 'cool-headed judgement that was once characteristic of British statesmanship.'[30] Churchill was under few illusions when he stated to the Australian Prime Minister, Robert Menzies: 'the real foundation for the expedition . . . was the estimate of the overwhelming moral and political repercussions of abandoning Greece.'[31] The New Zealand Prime Minister, Peter Fraser, agreed: 'we took the only course open to us, and any decision to the contrary would have involved dishonour.'[32] Three days into the German invasion of Greece, Churchill stressed that in North Africa 'military considerations alone must guide our generals'.[33] It is difficult to ascertain whether Churchill's statement was hypocrisy or an early acknowledgement of a lapse in judgement.

If Metaxas had survived his illness, British intervention in Greece might never have happened. Metaxas was a strong character and was under no illusion about the political motives of Britain and her limited resources. Metaxas was an unlikely collaborator with the British government. Historian André Gerolymatos wrote: 'as late as April 1940 he was still suspicious of British intrigues against him.'[34] In 1938 an Anglo–Greek alliance was rejected by the British, after which Metaxas confided in his diary that 'the refusal left him free to pursue his own policy, essentially one of neutrality'.[35] The preparation of the British campaign must be viewed against a background in which Greece, Turkey and Yugoslavia feared a German invasion, and could not bring themselves to compromise their neutrality, or risk provocation by openly aiding the British.

It is of interest to look at German foreign policy regarding the Balkans during this period. On 7 January Ribbentrop informed the heads of the German military mission in Moscow: 'The measures being carried out by us are aimed exclusively against the British forces gaining a foothold in Greece' but not 'against any Balkan country, including Turkey.'[36] The argument could be made that in trying to achieve a largely political objective in Greece, Britain induced German aggression towards the Balkans. Martin van Creveld has written that Germany's decision to invade Greece was: 'the result of offensive, not defensive, considerations.'[37] Papagos believed that Germany used the presence of British troops in Greece as 'extenuating circumstances for their aggression against a small nation'. Papagos wrote: 'irrespective of the presence or absence of British troops in the Balkans, German intervention would have taken place.' He concluded: 'the Germans had to secure the right flank of the German army which was to operate against Russia.'[38]

Mussolini attempted to recover some pride with an audacious attempt at claiming victory over the Greeks. In a broadcast to the British people, Churchill went some way to redress the balance. Commenting on the Italian dictator's public congratulation of his armed forces' 'victory', Churchill stated that it was: 'surely the world record in the domain of the ridiculous and the contemptible'. He said: 'This whipped Jackal Mussolini, to save his skin has made of Italy a vassal state of Hitler's empire.' The Prime Minister likened Mussolini to a jackal begging from the 'German tiger with yelps not only of appetite . . . but even of triumph'. Churchill concluded his damning tirade by stating that people in the British Empire and the United States should 'find a new object in life in making sure this absurd impostor will be abandoned to public justice and universal scorn'.[39] It seemed that Mussolini had taken on yet another battle that he could not hope to win, by entering a propaganda duel with Churchill who specialised in verbally destroying people.

On April 27 Churchill stated in a speech: 'There is only one thing certain about war, that it is full of disappointments and also of mistakes.' Describing Greece as a 'disappointment' or 'mistake' is slightly mis-leading as it would imply that an oversight, or a miscalculation was made. In Lieutenant Colonel Rich's report on Greece, he stated that prior knowledge of the campaign was such that 'it was accepted in London and the Middle East that the force would have to be evacuated again'.[40] After the battle, Churchill sent Wavell a message stating: 'we have paid our debt of honour with far less loss than I feared.'[41] Unfortunately the debt was paid by the blood of British and Commonwealth troops. General Freyberg had claimed: 'the effect of the Greek campaign turned the ANZAC Corps into a disarmed and totally disorganised force.'[42] Freyberg also stated that the 'rearguard battle and withdrawal had been a great feat of arms. The fighting qualities of the troops were beyond praise.'[43]

Churchill concluded that it 'remained to be seen' whether the Germans had made a mistake in 'trampling down Balkan states in making a river of blood and hate between themselves and the Greek and Yugoslav peoples.'[44] In the following years, Churchill actively encouraged an insurgence against the Germans in Greece to drain their resources. In an attempt to pacify resistance in Greece Hitler paid tribute to the Greeks stating: 'Towards the Greek people we feel a sense of genuine compassion.' He went on. 'Greece fought so bravely that the esteem of her enemies cannot be denied her.'[45]

The Greek population suffered grievously during the joint occupation by Germany and Italy between 1941 and 1943. The harsh regime of the Axis and the general dislocation of labour had resulted in a shortfall in the harvest. Axis forces' attempts to seize grain for their soldiers led to a revolt by farmers who refused to produce the true extent of their harvest. Inevitably a famine ensued which claimed the lives of thousands of Greeks; dead bodies filled the streets of every Greek city and town.

These conditions were ripe for the emergence of an organised resistance against the Axis occupation. Initially, groups manifested themselves by helping stranded British soldiers, who helped to develop them into organised units. A number of resistance groups had emerged in Greece by the autumn of 1941. The most prominent was derived from the Greek Communist Party, the EAM and its military wing, the National People's Liberation Army (ELAS). The emergence of the Communists was facilitated by the apathy of the Greek bourgeois towards the Axis occupation. The ELAS's strong connections with the Communist Party meant that the British were reluctant to afford too much support to them, as Churchill was concerned about facilitating the rise of Communism in Greece and thus aiding Soviet control of the eastern Mediterranean. Although the ELAS was the most effective fighting group, it was the anti-Communist EDES who were the principal recipients of British material and financial aid. Despite the rivalry between resistance groups (that would culminate in a Greek civil war) it did not diminish the impact on the occupying Axis forces. Hitler stated his concerns in a speech at the Rastenburg conference in December 1942. Hitler emphasised the need to pacify the Balkans or 'all the heroic courage of the Axis troops in Crete and the Peloponnese would have been in vain'.[46]

Italy was theoretically the predominant occupying power, but it was the Nazis who left their foul stamp of notoriety on the country in one of the most controversial episodes of the Second World War. During 1943 Marshal Badgolio displaced Mussolini as the Italian leader and promptly surrendered to the Allies. Hitler's troops quickly went about disarming their former allies and sending them to prisoner of war camps in northern Yugoslavia. The mass disarming of Italian troops was only resisted on some of the Greek islands, and only in Cephalonia did the resistance exceed forty-eight hours. The 9,000 Italian troops of General Gandin's Acqui Division could have defeated the 3,000 German soldiers stationed on the island. But there were conflicting orders from General Badgolio to resist, and from Gandin who wanted to surrender. The deliberation between Gandin and his officers went on for two days and the delay proved fatal. During that time two battalions of the 1st Mountain Division reinforced the Germans on the island. As some of the German landing craft were approaching Cephalonia, an Italian artillery captain gave the order to open fire on the Germans. The Greek partisans EAM–ELAS aided the Italians in their resistance for nine days. German airpower once again proved victorious and destroyed what little Italian artillery was remaining, and the Italian resistance ended on 24 September 1943.

Unable to imprison such a large number of troops on the island, the Germans proceeded to massacre their former allies in cold blood. The majority of the troops were herded into clearings in the hills above Argostoli, and cut down with machine-gun fire. The killings were alleged to have taken place over twenty-three sites across the island; the Germans were particularly calculating in their methods in order to eliminate survivors. The executioners would announce a promise of mercy to anyone who had survived the initial shooting; when they stood up they would be shot. A garrison of 1,500 Italian troops to the north of the island were dispatched in a more clinical way. After being marched to the west coast at Assos, they were forced to jump off precipitous cliffs at gunpoint where they plunged 1,000 feet to their death. In total, 371 Italian officers and around 4,750 soldiers perished in the slaughter. The bodies were heaped into large piles and burned; the fires could be seen for miles across the island. The remains were buried in mass graves or scattered out to sea. The surviving Italians troops were taken to Argostoli harbour where they were embarked on ships bound for mainland Greece. According to German records, two of the vessels hit a minefield and capsized, with the loss of nearly 3,000 Italian prisoners; many Greek and Italian veterans still believe that the ships were deliberately scuttled. The much-criticised novel by Louis de Bernières, *Captain Corelli's Mandolin*, has immortalised the events on Cephalonia, if somewhat loosely based on reality. After the closure of the inquiry into the incident in 1960 due to limited evidence, the Italians had been reluctant to talk of the massacre. Now files have been reopened and de Bernières' work has re-awakened the forum for debate. The incident has become a defining moment for the Italian people to come to terms with a difficult period in their history. It was a particularly heinous end for the Italian troops who had begun the campaign believing

101

that they had embarked on an innocuous march through Greece to victory.

NOTES

1   Beevor, Antony, *Crete – The Battle and the Resistance*, London: John Murray, 1991, p. 37.
2   Somerville, Christopher, *Our War – How the British Commonwealth Fought the Second World War*, London: Weidenfeld & Nicolson, 1998, p. 76.
3   Beevor, op. cit., p. 37.
4   MacDonald, Callum, *The Lost Battle – Crete 1941*, London: Macmillan, 1993, p. 109.
5   Stewart, I, *The Struggle for Crete*, London: Routledge, 1982, p. 17.
6   Beevor, op. cit., p. 39.
7   Buckley, Christopher, *Greece and Crete 1941*, London: HMSO, 1952, p. 54.
8   Hammerton, John, *The Second Great War*, Vol. IV, London: Waverly, 1950, p. 1626.
9   Ibid.
10   Beevor, op. cit., p. 35.
11   Ibid, p. 43.
12   Sir John White, interviewed by Jock Phillips, 25 January 2001, Tape One, Side A, Alexander Turnbull Library, National Library of New Zealand.
13   Dahl, Roald, *Going Solo*, London: Puffin, 1988, pp. 124–5.
14   Ibid, p. 151.
15   Ibid.
16   Buckley, op. cit., p. 123.
17   Hutching, Megan (ed.), *A Unique Sort of Battle. New Zealanders Remember Crete*, Auckland: HarperCollins, 2001, p. 51.
18   Beevor, op. cit., p. 48.
19   Ibid, p. 52.
20   MacDonald, op. cit., p. 111.
21   Hammerton, op. cit., p. 1626.
22   MacDonald, op. cit., p. 110.
23   Liddell-Hart, Basil, *History of the Second World War*, London: Cassell, 1970, p. 118.
24   Buckley, op. cit., p. 140.
25   Beevor, op. cit., p. 36.
26   Churchill, Winston, *The Second World War*, Vol. III, London: Cassell, 1950, p. 200.
27   Beevor, op. cit., p. 55.
28   Churchill, op. cit., pp. 207–8.
29   Roosevelt, Franklin, American Department of State Bulletin, 27 April 1941.
30   Liddell-Hart, op. cit., p. 15.
31   Stewart, op. cit., p. 14.
32   Fraser, Peter, CAB 44/120, *The Campaign in Greece*.
33   Churchill to the House of Commons, *New York Times*, 10 April 1941.
34   Gerolymatos, André, *Guerilla Warfare and Espionage in Greece 1940–1944*, New York: Pella, 1992, p. 45.
35   Ibid, p. 46.
36   Van Creveld, M, *Hitler's Strategy 1940–41 The Balkan Clue*, London: CUP, 1973, p. 14.

37   Ibid, p. 19.
38   Papagos, Alexander, *The Battle for Greece 1940–1941*, Athens: Alpha Editions, 1949, p. 317.
39   Churchill, op. cit., p. 200.
40   Rich, E E, CAB 44/120, Chapters P and Q, The Campaign in Greece, November 1940.
41   Beevor, op. cit., p. 54.
42   Freyberg, Bernard, CAB 106/701.
43   Ibid.
44   Churchill, op. cit., p. 200.
45   Cervi, Mario, *The Hollow Legions: Mussolini's Blunder in Greece 1940–1941*, London: Chatto & Windus, 1972, p. 303.
46   Howard, M, *History of the Second World War: Grand Strategy*, Vol. IV, August 1942–September 1943, London: HMSO, 1972, p. 338.

PART TWO

The Battle for Crete

In the dark blue sea there lies an island called Crete, a rich and lovely land, washed by the waves.

Homer, *The Odyssey* 19, 172–4

CHAPTER VII

Crete, Freyberg and ULTRA

Following the defeat of the Greek army, General Kurt Student had flown to visit Hitler to discuss the possibility of the capture of Crete. Less than twenty-four hours after the Allied withdrawal from Greece, Hitler sanctioned preparations for the invasion of Crete by airborne forces, backed by a small seaborne expedition.

Student was the head of both parachute and air-landed troops. German airborne forces were almost the unique creation of Student and were largely sustained by his continuing determination and drive. Student was a keen aviator and spent the First World War commanding a fighter squadron. In 1938, when Hitler was preparing for his invasion of Czechoslovakia, Student was given command of the first German parachute division. His intention was that parachutists would act as 'shock' troops, depending on surprise and confusion caused by a sudden attack from the sky. Historian Correlli Barnett has written that the use of airborne forces was an 'innovation which more than any other (except for the nuclear attack on Japan) sets the Second World War apart from other wars'.[1] Student was first given the opportunity to put his pioneering ideas into practice with the German invasion of the Low Countries.

The newly formed airborne troops were used in an attempt to capture the Belgian fortress of Eben-Emael, north of Liège. The fortress was heavily fortified with concrete emplacements burrowed into a cliff a hundred feet above the Albert Canal, which meant that artillery and aerial bombardment would prove useless. Therefore the airborne troops were used to infiltrate the fort's defences. The paratroops were dropped on four objectives: three bridges around the Albert Canal and Eben-Emael itself. Once landed on the fort, German troops raced towards the bunkers. They used explosive charges to breach the enemy's walls, and then followed up with automatic weapons and grenades through the embrasures to destroy the enemy. Despite being ultimately successful, the initial airborne assaults illustrated that heavy losses could be inflicted if paratroops were met with a determined defence during their descent. After the war, General Student described the assault on Eben-Emael as a 'deed of exemplary daring and decisive significance'.[2] The raid at Eben-Emael was an impressive feat, but there was a cautionary footnote to the victory. The Hague and Rotterdam fell with many losses to German paratroops and equipment. These cities were eventually taken by the land troops advancing behind Student's initial airborne attack.

As a result of the successful landings in Eben-Emael and Rotterdam, the head of the Luftwaffe, Hermann Goering, held Student in high regard. Goering shared Hitler's enthusiasm for using paratroopers, but was less concerned with spilling their blood. Goering repeatedly requested Hitler's approval for airborne operations against Crete. Student used his exclusive relationship with Goering to meet with Hitler and discuss the possibility of an airborne assault on Crete. During the operation in Rotterdam, Student was severely wounded by a stray bullet that struck him in the side of the head. After recovering in a Berlin hospital, Student was decorated by Hitler and promoted to General, taking command of the inaugural XI Fliegerkorps. Despite giving off an aura of a mediocre business executive, Student's inclination towards the unorthodox appealed to Hitler. This revolutionary form of warfare fascinated the Führer, who was enthused by the imagery of elite paratroopers descending on their enemies with guns blazing. Hitler told Rauschning: 'That is how the wars of the future will be fought, the sky black with bombers', from which 'leaping into the smoke the parachuting storm-troopers, each one grasping a sub machine-gun'.[3] Hitler constantly referred to the elite division of parachute troops but he could not bear to risk them in large-scale military operations. Churchill wrote that the German air corps 'represented the flame of the Hitler Youth Movement. And was an ardent embodiment of the Teutonic spirit of revenge for the defeat of 1918.'[4] Indeed, the Luftwaffe and the German airborne forces had become the embodiment of revulsion against the Versailles treaty.

Although Student had the backing of Goering, many high ranking officers in the army and the air force did not share his enthusiasm; most believed Student to be a dreamer whose career had been furthered only by his relationship with Hitler. Many traditionalists resented Student and believed he had plundered established army reserves. The prospect of occupying a whole island was a much greater undertaking than that faced at Eben-Emael. A successful airborne invasion of Crete would prove one of the great military feats of the war, but the operation was fraught with danger. Student's airborne troops would rely on the outdated and slow moving Ju 52 transport; limitations in the design of the German parachute meant that there were no shroud lines to pull for directional control, and to maintain accuracy over the drop point, jumps had to be made below 400 feet, therefore the aircraft were highly susceptible to fire from the ground. Student also advocated deploying his airborne troops from gliders. After release from its tug a glider's approach would be silent; when landed, it could unleash an initial assault group against specific targets ahead of the main body of troops. Paratroops would be landed on Crete largely unarmed; they would collect the majority of their weapons from containers dropped separately.

Hitler was less easily persuaded than his generals and foresaw heavy casualties and loss of equipment. As historian Antony Beevor has pointed out, Hitler's 'military and psychological intuition was often very accurate'[5] when not obsessed with an enterprise. Student envisaged the capture of Crete as part of a series of operations across the Mediterranean that would culminate in the capture of the Suez Canal. Student's plan of attack concurred with General Jodl's peripheral strategy of attacking Britain's interests in the Mediterranean. Hitler was sceptical of using Crete as a stepping-stone for the conquest across the Mediterranean, and envisaged the capture of the island only in terms of how it fitted with BARBAROSSA, which dominated the Führer's thoughts.

Historian Callum Macdonald has presented a strong case stating that Hitler hoped to use Crete as a diversion to distract attention away from his build-up of troops in the east. By alleviating rumours of an invasion of Russia, Hitler could lull Stalin into a false sense of security and delay an Anglo–Soviet alliance before he was ready to strike. Deception played an important role in Hitler's political method. He boasted to Halder in 1938: 'You will never learn what I am thinking,' concluding that: 'those who boast most loudly that they know my thoughts, to such people I lie even more.'[6] Orders issued on 15 February 1941 outlined the importance of keeping Moscow misinformed. The impression would be given that the build-up of forces in the east for BARBAROSSA was part of the most elaborate deception in 'the history of war … A cover up for the final preparations for the invasion of England.'[7] Crete fitted into this grand deception by being presented as a practice run for the invasion of Britain. On 29 March Goebbels remarked 'the big project' (the invasion of Russia) was being carefully camouflaged. 'We shall divert suspicion to all sorts of places, anywhere but the East.'[8]

With deception in mind, Hitler agreed to the operation in Crete but he warned Student: 'In the interests of other operations the attack should take place as quickly as possible. Every day earlier is a profit, every day later is a loss.'[9] On 25 April 1941 Hitler issued Directive Number 28 for the capture of Crete, codenamed Operation MERCURY. There was one proviso: 'transport movements must not lead to any delay in the strategic concentration for BARBAROSSA.'[10] Such was Hitler's obsession with preparations for BARBAROSSA that he handed Greece (excluding Salonika) over to the Italians.

Martin van Creveld described Operation MERCURY as 'Far from being part of any coherent strategy'. He attributed Hitler's support for the operation as a 'sop to Goering, whose air force was destined to play a subordinate role in the coming Russian campaign'.[11] Antony Beevor believes that van Creveld overemphasised Hitler's apathy for Crete. Beevor states that Hitler was indeed uninterested in Crete as the first of a series of stepping-stones across the Mediterranean, but points out that Hitler did recognise the strategic importance of Crete as a 'useful offshore rampart'[12] from which to conduct an air war against England, in the Eastern Mediterranean, and protection for the Romanian oilfields.

The invasion of Crete was to be undertaken primarily by Student's airborne forces. German airborne forces were not required for the early stages of BARBAROSSA, therefore they could be employed against the British in the Mediterranean. The airborne troops were to be augmented by a seaborne convoy of primitive craft that was expected to transport some heavier weapons. Student assumed that he would have full control over the operation under the command of Goering, but in fact he was to share the responsibility with General Richthofen under General Löhr's 4th Air Fleet. Löhr and other senior German military personnel were concerned that the operation in Crete might delay Operation BARBAROSSA. They were convinced that the British would defend such a strategically important island to the last man.

The German forces were divided into three main groups: the Centre group was known as 'MARS,' with 'KOMET' in the west and 'ORION' in the east. Group Centre under Major-General Süsmann consisted of the bulk of 7th Air Division. Western group was made up of the glider-borne assault regiment commanded by Major-General Meindl. General Bräuer had one parachute regiment and a mountain regiment at his disposal to lead Group East. The task of MARS was to land south of Canea and neutralise the defenders around Galatas and Suda. A sub-section was to be landed at Retimo who were to capture the airfield and town before pushing through to join up with the main body in Suda. A further sub-section under Colonel Heidrich would attempt to clear the area south-east of Canea before advancing on Suda. KOMET had the task of capturing the vital aerodrome at Maleme, before linking up with MARS on the Canea road. Group ORION's objective was to capture the airfield and town of Heraklion. Student hoped that by the end of the first day of the invasion, all three airfields would be captured, including the towns of Retimo, Heraklion and Canea. After the capture of the airfields, transport planes would fly in troops from the 5th Mountain Division. Then the invasion force would be in a position to attack Suda on the morning of the second day, whereupon heavy weapons could be landed from the sea by two convoys of ships that would make their way to Maleme and Heraklion.

Poor intelligence of the island's defences led German military planners to believe that Crete could be captured in three days. Bogus German intelligence stated that the island's garrison consisted of a mere 5,000 men. They believed Retimo was totally undefended and a mere 400 men were based at Heraklion. General Löhr, who directed operations from his

Athens headquarters, believed that the two divisions of elite troops should be able to successfully execute Operation MERCURY. The widespread belief was that the Cretan population would be sympathetic towards the invaders, or at least remain neutral, in exchange for favourable terms in the event of occupation. The assumption that Cretans would be apathetic towards their invaders was taken from the fact that most of the inhabitants of Crete were Venizelists and profoundly opposed to the Metaxas regime. But like the Italians before them, German military planners overlooked the fact, that above all other considerations, Cretans and Greeks were patriots.

Student's reconnaissance pilots reported that: 'Crete lay there as if dead.'[13] He commented after the battle: 'our information about enemy was scanty ... our pilots reported that the island appeared lifeless.'[14] It was against this background that Student formed his plan of attack for Crete that involved a perilously widespread distribution of troops over seven landing zones: Kastelli, Maleme, Canea, Georgeoupolis, Retimo, Heraklion and Askifou, all objectives for the first day. Student rejected outside advice to concentrate his forces on one objective; he had fought for the acceptance of his plan from its conception. Captain Heydte noted that the 'plan had become part of him, a part of his life'.[15]

By 14 May five hundred Ju 52 transports, slow tri-motor aircraft, were ready to attack Crete. German paratroopers travelled from their training grounds in north Germany to the Bulgarian border and down to the Aegean coast. Captain Freiherr von der Heydte commented that he felt 'rather on holiday than on a journey into battle'. When the paratroops arrived in Greece they began to see signs of war, including 'knocked-out tanks, gutted vehicles and freshly dug graves of soldiers'.[16] In Greece the Germans employed the use of forced labour from the local population who were ruthlessly conscripted. By mid-May the Germans had constructed operational airfields in the most advanced islands from the mainland. Some 2,500,000 gallons of aircraft fuel had to be transported by sea due to the damage caused to roads by the British evacuation; this meant that the German attack on Crete was delayed to 20 May.

After the Italian invasion of Greece, the Joint Planning Staff in Britain proclaimed that the preferred action would be to strengthen Crete and assist Greece by air and naval action. Wavell had himself stated to the Chief of Staff Committee: 'the policy of holding Crete in all circumstances should be maintained even if Greece gave way to pressures threatening her.'[17] Churchill stated: 'One salient strategic fact leaped out upon us – CRETE! The Italian must not have it. We must get it first – and at once.'[18] Churchill sent a telegram to Eden stating the importance of retaining control of 'the best airfield possible and a naval fuelling base at Suda Bay'.[19] Eden replied in full agreement stressing the need to prevent the Italians seizing the island.

Churchill wrote to Eden on 3 November 1940, stating: 'establishment of [a] fuelling base and airfield in Crete to be steadily developed into permanent fortresses [is] indispensable.'[20] On 1 December 1940 Churchill wrote to Ismay: 'Exactly what have we got done at Suda Bay.' Churchill's main concerns were: 'Anti-aircraft guns, coast defence guns, lights, wirelesses, R.A.F., nets, mines [and] preparation of aerodromes.' Churchill also advocated putting the local population to work: 'I hope to be assured that many hundreds of Cretans are working at strengthening defences, lengthening and improving the aerodromes.'[21] These questions from the Prime Minister got little response. The local population were not put to work and a reserve Cretan Division was not formed. The Greeks were holding the Italians in Albania and Wavell's offensive in the desert was looming; every gun sent to Crete was one less for Greece or North Africa. After visiting the island, Wavell concluded that the small garrison there was sufficient. It consisted of two British battalions, eight heavy and twelve light anti-aircraft guns with coastal artillery. The Greeks had only 1,000 men with a mere 659 rifles to arm them. Historian Ian Stewart (the Welch Regiment's medical officer in Crete) described Crete during the winter of 1940 as 'an obscure island in the Mediterranean where the local citizens dozed in their wicker chairs while taking the afternoon sun'.[22]

Although the Chiefs of Staff recognised the strategic importance of Crete, little had been done to enhance the defences of the island. Crete was far from the fortress that Churchill so desired. Churchill stated: 'to lose Crete because we had not sufficient bulk of forces there would be a crime.'[23] Yet it was Churchill's desire to prolong the Greek effort on the mainland that was partly hampering preparations for Crete. The heavy equipment and aircraft lost in Greece were literally irreplaceable. Anti-aircraft guns and RAF squadrons had been deployed to augment the Greeks on the mainland, thus depleting the reserves in the Middle East and leaving meagre resources for Crete. Wavell's apparent neglect of Crete was induced by Churchill's forward policy in Greece. Wavell had many demands placed on him during this period, not least the advance of Rommel in North Africa. The threat to Crete was not immediate; therefore serious preparations were not undertaken. Wavell did not believe Crete was in imminent danger as he was confident that the Royal Navy would prevent a seaborne invasion. Wavell wrote on 24 April 1941: 'It seems unlikely that the enemy will attempt a landing in force in Crete from the sea.' He concluded: 'Scale of air attack on Crete will, however, undoubtedly be heavy.'[24]

The common view is that the burden of Wavell's commitments at this point distorted his judgement. Rommel, whose forces were poised to advance on Alexandria, threatened Britain's territories. In Iraq there was a pro-German uprising, and in Syria the forces of Vichy France were actively co-operating with the Germans. All these events occurred in conjunction with the confused evacuation from Greece. Referring to the impending crisis in Iraq, Wavell complained to Churchill: 'my forces are stretched everywhere, and I cannot afford to risk part of them on what cannot produce any effect.'[25] With all the pressures facing Wavell, it was understandable that Wavell did not fully appreciate the opportunities arising from Crete.

On 18 April Churchill sent Wavell a list of directives concerning Crete: 'Libya counts first, evacuation of troops from Greece second . . . Iraq can be ignored and Crete worked up later.'[26] In issuing these directives it is clear that Churchill hoped that much of the necessary preparations for Crete had taken place in the preceding six months. Wavell had certainly ignored the island, despite repeated assertions by Churchill of the importance of Crete. Among the measures that needed to be implemented were landing facilities in southern fishing ports and the construction of roads leading to the north of the island. Churchill believed Crete could have been supplied from Egypt via the southern ports of Sfakia and Timbaki. However, this simple solution was flawed. Building roads over rough mountainous terrain would constitute a major engineering project; even then the winding roads would be dangerously exposed to the Luftwaffe. Churchill was guilty of a lack of realism of what could be achieved. However, his mood was lightened by intelligence sources that offered a rare opportunity for victory in Crete.

On 19 May a final conference between the German officers commanding the forces in Crete took place. As this meeting was in progress, ULTRA decrypts were being sent from London with details of the operation. Operation MERCURY was compromised almost from its conception. Due to the limited communications in the Balkans, messages were often relayed by radio, which were penetrated by code-breakers at Bletchley Park. Therefore, the British military had a comprehensive knowledge of the German invasion. It was this prior knowledge that convinced Churchill that Crete could be held and the elusive victory could be achieved against Germany. Crete, which was previously regarded as a 'receptacle of whatever can get there from Greece'[27], now became a priority in view of ULTRA intelligence.

By early May code-breakers confirmed that Crete was indeed a German target, with the growing German airborne forces in the Balkans. On 6 May the prospective date for the German invasion was revealed and the date of the attack was believed to be 17 May. British codenames were created to increase security surrounding the information; Crete was referred to as COLORADO and the attack itself as SCORCHER. The unique possibility of isolating German forces on the island was created by ULTRA. The prospect of slaughtering elite German troops fuelled Churchill's imagination and instigated his personal interest in the defence of the island. Once Hitler committed the bulk of his troops they would effectively be trapped. On 28 April Churchill sent Wavell a message stating that he was expecting a heavy airborne attack on Crete; he commented famously: 'It ought to be a fine opportunity for killing parachute troops. The island must be stubbornly defended.'[28] It was ULTRA signals intelligence that convinced Winston Churchill that the attack would offer the chance of inflicting a humiliating bloody nose on the Germans. Churchill never revealed the secret of ULTRA, but after the war he acknowledged that at no moment of the war had 'our intelligence [been] so truly and precisely informed'.[29] Churchill stated that he would particularly welcome the chance for British troops to engage the enemy without 'his usual mechanical advantages'.[30] Lightly armed infantry were highly vulnerable to assault from tanks; British I (infantry) tanks could even resist a blow from a German anti-tank gun.

Churchill was eager to land tanks on Crete. The British Prime Minister was the driving force behind Operation TIGER that involved a dangerous diversion of a convoy to Crete from a voyage bound for Alexandria in North Africa. When the convoy reached the relative safety within range of the RAF for the loss of only one ship, Churchill suggested to the Chiefs of Staff that the Clan Lamont head for Suda Bay to discharge twelve I tanks. The Chiefs of Staff deemed it 'inadvisable to endanger the rest of the ship's valuable cargo by such a diversion'.[31] Churchill insisted that the Clan Lamont, or another vessel, should deliver the twelve tanks to Crete after they had unloaded their cargo. Despite Churchill's best efforts, the I tanks were not delivered. Churchill stated to Wavell that he was increasingly impressed by the 'weight of attack impending upon COLORADO . . . Trust all possible reinforcements have been sent.'[32] Wavell stated that he had arranged for six infantry tanks and fifteen light tanks to be sent to the island, but these vehicles were old and battered, without proper cooling systems for the guns or sufficient wireless equipment. Ironically, the few I tanks that would have made such a difference in Crete were squandered in Operation BATTLEAXE, which turned out to be an ineffective offensive in the Western Desert.

From the initial stages of the campaign in Greece, Britain envisaged a German attack on Crete in terms of a heavy airborne assault. The advance party to Crete reported that the inhabitants of the island were pro-British and Suda Bay was suitable for landing heavy equipment. The island of Crete is 160 miles long and averages around thirty miles in width. It is bisected by a large mountain range that slopes precipitously on the southern slope. There were no railways on the island and civilian telephone facilities were underdeveloped. The main airfields were poorly situated from a British point of view. Airfields at Heraklion, Maleme and Retimo were all positioned on the north coast of the island facing Greece. 'The concentration of targets along the north coast was a German bomb-aimer's dream.'[33] The moat surrounding Crete provided a natural defence

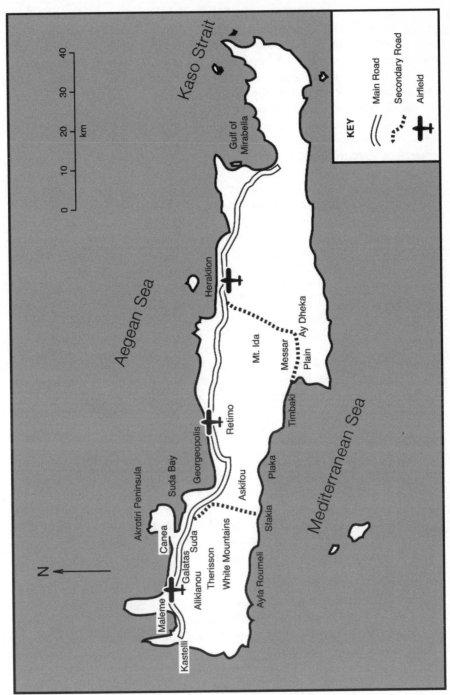

CRETE

that did not exist on the mainland. The situation in Crete dictated that tactical withdrawals were not an option. Churchill saw the conflict with his usual clarity and expected Commonwealth troops to fight with tenacity to overcome their opponents, a view that was not unfounded. Such a large body of troops on the island, if intelligently directed, could realistically inflict defeat on the Wehrmacht.

As Wavell devised no definitive plan, there was no common policy or guidance for local commanders to follow. Only vague consideration was given to Crete and this was not helped by a succession of local commanders. Five different commanders were appointed within a six-month period. The first of the commanders was Brigadier O H Tidbury who was tasked to defend Suda Bay. Tidbury identified the main German threat as coming from an airborne assault. He employed a programme of improving defences around the Suda Bay area, but digging tools and engineering equipment were in short supply. Tidbury was removed from the island in January 1941. The main instructions to the officers who succeeded him was to create an administrative base from which to defend Suda Bay.

In early April 1941 Major-General E C Weston took control of the island. Weston had originally commanded a group of Royal Naval and Royal Marine forces that made up the Mobile Naval Base Defence Organisation, which was designed to provide anti-aircraft support and protection for temporary harbours. Weston took the first military survey of Crete; the report was produced on 15 April, a week before the British evacuation of the Greek mainland. His report stated that the main threat was from an airborne invasion with the possibility of a seaborne landing, and an estimated enemy force of 3,000 men. The Joint Planning Staff backed Weston's appreciation and advocated that three brigade groups be brought to the island with adequate anti-aircraft and fighter support.

Despite the poor prospect of air support, airfields in Heraklion, Maleme and Retimo were worked upon to improve their facilities. The mining or destruction of Cretan aerodromes seemed a more prudent action, as there was no prospect of reinforcements by the RAF and it was imperative to deny the German invasion force use of the airfields. Air support for the defence of the island was almost non-existent. The fighter protection for Suda Bay consisted of a depleted squadron made up of ageing Gladiators and Fulmars. の the RN

The RAF had fought a hopeless battle against the Luftwaffe. By 18 May there were just five fighters remaining in Crete. Sergeant Reynish and Squadron Leader Howell described an air battle involving two Hurricanes against a horde of Messerschmitts: 'it was impossible to keep track of them. Everything was yellow tracer and crackling cannon, thumping bofors and rifle shots.'[34] Squadron Leader Edward Howell landed his Hurricane safely three and a half hours later. Sergeant Reynish was later rescued from the sea; they had shot down six of the enemy between them.

Ian Stewart noted that the brave men of the RAF died in meaningless battles with the Luftwaffe. 'Their sacrifice was no more than a gesture, their resistance a token resistance. Only their deaths were real.'[35] On the departure of the last aircraft from Crete, the remaining RAF crew fought as infantry. At Maleme 339 RAF servicemen were not enthusiastic about the prospect of fighting as ground troops; many refused New Zealand offers to instruct them in the cruder form of warfare.

On 27 April General Wilson arrived in Crete from mainland Greece and immediately made an appreciation of what was required for the defence of the island. In his report, Wilson described the defence of Crete as a 'dangerous commitment' stating that the island could not be held unless 'all three services are prepared to face the strain of maintaining adequate forces up to strength'.[36] Wilson was aware of the weakness of the RAF; therefore it was 'tantamount to saying that he did not think the island could be successfully defended'.[37] When Wavell met Wilson in Maleme, he explained that he wished him to 'go to Jerusalem and relieve Baghdad'.[38] Wilson replied that he was confused by the decision as he had no idea of what was happening outside Greece. Wilson's initial pessimistic view might have influenced the decision to relieve him of his duties in the Greek campaign.

In contrast to his ambiguous attitude towards the defence of Greece, Churchill's view on Crete was patently clear; he believed that the island must be held. Apart from the prospect of 'killing parachute troops', Churchill was lured by the chance to defeat the Nazi threat to Egypt and the Suez Canal. Churchill perceived Crete, Malta and Tobruk as vital positions for the flanks of the Axis offensive against Suez. On 28 April Churchill stressed that the loss of Egypt 'would be a disaster of the first magnitude to Great Britain'.[39] Churchill maintained that no surrender on Crete would be acceptable unless 'fifty percent casualties are sustained by the force in question', adding that 'Generals and Staff Officers . . . are to use their pistols in self-defence'. Churchill continued his brutal rhetoric stating that anyone who died taking 'a Hun or even an Italian' with them would have 'rendered good service'.[40] This was the spirit in which Churchill wanted the battle for Crete to be waged; further tactical withdrawals would simply not be tolerated. With this belligerent attitude in mind, Churchill secured the services of General Freyberg who had previously commanded New Zealand forces in Greece.

Freyberg was the embodiment of the 'man of action' that Churchill had desired in his generals. Churchill and Freyberg first met at the Admiralty in 1914 where Churchill secured Freyberg a commission in the Royal Naval Division. Freyberg had a reputation for reckless bravery in the First World War, in which he survived nine wounds and received the Victoria Cross. The British-born, New Zealand general appealed to Churchill's fascination with courageous and blood-spattered feats. At a party in 1919,

Churchill marvelled at Freyberg's twenty-seven scars and gashes; Freyberg modestly explained: 'You nearly always get two wounds for every bullet or splinter, because mostly they go out as well as in.'[41]

Churchill stated after the war that Freyberg would 'fight for King and country with an unconquerable heart ... and with whatever forces'.[42] Despite Churchill's obvious admiration for Freyberg, his appointment was of political merit. The number of New Zealand troops on the island far outweighed the British contingent; therefore, a New Zealand commander was good for morale. Moreover, Freyberg's appointment would improve diplomatic relations with the New Zealand government, given that the respective governments of ANZAC forces had not been kept informed about the use of their troops. Paradoxically, the presence of so many New Zealanders added to Freyberg's responsibilities and anxieties. Privately, Freyberg was disapproving of the way in which New Zealand forces were committed to the Greek campaign without proper consultation; also he was reluctant to sacrifice his men to another hopeless cause. New Zealand was a small country and could not afford large-scale casualties.

When Freyberg arrived in Suda Bay, he met with General Wavell who had flown in from Cairo. Freyberg recalled that Wavell looked 'drawn and haggard, and even more tired than any of us'. General Ismay commented: 'he had been tremendously affected by the breach of his desert flank.' Eden noted that Wavell seemed to have aged 'ten years'.[43] On meeting Freyberg, Wavell congratulated him on the performance of New Zealand troops in Greece and then went on to casually offer him the position of commanding forces in Crete. At the subsequent conference, Wavell stated that Crete would be attacked by an airborne assault landing in Maleme and Heraklion, supported by a seaborne landing. D'Albiac stated that the RAF had no resources with which to counter an airborne assault. Weston added to the discontent, stating that he could not envisage preventing a seaborne landing on the island. At this point, Freyberg rose from the conference table and asked Wavell for a private discussion. Freyberg told Wavell that the garrison on Crete was 'unprepared and unequipped' and in his opinion 'the decision to hold Crete should be reviewed'. Wavell explained that due to a shortage of ships, Crete could not be evacuated. This left Freyberg little option; he later recalled that there was 'nothing further to be said, and I accepted my task without more comment'.[44]

The British and Commonwealth troops on the island became known as CREFORCE. After an initial meeting with Wilson and Wavell, Freyberg headed for CREFORCE headquarters that had been established in a quarry on a hill outside Canea. Weston's term in charge of Crete had lasted just four days, a rebuke that he found hard to accept. Weston resentfully held on to his personnel, which meant that General Freyberg found himself without administrative staff in his headquarters, but Freyberg backed away from any conflict with Weston and accepted his predicament.

1. The newly arrived troops from the New Zealand Battalion halted for a spell on the roadside in Greece. Prisoners from the Albanian front are marching past.

2. Commonwealth troops are given a warm reception by the people of Athens.

3. Bill Crawley and Phil Tritt of the New Zealand 27th Machine Gun Battalion after an air attack, during the withdrawal from Grevena, Greece.

4. Commonwealth troops resting during the withdrawal in Greece.

10. German paratroopers landing at Galatas.

11. German assault troops lay dead beside their crashed glider transport.

12. An aerial reconnaissance photograph of Maleme. The aerodrome is strewn with the wreckage of German aircraft.

13. A German anti-aircraft gun protecting German troop carriers landing at Maleme aerodrome.

14. A German soldier enters Galatas. The aftermath of the New Zealand counter-attack litters the streets.

15. German mountain troops advance to the front in Crete.

16. Captured German paratroopers line the streets of Canea.

17. One of Roy Farran's light tanks disabled during the battle of Galatas.

Freyberg was popular among his men because of his obvious courage and genuine compassion. He dismissed the accustomed formal approach to leadership; his men often spoke their minds, to the surprise of the British officers who observed a more austere attitude towards their men. Despite being a man over six feet tall and with a large frame, Freyberg was affectionately known as 'Tiny'. Freyberg was legendary for being cool under fire. In Greece he had stood his ground under air attack while his men scrambled for cover. Although obviously brave, Freyberg was notorious for being stubborn and inflexible.

When Freyberg took command there was little that anyone could tell him. In the first days of his command, he studied the initial reports by Weston and the Joint Planning Staff, which laid emphasis on a combined sea and air invasion. Weston believed that the German attack would fail if the aerodromes held out. Freyberg was less inclined to envisage an attack in terms of airfields as he believed that transports could crash land in open country and he was unsure of the number of parachutists that would be used. He also remained confident that he could repel the paratroops if they came unsupported. Freyberg perceived seaborne invasion as the gravest threat to the defence of the island as German armoured units could be landed. Freyberg was unaware of the forthcoming offensive against Russia; he believed that Hitler would utilise the whole of his 12th Army if necessary, using the Luftwaffe to defeat the British navy. On 1 May Freyberg contacted Wavell maintaining that Crete could not be held without sufficient artillery, naval and RAF support. Wavell replied to Freyberg, insisting that Admiral Cunningham would provide naval support, and plans were being made for equipment to be sent to Crete.

Freyberg expressed his concerns to the New Zealand government: 'There is no evidence of naval forces guaranteeing us against seaborne invasion.' Freyberg went on to explain that the air force on the island consisted of six Hurricanes and seventeen other obsolete craft. In view of the 'grave situation' in which the 'bulk' of the New Zealand Division was placed, Freyberg appealed to the New Zealand government to 'bring pressure to bear' on the 'highest plane in London to either supply us with sufficient means to defend the island', or review the decision that 'Crete must be held'.[45] Freyberg intended to shock the New Zealand government into taking political action. Stating that there was no evidence of naval forces capable of protecting Crete was in direct contrast to that which Wavell had put forward at their initial meeting. The New Zealand government was concerned after Freyberg's pessimistic cable and sent Churchill a request for a review of the situation. Churchill replied, stating that a seaborne attack was unlikely to succeed against the Royal Navy and that an airborne attack would suit the New Zealand forces as they would be able to come to close quarters with the enemy.

In a message to Churchill, Freyberg expressed distinctly contrasting sentiments from those that he had communicated to his own government. In a bold statement Freyberg insisted: 'If he attacks us here in Crete, the enemy will be meeting our troops on even terms.' Freyberg then maintained his façade of confidence stating to Churchill: 'Cannot understand nervousness; am not in the least anxious about airborne attack ... Combination of seaborne and airborne attack is different.' He concluded: 'with a few fighter aircraft it should be possible to hold Crete.'[46] After the war Freyberg remarked: 'I hope that my attitude was soldierly' and that 'I managed to look the part of a man with complete confidence in the situation.' Freyberg stated that only 'four people on Crete ever knew what I really thought; my Chief of Staff (Brigadier Stewart), my personal assistant (Captain White) ... the cipher officer and myself.'[47] Freyberg's reluctance to express his reservations to the troops for the purpose of maintaining morale is understandable, but the fact that his personal opinions were directly opposite to those that he expressed to Churchill, again demonstrates Churchill's force of personality. Freyberg was loath to dispel Churchill's view of him as a willing general. Peter Coats, the ADC to Wavell, noted that Freyberg was a man 'of changeable moods; he could be easily elated and equally depressed'.[48] Freyberg believed that Wavell shared his pessimistic view about the prospects of defending Crete, but Wavell learned from the campaign in Greece that expressing negative opinions would only incur the wrath of the British Prime Minister.

On 10 May Churchill decided that Freyberg should be given the German plans for the attack on Crete. He specified: 'no one should be informed but the General, who would give his orders to his subordinates without explaining his full reasons.'[49] Freyberg received ULTRA intelligence as operational messages and as part of intelligence intercepted in London. Wavell briefed Freyberg on the importance of security surrounding ULTRA decrypts. Freyberg was told that he was prohibited from mentioning the existence of ULTRA to anyone on the island; also he was to take no action from what was learned from ULTRA alone. This was a 'fundamental rule which must be strictly obeyed',[50] lest the enemy realise their codes were compromised, and the secret of ULTRA be revealed.

On 11 May 1941 Freyberg received ULTRA intelligence stating that the attack would be concentrated on the aerodromes at Maleme, Retimo and Heraklion. The second objective would be Suda Bay and the port at Heraklion to enable German forces to land heavy equipment by sea. The intelligence report explicitly read: 'it will be noted that the entire plan is based on the capture of the aerodromes. If the aerodromes hold out, as they will, the whole plan will fail.'[51] The report concluded by acknowledging that sea landings 'must not be overlooked; but they will be of secondary importance to those from the air'.[52] Despite being informed categorically that the main threat of invasion came from the air, Freyberg was insistent on the threat from the sea. Moreover, this intelligence showed that the deployments along the beaches were wrongly placed to counter an airborne invasion directed against the airfields. When the original deployment was dispatched, the seaborne invasion was considered the most prominent threat, as the New Zealand Division based at Canea was stretched over ten miles to defend the coast.

Beevor maintains that Freyberg interpreted the term 'seaborne invasion' in the wrong context, which in turn distorted his plans for defending Crete. Freyberg's repeated use of the phrase 'seaborne invasion' suggested that he was expecting a major beach landing, rather than a major invasion from airborne troops. Freyberg's understanding of the situation was not helped by false ULTRA intelligence issued on 13 May, suggesting that the invading force would consist of 35,000 men with 10,000 being landed by sea. Despite being incorrect, the report still indicated that the more immediate threat was from an airborne landing. However, Freyberg remained insistent on the threat from the sea. He later acknowledged: 'We for our part were mostly preoccupied by seaborne landings, and not by the threat of air landings.'[53]

Freyberg divided the island into four sectors of defence. The Heraklion sector was defended by the 2nd Black Watch, two British battalions, an Australian battalion, three Greek battalions and 250 gunners armed as infantry, under the command of Brigadier Chappel. Heraklion is the largest settlement in Crete and is steeped in history, home to ruins of the ancient Minoan palace at Knossos excavated by Sir Arthur Evans, and the birthplace of Zeus. In 1941 Heraklion possessed excellent port facilities and the best aerodrome on the island. On 16 May Chappel received reinforcements from Egypt in the form of the 2nd Leicesters. At Heraklion, the problem was comparatively straightforward; the port and airfield would be defended within a five-mile radius. The Retimo sector, under Australian officer Vasey, was divided between the airfield and the town. In the airfield area there were two Australian and three Greek battalions; the town was held by the police and army reserves. Two Australian battalions defended the beach at Georgioupoli. The Mobile Naval Base Defence Organisation, along with the 1st Welch, two Greek battalions and some makeshift infantry units, protected Suda Bay.

In the Maleme area, the command structure was most complex. There were 12,000 men based at Maleme, which included 3,500 Greeks, many of whom were without arms. There were various units at Maleme, including RAF personnel who were unlikely to contribute as infantry in a battle. The Maleme sector was under the control of Brigadier Puttick. He had at his disposal the 4th and 5th New Zealand Brigades with three Greek battalions. The 1st Welch and 4th New Zealand Brigade were selected as reserve forces to be used as mobile units and directed to counter-attack paratroops. Freyberg did not have direct control of the reserve force in the area for the purpose of counter-attacking. He insisted that sector commanders could administer reserve forces by their own judgement. Stewart noted that: 'Much was to depend upon the foresight and enterprise of unit commanders.'[54] Poor communications meant that accurate information could not be easily conveyed to the commanders. Lack of transport and the ability to move without exposure to air attack, posed problems for the mobilisation of troops. Crete's communications were poor, as telephone wires were extremely vulnerable to air attacks and paratroopers. The only wireless sets that existed were those brought from Greece, which were in short supply.

The vital Hill 107 that overlooked Maleme aerodrome was sparsely defended by the New Zealand 22nd Battalion under Colonel Andrew. Andrew would be supported by Colonel Leckie who was dug in two miles away in Dhaskaliana around the foothills of a coastal road. Leckie's orders were to await a signal for a counter-attack against forces threatening Maleme aerodrome; he would be contacted by telephone, or if that failed, flares. Freyberg aimed to hit the parachutists hard just after they landed, when they were at their most vulnerable.

The slopes of Hill 107 commanded the road along the dry bed of the Tavronitis river. West of the river, the ground was flat and offered an ideal assembly area for descending paratroops. The undefended areas west of the Tavronitis led directly to the perimeter of Maleme airfield. This meant that if German troops landed in this area they would be unopposed and have an unhindered approach to attack Maleme airfield. Non-combat personnel were housed in the firing range of the vital bridge over the Tavronitis. Freyberg impressed upon Puttick the threat of a seaborne invasion around the Maleme area and they reached a compromise that resulted in Puttick's forces being thinly stretched over a wide area to guard against a simultaneous sea and airborne assault. Puttick was concerned that there were not enough troops to cover the area past the Tavronitis river where there remained a huge gap. At Kastelli Kissamos the 1st Greek regiment represented the only troops beyond the Tavronitis river and were dangerously isolated.

Five months previously, Tidbury had pointed out that Maleme airfield was badly positioned and asked for reinforcements in the west to cover the bed of the river. Freyberg personally witnessed the problem when he visited the Tavronitis area, but he failed to take any action. Due to lack of transport and the impending German invasion, it was decided by Freyberg that there was not enough time to carry out the movement of troops. The New Zealand Official History stated that the transport could not be undertaken because 'we realised that it would be impossible to do it and have them dug in before the attack came'.[55] Subsequent authors on the subject have argued that it is difficult to understand why this area had

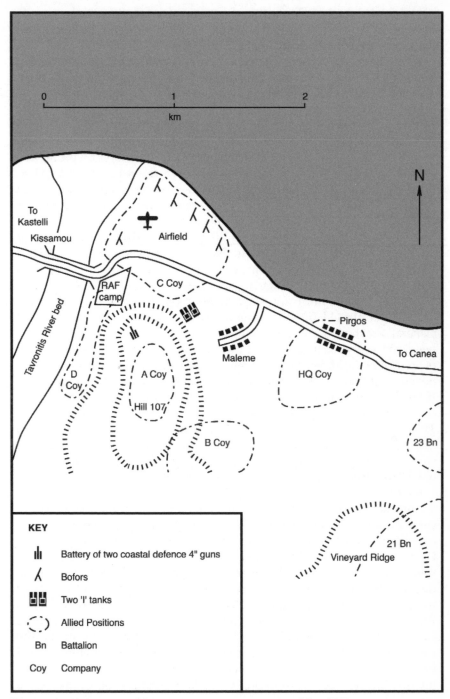

DEFENSIVE POSITIONS AT MALEME BEFORE THE INVASION, MAY 1941

not been adequately defended. Stewart maintained that the distance could have been 'covered in a night's march; the men had very little to carry. And some trenches had already been prepared.'[56]

Before he died, Freyberg offered a more contentious explanation for not moving the troops. After receiving detailed intelligence about the German invasion from ULTRA, Freyberg was shocked to discover his defensive positions along the coast, particularly in the Maleme area, were wrongly placed to counter a heavy air assault against the airfields. Freyberg decided to move the 5th New Zealand Brigade across the Tavronitis and withdraw the 1st Greeks from Kastelli. But Wavell apparently prohibited such a tactical reshuffle in order to preserve the security of ULTRA. Freyberg stated to his son Paul that Wavell wrote: 'the authorities in England would prefer to lose Crete rather than risk jeopardising ULTRA.'[57] Sir Harry Hinsley, a historian of British intelligence in the Second World War, commented on the use of ULTRA: 'the rules were if anything even more rigorous in the spring and summer of 1941.'[58] Freyberg was prohibited from keeping copies of the signals, thus removing the possibility of tracing or checking back on ULTRA decrypts.

Colonel Jasper Blunt appealed to Freyberg to bolster the defences around the airfield but Freyberg refused. Antony Beevor argues that General Freyberg's subsequent behaviour pointed to the fact that he believed a seaborne invasion was the main threat. Freyberg's relative lack of interest in the Maleme aerodrome until two days after the invasion does not suggest that he had a firm understanding of the impending invasion. If Freyberg fully appreciated the importance of the airfields it is hard to understand why did he not reinforce Maleme as soon as the battle began. The redeployment of troops after the initial German landing had taken place would not have compromised the security of ULTRA. Beevor goes so far as to suggest that Freyberg inadvertently helped uphold the security of ULTRA decrypts by misreading their contents.

Paul Freyberg maintains that his father realised the importance of the intelligence he received, and fully understood that no initial attacks would come from the sea. He points to the fact that no redeployment was made between the time of the report on the German invasion on 11 May, and the German invasion on 20 May, demonstrates that the restrictions surrounding the use of ULTRA were still in place, although there is no documentary evidence that the prohibition on redeployment of troops remained in place up until 20 May. Before Wavell could authorise Freyberg to take action on the information, he had to gain special clearance from ULTRA authorities in London. No instructions to relax the restrictions on ULTRA were forthcoming from London; therefore Wavell had no option but to continue to enforce these rules. Perhaps Freyberg interpreted the rules surrounding ULTRA too literally. Strict rules were observed in the battle for Cape Matapan, but the information was still used effectively. Cunningham had learned from ULTRA the location of the Italian Fleet, but was not allowed to take offensive action on this information alone, so he dispatched reconnaissance planes to confirm the position of the enemy before taking action.

Paul Freyberg has written that his father had an alternative plan for the deployment of troops at Maleme to deal with a purely airborne assault, which was not implemented. Major-General Sir Guy Salisbury-Jones stated that Freyberg refrained from using the alternative positions in Maleme to avoid 'controversy and possible security objections'.[59] After the battle, on 14 June 1941, Churchill complained about the 'slowness in acting upon the precise intelligence with which they were furnished'.[60]

In contrast to Wavell, Churchill was eager that Freyberg make effective use of the intelligence. Paul Freyberg wrote: 'it is clear that the Prime Minister wanted Freyberg to be given a free hand to defeat the impending German assault.'[61] Paul Freyberg explains that his father was under the misconception that the restrictions were supported by Churchill. Had Freyberg known that Churchill was in favour of utilising the information he would certainly 'have drawn Churchill's attention to the facts of the situation in Crete'.[62] If Freyberg believed the gap beyond the Tavronitis river was vital, why did he not press the issue with Churchill?

According to Freyberg's version of events, the restrictions that General Wavell administered were over-cautious and inconsistent. Wavell's strict policy regarding ULTRA did not apply to the RAF who had been allowed to bomb the airfields where Student's invasion force was massing. Indeed German intelligence deduced from the RAF raids that Britain was aware of the impending attack on Crete. Furthermore, British forces were already alerted to the threat of parachute troops after the attack at Corinth, an action ordered by Hitler that Student himself regarded as a serious compromise of security surrounding Operation MERCURY.

On 16 May the Royal Navy landed the 2nd Battalion Leicestershire Regiment in Heraklion. This was a clear breach of the security guidelines surrounding ULTRA, as Heraklion was one of the main German objectives. The argument was made that the order to reinforce Heraklion was given at the beginning of May before the information on the German landing had been disclosed, therefore the movement could take place. This was an obvious reinforcement that could have easily been observed by the enemy, while the redeployment needed at Maleme would have been much less conspicuous. Paradoxically, a greater risk was taken reinforcing the less important eastern sector of the island, while the vital area of undefended ground west of the Tavronitis river remained wide open.

Perhaps as controversial as the deployment of troops at Maleme was the decision not to mine the airfields. Despite having no aircraft on the island and inadequate defences, the airfields remained operational and the runways were still intact. As ULTRA decrypts explicitly stated, the airfields were of vital importance to the success of the German operation. Freyberg later admitted that the correct decision would have been to mine or plough the runway, but he maintained that the 'Middle East were insistent that they should be kept serviceable'.[63] At Maleme, preparations were under way for the demolition of the airfields by the Staff Captain of the New Zealand 5th Brigade. He had 300 mines available, but did not receive the order to use them. The Chiefs of Staff believed that the destruction of the airfields was 'an impossible task as the engineers, transport, quantity of explosives and detonators were not available.'[64] The decision to destroy the airfields should have been taken at an early stage, as the airfields were of little operational value.

Ian Stewart maintained that because Freyberg believed that planes could crash land anywhere 'he was not according supreme importance to the airfields themselves'.[65] ULTRA signals clearly indicated that the Germans wanted to utilise the airfields at Heraklion and Maleme for their fighters and dive bombers. Whatever the truth about the confusion surrounding ULTRA intelligence, it is true to say that the signal intercepts were not used to their full potential. Confusion also surrounded Freyberg's apparent concern over the seaborne threat. Brigadier Kippenberger wrote: 'I did not understand why our commanders were so worried about a seaborne invasion.' Kippenberger went on to say that none of the commanders had been down to assess the coastline. 'In many places there were rocks which would have made a landing impossible.'[66] He stated that apart from a bay around the 7th General Hospital, everywhere else was extremely difficult for landing troops. The nature of the coast had not been properly appreciated by the defending commanders, which led to muddled priorities and the dispersal of troops.

NOTES

1 Barnett, Correlli (ed.), *Hitler's Generals*, London: Weidenfeld & Nicolson, 1989, p. 479.
2 Ibid, p. 468.
3 Clark, Alan, *The Fall of Crete*, London: Cassell, 1962, p. 44.
4 Ibid.
5 Beevor, Antony, *Crete – The Battle and the Resistance*, London: John Murray, 1991, p. 74.
6 MacDonald, Callum, *The Lost Battle – Crete 1941*, London: Macmillan, 1993, p. 54.
7 Ibid, p. 58.
8 Ibid.
9 Ibid, p. 61.
10 Beevor, op. cit., p. 74.
11 Van Creveld, Martin, *Hitler's Strategy 1940–1941: Balkan Clue*, London: CUP, 1973, p. 168.
12 Beevor, op. cit., p. 74.

13 MacDonald, op. cit., p. 78.
14 Clark, op. cit., p. 50.
15 Beevor, op. cit., p. 78.
16 Ibid, p. 77.
17 Chief of Staff, COS 2 & 4 II, 1941.
18 Churchill, Winston, *The Second World War*, Vol. II, London: Cassell, 1949, p. 472.
19 MacDonald, op. cit., p. 114.
20 Churchill, op. cit., p. 476.
21 Ibid, p. 482.
22 Stewart, Ian, *The Struggle for Crete, 20 May–1 June*, London: OUP, 1991, p. 29.
23 Churchill, op. cit., pp. 477–8.
24 Connell, John, *Wavell: Scholar and Soldier*, London: Cassell, 1964, p. 419.
25 Clark, op. cit., p. 42.
26 PM personal telegram, Churchill Papers, 20/37, 18 April 1941.
27 Keegan, J (ed.), *Churchill's Generals*, London: Weidenfeld & Nicolson, 1991, p. 79.
28 Churchill, Winston, *The Second World War*, Vol. III, London: Cassell, 1950, p. 241.
29 Ibid, p. 240.
30 Ibid, p. 246.
31 Ibid, p. 41
32 Ibid, p. 246.
33 MacDonald, op. cit., p. 132.
34 Stewart, op. cit., p. 131.
35 Ibid, p. 130.
36 Clark, op. cit., p. 24.
37 Davin, D M, *Official History of New Zealand, 1939–1945 Crete*, Wellington: 1953, pp. 39–40.
38 Clark, op. cit., p. 24.
39 Gilbert, Martin, *Road to Victory, Vol. VI, Finest Hour 1939–1941*, London: William Heinemann, 1986, p. 1072.
40 Ibid.
41 Churchill, Vol. III, p. 242.
42 Clark, op. cit., p. 26.
43 Freyberg, Paul, *Bernard Freyberg VC – Soldier of Two Nations*, London: Hodder & Stoughton, 1991, p. 266.
44 Ibid, p. 268.
45 Ibid, p. 271.
46 Churchill, Vol. III, p. 246.
47 MacDonald, op. cit., p. 146.
48 Beevor, op. cit., p. 88.
49 Gilbert, op. cit., pp. 1085–6.
50 Freyberg, op. cit., p. 286.
51 Ibid, p. 284.
52 Ibid.
53 Beevor, op. cit., p. 91.
54 Stewart, op. cit., p. 112.
55 Ibid, p. 128.
56 Ibid.
57 Freyberg, op. cit., p. 286.
58 Hinsley, Harry, 'The Influence of ULTRA in the Second World War', Address to Security Group Seminar, 19 October 1993.

59 Freyberg, op. cit., p. 288
60 PM to Chiefs of Staff, PREM 3/109.
61 Freyberg, op. cit., p. 280.
62 Ibid, p. 286.
63 MacDonald, op. cit., p. 164.
64 Stewart, op. cit., p. 133.
65 Ibid, p. 135.
66 Ibid, p. 74.

CHAPTER VIII

Life on the Island

The garrison on Crete was bolstered by the arrival of over 25,000 survivors from the mainland. In wardrooms and decks of their evacuation vessels, men lay collapsed, exhausted from their ordeal in Greece. As they came into Suda Bay, men crowded around the deck rails to catch a glimpse of the White Mountains. Over the still blue water was the sight of beautiful green, tree-lined avenues and villas of the town of Canea. Behind the quay was a huddle of whitewashed houses and olive groves. A crimson glow from the sun rose behind the mountains, and there was a murmur of conversation as they quietly slipped into the harbour. The conversation was soon cut short and the serene atmosphere shattered, as two aircraft were spotted approaching; to their surprise the aircraft turned out to be British. The scream of sirens and blast of bombs were still fresh in the ears of the men evacuated from Greece. Personal assistant to Freyberg, John White, recalled: 'We saw two Hurricanes and felt absolutely secure again, but those two Hurricanes were the operational defence force of Crete.'[1]

As the ships drew closer it became evident that Crete had not escaped the attention of the Luftwaffe. Since the German campaign in Greece, Suda Bay had been subjected to perpetual air attack. The wrecks of HMS *York* and the *Eleanora Maersk* lay stranded in the port. The *Eleanora Maersk*, a 10,000-ton tanker, had been hit on 24 April and she lay beached, burning for five days. All subsequent transports coming into Suda Bay were forced to pass the flaming wreck, surrounded by bodies bobbing on the surface of the water. Several thousand unarmed British and Commonwealth servicemen arrived in Canea, a city that was made up of narrow streets coupled with old Venetian houses and villas with gardens of palm trees. Elderly men and women from the local villages offered oranges and ice cream. After they had eaten, men rested in the shade of a garden suburb, with wayside cafes, lined with trees. The soldiers arriving from Greece lacked even basic equipment such as entrenching tools and personal kit. One Australian recalled that half a battalion were landed without their boots after their cruiser was torpedoed. The deficiency in equipment was so severe that men were reduced to sharing blankets at night when it grew very cold. From the quay at Suda Bay exhausted troops disembarked and were sorted into units in the olive groves of Canea. The evacuees were a motley collection of soldiers unlike any that were to face German forces in the Second World War. Lice were rampant among the troops until they could find new uniforms; dysentery was also a common problem.

The British contingent that was already stationed in Crete provided a contrast to those evacuated in disorder from Greece. After a long march in sweltering heat, the 28th (Maori) Battalion halted at a refreshment point near Canea where hot tea, cigarettes, an orange and some chocolate were given to each man by troops of the Welch Regiment. A Maoris man wrote: 'Every man was very grateful to the Welsh regiment . . . for [the] sense of stability at the sight of the disciplined organization it provided.'[2] Their immaculate dress and confident manner provided a welcome sight for the ragged evacuees from Greece.

A British staff officer met the men as they disembarked in Suda Bay; he yelled instructions to pile all weapons (apart from rifles and sidearms) on the side of the jetty. Brigadier James Hargest refused to acknowledge the order, fearing that his men would not see their weapons again; however, military police endeavoured to gather up most of the heavy weapons. Men arrived without helmets and many were dressed only in rags. Lack of field bakeries meant that bread was scarce; the troops' diet consisted mainly of bully beef and hard tack biscuits with jam. Bully beef or 'corned dog' was eaten from the tin off a knife. Drinking containers were fashioned from empty bully beef tins and many soldiers cooked in empty petrol cans. Short rations of tea and sugar meant that the consumption of local wine increased. The locals were dumbfounded by the Anglo-Saxon desire to get drunk.

Among the regular troops brought from Greece were around 10,000 other evacuees landed on Crete; these included Cypriot pioneers, clerks and deserters. Many of these men were untrained for fighting and were a drain on resources. Soldiers not assigned to a unit were forced to sleep rough as there were no tents to accommodate them. As a result there was a revolt against military discipline. Soldiers resorted to looting military stores in order to bolster their resources. Men wandered into the country-side to see what they could scavenge; at night they would appear again, drinking local wine as if it was beer. Shots rang out through the night; several locals were injured and at least one killed. Outside the hours of daylight, some Australian troops took to shooting at any light they saw, whether a cigarette, or the dimmed lights of a truck. Dominion troops and British symbols of authority inevitably clashed. On one occasion a British officer was threatened by a pistol after he tried to stop a drunken Australian from robbing a Cretan fruit stall. A British officer reported that some of the toughest, least trained troops were 'living as tramps in the hills and olive groves'.[3]

After a tour of the troops Freyberg noted that the 'morale of the men from the unequipped and non-fighting Units was low'.[4] Freyberg was determined to rid the island of these disruptive elements and also wanted to dispose of the 15,000 Italian prisoners stationed on the island. Among the evacuees from Greece were many casualties, with over a hundred nursing sisters. The 7th General Hospital was established three miles west of Canea, and was filled almost immediately by the wounded evacuated from Greece. The shortage of shipping meant that Freyberg was unable to rid the island of those who were draining resources. However, many of those living like 'bandits' would soon prove their worth in a desperate struggle against German paratroops.

The life of the local Cretans assumed an air of normality. The men who remained in Crete kept to their usual routine of newspapers and Turkish coffee; they were largely traditional and middle-aged with heavy moustaches. The wives and grandmothers of the men fighting on the mainland were clad in black with only the head and hands revealed; younger girls favoured the modern European style with brightly coloured dresses. The Cretan character was proud and belligerent, instinctively generous to friends or strangers in need, but notoriously unforgiving of enemies. Blood feuds were not uncommon among villagers and the rifle was regarded as a symbol of manhood. Cretan characteristics were reflected in the contrasting landscapes in which the islanders lived, with harsh mountain ranges coupled with idyllic pastures and coastline. Simple mountain villages consisted of a few whitewashed houses and an Orthodox church; a mountain shepherd's diet consisted of sheep's and goat's cheese with potatoes and what meat he could find.

Cretans welcomed British soldiers as distant relatives and they were instantly united by their common cause. British troops received a warm welcome from the Cretan people and were overwhelmed by their hospitality; egg and chips soon appeared on the menus of tavernas around Canea and Galatas. Lloyd Johnstone from the 27th Machine Gun Battalion described the reception of the locals: 'On the day we arrived, the monks came down and gave us wine and arranged for females to scrub our backs.'[5] In the village of Platanias, the mayor welcomed a Maori battalion with tables laid with bread, goat's cheese and red wine.

The island of Crete was a haven for the soldiers evacuated from Greece who quickly began to enjoy the intoxicating beauty of their surroundings. Men bathed in the warm Mediterranean waters that surrounded the island and amazed the locals with their ability to consume vast amounts of Cretan wine. The only area of conflict between the local population and the troops landed on Crete came with the savage treatment administered to Italian prisoners by Cretans. Italian prisoners began to flood to the island; by January 1941 approximately 15,000 inhabited detention camps in Canea; many wore rags and were malnourished. The majority of the Italian prisoners were glad to be behind barbed wire in captivity such was the hostility of the local population.

Tidbury recognised Cretan hillmen as 'splendid soldiers' although it was noted that they had a tendency to individualism. Cretans had a turbulent relationship with the mainland and were opposed to the Metaxas regime. Metaxas had placed Crete under martial law after an abortive coup in Athens. The deployment of the Cretan V Division to defend Greece was also an area of contention between the Cretan population and the mainland. The Cretan Division had been deployed to Epirus in November 1940, where they distinguished themselves. The V Cretan Division's performance was a source of great pride, but the Cretan people suspected that the Metaxas regime had sent the division to Albania rather than risk arming them to defend their homes in Crete. The absence of Cretan troops only served to strengthen the affinity felt by the local population with British troops.

Churchill created the Special Operations Executive (SOE) in June 1940. On 5 June an SOE agent, John Pendlebury, was sent to Crete under diplomatic cover. Pendlebury, a Cambridge archaeologist, was sent to Crete to establish partisan resistance groups. Pendlebury was a popular figure among the Greek population and he was well known in many tavernas. He was the epitome of an English eccentric; he carried a swordstick, which he claimed was the perfect weapon against paratroops. He also had a glass eye that he left on his desk whenever he was away on secret business. Intelligence officer Patrick Leigh-Fermor commented that his 'slung guerrilla's rifle and bandolier and famous swordstick brought a stimulating flash of romance and fun into that Khaki gloom'.[6] Pendlebury recruited many potential guerrilla leaders, one of the most prominent of whom was a man named Gregorakes. He was known as 'Captain Satanas' due to the fact that 'nobody but the devil could have survived the number of bullets that he had in him'. Gregorakes had a fierce reputation. After losing a game of dice it was said that his anger was such that 'he shot off his rolling finger, forgetting ... that the offending object was also his trigger finger.'[7]

After the Italian invasion of the mainland, Pendlebury became the official liaison officer between British and Greek forces. Brigadier Whitely, personal representative of Wavell, stated that Pendlebury was the 'uncrowned king of Crete ... apparently beloved of all the principal Cretan leaders – a very tough lot it seems'.[8] John Pendlebury had accepted his death in advance; three weeks before the German invasion he wrote to his wife: 'love and adieu.'[9] Pendlebury was determined to carry the fight on if the Germans overran Crete, which he soon regarded as his second home. His work included finding sites for ambush and demolition targets; one of his projects included assembling snipers to cover wells and springs, as he knew that water would be a vital commodity for the paratroopers.

Pendlebury was initially able to work largely independently of London which had only a vague idea of what he was doing. When British troops were deployed in Crete his activities came under closer scrutiny from HQ in Cairo. Being under the microscope frustrated Pendlebury, as the British military did not appreciate that the civilian population could play a crucial role in the defence of Crete. Pendlebury had yet to receive any substantial assistance; his guerrilla army remained poorly armed and were largely untrained. The arms requisition by Metaxas had left the Cretan population largely unarmed, and lack of rifles was one of Pendlebury's chief concerns. Before the battle began, Cretans demonstrated contempt for their enemy and vented their anger on Luftwaffe pilots. At Maleme a German fighter pilot was shot down; when some New Zealand infantry found him he was in tears. 'The village ladies had stolen his engagement ring . . . His finger had been hacked off with a carving-knife.'[10] As the pilot told his story to the New Zealanders, he brandished the bloody stump. SOE officers had noted the belligerence of the local people and wanted to channel their aggression into organised resistance, but Pendlebury and his men did not receive the weapons they craved or deserved. Freyberg failed to comprehend the role of Pendlebury's operation. Being a professional soldier, Freyberg was reluctant to distribute weapons to a civilian militia who might act independently. The Cretan police were better prepared than other Cretan fighters; they were armed, disciplined and certainly the most organised of the home forces.

Although he appreciated the local Cretans' will to fight, Freyberg failed to integrate them into a conventional military force. The Cretans had a tradition of guerrilla warfare against the Ottoman Empire; this resilience was bred into the locals and there was little doubt that they would fight regardless. The failure to create a Cretan version of the home guard had tragic consequences. It effectively meant that resistance from local Cretans would be without the protection of military law; if captured they would face execution without trial. Against paratroopers, Cretan guerrillas could expect no mercy. In the 'Ten Commandments of a Parachutist' (see Appendix A), Commandment number nine read: *Against an open foe fight with chivalry, but to a guerrilla extend no quarter.* Something as simple as an armband might have deterred German troops from brutal reprisals. In Poland during the Warsaw Uprising in August 1944, British and American authorities declared that the Polish Home Army was a legitimate fighting force. Thus, the Polish prisoners were treated as legitimate prisoners of war. The Foreign Office stated after the war that military authorities on Crete bore: 'a heavy responsibility' for failing to turn the Cretans into a home guard 'with recognised markings to ensure they were not shot as franctireurs'.[11] The Greek authorities were not blameless in failing to protect the Cretan population with legitimate fighting status; the suspicion was that the Greek authorities were reluctant to arm the Cretan population for fear of reprisals against their regime after the war.

After their crushing defeat by the Germans, many of the Greeks who arrived on Crete were disheartened; they were short of equipment and their best troops remained on the mainland. Freyberg believed that the Greeks evacuated from the mainland could fight effectively if they were given the correct training and equipment, although Colonel Kippenberger described the Greeks as 'malaria-ridden little chaps from Macedonia with four weeks' service'.[12] Freyberg attempted to incorporate 11,000 Greek troops (whom he now commanded) into the defence of Crete. Subsequently, New Zealand troops demonstrated standard training and tactics to the Greeks.

The prized Cretan V Division remained stranded on the mainland. However their commander, General Papastergiou, who was from Greece, had deserted his men and fled to Crete. To arrive on the island without his troops was unwise; while walking in the streets of Canea the general was promptly assassinated. One British official commented that this was an 'excellent sign . . . something would have been very wrong if he had not been promptly shot'.[13] Members of the Metaxas regime arrived on the island, including Maniadakis, the secret police chief, along with fifty of his henchmen. They promptly left for Egypt, where it was said that they set about terrorising the Greek community in Cairo.

As munitions were landed at Suda Bay, shipping losses steadily increased, and thirteen ships were damaged or sunk. As a result of the air attacks the losses meant that supplies were falling way behind what was needed for the island. It was usually possible to unload around 500 or 600 tons a night; by 20 May, 15,000 tons had been landed at Suda Bay, but it only represented seventy percent of the estimated current total required to feed and maintain troops and civilians alike on Crete. The intensity of the German air attacks on Suda Bay meant that during the first three weeks of May, only 3,000 tons of munitions were landed, out of 27,000 tons sent to Crete. This was an appalling waste of resources and was due mainly to the lack of foresight regarding supply of the island, and the failure to construct a direct road down to the southern port of Sfakia (suggested by Churchill months earlier). German air superiority meant that the British fleet could only operate during the night around the island and severely hampered the use of Suda Bay and Heraklion. Suda Bay represented an apocalyptic vision. On 14 May an ammunitions ship was hit by Stukas and exploded in dramatic fashion, trees and telegraph poles were upturned, and the anchor chain was seen flying one hundred feet in the air. Plumes of oily smoke hung over Suda Bay and the flames lit up the Galatas olive groves.

Suda Bay was virtually unusable during the daytime; the air raid alarm system had been abandoned. Men unloading munitions faced constant aerial bombardment and the lack of advanced warning made the stevedores extremely nervous. The officer in charge of the port made the

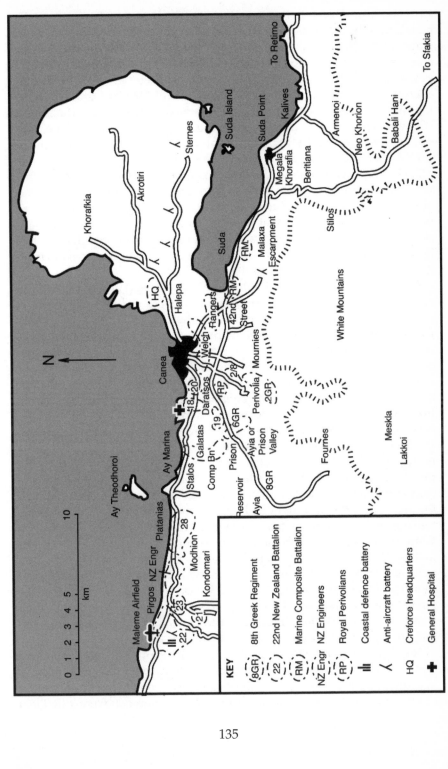

MALEME AND CANEA AREAS, MAY 1941

situation worse by refusing to allow the workers to take cover under attack; in some instances men were forced to unload high explosives when ships were on fire or even sinking. One officer's advice was hardly comforting: 'You can dive over the side if the ship you are on is hit by a bomb.' He told his men. 'Otherwise, you must keep right on with the job, even if the bombs are falling all around you.'[14] This had grave psychological repercussions on the men who mostly were not professional soldiers. The medical officers diagnosed eighty-one cases of nervous prostration, induced by the severity of the bombing. The men from the 1,005th Dock Operating Company were mostly shipping clerks from Manchester, Liverpool and London. To compound their fears their ship was sunk en route to Crete, only to be rescued by another ship that was also bombed but managed to reach Suda. Civilian crews had abandoned their posts, which meant that soldiers had to undertake their work as stevedores. Roy Farran of the Royal Armoured Corps noted that it was a 'terrifying job . . . Every bomb, however far away, sent concussion waves through the sea to crash against the hull.'[15]

Bombing intensified from 13 May and concentrated on the anti-aircraft defences of the island; men on the ground were ordered not to fire at German aircraft for fear of giving away their position. As long as they were concealed in bamboo or olive groves, they generally escaped aerial attack, but could do nothing other than cower in their slit trenches and endure the grim experience. The psychological effect on the men was more significant than casualties inflicted. Slit trenches provided effective cover against the air raids and generally they were regarded as a haven from air attacks. An example of the danger of leaving slit trenches occurred on the Akrotiri Peninsula. A swarm of German aircraft numbering around a hundred, returning from a raid on Suda Bay, attacked a narrow ravine where the Welch Regiment were encamped in their slit trenches. The air was quickly filled with the stench of cordite; clouds of dust and debris enveloped everything in their path as the planes strafed the area. After the onslaught had passed, five men left their slit trenches for some respite: 'In an instant a straggler Messerschmitt had swept upon them, scattering their limbs and brains around trees and rocks.'[16] Deaths in these circumstances, although few and far between, served to induce an atmosphere among the troops in which men were reluctant to leave their trenches. The quartermaster from the Welch Regiment, a veteran of the First World War, stated: 'I don't like to see these men cowering in their trenches.' He concluded: 'they've got to get out of them some time and they might as well start to learn how to do it now.'[17]

Tension grew on the island as the Luftwaffe preyed on any movement on the ground. Fighters would appear suddenly over the crests of hills, machine-gunning everything in their path. Occasionally men were caught out by random air attacks; an anaesthetist and a surgeon were killed in a bombing raid while swimming near the hospital. Those who drove ration trucks were in the greatest danger from air attack as they raised huge clouds of dust that could be easily targeted from the air. Transport on the island had been severely restricted by the Luftwaffe's presence; trucks could not be driven without sufficient spotters looking for aircraft.

Bofor gunners surrounding the airfields were instructed that: 'men [and] their weapons must be protected during the preliminary air attack'.[18] If they opened fire every time they spotted an enemy plane they would be quickly located and destroyed. Lieutenant Bert Dyson noted: '[Brigadier] Puttick wanted to stop all our ack-ack guns from firing. He had no control over them because the war was being fought in water-tight compartments. Most of these guns were under the direct control of the Mobile Naval Base Defence Organisation.'[19] The use of anti-aircraft fire was left to the discretion of local commanders. However, the majority of gunners showed remarkable restraint under heavy bombardment and their positions remained undetected. The hard work of camouflaging equipment and digging slit trenches paid dividends. Surprisingly little damage was inflicted by the Luftwaffe who carried out their low level attacks from as little as fifty feet from the ground.

Despite the threat from the air, the troops' surroundings were idyllic. Men continued to bathe in the sea, which amazed the local Cretans who rarely ventured near it. The air was invigorating and fresh. Brief storms would freshen the atmosphere; droplets would linger on fragrant shrubs and flowers sparkling in the sun's gaze. Steam rose from the earth as the heat of the sun drew the moisture from the ground until it was baked dry. All around in the mountains spring flowers were blooming; men were able to wash their clothes in the icy water that tumbled from the mountainside, where the slopes were speckled with daisies and thistles. The spirit among the men was one of being on holiday. One New Zealand soldier of the 23rd Battalion wrote in his diary: 'All we do is eat oranges and swim. Having a marvellous time.' He carried on: 'this holiday we're having seems too good to last. These swims in the old Mediterranean are great.'[20]

The majority of the men evacuated from Greece had recovered from their ordeal. The recently evacuated troops from Greece did not have their minds on another battle; many believed it was only a matter of time before they would be going to Egypt. The lack of military police meant that many were inclined to relax. They rested in the shade of olive-groves and were revitalised by swims in the clear blue sea of the Aegean. Many bought cheese and honey at local markets or relaxed in village squares. Some Cretan women even offered to wash the troops' clothes. The soldiers who fought on the mainland had felt a certain kinship with the stout-hearted people of Crete. They no longer believed that they were simply fulfilling a political obligation and felt genuine affection for the Cretan people.

On Freyberg's final inspection of the defences in Crete, he informed Wavell that: 'all ranks are fit and morale is high . . . I feel that at least we will give an excellent account of ourselves.' Freyberg's rhetoric was positive: 'With the help of the Royal Navy I trust Crete will be held.' Wavell replied: 'German blitzes take some stopping. But we have stout hearted troops, keen and ready to fight.' He concluded: 'I hope [the] enemy will find their SCORCHER a red-hot proposition.'[21] Brigadier Hargest, with perhaps a more honest assessment, commented that the prospect of the German invasion produced in him a 'sensation I never knew in the last war . . . I can only describe it as dread'.[22]

In the evenings the men had long conversations in the olive groves among a chorus of croaking frogs, and familiar tunes played on a mouth organ. At Galatas, music could be heard through the narrow streets and an accordion played near an RAF camp at Maleme. All along the coast of the Heraklion area men idly chatted while eating bully beef stew and drinking tea. A soldier recalled that the sunset that evening had been remarkably fine; the sun 'appeared to be sinking into a sea of blood against which the black branches of olive trees were strikingly silhouetted'. Finally the 'angry glow gradually faded and the calm stars appeared one by one'. [23] As darkness fell, men huddled in their slit trenches under blankets trying to sleep in the cold night air. On the night of 19 May New Zealanders gathered in Uncle John's taverna in Galatas. The noisy party had already lasted into the early hours of the next day when military police broke up the gathering, shouting that the Germans were on their way. As the party fell into silence, a New Zealander turned to the young waiter and said confidently: 'Don't worry John. We'll fight them.'[24] On the mainland Student's elite troops boarded their transports.

In contrast to the medley of Commonwealth troops on Crete, German forces stationed in Bulgaria were subjected to a strict regime designed to 'maintain efficiency'. Medical inspections were held daily at 09.00. Sport and walks were provided, although 11.00 to 15.00 was a siesta period, and sunbathing was only allowed during the hours 07.00 to 09.00 and 17.00 to 19.00. The instructions to German officers read: 'It will be impressed on the troops that the observation of discipline is a prerequisite of success in the forthcoming operation.'[25] The German paratroops were transported to Greece by train. All insignia was removed and special equipment was sealed in containers; even the singing of regimental songs was banned.

The 7th Parachutists and the 5th Mountain Division had three battalions each with three companies to a battalion. Each section incorporated one light machine gun and eight Tommy-gunners, with two champion snipers who wore special goggles in their descent to protect their eyes. There were also flamethrower crews among the assault groups and a company of heavy and light mortar groups. Anti-tank groups also operated among the infantry; their weapons were ineffective against the I tank, but they were useful against the lighter tanks and for shooting through walls. Medical officers and orderlies were dropped with a special sodium-caffeine salicylate solution to inject those who were suffering from exhaustion. Individual men were issued with pervitin or benzedrine tablets, which were used as a stimulant. Each soldier carried rations for two days including bread, chocolate, rusks and sugar. The storm-troopers wore leather jerkins with close fitting, skull-tight helmets and ribbed canvas kneepads. Most of the paratroops dropped with only pistols and long-handled knives; they would collect their heavier weapons from containers that were dropped separately.

The daring method of deployment into battle was dependent on young, fit troops. A large proportion of those who were to descend on Crete were volunteers; many were 17-year-olds who were enticed by magazine articles to be a part of this new elite. Nazi propaganda films that portrayed the war as a glorious procession inspired the confidence of these young men. Many volunteers were former members of the Hitler Youth, who had been indoctrinated with national slogans. However, the parachute regiment was not solely made up of Nazi Youth; soldiers also came from a number of Prussian families. The most prominent example was three brothers from the von Blücher family who had a proud military heritage. The oldest was 24, the youngest 17; and all three were to die fighting the Black Watch in Heraklion. Many of the young paratroopers who were to die in Crete had not been in battle before and were unaware of what awaited them; Nazi propaganda did not show German corpses.

The majority of troops were not informed of their destination until an hour before their transport took off; some were still unaware even when they were in the air. It was instilled into the men that they were to take their objective within forty minutes of landing, although few of them knew the names of the positions they were about to attack. Phrase books were issued containing crude sentences. Von der Heydte described the scene as they prepared to leave for Crete: 'we were greeted by the ear splitting roar of 120 air transports as they prepared for the take-off.' Only the silhouettes of men could be made out in the clouds of dust as: '120 officers and NCOs of my battalion tried their best to make themselves heard above the thundering of the engines.'[26] The first of the transports were airborne by 05.00. As the Ju 52s rumbled along the runway they bounced heavily against the weight of the paratroopers inside, their engines straining at full throttle to lift their heavy burden off the ground. Dust created by the propellers obscured the view of pilots in the next wave. Seventy gliders had taken off before the troop carriers at 04.00. The gliders were claustrophobic and provided a strange sensation for those inside, first a drifting motion coupled with a sudden jerk as the cable pulled against the tow-plane.

The slow moving Ju 52s flew low over the Aegean, its surface glimmering as the sun began to rise. The first sight the dozen young paratroops saw from inside their corrugated metal transports was the silhouette of the White Mountains, and then the coastline of the island itself, a 'thin black spine of rock in the blue, with smoke from the bombardments thickening the haze'.[27] As the transports headed towards their destination they saw returning bombers from Crete thousands of feet above them.

The hypnotic drone of the engines was suddenly punctuated by a violent gust of air as the door in the side of the fuselage was opened. Each man began to nervously check weapons and adjust chin straps and helmets. The command was given to stand up and they attached their safety clips to a bar above their heads. The plane began to shudder as they gained altitude and lurched to one side as they turned for the dropping zone. As the men stood in a line some strained to catch a glimpse of the island, others simply stood with their eyes shut in an effort to keep their composure. Then a klaxon sounded and the order was given, 'Go!' The men moved forward closely together with their lines attached to the rail above their heads. They began to jump in quick succession, grabbing handrails either side of the door, to fling themselves spread-eagle in the 'crucifix' position, which they had practised so many times in training. As the men jumped, the slipstream hurtled them towards the tail of the plane where they began the descent to their fate.

NOTES

1   Sir John White, interviewed by Jock Phillips, 25 January 2001, Tape One, Side A, Alexander Turnbull Library, National Library of New Zealand.

2   Stewart, Ian, *The Struggle for Crete 20 May–1 June*, London: OUP, 1991, p. 58.

3   MacDonald, Callum, *The Lost Battle – Crete 1941*, London: Macmillan, 1993, p. 149.

4   Freyberg, Paul, *Bernard Freyberg VC – Soldier of Two Nations*, London: Hodder & Stoughton, 1991, p. 273.

5   Hutching, Megan (ed.), *A Unique Sort of Battle. New Zealanders Remember Crete*, Auckland: HarperCollins, 2001, p. 46.

6   Beevor, Antony, *Crete – The Battle and the Resistance*, London: John Murray, 1991, p. 96.

7   MacDonald, op. cit., p. 128.

8   Ibid, p. 129.

9   Beevor, op. cit., p. 71.

10   MacDonald, op. cit., p. 154.

11   Ibid, p. 156.

12   Beevor, op. cit., p. 95.

13   MacDonald, op. cit., p. 150.

14   Buckley, Christopher, *Greece and Crete 1941*, London: HMSO, 1952, p. 168.

15   Farran, Roy, *Winged Dagger*, London: Cassell, 1948, p. 86.

16   Stewart, op. cit., p. 136.

17   Ibid, p. 137.

18   Freyberg, op. cit., p. 284.

19   Hutching, op. cit., pp. 52–3.
20   Stewart, op. cit., p. 77.
21   Churchill, Winston, *The Second World War*, Vol. III, London: Cassell, 1950, p. 250.
22   MacDonald, op. cit., p. 165.
23   Stewart, op. cit., p. 143.
24   MacDonald, op. cit., p. 166.
25   CAB 106/511. 'Greece's campaign against the Axis, October 1940–May 1941'.
26   Clark, Alan, *The Fall of Crete*, London: Cassell, 1962, p. 53.
27   Ibid, p. 54.

CHAPTER IX

The First Day

Tuesday 20 May was another beautiful summer's day in Crete. The strong sun burnt off the early morning mist and the skies were clear. At 06.00, as the troops stirred in their slit trenches, they were subjected to what seemed like a customary air attack. The whistle through the air and thud of falling bombs, coupled with the rattling of machine-gun fire, was now a familiar experience for the troops on Crete, so they suspected nothing out of the ordinary. The first aircraft to arrive were from Richthofen's VIII Fliegerkorps, their purpose to deliver a devastating attack on the defenders, strafing gun positions and the slopes of Hill 107. At around 07.30 the aircraft vanished over the horizon and the all clear was given. The troops on the ground believed it to be a regulation air raid and started to turn their thoughts to breakfast. After a lull of about twenty minutes, a second, more intense, phase of the bombardment began. 'The skies were full of German planes.' An eyewitness recalled: 'hundreds of them, diving zooming and criss-crossing as they bombed and machine-gunned all over the place.'[1]

Maleme was saturated with high explosives and strafing machine-gun fire. Colonel Andrew stated that it was more intense than anything he faced in the First World War; lines of communication were severed and fox-holes collapsed. Squadron Leader Edward Howell, the senior RAF officer at Maleme stated: 'The noise was indescribable. The ground shuddered . . . Our eyes and mouths were full of grit.' Howell continued: 'We were shaken . . . till our teeth felt loose and we could hardly see.' Howell and his men lost track of time as the attack continued. 'Debris continued to crash around us and the sides of the trench crumbled.'[2] Geoffrey Cox, an intelligence officer on Crete, described the climax of the bombardment as a line of thousand-kilo bombs were dropped in the Galatas area. 'Great brown geysers of earth' flew up in the air. 'Noiselessly for a second, till you wondered what had happened. Then came the noise and the blast, and you knew.'[3]

The intensity of the second wave indicated that an invasion was imminent and German transport aircraft quickly followed. Freyberg was reported to have commented on the precise timing of the Germans, a remark that only made sense to those aware of ULTRA. After a brief pause, in which birds could be heard singing, there suddenly came an overbearing noise of the throbbing engines from the Ju 52s. Private Arnold Hammond of 18 Battalion noted: 'There was a sense of foreboding when the air blitz ceased. Next thing, over our reserve area, a flight of silent, evil-looking gliders drifted over us. We could also see handy to us the Junkers troop carriers dropping their loads of parachutists. Unfortunately, I think in hindsight, we were under orders not to open fire unless under direct attack. We could have severely checked the gliders with rifle fire.'[4] Some of the defenders were under orders not to fire at German aircraft so they would not give away their positions.

Allied gunners were in a perilous position as they manned their Bofors guns. Apart from the obvious danger of air attack, huge clouds of dust and grit were thrown up by explosions, which hopelessly obscured their vision. But Bofors gunners pumped alternate tracer and incendiary high into the air regardless. A Royal Marine described a direct hit on one of the transports: 'you could actually see the shot breaking up the aircraft and the bodies falling out like potato sacks.'[5] Others at Maleme suggested that the anti-aircraft fire was creating little damage; an eye witness observed that the gliders were 'much slower than an ordinary plane and I reflected what a hash a few of our Hurricanes would have made of them if only they had been there'.[6] Of the gliders he noted: 'They passed as silently as ghosts with just a swishing sound instead of the usual roar, and their wings very long and tapering.' Geoffrey Cox noted: 'They were close enough for me to glimpse faces peering through the windows.'[7]

Many of the defenders had never seen gliders or parachutists before and found themselves captivated by the spectacular sight as the men fell like confetti from the slow moving aircraft. Bill Boyce from the 4th Field Ambulance commented: 'I was astonished. Some of our late arrivals from Greece told us of the parachutists at Corinth. "Bullshit," we said – all the more realistic when the Deutsch did arrive.'[8]

Joseph Highet of the 19th Battalion recalled: 'It was an awe-inspiring sight with the sky filled with parachutists, who were landing all around.'[9] Private George Heasley of 20th Battalion described the scene: 'The Junkers 52 planes were full of troops and also towing large gliders full of troops. The sky was completely blanketed by parachutes dropping fully equipped men as far as the eye could see. It was an awesome spectacle.'[10] Cox commented that even if he was killed, he had 'seen one of the most remarkable moments in history. I had witnessed the first airborne invasion of all time'.[11]

The paralysis of the defenders was only momentary as they watched the display. Private Thomas Foley commented: 'After the initial shock we realized the paratroopers were restricted, being strapped into the parachutes, and became sitting ducks. Those who dropped on top of us just did not survive.'[12] For the twenty seconds that the parachutists were in the air, they were extremely vulnerable to small arms fire, and many paratroops were killed before they reached the ground. An Allied soldier recalled the manner in which the men died in the air: 'Suddenly you'd see one go limp, then . . . straighten up with a jerk, and then go limp again.'[13] Some men aimed for the parachutes with incendiaries; the bullets tore through the silk and set it alight, the paratroopers falling heavily to the ground, breaking ribs and legs. Some considered hitting parachutists as impossible with a rifle, but possible with a captured Tommy-gun, if close enough. Others described aiming at the parachutists' feet as an almost certain method of hitting them. Many of the parachutists fired randomly at the defenders in desperation as they descended.

Where the German troops dropped on the coastal road between Maleme and Platanias, they fell directly into the positions of the 22nd and 23rd New Zealand Battalions. Men were caught up in trees with their parachutes or killed in the air. Private Archibald Sears recalled: 'Parachute troops dropped right over our area. One parachute caught in a tree and swung over my slit trench; the sergeant yelled: "Don't shoot! I'll get him." He fired and hit his grenades and he blew to pieces and his internals sprayed over me as he landed.'[14] After the main body of troops had been eliminated, the defenders remained vulnerable to enemy snipers. Private Thomas Foley was one of the many victims of German sniper fire. 'We had cleared our area and settled down in our defensive position and we found that those of the enemy who had come down in amongst the olive trees, used their parachutes as a hide where they sniped at us. We systematically shot them up with the Bren gun we had. They had wounded four or five of us, including myself. I had carried my mate, who had a thigh smashed, up to the R.A.P. [Regimental Aid Post] and returned to my position when I got shot by one of these snipers. I was lying down on a small parapet the sniper was in the top of a tree under his parachute. He must have aimed at my head, for the bullet went in my collarbone and out halfway down my back.'[15]

The opening stages as the German paratroops landed were vital. During the initial period the parachutists were most vulnerable as they scurried around to find their weapon containers. Many of the weapon containers fell into the hands of New Zealanders. Thomas Foley commented: 'The equipment, which came down in separate parachutes helped us tremendously, as we were very short of supplies and equipment.'[16] Augmented with German weapons, the New Zealanders defending Maleme made a concerted effort to repel the paratroops. Cretan civilians also took up the fight, although there were few able bodied men who had not left the island for Albania. As men stalked each other among the olive groves, old men, boys and women took up arms against the Germans, using ancient rifles, knives and sticks. German casualties mounted at an alarming rate. When asked if he needed assistance, a New Zealand commander replied: 'They'll all be dead before you can get here.'[17] Captured German documents revealed that one company of paratroops had lost 112 men killed out of 126; New Zealand sappers fighting as infantry accounted for the majority of them.

The initial German attack focused on Maleme airfield and the Canea area. The glider-borne and parachute troops had suffered heavy losses at the hands of the defenders but they gained a foothold in two areas. There was a large concentration of paratroops in what became known as Prison Valley (due to the prominent white buildings of the Ayia jail). Substantial German forces had also landed in the undefended territory beyond the Tavronitis river, west of the airfield at Maleme. The common view was that if Freyberg had moved the desired troops beyond the Tavronitis, then the paratroops landed there would have suffered the same fate as the other detachments that landed directly on top of the defenders. At approximately 08:15 paratroops began dropping to the west, south and east of the Maleme airfield. Those paratroops who landed to the east and south of the airfield were heavily attacked. Paratroops were also landed near Hill 107; others came down near Maleme village on roof-tops and in narrow streets.

At 10.55 Andrew sent Brigadier Hargest news that a total of 400 paratroops had landed in the area, 100 near the airfield with 150 to the east and 150 to the west. What Andrew did not know was that a total of 1,000 paratroops had landed unopposed on the pebbly bed of the Tavronitis river. A huge swirling cloud of dust had obscured Andrew's vision. Ian Stewart likened the battle to the days of Wellington, when his foot-soldiers searched the slopes of Waterloo while French cavalry appeared and vanished in between the belches of cannon smoke which drifted across the battlefield.

The first German troops on the ground were the 1st Battalion of the Assault Regiment's glider detachment. The elite Storm Regiment under General Eugen Meindl (Group West) was tasked with the capture of Maleme and had delegated three glider groups to lead the attack. Lieutenant von Plessen had 108 men with which to attack the west of the airfield at the Tavronitis river. One hundred and twenty men under Major Koch were to assault the slopes of Hill 107, and Major Braun led seventy-two men to seize the Tavronitis bridge. Captain Gericke landed with heavy weapons in the open ground west of the river, near the Tavronitis. Major Stenzler and the 2nd Battalion landed south of the airfield to act as a reserve force. The 3rd Battalion under Scherber landed beyond Maleme along the coastal road to attack from the east. It was intended that after Maleme was captured the entire force would join up with Centre Group in Canea.

The gliders landed in the midst of the bombing, through heavy clouds of dust. One of Plessen's glider detachments immediately came under fire from the Bofors; one caught fire in the air, another was hit at point blank range and was obliterated. On the ground, Plessen's men advanced quickly to overrun a Bofors battery (the personnel manning the battery had rifles but no ammunition). Advancing to the west of the airfield, Plessen and two of his men were killed after being subjected to heavy gunfire. Scherber's group ceased to exist as a fighting force before they reached the ground. As the men leapt from their transports, they were met with a cacophony of small-arms fire, like a thousand firecrackers being set off. Those who were not killed or injured in the air found it impossible to link up with their comrades or locate their weapons containers, which mainly benefited the defenders. Scherber's men paid a high price for the bogus intelligence they received prior to the invasion. Scherber was led to believe that the area was undefended; in reality the New Zealand 21st and 23rd Battalions defended the position and they were well dug in. Captain Wilson was observing the 21st Battalion area when 'a pair of feet appeared through a nearby olive tree. They were right on top of us.'[18] Lieutenant Colonel Leckie was reported to have shot five paratroopers in the opening minutes of the invasion; two without rising from his desk.

Captain Witzig, a veteran of the landing on Eben-Emael, was shot through the lungs and lay in a ditch for three days before he was discovered. Another paratrooper, Helmut Wenzel, was hit in the neck and chest during his descent. On the ground Wenzel attempted to organise the remnants of his platoon when he was struck by another shot that pierced his helmet and tore through his scalp fracturing his skull. Wenzel and four others proceeded to defend a small patch of ground with pistols and hand grenades. During the ensuing mêlée Wenzel was hit again, shot through the ankle. One of his fellow paratroopers was killed moments later. Wenzel heard a shot ring out and then, as the man slumped forward, the clang of his steel helmet hitting against his rifle. 'I then saw his blood dripping from beneath his helmet. He died without uttering a word.'[19] Wenzel recalled how his shirt was drenched in blood and a nauseating stench emanated from his wounds, which had not been properly dressed; the heat of the day tortured him with thirst as he battled to stay conscious. Nightfall brought Wenzel's small group a reprieve and the survivors were able to crawl under the cover of darkness through the New Zealand positions to safety on the western side of the airfield. In total approximately 400 men were killed, including Scherber. One battalion had all of their officers and two-thirds of their number killed.

A group led by Lieutenant Mürbe landed outside Kastelli, which was defended by the 1st Greek Regiment who were backed by local villagers armed with a medley of weapons. The Greeks were poorly armed; they had 600 rifles among them with only three rounds of ammunition each. Despite the lack of weaponry their irrepressible spirit shone through and the Greeks quickly seized the initiative. The Greek and Cretan fighters knew the area impeccably and stalked their enemy flat on their stomachs, before rising from the earth and charging. Many Germans were knifed or beaten to death in the olive and almond groves. Armed with German weapons, the Greeks forced the surviving paratroops into a stone-walled farmhouse. Major Bedding, who was advising the 1st Greek Regiment, suggested that they besiege the farmhouse until the Germans were forced to surrender. But Bedding found it impossible to contain the passionate Cretans, and under heavy machine-gun fire they broke from cover and stormed the farmhouse en masse. Despite suffering many casualties, the Cretans overwhelmed their German opponents by sheer force of numbers. By the time Bedding had organised the 1st Greek regiment to restore order, only seventeen of Mürbe's men remained alive. Their wounds were treated and they were taken to the local police station for their own safety.

Cretans were demonstrating the same guerrilla instincts that had served them so well in past conflicts with the Turks. In Maleme it was reported that an elderly man beat a German to death with his walking stick before he could disentangle himself from his parachute harness. Some priests on the island led their parishioners into battle. At Retimo, a monk was reported entering battle with a rifle and an axe in his belt; he was later seen with a Schmeisser sub-machine gun. In encounters throughout Crete, the local population, armed with knives, rocks and clubs, were taking on an enemy with machine guns that could 'fire at the rate of three hundred a minute; with five different choices of grenade'.[20] Alan Clark speculated about what might have happened if a year before 'the inhabitants of the West had shown the same fierce courage when their villages were invaded'.[21] It was the first time during the war that the Germans encountered civilian resistance on such a savage scale. Many of the invasion force were shocked after being lulled into a false sense of optimism by German intelligence that Cretans would welcome them, or be neutral at worst. Private Colin Burn from 18 Battalion stated: 'The paratroopers had been told that they would be welcomed with open arms by the Cretan population and that there'd be very limited opposition. They were absolutely astounded when they were confronted by angry Greek men and women with pitchforks and tomahawks. We had one old man come through where we had our lines who had what looked like a muzzle-loading rifle. We told him to clear out and get back to the village. He said, "Germanos" – Germans, it was all he was after.'[22] The Germans were reeling from what they had experienced, but they would soon take brutal retribution against the Cretans.

Major Braun's detachment succeeded in capturing the bridge over the Tavronitis. As the defenders recovered from the initial assault, the bridge came under heavy fire. German troops found themselves pinned down by the well directed fire brought against the bridge. Braun was shot through the head and killed. Captain Gericke's troops landed west of the Tavronitis on the undefended ground with only slight casualties; much of the heavy equipment that was landed was damaged in the process. Meindl ordered Gericke's 4th Battalion along with Stenzlers's companies to reinforce Major Koch's group who were suffering on the slopes of Hill 107. Meindl, who had jumped with Gericke's group, attempted to make contact with Koch by a series of flag signals. As Meindl raised his flag he was shot through the hand; seemingly undeterred Meindl got to his feet and was immediately hit in the chest. Mortally wounded, Meindl was carried to cover under the bridge.

Many of the gliders from Major Koch's group crashed into rocks or olive groves. Comeau recalled a glider landing near the RAF camp. As the door of the glider opened it revealed a dazed German. Impulsively Comeau fired at point blank range; his adversary fell onto a second man behind him who was holding his head in his hands. Comeau shot the second man who spun round before collapsing, his body blocking the doorway. Comeau made his escape through the olive groves after his rifle jammed. Koch's men were surprised by the number of defenders who were well concealed in camouflaged trenches. His group suffered heavy losses and were forced to retreat back to the bridge; Koch himself was shot through the neck and killed.

The RAF camp represented a weak point in Colonel Andrew's defences. The camp was positioned between C Company around the airfield and D Company along the dry riverbed of the Tavronitis. Squadron Leader Howell assembled an improvised force of RAF personnel to defend the camp, but the initial bombing raid had dispersed the group. The RAF personnel and New Zealand troops defended the slopes of Hill 107 in chaotic circumstances. Many of the defenders were without weapons and came under fire from both friend and foe. An eye witness recalled: 'People were frightened at times to shoot because they couldn't tell whether it was your bloke or a German . . . People moved around wherever the fighting was . . . they'd shoot . . . and hope to God they weren't shooting their own men, because some did get hit by their own chaps.'[23] Haddon Donald described a remarkable act carried out by one of the members of C Company, after a German had thrown a grenade into their slit trench. 'He took off his helmet and stood on [it] over this hand grenade, he had his feet blown off, but he saved the rest of them. He died fairly soon afterwards.' The Germans began to 'build up their forces over the western side of the Tavronitis river, and they started to advance towards us. They took over a camp the air force were manning . . . They were not really equipped as infantry.'[24]

Around the RAF camp it was reported that the Germans had used air force prisoners as a screen to shield them from the defenders' fire. Harold Wilkinson stated: 'We were made to line up with our hands above heads.'

The group were forced to advance towards C Company in front 'of the advancing Germans, who threatened us with their sub-machine guns'.[25] When they came within view of the New Zealand troops, the Germans opened fire. Haddon Donald recalled: 'We were manning our slit trenches, and a line of British prisoners, air force personnel and Bofors gunners came towards us unarmed, being driven by the Germans with Tommy guns as a screen in front of them. I quietly said to the boys, "Hang on, hang on. Wait a bit." Then when they got to within about 40 yards of us, I shouted out to the Brits, "Drop! We're going to fire." And they did, and we shot up the Huns and they retreated.'[26] Some of C Company mistook the navy blue RAF uniform for that of their enemy. Wilkinson noted six or seven of his party were killed around him. By the time the New Zealanders realised, over half of the prisoners were killed. The surviving Germans fled leaving behind them a ragged row of corpses.

The Assault Regiment had paid a heavy price for this small gain; of the commanders who led the attack only Stenzler and Gericke remained standing. The intense heat tortured both sides, especially those who lay injured on the slopes baking under the gaze of the sun. Some screamed for help and others lay on the brink of consciousness. Squadron Leader Edward Howell was badly wounded as he returned to the camp to ensure that secret ciphers had been destroyed. Howell recalled lying in a pool of blood near the RAF camp. 'I craved water as I had never craved anything before.' He did not experience his life flash before him; in fact Howell was well aware of his position: 'I was alone and dying from loss of blood and thirst. It was a race to see which won. I only desired the race to end.'[27] After capturing the RAF operations office, the Germans discovered valuable documents giving precise details of the strength of Freyberg's forces. The German troops had succeeded in gaining a foothold at the base of the slopes of Hill 107. By noon the Germans to the east of Maleme had been largely mopped up, but in the dry riverbed of the Tavronitis in the west, the paratroops were regrouping. Due to the unopposed landing and failure of the landings elsewhere, the main thrust of the German attack came from west of the Tavronitis defended by the New Zealand 22nd Battalion under Colonel Andrew. Andrew's men had repulsed two German attacks despite being dive-bombed throughout the morning, but his platoons were gradually being depleted and suffering from the heat.

Group Centre under General Süssmann were tasked with attacking Canea. Two glider detachments led the assault; the 1st Battalion under Captain von der Heydte were due to advance through Suda to link up with Lieutenant Genz who would land south of Canea. The operation in this area started badly for the Germans, as General Süssmann's glider crashed on the island of Aegina before the invasion had begun. As they passed over Athens a passing bomber overtook Süssmann's glider, which left the tug bumping in its slipstream. The tow cable snapped which released the glider from the tow, and as the glider drifted away, its wings folded under the pressure. The fuselage fell to earth on the island of Aegina, killing all its passengers.

Despite missing his landing zone, von der Heydte emerged from his glider unscathed. He was able to assemble the remainder of Centre Group and advance on the town of Perivolia south of Canea. Other sections of the regiment landed on the Akrotiri Peninsula; one unfortunate group were dropped into the Alikanos reservoir and drowned. A total of 350 men survived the drop and regrouped near the prison. Local partisans killed those paratroops who had splintered from the main body of troops with axes and spades. The survivors linked up with von der Heydte's 1st Battalion. Lieutenant Neuhoff and the 7th Company landed south of Galatas and made a failed attempt to take Pink Hill (so named because of the colour of the earth). Here the New Zealand Petrol Company held their position grimly among the trees. The accurate rifle and Bren fire from the New Zealanders kept the Germans pinned down and they were not able to collect their heavier weapons. The only German gain came when the 12th Company were able to overrun the 6th Greeks and take control of Cemetery Hill. The remainder of Group Centre were landed around the town of Perivolia.

On the day of the German invasion, King George of Greece and his attendants watched from their garden in the small village of Perivolia, a couple of miles away from Canea. They saw the gliders and Ju 52s pass serenely overhead before dispersing an array of white, green and red spots of silk. Paratroops landed in strength around Perivolia, approximately 200 men descending around the king's villa. It was reasonable to assume the paratroops were briefed on the whereabouts of the king and he would be one of their main objectives. In fact the troops who landed in Perivolia did so in error; their landing zone was intended to be in Galatas and they had no prior knowledge of the king's location.

The king's evacuation party numbered around forty men including the king's cousin, Prime Minister Tsuderous, and men from the New Zealand 18th Battalion under Lieutenant Ryan. As they set out, they immediately ran into a group of a dozen paratroops, who were driven off by fire from Ryan's men. On many occasions the king and his escorts were forced to fling themselves to the ground to avoid attack from low-flying German aircraft. The planes flew so low that the pilots' faces were visible. Ryan wisely persuaded the king to remove his tunic that was covered in gold braid and ribbons, for fear of attracting the unwanted attention of a more observant German pilot. Danger also came from local Cretans who fired on the group and took some convincing of the king's true identity.

The royal party eventually took refuge in the mountains where they accepted the hospitality of the sparse inhabitants and sheltered in caves. As they reached higher into the snowy mountain peaks, they were forced to sleep in the bitter cold. Many of the New Zealanders were clad in summer kit of thin shirts and shorts so they huddled around fires to warm themselves and roasted lean mountain sheep. Tsuderous paid tribute to the king's resilience, stating that he accepted the hardships: 'With majestic simplicity . . . He slept on the cold ground, and shared with us the scant food and snow.'[28]

On their descent towards the sea, the party limped into the village of Samaria with tattered boots and bleeding feet. They moved on to the coastal village of Ayla where they endeavoured to contact the Royal Navy. The Royal Navy was suspicious of SOS signals and were reluctant to move closer. In the evacuation of Greece, Germans had used similar signals to lure warships into shore to attack them. After an hour of waiting, a fishing boat appeared out of the darkness and came to shore. The party were promptly transported to HMS *Decoy* and set sail for Egypt; they arrived in Alexandria late that night.

The German 10th Company under Nagele landed by the 7th General Hospital near the coast behind Galatas. The hospital consisted of a large number of tents with beds for 500; that were already filled with men evacuated from Greece and victims of the air attacks on Crete. Wounded German airmen housed in the hospital crawled from their beds and signalled to the paratroops with hand-mirrors. Some hospital tents were set ablaze by the intense bombing and others were torn apart by machine-gun fire. Patients who were mobile made their way to slit trenches for cover, while those who were unable to walk lay helpless in their beds; many of the wounded were hit again by machine-gun fire or shrapnel. Lance Corporal Allan Robinson from the 6th Field Ambulance described the scene: 'They strafed up and down our lines for two hours . . . There's nothing worse than to sit in your slit trench . . . the bits of bark and everything come down on top of you, and see the clouds of dust around the top of your slit trench as the bullets go round. To say that I was scared would be an understatement.'[29] As parachutists dropped on the area the devastation from the bombing raid was still evident, clouds of smoke from burning tarpaulin were still drifting across the hospital grounds. By 11.00 the Germans were in complete control of the hospital. The hospital area provided German paratroops with the perfect platform to attack Canea, cutting out the Canea–Maleme road.

Lieutenant-Colonel Plimmer was killed as he attempted to surrender. Robinson stated: 'I'd just got out of the slit trench, hands on my head, when the next thing I heard was bang! Crack! A shot.' As Plimmer stood up in his slit trench, with his arm in a sling, he was shot dead. 'As he was told to get out, he must have put his arm down to help himself out, and they must have thought that he was reaching for his [pistol] and they shot him. He just went back into the slit trench. He didn't die straight away. We tried to comfort [him] but he died.'[30] The hospital was subjected to a strafing attack by German aircraft before the paratroops made one of their captives climb a tree and attach a white flag. Roy Farran recalled: 'I never really understood the German callousness towards the Red Cross at this period of the war', all the more perplexing to Farran as 'generally speaking they were most meticulous in their observance of the rules.'[31]

In a counteer-attack Roy Farran's light tanks moved into the vicinity of the hospital, firing careful bursts of machine-gun fire at the German captors, who fell dead in a shower of bullets. The party of 300 Germans who guarded the hospital were panicked by the arrival of British light tanks. Fearing that more armour might arrive soon, Nagele decided to fight his way through to Prison Valley and link up with the rest of Group Centre. The Germans endeavoured to move the wounded men from the hospital. Lance Corporal Robinson recalled: 'We were told we were on the move. We were going to be used as a shield to go into some of the lines held by the New Zealanders.'[32] The procession of wounded men made their painful progress towards the New Zealand lines, many of the patients barefoot or in dressing gowns. As they came to a halt at the brow of a hill a New Zealand patrol came into sight a hundred yards away. As the patrol passed the Germans compelled their prisoners to remain quiet. One New Zealander from the patrol was heard saying: 'There are no bloody Huns here.'[33] Nagele and his men allowed the patrol to pass, but the New Zealanders soon returned and this time they fired a random shot. A nervous Luftwaffe pilot, who had attached himself to the parachutists, returned fire and the alarm was raised. A fire-fight ensued which lasted around half an hour. At first the New Zealand patrol did not know that their wounded comrades were among the Germans and began firing into the group. Robinson described the scene: 'they started firing straight through us . . . the 19th Battalion had Bren guns . . . they put it on a fixed trace and they fired it. I got behind a decent-sized olive tree, and I was sheltering . . . Bits of bark [were] flying around. It was scary.' An unfortunate Cretan boy, who had previously befriended Robinson, visited the hospital during that morning. Robinson recalled that the Germans caught the boy and 'of course, he was herded like the rest of us'. Shortly after the firing began, Robinson heard the boy moaning. 'I pulled up his shirt and I could see a black hole . . . He'd been shot in the stomach and he was moaning. I couldn't do a damn thing . . . I didn't have a field dressing. I had nothing at all. And this poor blighter beside me, he died. He died.'[34]

After they had realised there were prisoners among the Germans, the New Zealanders acted with the greatest prudence. A British officer commented: 'the New Zealand troops developed their attack with the utmost regard for our safety.'[35] The New Zealand troops managed to pick off the German captors, with minimal casualties among the prisoners. At the same time the hospital itself was won back by the New Zealanders with assistance from the 3rd Hussars. Nagele and many of his men were killed, the surviving Germans were taken as prisoners and the patients were freed. After the war it was claimed that the Germans had used their captors as a screen, but a subsequent investigation discounted the accusations. It was noted that the conduct of Nagele and his men was no worse than might 'be expected of worried men in an awkward position, not sure where the defenders were or where they were themselves'.[36] The Germans did not push their captors ahead of them, but moved them as a column surrounded by guards.

With the arrival of Australian forces in Perivolia, von der Heydte was forced to abandon his early gains. To recover the initiative in this area, Lieutenant Genz was ordered to break through to the Prison Valley by nightfall. Before Genz had boarded his transport in Greece, a signaller ran across the airfield grasping a piece of paper. The message was an ill-timed intelligence report that showed a revised number for the defending garrison on Crete – from 12,000 to 48,000 men. Although shaken by the news, Genz knew that at this late stage he was compelled to carry out the operation. On the approach to Canea two of the gliders from Genz's group broke their tows under anti-aircraft fire and crashed. Another glider was hit as it landed, killing the majority of the crew.

With only fifty men remaining in his group, Genz's detachment was able to overrun a heavy anti-aircraft battery. It was reported that all but seven of the garrison were shot by the paratroops. Some accounts state that the defenders were machine-gunned in their slit trenches where they had taken refuge after the bombardment. A survivor of the battle described the encounter to Ian Stewart, who wrote that ten men from a solitary glider overwhelmed the 180 gunners from the anti-aircraft position. The defenders had only a dozen rifles among them and they were soon crushed by the superior firepower of the Germans. Stewart claimed that the: 'Germans then lined up their unarmed adversaries and shot them to death against the sandbags'.[37] Later in the battle a force consisting of the Rangers, the 1st Welch Regiment, Royal Marines and the 2nd Greek Regiment, succeeded in recapturing two heavy anti-aircraft guns. Meanwhile Genz and his men moved on to their second objective, the nearby radio station, where the Rangers and Bren carriers of the Welch Regiment halted their advance. Genz decided to consolidate his position and waited to be joined by further paratroopers. Of ninety men who began in the group only thirty-four remained fit for battle.

By the Canea–Alikianou road to the south-west, a series of disjointed and isolated battles continued. Paratroops descended among a group of 3.7-inch howitzer guns, the gunners tried to put the guns out of action before they fell into enemy hands, but they were quickly overwhelmed. At Alikianos the 8th Greek Regiment had established a stronghold at a water-pumping station. As the paratroops broke from the cover of cactus groves to recover their weapons containers, they were subjected to savage attacks from men, women and even children, wielding all manner of crude weapons. The 8th Greek Regiment fought entirely alone as the New Zealand Divisional Cavalry had been withdrawn to the heights of Galatas. The defenders who occupied the summits of Pink Hill and Cemetery Hill surrounded Heidrich's men. Colonel Heidrich of the 3rd Parachute Regiment quickly reached the conclusion that the battle for Galatas could be won if they gained control of the high ground. He ordered his men to support the remnants of Neuhoff's men at Pink Hill.

Colonel Kippenberger and the men of the 10th New Zealand Brigade held the high ground. When the assault began at Galatas, Kippenberger was still finishing his breakfast in his billet. With the sight of paratroops dropping from the sky, Kippenberger raced for his headquarters, which were based in a villa on Pink Hill. On reaching the villa, Kippenberger was fired on by a lone German paratrooper hiding in the grounds. As the barrage of bullets splintered the hedgerows around him, Kippenberger took evasive action and flung himself to the ground and rolled down the bank. Seemingly unconcerned by what had occurred, Kippenberger picked himself up and climbed back up the hill towards the rear of the villa; he crept into the house and sighted the intruder through the window. He then stalked his enemy round the side of the house and shot him clean through the head from ten yards. Kippenberger commented that the 'silly fellow' was still looking down the bank through a gap in the hedge. Kippenberger then armed himself with the dead German's Tommy-gun and began to assess the situation. From his vantage point on the hill Kippenberger saw the Germans overrun the Greeks at Cemetery Hill. He had always questioned the ability of the commander of the 6th Greek Regiment, and his suspicions were justified when it was revealed that the Greek colonel, Gregoriou, had not issued ammunition from a nearby dump, which left the Greeks to fight with a mere three rounds each.

Kippenberger immediately ordered his brigade major, Captain Bassett, to halt the Greek retreat at Cemetery Hill. Bassett managed to rally around 400 men and began to push the paratroops back in a concerted attack. Sensing the Germans were on the back foot, Kippenberger was pushing for permission from Puttick for a counter-attack but his request was refused. Kippenberger's men had fought well during the morning; the New Zealand 19th Battalion to the east had reportedly killed 155 parachutists with only nine captured, although they 'apologized for having shot [the] Greek Colonel [Gregoriou] who was creating a nuisance by throwing grenades at them.'[38] Second Lieutenant Peter Wildey, who was involved in the fighting around Cemetery Hill, stated: 'The 19th Battalion was above us and that was the trouble. The Germans arrived amongst us, and they [the 19th] were firing down at the parachutists, but they were firing amongst us too ... I think they killed a lot of Greeks, because the Greeks had little wee helmets that looked something like a German helmet.'[39]

At the aptly named Cemetery Hill, the dead lay next to a graveyard wall huddled against one another. Along a narrow ravine there were three mounds known as Ruin Hill, Wheat Hill and the much fought over Pink Hill. German attempts to seize Pink Hill failed, resulting in fifty percent losses; those who had survived were running short of ammunition. The hill was subject to such an intense barrage of fire that all cover in the form of foliage was cut to pieces. Without cover, the New Zealanders were quickly pushed back again after being subjected to murderous mortar fire. 'Poor devils were blown up all around us.' Captain Basset recalled 'fellows with their chests blown in . . . and bloody stumps where their forearms had been'. The area around Pink Hill and Cemetery Hill became a no-man's land. Of Cemetery Hill Basset noted: 'Every time Jerry tried to occupy it and overlook us we wiped him off it, and it deserved the name.'[40] Later in the battle, von der Heydte's men played dance tunes on a looted gramophone between bombardments; it was reported that on the resumption of firing after a lull, a German soldier shouted towards New Zealand positions: 'Wait a moment while I change the record!'[41]

An unseen paratrooper who lay wounded on the slopes did not help the spirit of the paratroopers; during a lull in the fighting he cried out in a high-pitched wail over and over again. It was a stark reminder to the men that they could suffer the same fate in an instant. The paratroops had jumped from their transports expecting minimal resistance from a minor garrison, and the remnants of a weary group of soldiers who had been defeated in Greece. The unbearable heat undoubtedly magnified the psychological impact of the battle. The cold of the morning had been transformed into blistering heat. The sun blazed down on the sweating soldiers who were struggling up steep ravines or diving for cover among the dust and rocks. Von der Heydte described the moment as one of his commanding officers lay seriously wounded and his second-in-command leapt up and down in pain across the road with 'a blood sodden sleeve.' Von der Heydte recalled: 'I suddenly felt fear crawling into my heart. It literally crawled.'[42] Many of the young paratroops were glad to be captured; some stated that they had shown the white flag but were compelled to continue fighting as it had not been recognised by the defenders. A regimental officer described the paratroopers in battle: 'Some were so tough that they never gave in [and] fought on hopelessly until we killed them.' Others 'after wandering round for 48 hours, more or less gave themselves up with cries of "give me water."'[43] Thirst remained a problem for the paratroopers; the little water there was to be found in streams was often contaminated; the effect of the Benzedrine tablets designed to keep the troops alert only accentuated their thirst.

Where the paratroops had literally landed on top of the New Zealand positions, they were annihilated. Some German paratroops appeared to be very resentful of the reception they experienced on their descent. They complained that the defending troops had not fought fairly and should have allowed them to reach their weapons before opening fire on them. Buckley noted that the German paratroops took exception to being fired upon while helpless in the air because they believed that it was the accepted practice not to shoot at airmen while they were bailing out. However, the accepted conduct towards airmen was based on the assumption that they would be on their way to surrender. Crete was different; the troops were being dropped from aircraft with hostile intent. Freyberg stated that the 'indiscriminate' way in which paratroops had used their Tommy guns and grenades during their descent 'hardly invited lenient treatment'.[44]

As troops fought at close quarters in stifling heat there was little time for rational thought. The intensity and confusion of the situation meant that in order to preserve their own lives, many shot first and asked questions later. The close proximity of the enemy and the erratic nature of the battle confused all sense of direction; it was a challenge of one's nerve and discipline. As the battle started, Roy Farran found himself under fire in his light tank from an unseen paratrooper. Farran recalled: 'Indiscriminately we raked the trees with fire, pouring long bursts into the black shadows.'[45] Further fire came from the olive trees. Among the confusion a figure appeared in a long grey overcoat. Farran instinctively ordered his gunner to open fire. He soon realised the figure was in fact a civilian woman with 'a long grey dress' and grey hair 'in a bun'. The woman was screaming and 'holding out her hands for mercy'. Farran noticed that he had shot her. 'Her shoulder had been shattered by a bullet, splashing her dress and her wrinkled face with blood.'[46] They tried to help the woman but she carried on running up the road. After the woman had disappeared the hidden Germans resumed their fire and Farran was forced to withdraw.

Later that day, driving through Galatas, Farran was stopped by a local civilian who 'put one finger to his lips and pointed with the other hand to a figure lying prone in [a] ditch'.[47] As Farran looked towards the ditch he was shocked to see a German paratrooper in full kit – camouflage jacket and steel helmet. After firing a warning shot, he saw the German flinch, and Farran shouted: 'Come on, surrender you jerry bastard.'[48] Farran fired four further warning shots from his pistol, before he ordered his gunner to turn his Vickers gun on him. Farther down the road two more paratroops perished from the Vickers gun in similar circumstances before five more parachutists appeared from the olive groves with their hands in the air. Farran recalled. 'I was not in any mood to be taken in by any German tricks . . . I ordered the gunner to fire.' Three were killed outright and two others managed to limp into the trees. After the battle Farran concluded: 'I do not think that I would make a practice of shooting prisoners', but he observed 'Crete was different, and in the heat of the moment I had not time to think'.[49] The ferocity of the battle for Crete was such that neither side gave much heed to the Geneva Convention and prisoners were killed.

George Heasley recalled: 'We knew the night before so were partially prepared, but the actual event was more frightening than anticipated. We were told that the Germans would take no prisoners so it was a case of kill or be killed.'[50] In some instances New Zealanders bayoneted wounded paratroopers where they lay. Corporal Rudolf Dollenberg observed an incident when a New Zealander took a wounded German's rifle away from him, as he lay helpless on the floor, and proceeded to kill him with the butt. Private Ted Martin-Smith from 18th Battalion recalled an incident when his platoon captured three German paratroopers. 'The history of the battalion says that 10 Platoon got three snipers, but they weren't snipers – they were frightened boys, young parachutists. They couldn't speak too much English, but one fella had high-school English, and I remember explaining to him that we didn't treat our prisoners badly. They had been there . . . two or three days, because they didn't have any water with them. They were just frightened boys. If they were snipers they could have got the whole 10 Platoon, because they were well-hidden.' Unsure of what to do with their young prisoners, Martin-Smith and 10 Platoon left the paratroopers under the supervision of some elderly Cretans. The platoon went in search of a German patrol that was reported to be in the area. When Martin-Smith returned to where the prisoners were being held, he was shocked to find that the Cretans had gone and the young paratroopers were lying dead with their throats cut. Martin-Smith noted: 'I went off the Crete [sic] people after that. I wouldn't join the Crete Veterans' [Association] until after twenty years [when] I realised that the Cretans weren't as hard-hearted and violent as I thought they were. If we had been proper soldiers, instead of amateur soldiers, we should have shot them ourselves. What could they do with prisoners? And the fact that they'd cut their throats, they were husbanding their bullets.' Neither side could afford to take prisoners, as there was no effective means of securing them. Later in the battle Martin-Smith witnessed some of the defenders surrendering to the opposition. 'The biggest shock I ever had in my life was [to] see our blokes, not very far away from us surrendering. All their senior people were killed. It hurts me to think of it because I knew they didn't have to; they could have just sneaked away. The Germans weren't taking any prisoners . . . they took a lot of prisoners but not just at that time. They'd just arrived, and they were fighting for their own lives.'[51] Colin Burn from the 18th Battalion observed that: 'Originally the Germans were told not to take prisoners [because] they didn't have the facilities to handle them. Various New Zealand troops had captured a few paratroops who were wounded and they'd been looked after . . . when the Germans recaptured them, they were told what happened so, they changed their ideas. They took prisoners where they could.'[52]

The fierce partisan resistance on Crete has been well documented with evidence of women and children entering the fray. This was not the case for a great many Cretans who were deeply traumatised as the tragic events unfolded. Lance Corporal Eric Oliver recalled: 'When the blitz started an old Greek woman arrived to collect any washing that we wanted doing. She was shaking badly and we did not know what to do with her. We decided to lead her down into our Sergeant's elaborate dugout, which had a roof over it. She remained there all day. We gave her a bite to eat and a drink at lunchtime. During the evening when things quieted down we were told to take her out of our company lines and help her on her way home. Later on that night we went down below our section position and buried our two mates and our OC, Captain Webster.'[53]

Haddon Donald described a member of his platoon who was suffering from nervous exhaustion in the days leading up to 20 May. Donald described him as a 'physical wreck . . . we had no means of getting him out'. The man was taken to a distant cave until the battle was over. The day before the battle began they went to the cave to check on him: 'he was stone dead. He died of fright. Not a mark on him. I've never heard of it happening before, but I can put forward no other explanation . . . It was a quite extraordinary thing.'[54] Ned Nathan from the 28th (Maori) Battalion described how he struggled to contain his fear. 'When you're hard at battle it's far from your mind, but if you are in the circumstance where you've got to wait . . . that's when it's very hard to control your nerves, and even to control your breathing.' Nathan highlighted the fighting qualities that the Maoris became famous for in Crete. 'Most of the warfare . . . was either at rifle range or almost hand to hand. [The Germans] didn't face us hand to hand. They ran. Not that I'm saying that we didn't have our frightened soldiers – let any man tell me he wasn't afraid, he's a liar, because we all fear at some stage or other . . . When you've got to act swiftly, things happen and there's no time to think whether you're a coward . . . you fight instinctively to survive, and as a result, because you survive you're a good soldier.' It was impossible to gauge how a man was going to react in the heat of battle. Nathan observed that: 'Sometimes bravery came to those least expected to be brave soldiers.'

Many soldiers were shocked at their own capacity to kill, Ned Nathan noted: 'How brutal a man can become in that kind of situation. We were like animals, absolutely like animals. It wasn't so bad if you were angry, but sometimes it was a cold-blooded situation, and I sometimes wonder even now, how we psyched ourselves up to doing it . . . I felt terrible about firing at a man who was helpless, dangling in the air, and didn't have a chance to protect himself.' Nathan continued to describe instances where he had to make terrible decisions when he witnessed German troops creeping up on his fellow soldiers. 'You might be able to fire a shot to save him, but in some instances you can't. I've seen a lot of instances where men have lost their lives through trying a little haphazardly to save the other person . . . These are things that cause you a lot of sweat and fear and pain, and so you look at yourself and berate yourself if you don't measure up in your own estimation.'[55]

Surrounded by death, many troops turned their thoughts to their own mortality. Arnold Ashworth described how he found a wounded German man who was begging to be shot. The man had been hit by a high calibre anti-tank rifle and half of his hip was blown away. Ashworth reflected how moments earlier the young paratrooper had been 'a fine specimen of manhood' but 'now he lay at my feet pleading with me to put an end to his horrible suffering and wasted life'. As Ashworth looked at the personal belongings scattered among the corpses, he wondered if someone would soon be standing over his corpse looking at his own photographs. He commented: 'It was a sobering thought and didn't cheer me up at all.'[56]

Fighting at such close quarters dispelled much of the propaganda that surrounded the elite of the Nazi war machine, many whom were still in their teens. For British and Commonwealth troops the killing had become much less impersonal. The paratroops who initially represented mere targets in the sky took on a much more human guise; a 17-old boy whimpering in pain was no longer an elite storm trooper. The paratroopers were no longer a faceless enemy, but ordinary men with families. Kenneth Forbes-Faulkner, a Corporal from the 22nd Battalion recalled: 'I shot a German at 25 yards and was very upset in looking at his paybook to find a photo of his wife and two small children. The action was pretty hectic all day and we were subject to dive-bombing and machine-gunning. I lost half of my section.'[57] Thomas Foley commented: 'After the physical and mental shock and we had settled back into our defensive positions, I went down a gully nearby where a glider had landed and was horrified to see that nearly all the occupants were dead in their seats or piled near the door at the rear. The glider was completely covered with bullet holes.'[58]

As part of the Centre Group, the 2nd Parachute Rifle Regiment under Colonel Sturm was tasked with taking the airfield and town of Retimo. Captain Wiedemann would lead the whole of 3rd Battalion, along with artillery and heavy machine-gun sections to capture the small hamlet of Perivolia (not to be confused with Perivolia town south of Canea) and then advance on to Retimo town. Major Kroh's force was to head the weakest of the groups in the invasion to capture the airfield at Retimo. Although lacking in numbers, Kroh's detachment had heavy weapons including flamethrowers and motorcycle combinations. German aerial reconnaissance had reported that the defences at Retimo were almost non-existent; the absence of anti-aircraft guns and excellent use of camouflage by the defenders had deluded the enemy. German intelligence failed to detect that Retimo was in fact held by two Australian and two Greek battalions under Lieutenant-Colonel Campbell. Campbell's headquarters were positioned on Hill D. The landscape was thick with olive groves and vineyards, ideal for concealing the defenders. The Australians held the strategic vantage points of Hill A and Hill B, with the Greek battalions protecting the connecting ridge. Although not adequately armed, the Australians were tough, experienced soldiers who had seen action in the Western Desert as well as in Greece. At Retimo the terrain was similar to Maleme with a narrow coastal strip and a main road overlooked by steep terraces. Two *I* tanks were situated to the west of the airfield covering the runway. The 5th Greeks were to be used as a reserve in the valley to the rear of the hills.

The initial aerial bombardment on Retimo began at 16.00; as at Maleme, the cumbersome transport aircraft appeared soon after the air raid had abated. It was reported that 161 transports were in the air at one time. Despite having no anti-aircraft guns at Retimo, German transports were subjected to machine-gun fire. The Ju 52s were subjected to fire at close range from Bren guns, mounted on high-angle tripods, as they laboured past Australian positions dug in on the heights. Bullets tore through the fuselage and caused terrible damage to those inside; in some instances only two or three men jumped from their transports. Two transports collided in mid-air. Seven others were shot down in quick succession, reeling away towards the sea trailing smoke and flames. As the transports made evasive manoeuvres, some of Kroh's men were dropped in the sea and drowned under their silk canopies. Many troops died while they were in the air; a platoon commander was shot before he jumped in the doorway of his transport and fell back onto his men. This unnerved his fellow paratroopers who refused to jump; soon the plane was hit and was ditched in the sea and only two men escaped. Those paratroops who landed on Hill A were cut down with lethal fire from the four Vickers guns positioned there. It was reported that Australian troops had discovered a line of twelve dead parachutists in a clearing 'riddled with bullets'.[59] Gunner Lew Lind noted that those shot in the air folded up 'like clasp knives as they hit the ground'. Three parachutists whose chutes failed to open landed with 'crunchy thuds'.[60] Perhaps those who suffered the worst fate were a group of parachutists that were dropped above a bamboo grove where they were impaled on landing.

Wiedemann's troops landed to the east of Retimo and approached the walled town at 18.00, where they encountered fierce resistance from 800 Cretan police and civilians. Faced with determined local resistance, Wiedemann was forced to call off his attack and moved back to Perivolia. Farther east at Hill B the Australians rose from their positions and the paratroops were also forced back onto the flat country and vineyards of Perivolia where they dug in for the night. Despite suffering heavy losses in the air around Hill A, German troops landed in great strength. German

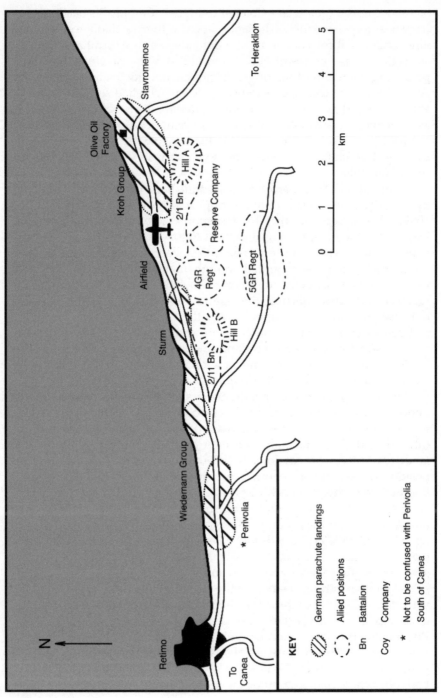

RETIMO, 20 MAY 1941

numbers were boosted in the area as two companies that should have landed in the west were mistakenly dropped there. Those who reached the ground unharmed managed to reach their weapons containers, which held heavy weapons such as mortars and armour piercing machine guns. Bitter fighting ensued and many Australians were killed, some of whom were defending their positions on the hilltop with picks and shovels. The shortage of armament meant that Australian gunners were forced to fire artillery at single German paratroops. Vickers guns soon ran out of ammunition, or jammed with heat, and the defenders were gradually overwhelmed. The situation quickly became untenable and the Australians were forced to concede Hill A to the Germans.

Campbell was quick to engage his two *I* tanks in a counter-attack. The sound of tanks sent Kroh's men into a state of panic and many were prepared to surrender, but the success of the counter-attack was short lived. The two *I* tanks that were sent into the fray against German concentrations in the east of the airfield became bogged down and the attack was called off. The German troops captured the tanks and their crew. The Germans proved more adept than their British counterparts at re-starting the tanks and were soon using them. Despite the failure of the counter-attack, the Germans were seriously disrupted by the strength of the defenders and were repulsed at every point except one.

Heraklion was the objective of the eastern group under Colonel Bräuer. Group East represented the strongest force deployed in the invasion of Crete. Their objective was to capture the walled city and airfield while establishing a beach-head for the landing of 85th Rifle Regiment from the 5th Mountain Division. German intelligence severely underestimated the strength of the garrison at Heraklion, which was thought to number 400 men. Stationed at Heraklion were three battalions of British regulars, an Australian battalion and an artillery regiment acting as infantry.

The area defended by Allied troops stretched from an open beach a mile beyond the airfield and east of the town itself. The 2nd Black Watch held a rocky hill over the south of the landing ground, 'East Hill'. The 2/4th Australian Battalion held two mounds near Aghiai Pandes known as 'The Charlies' while men of the 7th Medium Regiment Royal Artillery were acting as infantry near the sea in Nea Alikarnassos. At the rear of the Australians lay the 2nd York and Lancaster, alongside the 2nd Leicesters south-east of Heraklion. Heraklion town was under the protection of the 3rd and 7th Greek Regiments. A platoon of Black Watch and two Greek reservists held a position outside the main defences overlooking the beach from the south-east. Another platoon of Black Watch held a roadblock at Knossos, across the main road from the central mountain ridge inland. Two Bofors covered the airfield and two *I* tanks were concealed at each end. Captured Italian guns were in position over the high ground to the south-west, and six light tanks of the 3rd Hussars were stationed to the

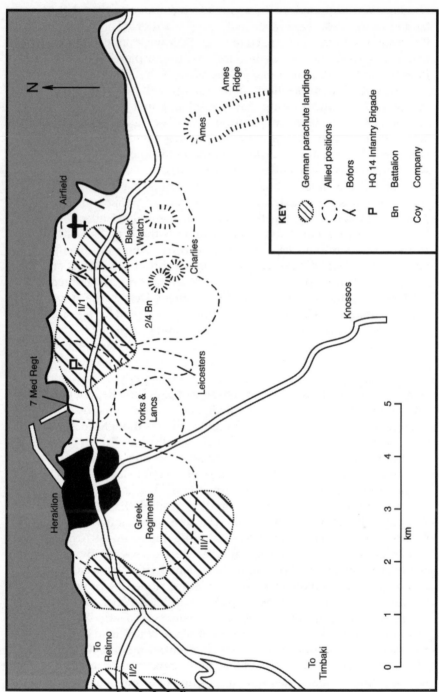

HERAKLION, 20 MAY 1941

south-east. The concentration of troops and guns was far greater than the makeshift arrangements at Maleme.

The 1st Parachute Regiment was tasked with capturing the town and airfield of Heraklion. The landing at Heraklion followed the same pattern of intense air attack, designed to keep the defenders under cover for the parachute drop. Due to dust storms and poor communication, the bombardment did not begin until 16.00, two hours after the proposed starting time. Some 750 aircraft took part in an air assault that lasted an hour, after which the German transports promptly appeared. The defenders' anti-aircraft gunners, who had observed the utmost discipline by not giving away their positions throughout the bombardment, now opened up in a crescendo fire. Under fire from Heraklion's anti-aircraft defences the German aircraft simply exploded in mid-air. As the Ju 52s lumbered past, the Australians dug in on the high ground were 'firing almost horizontally'[61] into the aircraft. The Australians could make out the faces in the transports: 'They looked so close, it felt as if you could almost touch them.'[62] A British regimental officer at Heraklion stated: 'the troop carriers are huge ugly black beasts with yellow noses. They fly slowly and almost sluggishly.'[63] The anti-aircraft defences had not suffered in the preliminary bombardment; out of over 150 Ju 52 transports, fifteen were shot down in the air, and many parachutists were killed on their descent. Men jumped in desperation as their transports were engulfed in fire; with their parachutes ablaze they plummeted to earth. One gunner stated: 'I saw planes burst into flames, then the men inside feverishly leaping out . . . Some were burning as they dropped to earth.'[64] An Australian corporal recalled an aircraft flying out to sea with six men trailing from their parachutes entangled in the fuselage. 'The pilot was bucketing the plane about in an effort to dislodge them.'[65] Another parachutist dropped into a cornfield screaming to his death as eight British soldiers revealed themselves with bayonets fixed.

The majority of the western group under Captain Dunz had been eliminated in the air. Tanks and infantry engaged those who landed as they attempted to reach their weapons containers. Without cover, the fighting was concluded in twenty minutes, and the paratroops were crushed by tank tracks or cut down by machine-gun fire. Those landed in the east of Heraklion also suffered; Lieutenant Hermann led a fraught charge towards East Hill. Hermann and his men were caught in a cross fire from the Black Watch, that killed Hermann and repelled the attack. Freyberg issued orders for the defenders to push forward and annihilate the enemy during the initial landing. The parachutists were astonished to see streams of men emerging from their slit trenches running to engage them. Close-quarters combat was an effective tactic against the Luftwaffe as they could not distinguish friend from foe.

The Germans deployed an entire battalion at Heraklion, half to the east and half to the west; it was practically annihilated before evening. Some paratroops sought refuge in a field of barley, which stood about three feet high and gave good cover. From the field the paratroops sniped at Allied troops who could only fire back at random at their concealed enemy. Suddenly there was a cry of : 'Let's set the bloody barley on fire boys.' A brisk wind set the flames dancing through it at high speed. The Germans hiding in the barley leapt up from their cover and 'ran like rabbits smoked out of their burrows. They were machine-gunned and picked off with rifles as they ran.'[66]

Major Schulz's 3rd Battalion suffered heavy casualties in the air and he was the sole survivor from his transport. Schulz leapt to safety moments before it exploded in mid-air. Cretans swarmed around parachutists caught in trees struggling to release themselves from their parachutes. Schulz regrouped his men and attempted to breach the walled city of Heraklion from the north and west gates. One British officer likened the attack to a medieval siege. As Greek forces ran low on ammunition, German troops were able to fight their way into the narrow streets. Flashes of gunfire illuminated the streets of Heraklion deep into the night; intermittent shots were heard followed by a tirade of running feet, then screams and an incomprehensible shriek of orders. German troops were amazed at the strength of Cretan resistance both in the walls of the town and in the hills. The local resistance grew as local Cretans joined the fray from neighbouring villages. Although unorganised, it was said that the Cretans would follow anyone who showed more courage than the rest. Pendlebury and Captain Satanas were at the forefront of the street fighting in Heraklion town.

At 19.20 German bombers returned to attack British concentrations. Further parachutists were dropped at this point, as they expected the airfield to be taken. The paratroops were met with fierce resistance from the Greeks, Australians, York and Lancasters and the Black Watch. The fresh German troops succeeded in pushing a small number of defending troops to the harbour where they were forced to escape by rowing boat to sea. A British destroyer, which was searching for the enemy invasion fleet, eventually picked them up.

Halder told those present at a conference in German headquarters that the initial landings in Crete had been unopposed. Lacking detailed reports, Student was unaware of the situation at Maleme and presumed that the airfield had been taken and he started preparing for the second phase of the invasion, the landing of the mountain troops. Albert Snowadzki led an airfield control party to Maleme to prepare the airfield for the landing of troops from the 5th Mountain Division. Snowadzki's party was carried in two Ju 52s. As his plane approached Maleme, Snowadzki spotted a Swastika flag laid out on the western side airfield. The pilot took this as a sign that the airfield was under German control, and proceeded to land; as the plane touched down it was subjected to a hail of small arms fire. The aircraft was hit by rifle and machine-gun fire from every side, which riddled the corrugated fuselage with bullet holes and smashed the windscreen. The pilot quickly fired up the engines and the plane limped back into the air. Student was quickly informed that Maleme had not fallen.

On the evening of 20 May Student sat at his headquarters in Athens as the tragedy of the first day started to unfold. He was based on the second floor of the Hotel Grande Bretagne that was draped in Edwardian decor. Developing baths were set up for the aerial photographs that arrived hourly and a large map of Crete dotted with flags dominated the room. The heavy nineteenth-century furniture was covered in telephone wires and teleprinters that constantly rattled away; ash trays were filled with half smoked cigarettes. The atmosphere was tense; aircraft reconnaissance had reported 'no sign of concerted activity'.[67] By midnight it was clear that the Germans held none of the airfields and that they had suffered terrible losses. Scherber, Koch, Süssmann, Braun and Plessen were all killed, and Meindl lay mortally wounded. Scherber's battalion had disappeared completely. The situation was desperate for the Germans as their medical supplies, food and water were all running low.

German intelligence severely underestimated the strength of the Anglo–Greek forces on Crete. Student wrote after the battle: 'It was obvious that the British were stronger and tougher than expected.'[68] At Canea 2,000 Germans were deployed and had suffered terrible casualties, although south-west along the Alikianou road (Prison Valley) there was a considerable force. At Maleme 2,000 troops landed with heavy losses, but they succeeded in forcing Commonwealth troops off the airfield towards the eastern perimeter and they controlled the western fringe. Maleme airfield itself was effectively no-man's land. At Retimo and Heraklion the defenders had successfully repulsed their enemy. To compound Student's misery, long-range RAF bombers were now in the process of bombing Luftwaffe bases in Athens, in an attempt to destroy the source of the paratroopers.

When Student realised the gravity of the situation he decided on a drastic course of action. In a last ditch attempt to save the operation from disaster, Student decided to gamble, using all his remaining resources to gain control of Maleme airfield. Student wrote that he had decided 'to concentrate all our forces against one spot. We selected Maleme because here, at least, we could see a glimmer of light.'[69] Only Storm Regiment at Maleme looked capable of challenging for an airfield, but it was not capable of securing the perimeter to protect the runway for the landing of the 5th Mountain Division. It was decided at an emergency meeting on 21 May that a parachute battalion under Colonel Ramcke would be dropped to the east and west of Maleme to reinforce Group West. The seaborne

167

landings were now also directed towards Maleme. Student knew that Ramcke's parachute battalion alone would not be enough to win the battle. Unless Student could secure the capture of an airfield to land fresh troops from the 5th Mountain Division, the invasion of Crete would be lost. The success of Student's plan depended on Meindl's men holding their position at Maleme throughout the night. If a counter-attack dislodged Meindl's group, then it would mean certain failure for Student's contingency plan. Student later admitted: 'I waited with my pistol continuously by side waiting to use it on myself, if the worst came to the worst.'[70]

NOTES

1 Buckley, Christopher, *Greece and Crete 1941*, London: HMSO, 1952, p. 174.
2 MacDonald, Callum, *The Lost Battle – Crete 1941*, London: Macmillan, 1993, pp. 169–70.
3 Cox, Geoffrey, *A Tale of Two Battles*, London: William Kimber, 1987, p. 68.
4 Hutching, Megan (ed.), *A Unique Sort of Battle. New Zealanders Remember Crete*, Auckland: HarperCollins, 2001, p. 59.
5 Clark, Alan, *The Fall of Crete*, London: Cassell, 1962, p. 55.
6 Buckley, op. cit., p. 174.
7 Cox, op. cit., p. 70.
8 Hutching, op. cit., p. 58.
9 Ibid, p. 59.
10 Ibid, p. 72.
11 Cox, op. cit., p. 70.
12 Hutching, op. cit., p. 73.
13 Buckley, op. cit., p. 176.
14 Hutching, op. cit., p. 58.
15 Ibid, p. 73.
16 Ibid.
17 Buckley, op. cit., p. 181.
18 Davin, D, *Official History of New Zealand in the Second World War*, Report by Captain Wilson, Wellington, 1953, p. 123.
19 MacDonald, op. cit., p. 176.
20 Ibid, p. 177.
21 Clark, op. cit., p. 82.
22 Hutching, op. cit., p. 194.
23 Ibid, pp. 67–8.
24 Ibid, p. 80.
25 Wilkinson, Harold, WO 208/4650, 24 November 1945.
26 Hutching, op. cit., p. 82.
27 MacDonald, op. cit., p. 174.
28 Buckley, op. cit., p. 215.
29 Hutching, op. cit., p. 156.
30 Ibid.
31 Farran, Roy, *Winged Dagger*, London: Cassell, 1948, p. 91.
32 Hutching, op. cit., p. 157.
33 Buckley, op. cit., p. 191.
34 Hutching, op. cit., p. 157.

35 Buckley, op. cit., p. 192.
36 Davin, op. cit., p. 479.
37 Stewart, Ian, *The Struggle for Crete 20 May–1 June*, London: OUP, 1991,p. 158.
38 MacDonald, op. cit., p. 187.
39 Peter Wildey, interviewed by Megan Hutchings, 9 November 2000, Tape Two, Side B, Alexander Turnbull Library, National Library of New Zealand.
40 Davin, op. cit., p. 200.
41 MacDonald, op. cit., p. 213.
42 Ibid, p. 184.
43 Buckley, op. cit., p. 176.
44 C-in-C Middle East to War Office, WO87911/297/49, 7 July 1940.
45 Farran, op. cit., p. 88.
46 Ibid, p. 89.
47 Ibid.
48 Ibid.
49 Ibid, p. 90.
50 Hutching, op. cit., p. 72.
51 Ibid, pp. 182–3.
52 Ibid, p. 195.
53 Ibid, p. 72.
54 Ibid, p. 80.
55 Ibid, pp. 230–1.
56 MacDonald, op. cit., p. 180.
57 Hutching, op. cit., p. 59.
58 Ibid, p. 73.
59 Clark, op. cit., p. 88.
60 MacDonald, op. cit., p. 190.
61 Stewart, op. cit., p. 205.
62 Beevor, Antony, *Crete – The Battle and the Resistance*, London: John Murray, 1991, p. 136.
63 Buckley, op. cit., p. 174.
64 Ibid, p. 205.
65 Ibid.
66 Ibid, p. 206.
67 Clark, op. cit., p.100.
68 Ibid, p. 65.
69 Ibid, p. 100.
70 MacDonald, op. cit., p. 197.

CHAPTER X
The Tide Turns

As the fighting of the first day came to a halt the defenders sank into their slit trenches exhausted and caked in sweat and dust. The cool of the night air brought a welcome respite from the blazing sun. After the chaotic events of the day, an uneasy stillness prevailed over the battlefield; the fighters and bombers had departed north an hour before sunset. At Maleme there was almost silence apart from a hypnotic chorus of croaking frogs, and a group of restless donkeys. But the night soon came alive. With darkness came the fear of the unknown; each unexplained noise provoked a rattle of machine-gun and tracer fire. Many German paratroopers lay under bushes in isolated positions, praying that local Cretans who stalked the battlefield would not find them. Some attempted to contact their colleagues with a series of hoots and whistles reminiscent of animal calls. Shadowy shapes of stragglers from opposing sides slipped past each other instinctively avoiding confrontation.

All the wounded could do was wait to be found. On the northern face of Hill 107 lay Squadron Leader Howell who was still battling for consciousness. He had attempted to shoot himself but the broken tendons in his forearms, which had been shattered by bullets, failed to pull the trigger. He now lay back against the earth wall of his slit trench in misery, taking shallow breaths, barely alive. West of the Tavronitis river lay Meindl in an improvised casualty station among the bamboos. Meindl was in an even more critical state; he grew progressively breathless as his chest began to fill with blood.

At CREFORCE headquarters General Freyberg sought news of the first day. By midnight, he had received a bloodstained document outlining German plans for the attack on Crete. It was clear from reading the document that none of the objectives had been met for Retimo, Heraklion and Canea. With a grenade within reach of his right hand, Freyberg sat at his table in CREFORCE headquarters and completed his report to Wavell by torchlight. The report read: 'We have been hard pressed. I believe that we hold the aerodrome at Maleme, Heraklion and Retimo and two harbours.' Freyberg qualified these statements with a cautionary footnote: 'the margin by which we hold them is a bare one', concluding: 'it would be wrong for me to paint an optimistic picture.'[1] By the time Freyberg had drafted his report to Wavell, the initiative was beginning to tilt towards the Germans.

The German officers who survived the massacre of the first day believed that they had lost the battle. As the paratroopers dug shallow slit trenches and bedded down in their parachutes, they expected the British to deliver a decisive counter-attack that would scatter their number and settle the battle for Crete. Throughout the night, Freyberg and his commanders failed to mobilise their troops for a dynamic counter-offensive. Freyberg had released the 4th New Zealand Brigade to be used as a reserve counter-attacking force, but during the afternoon at Prison Valley and Maleme, a counter-attack failed to materialise. Only one ineffective counter-attack was attempted during the night on Brigadier Puttick's orders. Puttick was the commander of the Maleme and Prison Valley sector. Hitherto, he had prevented Kippenberger from using the 4th Brigade to clear the Germans out of Prison Valley and Maleme, with the apparent support of Freyberg. At 18.20 Puttick gave the order for the 4th New Zealand Brigade to use one battalion to clear the area around the prison. This decision was only taken after Kippenberger submitted a report incorrectly stating that the Germans were building an airfield. However, Inglis, the commander of the 4th New Zealand Brigade, did not recognise the greater strategic importance of the counter-attack; he understood the order within the context of a local action with a limited objective. Inglis took the decision to leave his uncommitted battalions for a counter-attack the following day and proceeded to use just the 19th New Zealand Battalion, who had been involved in fighting around Galatas. Furthermore, the number of men used in the counter-attack was left to the discretion of the local commander, Major Blackburn. Blackburn felt that he should only use two companies, as he feared that using his entire force would leave a dangerous gap in his defences.

When Kippenberger learned the details of the plan, he feared that the counter-attack might be too weak to succeed and tried to prevent it, but the infantry had already been set in motion. From the onset the two companies from the 19th Battalion lost contact with each other and fumbled around in the dark until they came across random pockets of paratroopers around Pink Hill. In the skirmish twenty paratroops were killed and three mortars destroyed. The sound of firing and tank tracks seemed to have panicked the Germans and that night they withdrew, leaving Pink Hill to be occupied by the New Zealanders once again. However, this was the solitary success of the counter-attack as Blackburn's men found it impossible to locate the defenders around the Prison Valley area. Runners were eventually sent out to recall Blackburn's men back to New Zealand lines.

At Maleme the need for a counter-attack during the night was even more desperate. According to a German war correspondent only fifty-seven paratroopers remained fit for action around Maleme. Despite the heavy losses suffered by the enemy, the margin by which the defenders held Maleme was slipping away. Brigadier Hargest, the commander of the 5th New Zealand Brigade, was reluctant to utilise his reserves to assist Lieutenant Colonel Andrew who was the commanding officer of 22nd Battalion on Maleme airfield. The 22nd Battalion were subjected to constant air bombardment and concerted attacks on the RAF camp. During the afternoon Andrew was able to establish that the main German effort was directed at Hill 107 from the Tavronitis riverbed, and that he needed assistance to eliminate the threat. One of the main problems for Andrew was that he was unaware of what was happening to his companies in the vicinity of the airfield. The intense bombing severed lines of communication to his headquarters on the slopes of Hill 107, which also meant that British artillery batteries had communications with observation officers broken. By the early afternoon of the first day, Andrew fired emergency flares to signal that he needed assistance. The flare signal was lost in the smoke and debris around Maleme, which left Andrew with his only alternative, to request help via radio. At 17.00 Andrew contacted Hargest and requested forces for a counter-attack. Hargest informed Andrew that this was not possible as the 23rd Battalion were already engaged in fighting. In fact the 23rd Battalion was faced with no immediate threat and were only engaged in light skirmishes. It was evident that Hargest did not believe that Andrew's situation was serious enough to warrant the use of the 23rd Battalion.

Denied reinforcements, Andrew decided to create his own counter-attacking force from the 22nd New Zealand Battalion late that afternoon, when it was still daylight. The force was made up of two I tanks and some infantry led by C Company's Lieutenant Donald. Donald recalled: 'two I-tanks trundling up the road down in front of us. My platoon of about 28 blokes was supposed to go with the tanks and protect them, [but] we hadn't talked to them or made a plan.' Donald came up with an improvised plan. 'One section [was to go] on the right of the road, one section on the left . . . the other section on the road itself [to] protect the tanks.'[2] Donald's group initially made good progress, reaching the outer perimeter of the airfield without loss. They ignored the paratroops around the airfield and in the RAF camp; instead the tanks advanced towards the Tavronitis riverbed. 'It was pretty hopeless because it was broad open daylight. It was like the First World War – over the top in broad daylight . . . the first tank trundled off down the road being shot in every direction . . . [although the I tank was] fairly impervious to small-arms fire.' The first tank reached the riverbed where it engaged the enemy with its machine gun. The tank crushed a German mortar crew under its tracks, sending other paratroops running, before it became stuck among boulders on the edge of the Tavronitis where its turret jammed. Donald observed that the *I* tank 'got bogged down, and we saw them get out and surrender to the Germans. We'd counted 200 Germans at one time down there, [against] my platoon of 28 or thereabouts.' Without tanks, the infantry lacked cover and succumbed to withering fire. The counter-attack had failed and Donald's infantry suffered badly in their retreat. 'We hadn't caught up with the tanks at all. We tried, but we were shot at and [had] a number of casualties. I think we finished up with eight who weren't either wounded or killed out of 28 that we started with.' Donald's group eventually made contact with the second tank. 'The tank commander put his head out of the turret and said that an anti-tank shell had hit their turret and they couldn't turn it . . . I loaded several of my wounded blokes onto the lee side of the tank and the rest of us walked alongside with the tank to shelter us and we managed to get back to company headquarters . . . the attack was aborted. It was futile to start with.'[3]

The counter-attack had taken place around 17.00, and by 19.00 Donald's force had returned to company headquarters. Donald noted that their position at company headquarters was surrounded: 'I suppose we only had about ten or a dozen fighting troops left that weren't wounded or had been killed. Some were signallers and stretcher-bearers and that sort of thing, so it was fairly dicey. At this stage we couldn't make contact with our 13 Platoon. We knew 15 Platoon had been over-run. 13 Platoon [were still there] – and we couldn't make any contact with battalion head-quarters.'[4] The condition of each platoon varied greatly; some were running low on ammunition and had suffered heavy casualties, while others remained intact. After hearing about the failed counter-attack, C Company's commander, Captain Johnson, had reported to Andrew that he could probably hold on until dark but needed reinforcements. Andrew insisted that he must hold on at all costs, and that was the last com-munication from C Company. Andrew feared the worst after he had lost contact with the men directly concerned with the protection of the airfield. Although C Company had suffered heavy casualties, they were still holding their position and maintaining fire on the airfield. Andrew had also lost contact with D Company on the Tavronitis and assumed that they had been destroyed. D company had one of its members contact Andrew directly claiming that he was the sole survivor, therefore Andrew believed that there were only 200 men available to defend the area. D company was in fact holding their position on Hill 107, with one platoon intact and rallying survivors from others.

With his reserves expended and not much hope of further resources, Andrew decided that his only option was to abandon Hill 107. Tragically, there was plenty of unused support available from the 23rd and 28th (Maori) Battalions who had cleared nearly all of the parachutists in their area. At 18.00 Andrew reported to Hargest that the counter-attack had failed and stated his intention to withdraw. Hargest replied: 'If you must you must.'[5] A few minutes later, Hargest thought better of his remark and informed Andrew that he was belatedly sending two companies from the 23rd and 28th Battalions to help. No clear picture of the situation could be formed from the weak radio signal on Hill 107, so Hargest sent forward only two companies rather than the full battalion that Andrew demanded, and the situation required. Hargest's judgement suffered from poor communications as he was too far behind Andrew's position to contact him in person. The enemy were weaker than Hargest realised; a swift counter-attack from a full battalion could have cleared the enemy from the Tavronitis riverbed and removed the threat to Maleme airfield.

Andrew did not intend the withdrawal from Maleme to be permanent, and he planned to retake Hill 107 with the two fresh companies sent by Hargest, with his own exhausted men resting at the rear. However, Hargest's reinforcements failed to appear before dark, and Andrew took the decision to withdraw to B Company on the edge of Hill 107. Troops from the 23rd Battalion under Captain Watson arrived at Andrew's position at 22.00. Andrew immediately ordered Watson and his men to reoccupy the summit of Hill 107, which they accomplished without resistance. Shortly after they reached Hill 107, Watson's men engaged a German patrol, which left several wounded. The Maoris from the 28th Battalion, under Captain Rangi Royal, were the second company of troops intending to join Watson on Hill 107. But the Maoris failed to find Andrew's headquarters in the dark, and they clashed with German troops on the eastern edge of the airfield. After a brief battle they took the decision to return to the 21st Battalion. Fearing his position would be surrounded, the non-appearance of the second company pressed Andrew to take the fatal decision to recall Watson from Hill 107 and to fall back on New Zealand positions to the east. 'At that moment the best chance of holding Crete had been given up.' Geoffrey Cox commented; 'not because of any lack of courage or determination, but because of lack of knowledge.'[6]

As Andrew's men withdrew from their positions, they came across the bodies of Scherber's 3rd Battalion strewn across the battlefield. 'Crumpled German corpses littered the countryside . . . We stumbled over them . . . treading on stomachs, gargling hollow moans from lifeless lips.' Comeau noted: 'A few bodies hung from trees, twisted in their harnesses; unpleasant, yielding, fleshy obstacles to blunder against in the darkness.'[7] The delicate scent of thyme was progressively contaminated by the pungent stench of rotting flesh that was accelerated by the strength of the sun. The swollen black corpses were covered in swarms of flies where they lay; others hung from telephone wires and trees. Almost all of the dead were without equipment that had been looted by the defenders in search of decent boots and weapons. Some of the dead had single bullet wounds to the head, indicative of executions.

At 02.00 Andrew reached Colonel Leckie and the headquarters of 23rd Battalion near Dhaskaliana. It was still not too late to move the 23rd and 21st Battalions to retake Hill 107, leaving the remnants of the 22nd Battalion to act as a reserve. Crucially this decision was not taken; the local commanders did not put the policy of immediate counter-attack into practice and Hargest had not grasped the importance of the airfield. Despite suffering heavy losses, Andrew's C and D Companies were holding their positions, and the German assault had lost momentum. The forward companies could not be contacted by runners and thus had no idea that Andrew had withdrawn.

That evening Captain Campbell of D Company heard that the battalion headquarters had been withdrawn. In disbelief, Campbell ventured to the front to see for himself. When he got there he was shocked to discover that battalion headquarters had indeed withdrawn from Hill 107. Campbell felt that he had no alternative but to fall back. C Company under Captain Johnson remained on the airfield and was also unaware of Andrew's decision to withdraw. Haddon Donald of C Company noted: 'By this time it was getting dark and my runner, Jimmy Christian, [found his way through German lines] up to battalion headquarters, and came back and reported that there was nobody there.'[8] Donald was not convinced that battalion headquarters had disbanded and sent Christian back to check. At approximately 02.00 Christian returned after a thorough search of battalion headquarters convinced that they were deserted. Johnson was faced with a difficult decision, as he knew that his position was crucial to prevent German transports from landing by bringing direct fire on the airfield. However, with Andrew's force withdrawn, Johnson's group would be the focus of attack for the remainder of the paratroops and the Luftwaffe. Johnny Johnson finally decided that his company had little choice but to leave their position under the cover of darkness. After the battle Donald stated: 'Thank goodness he made that decision, because it was the right one.'

In the early hours of the morning, Johnson ordered his men to take their boots off and tie them around their necks. Silently, they made their way through groups of snoring Germans to the 21st Battalion position. Effectively the airfield was lost before the second day's fighting had begun and it was only possible to bring fire onto the eastern side of the airfield. Donald recalled the journey back to the 21st Battalion: 'I think we started moving at about 04.30 . . . By the time we got near the top of Point 107, it was starting to get light . . . and I saw a German helmet only about ten yards away, looking over a terrace . . . I couldn't restrain myself so I shot just below the helmet thinking there was a head there. The Germans were doing this on purpose trying to draw fire, which I hadn't realised . . . So I hauled out a grenade, and tossed it over. There must have been a few of them there because there were screams and yells . . . We disappeared smartly after that.' As they reached the top of the ridge in broad daylight, Donald spotted Ju 52s coming in very low over the sea. Donald raised his Tommy gun and started to shoot: 'you could see bullets holes going into the fuselage all the way down to the tail of the aircraft – I peppered it at about chest height. I could see the Germans sitting at each port hole . . . when we got back to Egypt, some of the boys who'd seen this said they'd crashed on the other side, and they'd watched it and nobody had come out, so they must have been pretty well annihilated.'[9] Donald and his men eventually joined up with 21st Battalion.

Captain Gericke admitted after the battle that his paratroops could not have endured a determined counter-attack; they were exhausted and without ammunition. The Germans waited throughout the night for the decisive assault on their position, but it did not materialise. Indeed it was the lack of German aggression during the night that allowed C and D Companies to withdraw without loss. At dawn the following morning, the paratroops around Maleme airfield were heartened to discover that Hill 107 was deserted. According to some German reports, Hill 107 fell after fierce resistance in the morning. In reality the paratroops were fighting each other as they ventured up either side of the slope.

Andrew and his men were subjected to intense bombardment during the day, and he had overestimated the strength of the enemy and under-estimated the willingness of his own men to stay and fight. However, Colonel Andrew stated after the battle: 'looking back now . . . I am convinced that the withdrawal at that time was the only possible action to take.'[10] Historian Christopher Buckley maintained that the airfield could not have been held had Andrew remained. He wrote that Andrew's force was too weak to hold the five-mile perimeter. Andrew was short of officers, and communications were poor due to damaged cables and lack of signals equipment. Headquarters was generally thought to be too far away from the front, situated near Platanias, which was at a distance of four miles from Maleme airfield. Corporal Michael Hanan, who was involved in the fighting around Maleme stated: 'The front was crying out for leadership. The conditions couldn't be assessed from the comfort of headquarters!'[11] Runners were unreliable as a form of communication; they were either hunted from the air or ambushed on the ground. Historian Ian Stewart claimed that it was the tendency for the com-manders in Crete to stay in their headquarters. On Crete, where the communications were so poor, it was vital for the commanders to keep in close contact with their forces. Stewart stated that in 'subsequent campaigns it was the accepted practice in the Division for commanders to be well forward'.[12]

Kippenberger and Andrew were sent too little too late. Both Hargest and Puttick were slow to react to the situation and left their reserves unengaged at the decisive point of the battle. Fresh troops directed at West or Centre Groups could have driven the paratroops from their positions into disarray. Moreover, during the night the Germans did not have the air support that had shaken Andrew's men during the first day. The possibility of a seaborne invasion seemed to paralyse the senior commanders who were reluctant to use reserves that they would store for future emergencies. Freyberg was also guilty of being too cautious; he supported Puttick in his decision to veto the plan to use the 4th Brigade to clear Prison Valley. Freyberg placed too much faith in his local commanders and failed to enforce his own convictions. The Official New Zealand History read that Freyberg 'gave his battalion commanders too much choice of a role with too little guidance',[13] the result being a premature withdrawal from Maleme, which handed Student the break he needed for his unlikely plan to work. Haddon Donald from the 22nd Battalion stated that the first German planes did not begin to land on the aerodrome until late in the evening on 20 May. 'The first German plane came . . . so I shot him up with this Browning [machine-gun taken from a Hurricane] and he crash-landed at the far end . . . The rest turned and flew off . . . nothing landed that evening, but they started to pour in next morning when we'd pulled out.'[14]

The capitulation of the defenders at Maleme meant that the German paratroops were given the hope of reinforcements. At 07.15 on 21 May an urgent signal was sent back to Athens which indicated salvation for Student. It read: 'Group West has taken the south-east corner of the airfield and the height 1 km to the south.'[15] Captain Kleye, a courageous pilot, was asked by Student to carry out a test landing on the western edge of Maleme airfield. Kleye arrived in Maleme later that morning and was able to land with relative ease, being subjected to only sporadic small arms and artillery fire. Shortly afterwards a second Ju 52 loaded with ammunition was flown to Maleme aerodrome by two pilots, Koenitz and Steinweg. The pilots had flown over the Aegean without permission after receiving a radio message from the survivors at Maleme stating that they were running out of ammunition. The appearance of the aircraft was greeted with cheers from the parachutists on the airfield. As the ammunition was being unloaded, Koenitz went in search of General Meindl, whom he found lying on a stretcher, delirious from his wounds. Meindl's confused mutterings about snow indicated that he thought he was back in the Norwegian campaign. Meindl, along with seven other wounded men, was taken aboard and successfully evacuated.

On hearing of Kleye's successful landing, Student immediately ordered General Ringel of the 5th Mountain Division, to prepare his troops to fly to Crete. The 5th Mountain Division had fought well in Greece and managed to break through against the Greeks at the Rupel Pass. The mountain troops had been held in reserve at Athens to be used in the battle for Crete. General Ringel's men were mostly Austrians and

Bavarians; they were brave and well disciplined but the majority were inexperienced and uncomfortable in their new aviation role. Student intended the mountain troops to perform an auxiliary role, but after the failure of the initial landings the fortune of the 5th Mountain Division was crucial for the success of the invasion of Crete.

Student's plan was to reinforce the original Assault Regiment at Maleme with his final parachute battalion before the landing of the mountain troops. The battalion was to be led by Colonel Bernard Ramcke, one of Student's toughest officers, who was described by the British as 'a fanatical Nazi'.[16] Ramcke was taken to Greece and assigned to instruct mountain troops in the techniques of air landings. On 20 May Ramcke formed a reserve parachute battalion from the remnants of Group East, who were now called into action. Ramcke was to assume command of Meindl's Storm Regiment (Group West) and secure the airfield at Maleme for the vital landing of troops from the mountain division. Colonel Ramcke and his reserve group of parachutists were to be dropped west of the Tavronitis under the protection of the surviving paratroops on the western section of the airfield. Two remaining companies from the 2nd Parachute Regiment were to be dropped east of the airfield perilously close to where the 5th Brigade were reorganising Colonel Andrew's survivors into the 21st and 23rd Battalions.

On the morning of 21 May Maleme, Prison Valley and Galatas were bombed and strafed to pave the way for the drop of parachutists consisting of 300 men, landing to the east and west of Maleme. When the air attack abated, the ominous drone of the transports could be heard. Twenty-four Ju-52 transports appeared in their customary formations of three, and the parachutists began to emerge. The parachute drop to the east of Maleme was as disastrous as that on the opening day of the battle. Faulty German intelligence once again landed their paratroops directly among the New Zealand 21st and 23rd Battalions, west of Platanias. Out of two companies dropped, only eighty men survived from the 2nd Parachute Regiment. On noticing the transports above them, the Maoris fixed bayonets and headed directly for the dropping zone. One eye-witness stated that he felt 'almost pity' for those who fell among the Maori lines; they slaughtered their enemy 'with fixed bayonets in a terrible skirmish, wiping out every invader'.[17] A New Zealand officer, armed only with a pistol, described how he ordered a Maori to bayonet a German who was playing dead. 'As he did so, he turned his head away not bearing the sight.' As they advanced farther they came across a 'giant of a man' [who was shouting] "Hants Oop!" with his hands in the air. The man fell to the rifle of the Maori as he was ordered by the officer to "shoot the bastard".'[18] Fresh German corpses now lay among Scherber's fallen men who had perished on the previous day. Many were shot in the air or as they struggled to free themselves from their harnesses. The majority did not have a chance to reach their containers, and the survivors who scrambled to safety established themselves at a farm in Pirgos. Among those killed was Dr Hartmann, whose medical section ceased to exist. Cornered in a ditch, Hartmann was shot through the head as he stood to fire his final two rounds. With this fresh slaughter of his remaining parachutists, the situation seemed even worse for Student. His motive for dropping these two companies behind 23rd Battalion lines seemed logical enough as he explained after the war. Student stated that it was reported to him that the 22nd Battalion had withdrawn during the night; Student assumed that the absence of a counter-attack meant that Freyberg's reserves had been expended and that the area would be empty. The irrational tactics of the Allied commanders on Crete had lulled Student into a false appraisal of the strength of the defenders, and a fresh slaughter of his paratroops.

An hour later at around 19.00, Ramcke's western group landed un-molested west of the Tavronitis, although forty men drifted out to sea and were drowned. As they plummeted into the waves, their canopies rested gently on top of the water. Despite Andrew's withdrawal, there was still intermittent sniper fire coming from the area around Hill 107, and several of the German reinforcements were hit as they rushed across the iron bridge over the Tavronitis. As Ramcke and his men approached the airfield they could see the first of the transports loaded with mountain troops beginning to land; their arrival had been delayed until early evening due to artillery fire on the dusty red runway. However, the nine field guns of the 5th Brigade to the east of the airfield remained in operation and maintained firing. Despite the failure to destroy the artillery shelling the runway, Student was forced into landing the mountain troops before darkness halted air operations. Some mountain troops disembarked from moving transports, other aircraft stopped on the runway with their engines running, unloaded and then quickly took off again, and many were destroyed by shellfire. Approximately twenty aircraft were destroyed by random artillery fire from the sightless guns of the defenders. The first of the transports received a direct hit and burst into flames, others simply crash landed and scraped along on their under-carriage breaking up in the process. A German war correspondent with the mountain troops commented that hours earlier they had been 'lying in the shade of our planes on the mainland and now we were being fired at from everywhere'.[19] For the mountain troops it was a disorienting experience; as they left their transports they were faced with the deafening noise of the engines, coupled with the burst of mortar bombs and the hollering of ground crews. The propellers of the aircraft threw up a blinding storm of red dust. Disembarked mountain troops were shaken by the shockwaves of the bombardment and they immediately dived for cover among a hellish confusion of exploding shells and burned out aircraft. To the defenders' astonishment the transports began to land with almost suicidal tenacity. As the wreckage on the airfield mounted, the Ju 52s began to crash land on the beaches or wherever they could find an open space, although the German pilots soon realised that those crash landing along the shore were sustaining heavy casualties and it was safer to land on the congested runway. With a ruthless determination, and disregard for casualties, the Germans endeavoured to keep the runway operational.

Despite the chaotic scenes and numerous losses at Maleme, Ramcke managed to land 650 fresh men by nightfall. As the troops of the 5th Mountain Division arrived, they were shocked by the state of the airfield and the men who defended it. The men of the 7th Parachute Division and Assault Regiment, who made the initial landings, were exhausted. No system of relief had been put in place, and many had not eaten for twenty-four hours; they were short of both ammunition and water. Ramcke divided his men into two sections; the first section would support the paratroopers engaged with Cretan partisans on the Paleochora road; the second section would defend the southern and western areas of the airfield, silencing the defenders' artillery. The Assault Regiment advanced along the coast towards Pirgos. As they moved towards Hill 107 they came under heavy counter-attacks from New Zealand stragglers and local Cretans. At Pirgos a German patrol encountered the New Zealand 23rd Battalion which left 200 Germans dead.

German patrols relied heavily on the assistance of dive-bombers. German observation aircraft circled constantly overhead waiting to unleash a devastating air attack on anything that moved. The omnipresent Luftwaffe had a debilitating effect on the defenders and German dominance in the air started to take its toll. Comeau stated: 'One by one in leisurely fashion, they peeled off screaming down in a vertical dive, air brakes extended, siren wailing.' After the bombs were released the chosen area would be 'plastered with high explosives, the torn and bleeding men dragged out of the line like bundles of blood stained rag'. A doctor from the Pioneer Corps noted the psychological effects: 'The continuous noise and concussion made one feel sick and dazed . . . the roar of its engine . . . the screech of its approach.'[20] The incessant tension undoubtedly affected the men on the ground. Nervous exhaustion was caused by the persistence of German bombers that circled in the sky like birds of prey; some would circle overhead for over an hour before retiring. The absence of the RAF caused resentment among the troops on the ground, who referred to them as 'Rare As Fairies'. For many the air attacks took on a personal tone. Private John Ede from the 23rd Battalion, recalled: 'I shall never forget the pilots' laughter as they dropped bombs and grenades on us.'[21] Stuka pilots had developed a special bomb with a proximity fuse to ensure a lethal spread of shrapnel from the rocky Cretan soil. A metal rod protruded from the bomb, so that it would explode above ground, thus spraying a more devastating array of shrapnel. From strafing aircraft alone, Sid

Raggett noted: 'We estimated that each bullet was having five goes at us as it ricocheted from rock to rock.'[22] That afternoon a German bomb hit an ammunition and petrol dump which reaffirmed the Luftwaffe's aura of power among the defenders as their surroundings took on an apocalyptic scene. Olive groves began to burn and the billowing smoke darkened the sky prematurely.

Student believed that the successful landing of the mountain troops had averted the crisis of the first day. However, in his original plan, Student had purposely limited the role of the mountain troops in the operation. General Ringel, who led the 5th Mountain Division, considered his men the elite of the German infantry and resented the pretensions of the Luftwaffe parachute troops. Rivalry between the two factions was endemic and conflict erupted in Athens between both soldiers and commanders. The rivalry was evident in Student's plan of attack; Ringel was the only commander not to be dropped in the initial landings. The 5th Mountain Division was originally intended to remain in Greece until the airfields were captured. Student hoped to establish his own headquarters on the island and thus assume direct control of the battle. If Student's operation had gone to plan, Ringel and the 5th Mountain Division would have been assigned to perform a mere mopping up role after the battle had been won by the parachute troops. It was assumed by Student that his parachute troops would take the glory and reinforce his standing within the military hierarchy of the Third Reich.

With the disastrous start to the campaign in Crete, Student quickly found himself under great pressure. Many of the German military hierarchy voiced their concerns over the obvious implications for BARBAROSSA. It was decided at a meeting attended by both Hitler and Goering that they would be forced to ask the Italians for assistance. Mussolini agreed to land troops from Rhodes on the eastern side of the island, but refused to risk naval action against the British. Goering was furious at the humiliating experience of having to ask Mussolini for assistance. After the losses of the first day both Hitler and Goering started to question Student's judgement. It was inconceivable that Student could be dismissed because of the impact on morale, but it was unofficially decided that he would no longer continue in his operational role. Student was subsequently ordered to remain in Greece and was refused permission to land in Crete. To add to Student's humiliation, General Ringel of the 5th Mountain Division was chosen to direct operations in Crete in his place. Ringel's military approach was summed up by his saying: 'Sweat saves lives.' In contrast to Student, Ringel was an Austrian Nazi who valued the traditional virtues of the soldier and had been sceptical of Student's plan from the outset. Ironically, Student had to accept that his rival would take control of his operation at a time when perhaps the balance of the battle had tilted in the Germans' favour.

The fluency of the landing of air transports at Maleme was increasingly worrying for the defenders. A staff officer at CREFORCE headquarters observed through binoculars that it took a transport 'seventy seconds to land and clear its men and gear'.[23] As the afternoon wore on, the gravity of the situation eventually hit Freyberg and he began to make plans for a decisive counter-attack that would commit the whole of 5th New Zealand Brigade. At 16.00 on 21 May Freyberg summoned a conference in CREFORCE headquarters to establish plans for the forthcoming operation. Brigadiers Puttick and Inglis attended along with the senior Australian officer, Brigadier Vasey. Hargest discussed the matter at length with Puttick, and by 18.00 the senior officers finally acknowledged the need for a counter-offensive. A counter-attack was to be launched with two battalions under the cover of darkness, with the objective of recapturing Maleme airfield before dawn. Freyberg also requested an RAF bombing raid from Cairo, but his request was not acted on immediately. The mission was flown the following night and was largely ineffectual.

The inadequate force devoted to the attack undermined the operation from the outset. Only two battalions from 5th Brigade would be used for the counter-attack, the 28th (Maori) and the 20th Battalions, supported by three light tanks. The start-line was to be to the west of the Platanias river. Lieutenant Colonel Dittmer, who commanded the Maoris, was concerned about possible delays caused by enemy pockets of resistance between the start-line and Pirgos, where fresh paratroops had taken refuge earlier that morning. Dittmer suggested that an advance party be sent to clear the area in advance. However, it was determined that 'it was too late for any clearing up activity'.[24] The 20th Battalion would advance along the Maleme to Platanias coastal road where enemy parachutists awaited them, lodged in houses and dug in behind walls and ditches.

The 20th New Zealand Battalion was tasked with clearing the airfield while the Maoris attempted to capture Hill 107. The two battalions were to move parallel to each other along the road with the three light tanks in between. Once they reached and cleared the village of Pirgos, there would be a thirty-minute rest period before the 20th Battalion cleared the airfield and the Maoris re-captured Hill 107. These two battalions were expected to defeat a well-armed battalion of freshly landed mountain troops. Hargest stated that after these objectives were met, the Maoris were to withdraw to Plantanias. This meant that the 20th Battalion had to occupy and defend both Hill 107 and the airfield. It is hard to comprehend Hargest's thinking, which seemed wildly optimistic. If Andrew's battalion failed to hold on to the position on the first day, it is difficult to understand how the 20th Battalion could achieve the feat after fighting a prolonged counter-attack throughout the night. Moreover, they were faced with an enemy that was twice the strength of that on the first day after being reinforced by fresh troops. If the 20th Battalion and the Maoris joined the rest of 5th Brigade, their cumulative strength would have been five battalions. If this force moved as a solid group, there was a good chance of pushing the enemy off the airfield and into the Tavronitis. However, in the event of the first stage of the counter-attack proving successful, there is no record of orders for the three remaining battalions of 5th Brigade to move forward and support the 20th Battalion. The only instructions given to the remaining 21st and 23rd Battalions in the event of a successful counter-attack were vague orders for a consolidation role.

The operation laid a heavy burden on the infantry of 20th and 28th (Maori) Battalions; their main hope lay in speed of execution and utilising the dark hours when the Luftwaffe could not operate. However, the counter-attack was to be carried out under debilitating conditions that dictated the timing of the operation and fatally restricted the chances of success. The Australian 2/7th Battalion, based in Georgioupolis, was to be redeployed to replace the 20th Battalion guarding the western coast of Canea. This meant transporting the Australian battalion eighteen miles before the counter-attack could begin. To make matters worse, the Australians were lacking adequate transport and were not in direct contact with headquarters. It was presumed that this manoeuvre would not be completed before midnight; therefore the attack was scheduled to take place at 01.00, giving them only a few hours of darkness before the Luftwaffe appeared again.

If the second counter-attack failed and German strength continued to grow, the defending troops in the Maleme area would be forced to fall back and concede the aerodrome. With the aerodrome under German control, they could increase their strength at will by landing aircraft and ultimately win the battle for the island. Freyberg's acceptance of the deficient arrangements surrounding the counter-attack could be explained partly by the faith placed in his local commanders, but also by his insistence on covering an invasion from the sea. One of Freyberg's staff officers wrote that the 'counter-attack was overshadowed by an impending event closer at hand. The seaborne invasion was under way.'[25]

On the morning of 21 May Freyberg received an intercept that made reference to seaborne landings: 'Arrival of the seaborne contingent consisting of anti-aircraft batteries as well as of more troops and supplies.'[26] As with the other intercepts, the signal was looked at by Freyberg alone and then destroyed. Freyberg was not confident that the Mediterranean Fleet was capable of protecting Suda Bay from a seaborne invasion, although the message did not suggest that the Germans, or the Italians, possessed landing craft or ships. Furthermore, the operational plans captured from the Germans clearly indicated that operations on the island did not refer to a large seaborne invasion, but instead indicated that a 'light ships' group would land west of Maleme. A further signal received on the afternoon of 21 May stated that later that day there would be an 'air landing [of] two mountain battalions and attack[on] Canea. Landing from [a] echelon of small ships depending on situation at sea.'[27] Historian Anthony Beevor maintains that Freyberg appeared to have disregarded the phrase 'air landing', and put emphasis on the words 'Canea' and 'Landing', missing out the full stop in between. Therefore Freyberg believed the attack on Canea would be from the sea rather than from the paratroopers in Prison Valley, or a bombing raid. Regardless of Beevor's theory about the missing full stop, it is difficult to understand how Freyberg calculated that an 'echelon of small ships' could mean a significant invasion force with armour. Soon after receiving the information from ULTRA, Freyberg issued the order: 'Reliable information. Early seaborne attack in area [of] Canea likely.'[28] Freyberg went on to state that the New Zealand Division would hold the coast from the west to the Kladiso river and the Welch Battalion, his largest and best equipped battalion, would remain in Canea to secure the coast. Also he would only allow Inglis to release the 20th Battalion from his 4th Brigade after it had been replaced by the Australian 2/7th Battalion based at Georgioupolis, thus seriously undermining the chances of success for the counter-attack. Of the belated release of the 20th Battalion he wrote: 'I could not leave this covering position near Canea unheld.' Freyberg maintained that had the Germans landed at Canea as planned 'we should have lost all our supplies and ammunition'. Freyberg assumed responsibility: 'I gave the order; neither Puttick nor Inglis was responsible for the delay.'[29] Freyberg later stated that the reason that he could not leave the Canea beach unprotected was that intelligence reports had given him 'precise information about the enemy seaborne attack . . . We knew that a seaborne force was en route for the coast near Canea.' Freyberg recalled that he had placed 'the 20th Battalion specifically to meet it. I felt that the Australians . . . could not occupy the defences without a proper handover.'[30] Freyberg's comments seem to discount the claim that he was never specifically concerned about the seaborne landings. After the war, Freyberg still did not realise that the German flotilla had been directed at Maleme not Canea. Freyberg misread the ULTRA signals and was not prepared to trust the Royal Navy to protect the island.

Far from the invasion fleet that Freyberg feared, the seaborne landing consisted of only nineteen caiques (long narrow rowing boats used in the eastern Mediterranean) and two small rusty steamers, escorted by an Italian light destroyer, the *Lupo*. The convoy transported only the 3rd Battalion of the 100th Mountain Regiment with heavy supplies along with flak batteries. Another Italian destroyer, the *Sagittario*, escorted a second convoy, which carried the 2nd Battalion of the 85th Mountain Regiment. An Italian escort was necessary as the German fleet were unable to pass the British guns at Gibraltar. ULTRA had built up a good picture of the

German flotilla and at dusk Cunningham received crucial signals intelligence stating the precise nature of the German convoy of slow moving caiques, and had picked their course from Milos to Maleme. Cunningham followed the security precautions surrounding ULTRA by sending out a Maryland aircraft to sight the flotilla before the fleet made contact.

The engagement lasted around two and a half hours, during which time the steamers and around a dozen caiques were sunk. Geoffrey Cox described the battle as he saw it from the shore. 'Suddenly on the horizon . . . came the flash and thunder of guns, and the dull red glow of burning vessels.'[31] As the deep booms resonated across the island, Von der Heydte watched the battle at sea from the summit of a hill. He likened the destruction of the German convoy to a giant firework display: 'Rockets and flares were shooting into the night sky . . . searchlights probed the darkness . . . distant detonations lent sound to this dismal sight.' Von der Heydte recalled that it was 'too easy to guess what had happened. The British Mediterranean Fleet had intercepted our light squadron and . . . destroyed it.'[32] Freyberg was reported to be 'bouncing up and down' like an excited schoolboy at the destruction of the caiques.[33] The seaborne expedition had been a failure; only a single caique had reached Crete intact. In the caves of CREFORCE headquarters there seemed little doubt that with the seaborne landing smashed, and with the decisive counter-attack planned, the battle for the island had been won. Freyberg turned to Brigadier Stewart and said: 'Well, Jock, it has been a great responsibility.'[34] Freyberg and his comrades in headquarters had gone to bed that evening relieved that their main fear of a seaborne invasion was alleviated. Cox recalled: 'I for one climbed into my sleeping bag in Bell's dug-out with a feeling of profound thankfulness.' Cox admitted to feeling almost disappointed 'that it had all been over so swiftly'.[35] Freyberg did not ask for a progress report before retiring; he 'clearly thought the battle was as good as won'.[36] Unknown to those at CREFORCE headquarters, the decisive battle for Crete had yet to be fought. The fixation with the seaborne landings had already tilted the battle in favour of the Germans.

While the battle at sea was taking place, the final preparations for the vital counter-attack on Maleme airfield were being completed. Roy Farran led his light tanks along the coast towards Maleme, where he could make out the burning wrecks out to sea of the failed German flotilla. Farran's tanks were to be used to spearhead the counter-attack. On reaching brigade headquarters, Farran met with Brigadier Puttick whom he described as a 'red open faced man, who looked like a country farmer: it was obvious that he was suffering from acute fatigue'. Puttick asked Farran to wait outside while he had some sleep. Farran was himself in need of sleep; he had been fighting non-stop for almost forty-eight hours. Farran recalled: 'Disgusted, intolerant we sat on the steps until he was ready.' Farran regarded the counter-attack as 'almost certain suicide'.[37] The counter-attack would be attempted with no artillery support, which meant that they would have to advance without a barrage. To make matters worse Farran was warned that the enemy had captured two Bofors guns. When Farran pointed out that his tanks were thinly armoured and the job was more suited to I tanks, he was told that 'beggars cannot be choosers'.[38] The I tanks had been put out of action the previous day. Farran's reservations were exacerbated after the transfer of the 2/7th Australians cast doubt on whether the operation should have taken place at all.

The Australians, under Major Marshall, endeavoured to complete the transfer with the 20th Battalion as quickly as possible. They drove along a winding coastal road and made good progress despite being under fire from Messerschmitts. Marshall's forward party reached the New Zealand 20th Battalion at 20.00. However, the rear of the column became lost in the narrow streets of Canea, which caused a fatal delay. Colonel Dittmer of the 28th (Maori) Battalion implored Hargest to bring the 20th Battalion up to the start-line before the arrival of the Australians. Hargest contacted Puttick to ask his permission to release the 20th Battalion. Despite having witnessed the destruction of the German flotilla, Puttick refused on the grounds that a seaborne landing might be attempted in 20th Battalion's area that night. Brigadier Burrows from the 20th Battalion had also asked to move his battalion before the arrival of the Australians but he was refused. The handover between the Australians and the 20th Battalion was not complete until after 23.30, when the New Zealanders made their way towards the Platanias bridge. It was 02.45 before the first companies from 20th Battalion reached the start-line; the Maoris had been kept waiting for three hours. At this stage only Companies C and D had arrived. Brigadier Burrows decided if the attack was to get underway before daylight 'there was no option but to put in the attack with the two companies only'. At this point Hargest's optimism faded fast and he questioned 'whether the plan could be carried through at all'.[39] Puttick insisted that the attack must go ahead. The march from Platanias began at 03.30, two and a half hours later than scheduled. This meant they would be exposed to air attacks and had lost the advantage of night operations. The 20th Battalion advanced along the right side of the road along the coast with the 28th (Maori) Battalion on the left of the road covering inland. The three light tanks clanked down the road between them; a section of the Maori infantry followed them who were detailed to protect the tanks from Molotov cocktails.

On the left of the road the 28th (Maori) Battalion made easy progress. The 23rd Battalion had previously cleared their path of parachutists who had withdrawn northwards towards the coastal strip where the 20th Battalion were advancing. The 20th Battalion encountered enemy resistance almost immediately; a burst of German machine-gun fire accounted for four of the battalion before they could take cover. The Germans were using explosive bullets and they erupted in a shower of flames as they hit trees. Arcs of tracer fire poured out of various buildings and lit up the night sky. The New Zealanders of the 20th Battalion did their best to clear the resistance quickly, but every other vineyard or isolated farmhouse seemed to contain parachutists equipped with machine guns. The commander of C Company, Lieutenant Charles Upham, led a frontal assault despite suffering from dysentery. Much of the German machine-gun fire was high, and the tracer bullets enabled Upham to locate his targets. Using this method he crawled within yards of the enemy before hurling grenades through windows and into ditches. Upham recalled that there were: 'plenty of grenades and a lot of bayonet work which you don't often get in war'. Upham single-handedly destroyed three machine-gun nests for which he won a Victoria Cross. Upham recalled that the Germans were unprepared. 'The Germans were helpless in the dark . . . Some were without trousers, some had no boots on.'[40] He also noted that his men had taken heavy casualties but the Germans had suffered much more heavily.

As Farran's group advanced they came under fire. His light tanks returned fire. Farran recalled: 'I sprayed the front with my tracers and was lucky enough to hit an ammunition dump.' Farran likened the explosion to: '"Golden rain" at the Crystal Palace'.[41] The section of Maoris assigned to Farran had suffered heavy casualties in the dark. Farran was unaware that they were under such heavy fire and was surprised to see his group depleted. The tanks soon approached the village of Pirgos, where the Germans had established strongly held positions. Farran noticed that the lead tank was advancing too quickly towards the village and was leaving his group behind. As they turned the corner of the street, the lead tank was hit by a captured Bofors gun fired from a churchyard, the tank tried to retreat, but was immediately struck by another shell. The tank's gunner was killed instantly, and the tank commander, Sergeant Skedgewell, was 'mashed in his seat'. The driver had a serious foot wound and astonished Farran by his ability to continue to operate the tank. Still ablaze, the tank was driven to safety. Skedgewell was 'writhing in mortal agony' and screaming for Farran to get him out. Farran attempted to pull Skedgewell out, but his sweat-soaked shirt tore in his hands. Skedgewell was in great pain and: 'obviously beyond all hope' so Farran administered some morphia '(perhaps too much)' to ease the pain.[42] Stretcher-bearers told Farran that Skedgewell had died twenty minutes later.

As day broke, the sky was filled with hundreds of aircraft, a: 'swarm of Me 109s like angry buzzing bees'. They set their sights on Farran's remaining two tanks. Hot flakes of metal ricocheted around Farran's turret from the impact of the German fighters' bullets. In an attempt to escape the onslaught, 'like a wounded bull trying to shake off a cloud of flies', Farran drove his tank through a bamboo grove damaging a wheel in the process.[43] Farran faced a terrifying wait as the wheel from the wreck of Skedgewell's tank was fitted to his own vehicle. A fire started by strafing aircraft had burnt away the bamboo surrounding Farran's tank, leaving it exposed. In between running for cover from strafing aircraft, the tank was eventually made roadworthy. Farran was then ordered to return to Maleme to assist D Company at the aerodrome. The third tank in Farran's party was ordered to withdraw, leaving the infantry with no armour.

The Maoris bypassed Pirgos village to the west and approached the rear slopes of Hill 107, where they were pinned down in broad daylight by heavy machine-gun fire. The Maoris advanced towards Hill 107 under a deadly cross fire from the lower slopes of the hill and from houses on the fringe of Pirgos. Major Dyer reported: 'Men were hit, men were maimed. The din of the fight was incessant.' The Maoris were outnumbered against an enemy with four or five times their firepower. German machine-gunners were seen running through the trees. Dyer noted: 'bullets and mortar bombs were cracking around us . . . There seemed to be German machine-guns behind all the trees.'[44]

The Maoris mounted repeated bayonet charges under incessant air attack and effective enemy fire. Colonel Dittmer led by example; he encouraged to their feet men who had been driven to ground from enemy fire, and so the attack went on. Major Dyer described how the Germans had raised a counter-attack: 'the red nazi banners erected on poles before they came at us'. As the Germans advanced, the Maoris emerged from some trees and charged to meet them 'crying "Ah! Ah!" and firing from the hip'. The Germans ran for their lives down a nearby gulley. Dyer marvelled at the spontaneous nature of the charge and stated: 'the ancestral fighting urge was a truly magnificent thing.'[45] Ned Nathan recalled: 'At times we ran into our own troops and fired upon them. That was very sad.'[46] Despite the bravery of the 28th Battalion they were unable to advance any farther due to the sheer volume of enemy fire against them. Nathan stated that the Maoris suffered considerable casualties. Nathan himself was shot through the hip and jaw, losing the sight in one eye. When Nathan regained consciousness he found himself surrounded by dead and wounded. Stretcher-bearers took Nathan away from the immediate battle, but they had no medication for so many wounded. They advised the walking wounded to head for the advanced dressing station. Those who were incapable of walking were left by the side of the road. On reaching the dressing station, Nathan discovered that it consisted of a single slit trench. The doctor had been wounded, which left the sergeant of the medical section to deal with all the wounded on his own.

In Pirgos itself, A and C Company from 20th Battalion had entered the village and were involved in bitter house-to-house fighting. The attackers missed the tanks of Farran badly as they fought their way through a maze of streets. Some Germans ran along the roofs of houses dropping grenades as they passed; others hid in cellars until their enemy advanced beyond them, and then emerged to attack them from behind. Despite a valiant effort from the attackers, they were too few to clear the village. C Company could not afford to expend their reserves clearing each hiding place, so they endeavoured to push on through hoping that the 23rd Battalion would be following up behind them. However, the 23rd Battalion under Colonel Leckie made no move for the third day running.

D Company advanced from the coast to the edge of the airfield where they were held up by mortar and machine-gun fire. As D Company approached the airfield only one officer, Lieutenant Maxwell, remained uninjured. Maxwell reported seeing 'stacks of aircraft, some crashed some not'. In broad daylight and with clear ground in front of them, D Company was pushed back after being subjected to intense machine-gun and mortar fire from Colonel Ramcke's paratroopers. B Company arrived belatedly and were ordered to assist D Company maintain their position on the edge of the airfield. B Company found little natural cover and was exposed to strafing German aircraft and fire from German positions on the slopes of Hill 107. B Company was effectively paralysed, pinned down by enemy fire. Captain Rice of B Company was killed and one of his lieutenants fatally wounded.

The 21st New Zealand Battalion, under Lieutenant-Colonel Allen, attempted to support the counter-attack by moving towards the southern slopes of Hill 107 on the left flank. While the 20th and 28th Battalions had fought to a standstill, a tremendous effort by the 21st Battalion pushed the German mountain troops back. The 21st Battalion benefited from little interference from the Luftwaffe whose attention was drawn by the more immediate threat of the 20th and 28th Battalions. However, Ramcke's men were able to recover from the shock of the New Zealand counter-attack and were pushing hard against positions on Vineyard Ridge. By mid afternoon, Allen's men were in desperate need of support and were eventually pushed back to their original positions on Vineyard Ridge. Shortly afterwards a German officer approached Allen with a white flag and passed over a note demanding the surrender of his men. Allen screwed the note up and threw it in the messenger's face and the German officer quickly retreated.

Major Burrows of the 20th Battalion decided that the only way to change the course of the battle was to bring his men to the aid of Dittmer and the Maoris attack on Hill 107. By midday, Burrows had disengaged and manoeuvred all his men south of the road behind the Maoris, all except D Company under Maxwell who had misread the order and retreated to Platanias. When contact was made with the Maoris, it was learned that all four Maori companies were pinned down by enemy fire. The regimental aid post had run out of medical dressings and was full of wounded from both sides. The New Zealanders were short of Bren ammunition, grenades and mortar bombs. The failed tank attack was the centrepiece on which the success of the other companies hinged. The counter-attack had lost its momentum and the Germans increased the pressure after bringing forward three fresh companies from the 85th Mountain Regiment's 2nd Battalion. Without further infantry support the attack could progress no further.

Realising the seriousness of the situation, Colonel Dittmer contacted Leckie and Andrew, asking for support for a renewed attack. This was a reasonable request considering the 23rd Battalion had thus far seen little action, and three companies of the 22nd remained intact. However, neither Leckie nor Andrew had shown the qualities of Dittmer's aggressive leadership, and they decided that the best course of action was to 'hold what ground they had, and stop the enemy infiltration that was constantly going on'.[47] This decision effectively brought the counter-attack to a halt. Leckie and Andrew had shown a lack of understanding of what Dittmer was trying to achieve; whether this was due to bad leadership or a result of poor communication, the fact remained that consolidation of their position was irrelevant in the wider context of the battle. Historian Dan Davin wrote: 'Ultimately the withdrawal from Maleme was to entail the loss of Crete.'[48] Maleme airfield represented the Germans' only source of effectively reinforcing their troops. Student had expended the last of his parachute reserves and without the airfield they would be forced to crash land transports in open country, which their resources could not sustain. If denied the airfield, the Germans were isolated, but with the airfield in their possession, it was only a matter of time before Freyberg's men were overwhelmed.

At Maleme airfield, German troops continued to land amidst exploding shells and gunfire. ULTRA revealed that one squadron had lost thirty-seven aircraft. Von der Heydte recalled: 'They lay there immovable, like giant captured birds.'[49] Maleme airfield was littered with the burnt out wrecks of German transports, many of which were on fire, sending plumes of smoke into the evening sky. Albert Snowadzki's airfield control party laboured to clear the runway of wrecks with a captured Bren Carrier, which made an effective bulldozer. Snowadzki resorted to ruthless methods in order to keep the runway operational. In contravention of the Geneva Convention, British prisoners were forced to work at Maleme, unloading planes and repairing shell holes. Robert Julian Lawrence stated that the Germans had other motivation for taking prisoners: 'There was an order from higher authority to take no prisoners on the island.' However, 'the local commander had ordered the taking of prisoners in order to provide himself with forced labour for unloading supplies.'[50] Forty prisoners of war were forced to work at the aerodrome; one prisoner who refused to work was 'shot dead before the other prisoners'.[51] It was reported that several other men who refused to work were also executed. 'The aerodrome was under shellfire ... and the prisoners suffered heavy casualties. They were not allowed to attend their own wounded.'[52] Flight Sergeant Wilkinson stated that the only food he ate in three days was what he had looted from German dead. Despite suffering from a knee injury, Wilkinson was forced to repair shell craters and unload ammunition. Wilkinson described the German attitude towards the prisoners as 'entirely callous and indifferent'. However, Wilkinson noted that the behaviour of his German captors 'appeared to be dictated by a general and official policy rather than vindictiveness on the part of the individual'. When not in the presence of their superiors the German troops behaved humanely towards their prisoners, but they 'conformed, it seemed, to orders from higher authority in the presence of officers or NCO's'.[53]

As the morning wore on, Hargest's positive frame of mind returned and he formed the ludicrously optimistic notion that the Germans were preparing to evacuate the island. Hargest reported: 'Steady flow of enemy planes landing and taking off. May be trying to take troops off. Investigating.' Hargest's message to headquarters read: 'it appears as though the enemy might be preparing evacuation.'[54] Hargest reported seeing men running towards aircraft before they took off; these were in fact unloading parties. As the day developed, the reality of the situation was relayed to Hargest and his optimism quickly faded. Hargest began to exaggerate the exhaustion of his men and claimed that they were incapable of further action. Hargest formed his opinion without visiting the front; whether the realisation that the Germans were not leaving the island had interfered with his judgement is unclear.

At 17.00 Freyberg was informed that the counter-attack at Maleme had failed. With the threat from the sea abated, it seemed that he grasped the idea that it was vital to dislodge the Germans from the aerodrome at Maleme. Freyberg ordered a further counter-attack with two fresh battalions from 4th Brigade, the 2/8th Australian and 18th New Zealand Battalions. During the afternoon Puttick was met by Hargest who stated that the troops of 5th Brigade were: 'exhausted, and certainly not fit to make a further attack.'[55] At the end of the conversation with Hargest, Puttick decreed that the 5th Brigade was unfit to take any further part in the assault and should be withdrawn from their positions. Around 19.00 Puttick contacted CREFORCE headquarters and recommended the withdrawal of the 5th New Zealand Brigade to Platanias, even though it meant the loss of the island. Freyberg apparently did not argue.

Puttick was extremely concerned about reports of enemy activity around Galatas and Prison Valley. Movements in the hills north of Prison Valley provoked fears that Heidrich's forces were attempting to encircle Freyberg's forces at Maleme. The prospect of six battalions being cut off

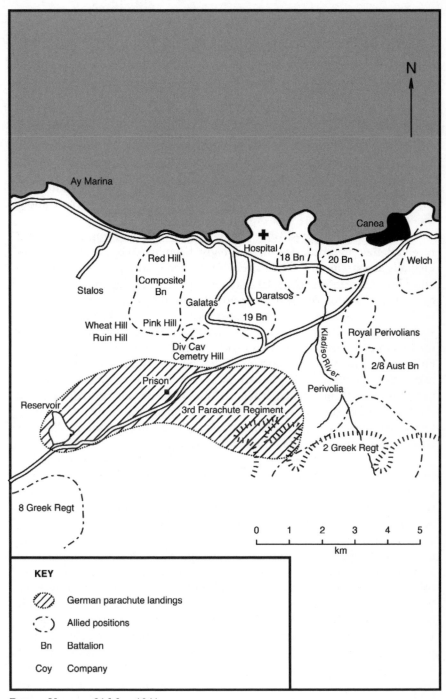

N

Ay Marina

Canea

Hospital

Red Hill   18 Bn   20 Bn   Welch

Composite
Bn

Stalos   Daratsos

Galatas

Wheat Hill   Pink Hill   19 Bn

Ruin Hill

Div Cav
Cemetry Hill

Royal Perivolians

2/8 Aust Bn

Prison

Reservoir   3rd Parachute Regiment

Perivolia

2 Greek Regt

8 Greek Regt

Kladiso River

0   1   2   3   4   5

km

KEY

German parachute landings

Allied positions

Bn   Battalion

Coy   Company

PRISON-VALLEY, 21 MAY 1941

193

and forced to surrender at Maleme would have signalled the destruction of Freyberg's forces in Crete, and had profound political implications. Puttick's concern with enemy movements in the Prison Valley area was in fact a scout group looking to make contact with the freshly landed mountain troops. Freyberg had retired to bed the previous night believing the battle was won, so the news that the counter-attack had failed would have been a shock. The unexpected turn of events, coupled with Hargest's pessimistic account, meant that Freyberg did not consider his options. It was clear that Freyberg did not want to be responsible for the destruction of his fellow countrymen's division. Therefore, Freyberg and his senior commanders decided to preserve the New Zealand 5th Brigade as a fighting unit and withdraw them to Platanias. Beevor described Freyberg as not the sort of general from the First World War who did not care about the 'Butcher's Bill' [but] 'was curiously soft-hearted'.[56]

Von der Heydte noted on 22 May: 'What little ammunition we had received the previous day had already been used up, and food was virtually unobtainable.'[57] In Prison Valley the Germans were contained and Heidrich continued to drive his 3rd Parachute Regiment in attacks against the heights of Galatas. Heidrich ordered a group led by Major Heilmann to manoeuvre to the north-west of Galatas through Stalos to seal off the coastal road and make contact with Storm Regiment. As cover for Heilmann's group, Hedrich ordered Major Derpa to recapture Pink Hill and storm New Zealand positions on the Galatas heights. Derpa expressed doubts and explained to Heidrich that he foresaw an un-necessary loss of life. Heidrich accused him of cowardice; von der Heydte recalled the blood draining from Derpa's face; after a momentary pause, Derpa saluted and replied: 'I am considering the lives of the soldiers for whom I am responsible. My life I would give gladly.'[58]

Derpa launched the attack with strong air support and succeeded in reaching the summit of Pink Hill where he established machine-gun positions. Kippenberger was faced with committing his last reserves when suddenly there came a terrific clamour from behind. Out of the trees appeared Captain Forrester clad in shorts, without a helmet, and in a long yellow army jersey to the bottom of his shorts, brass polished and gleaming. Kippenberger described Forrester as the 'the very opposite of soldier hero; as if he had just stepped onto the parade ground'. Forrester rallied the support of over 400 Greeks before leading them on a frenzied bayonet charge, 'tooting a tin whistle like the Pied Piper.'[59] Waving his revolver in the air, Forrester led a disorderly charge of Greeks including women. Kippenberger recalled Forrester's men appearing over an open plain, 'bounding and yelling like Red Indians . . . led by Michael Forrester twenty yards ahead'. Captain Smith witnessed Forrester's charge as they jogged forward, 'yelling "aera" or something like that, which I was told was the Evzones' war-cry'. Faced with this chaotic onslaught, the

Germans turned and ran without hesitation. Smith recalled: 'It was very effective, and the whole show was the most thrilling moment of my life.'[60] Forrester inspired great admiration among the New Zealanders who tended to view British officers as stereotypically conservative. Michael Forrester had trained a band of 200 Greeks in the basics of warfare and tactics. He overcame the language barrier by operating a series of simple whistle signals. Beevor described Forrester as 'an almost mythical leader of irregulars in the battle against German paratroopers'.[61]

Von der Heydte watched through his binoculars as his men suffered heavy casualties and tumbled back down the hill. Among the German casualties was Major Derpa, who was buried in a small Greek cemetery near the prison in Prison Valley. Forrester's small victory in Prison Valley was to be short-lived. The withdrawal of 5th Brigade would allow the Germans advancing from Maleme to join with those at Prison Valley, who had not been reinforced since the first day's fighting.

Later that evening General Ringel arrived in Crete with a large fighter escort. Ringel immediately went about deploying his troops in offensive positions, a sign that the German military hierarchy required a swift ending to the conflict. After the failure of the counter-attack, Ringel was confident of victory and was eager to enforce German domination of the island. Ringel divided his forces into three sections; the first was a battalion of mountain troops under Major Schätte. Schätte's group were to advance towards Kastelli to secure the landing of tanks. The surviving paratroops around Maleme were merged into a battle group under the command of Ramcke, who were to defend Maleme airfield and advance along the coastal road towards Canea. The third group under Colonel Utz was made up of the remainder of the mountain troops. They were under orders to outflank New Zealand positions on Vineyard Ridge.

At 00.15 the orders for the withdrawal were finalised. Captain Dawson arrived at 23rd Battalion headquarters and informed Leckie that they were to withdraw to Platanias. Leckie's reaction was one of surprise; he stated that no 'unit representatives present considered they would have any difficulty disengaging [although] All were of the opinion that we could hold the position.'[62] The 5th New Zealand Brigade could not believe the order to withdraw. Sandy Thomas, a platoon commander of the 23rd Battalion, wrote of his troops: 'They had seen so many of the enemy dead that their morale was quite unshaken by the terrific air attacks by the day.' Thomas concluded: 'Man for man they considered that they could lick the German despite his superior weapons and equipment.'[63] From the moment the withdrawal was promulgated to the troops, the scent of victory was replaced by the stench of defeat. The defenders believed they were more than a match for the Germans, but the order to withdraw undoubtedly stirred memories of Greece. As had occurred on the mainland, the wounded were taken away on improvised stretchers and artillery was destroyed.

Dittmer's Maori battalion, which bore the brunt of the counter-attack, were dealt a final indignity when the 28th Battalion was selected to act as rearguard for the withdrawal. Dittmer commented: 'I knew that the enemy would see other units going over high ground to the east and then the 28th Battalion would catch it.'[64] The Germans followed the Maoris closely, towing captured Bofors with Volkswagens. The Maoris stopped on three occasions and fought brave running battles with their German pursuers.

In the morning of 23 May weary troops began to disengage and filter back towards Platanias. The withdrawal to Platanias was the crucial turning point of the battle that effectively gave Ringel control of the airfield, which was now out of range of artillery fire. Freyberg argued that even if he used all of his available forces for a counter-attack on 21 and 22 May, they still could not have forced the Germans off the airfield. The delay of the counter-attack, caused by the movement of troops to secure the sea defences, was dismissed by Freyberg who stated that if the counter-attack was successful: 'We might have driven a wedge into the enemy's position but we still could not have broken the core of his defence.'[65] Beevor maintains that Freyberg had not appreciated the gravity of the situation at Maleme. Freyberg had three uncommitted battalions, the New Zealand 18th Battalion, the Australian 2/7th and the Welch Regiment. Had these battalions joined the 23rd Battalion and the Maoris in an all-out counter-attack, they could have forced the Germans from the airfield.

By 14.00 on 23 May the withdrawal was complete. During the morning Churchill sent Freyberg a message stating: 'The whole world is watching your splendid battle, on which great events turn.'[66] During the afternoon Churchill contacted General Wavell and was typically direct: 'Crete must be won. Even if [the] enemy [has] secure[d] good lodgements.' Churchill demanded: 'Is it not possible to send more tanks and thus reconquer any captured aerodrome?' The Prime Minister concluded by stating that the 'enemy's exertions and loss in highest class troops must be very severe. He cannot keep it up forever.'[67] Unknown to Churchill, the time for recapturing territory had been passed up by those in command on Crete. The best outcome now would be a prolonged stalemate that forced Germany to withdraw in preparation for their impending attack against Russia.

When Puttick and Hargest ruled out the prospect of a further counter-attack on the 22 May, all hope of a clear-cut victory went with it. Given the opportunities that had been spurned, it is true to say that a second counter-attack was a gamble, but surely it was worth taking. The failure to counter-attack meant that the island was lost. The question now was, how extensive would the defeat be in Crete?

Throughout the battle Freyberg, Puttick and Hargest had the

opportunity to affect the course of the battle and repel the enemy. The commanders of Crete were accustomed to the positional warfare of the First World War and put emphasis on securing their defensive line and flanks. Also the commanders were reluctant to use their reserves early on in the battle. They failed to realise that the key to victory was to destroy the enemy before they established themselves on the island. Before the battle began, Freyberg's orders encouraged the defenders to rapidly counter-attack when possible; the commanders on the ground had not put this into practice when the situation warranted it. Freyberg admitted after the battle that he should have appointed younger men as his senior commanders. Freyberg described his commanders as 'too old . . . to stand up to the strain of an all-out battle of the nature that eventually developed around Maleme Airfield'.[68] Freyberg had not imposed his leadership on his commanders. Some historians believe that the fact that Freyberg had been promoted over the head of other senior commanders might have affected his ability to lead them. Churchill appointed Freyberg for his aggression and verve, but these qualities were not evident in his leadership in Crete. Freyberg was a New Zealander who lived in London, but he felt an obligation not to risk the destruction of the New Zealanders. However, the difficulty of communications must be considered when analysing the commanders on Crete. There was a desperate shortage of wireless equipment and communications were severed by aerial bombardment.

The failure to mount a successful counter-attack sealed the fate of Crete and its inhabitants. Historian Alan Clark described the failure as the third, and final, major crisis in the battle for Crete, the first being the withdrawal of the 22nd Battalion from Hill 107 on the first day, and the second being the bungled plan for the counter-attack on the second day. But this third error proved to be fatal. Given that the Royal Navy had proved more than effective in protecting the island from a seaborne landing, the decision not to support the counter-attack is all the more indefensible. The Royal Navy had created the opportunity for the counter-attack at great cost.

NOTES

1   Freyberg, Paul, *Bernard Freyberg VC – Soldier of Two Nations*, London: Hodder & Stoughton, 1991, p. 299.
2   Hutching, Megan (ed.), *A Unique Sort of Battle. New Zealanders Remember Crete*, Auckland: HarperCollins, 2001, p. 83.
3   Ibid.
4   Ibid, p. 84.
5   Davin, D, *Official History of New Zealand in the Second World War*, Wellington, 1953, p. 110.
6   Cox, Geoffrey, *A Tale of Two Battles*, London: William Kimber, 1987, p. 78.

7 MacDonald, Callum, *The Lost Battle – Crete 1941*, London: Macmillan, 1993, p. 201.
8 Hutching, op. cit., p. 85.
9 Ibid, pp. 85–6.
10 Buckley, Christopher, *Greece and Crete 1941*, London: HMSO, 1952, p. 188.
11 Hutching, op. cit., p. 104.
12 Stewart, Ian, *The Struggle for Crete 20 May–1 June*, London: OUP, 1991, p. 162.
13 Davin, op. cit., p. 138.
14 Hutching, op. cit., p. 82.
15 MacDonald, op. cit., p. 203.
16 Ibid, p. 196.
17 Ibid, p. 207.
18 Davin, op. cit., p. 90.
19 MacDonald, op. cit., p. 208.
20 Ibid, p. 206.
21 Hutching, op. cit., p. 59.
22 MacDonald, op. cit., p. 206.
23 Cox, op. cit., pp. 80–1.
24 Davin, op. cit., p. 199.
25 Cox, op. cit., p. 81.
26 Beevor, Antony, *Crete – The Battle and the Resistance*, London: John Murray, 1991, p. 156.
27 Davin, op. cit., pp. 195–6.
28 Beevor, op. cit., p. 157.
29 Stewart, op. cit., p. 309.
30 Freyberg, Bernard, comments on Churchill's *History*, CAB 106/701.
31 Cox, op. cit., p. 82.
32 MacDonald, op. cit., p. 221.
33 Cox, op. cit., p. 82.
34 Clark, Alan, *The Fall of Crete*, London: Cassell, 1962, p. 123.
35 Cox, op. cit., p. 83.
36 Beevor, op. cit., p. 162.
37 Farran, Roy, *Winged Dagger*, London: Cassell, p. 94.
38 Ibid.
39 Davin, op. cit., p. 215.
40 Ibid, p. 216.
41 Farran, op. cit., p. 94.
42 Ibid, p. 95.
43 Ibid.
44 Davin, op. cit., p. 220.
45 Ibid, p. 229.
46 Hutching, op. cit., p. 232.
47 Clark, op. cit., p. 133.
48 Davin, op. cit., p. 114.
49 Clark, op. cit., p. 122.
50 Lawrence, R J, WO208/4650.
51 WO311/372, Charges against German War Criminals.
52 Ibid.
53 Wilkinson, Harold, WO208/4650, 24 November 1945.
54 Clark, op. cit., p. 132.
55 Ibid, p. 138.
56 Beevor, op. cit., p. 174.

57   Clark, op. cit., p. 137.
58   Beevor, op. cit., p. 172.
59   Davin, op. cit., p. 156 (Report by Captain Wilson).
60   Ibid (Report by Pope).
61   Beevor, op. cit., p. 9.
62   Davin, op. cit., p. 251.
63   Thomas, W B, *Dare to be Free*, Allan Wingate, 1951, p. 14.
64   Davin, op. cit., p. 252.
65   Freyberg, Bernard, comment on Churchill's *History*, CAB 106/701.
66   Clark, op. cit., p. 141.
67   Ibid, p. 142.
68   Freyberg, Paul, op. cit., p. 304.

CHAPTER XI

The Battle at Sea: A Trial of Strength

As the battle raged on the island, the Royal Navy was engaged with the enemy, protecting the waters surrounding Crete. Admiral Cunningham's British Fleet was subjected to a protracted ordeal during the first six months of 1941. During this period the Mediterranean Fleet had to sustain the garrison in Malta, supply Tobruk, battle against the Italian Fleet and evacuate 50,000 men from Greece. This schedule had stretched Cunningham's fleet to breaking point, and all of his cruisers and destroyers were in desperate need of a refit. Navy personnel were exhausted; none of the crew had been allowed any leave. Cunningham had received reports of stress among the officers, particularly those from anti-aircraft cruisers. The life of the crew from the Mediterranean Fleet was one of endurance; they rarely had the satisfaction of a ship-to-ship encounter, as the Italians would run at the first sign of a British destroyer. The main threat came from the mounting power of the Luftwaffe, which the British Fleet faced on many occasions without fighter cover. While the British dominated the sea around Crete, the Germans controlled the air. Navy personnel had been highly critical of the RAF, and it was unwise for RAF personnel to show themselves around the naval base at Alexandria. Cunningham was vocal in his criticism of the lack of aircraft available to cover his fleet. However, he did not blame Air Chief Marshal Longmore; on the contrary, he supported Longmore's demands for more fighters and bombers, much to the annoyance of Churchill.

Cunningham stated on 15 May 1941: 'We are trying to make headway against an air force which outnumbers ours vastly.' Cuningham argued that the navy was short of fighters and anti-aircraft ammunition and there was 'practically no reconnaissance, whereas the Germans and Italians report us as soon as we put our noses out of port'.[1] However, Cunningham's argument regarding aircraft reconnaissance did not take into account the huge advantage the navy derived from ULTRA decrypts, which led to victory in the battle of Cape Matapan. Despite his reservations, Cunningham had no option but to endure the wrath of the Luftwaffe if the island was to be saved. Vice-Admiral Pridham-Wippel took operational command as Cunningham stayed in Alexandria to co-ordinate the movements of the fleet. The navy's first objective in the battle for Crete was to protect the island from a seaborne invasion.

Without sufficient air cover, it was decided that the Aegean should be patrolled at night with a mobile force of destroyers and cruisers. Force A comprised the battleships *Warspite* and *Valiant*, the cruisers *Gloucester* and *Fiji*, and ten destroyers. Force A was led by Vice-Admiral H B Rawlings who was stationed to the west of Crete, with the objective of intercepting Italian heavy ships. The task of directly repulsing the seaborne landing was reserved for the cruisers of Forces C and D. Force D, under Rear Admiral Glennie, consisted of the cruisers *Dido*, *Orion* and *Ajax* with four destroyers, *Janus*, *Kimberley*, *Hasty* and *Hereward*. Force C, commanded by Rear Admiral King, was made up of the cruisers *Naiad*, *Calcutta*, *Carlisle* and *Perth* with four destroyers, *Kandahar*, *Nubian*, *Kingston* and *Juno*. Force C were to patrol the eastern half of Crete's north coast around the Heraklion area.

On 20 May the destroyers *Jarvis*, *Nizam* and *Ilex* bombarded the Skarpanto airfield (an Italian aerodrome used by the Luftwaffe.) Through-out the night of 20/21 May British ships were subjected to heavy bombing raids by the Luftwaffe, with the obvious objective of clearing a path for the seaborne landing. During one of the raids Admiral King's force to the east lost the *Juno* which was hit by three bombs, one of which had struck her magazines; the explosion broke the ship in two and she sank within minutes. The destroyer *Nubian* managed to pick up the majority of the survivors, but 121 men were lost, including Admiral Cunningham's nephew. Stukas attacked Force D at dusk, but they retaliated with an intense anti-aircraft barrage, shooting down two aircraft.

Despite destroying the *Juno*, the Luftwaffe failed to break the protective barrier of British ships. With only one ship lost in the four-hour bombing raid, German shipping would still have to take their chances against the British Mediterranean Fleet. Student intended the seaborne landing to act as a contingency plan in case the airfields had been rendered inoperable by the defenders. The Germans themselves had paid little attention to the seaborne expedition. The mountain troops who boarded their caiques regarded them as 'death traps'. According to General Ringel, the navigational aids of the caiques consisted of 'a 1/500,000 map and a pocket compass'.[2] On 18 May the mountain troops boarded the wooden caiques at Piraeus docks. The flotilla made its slow journey towards the island of Milos; apprehension was etched on the faces of many of the mountain troops. By the evening of 20 May the caiques reached Milos. The German flotilla now faced seventy miles of open sea before they reached Crete. They planned to cross the Aegean during daylight hours under the protection of the Luftwaffe, and using their sails to aid the weak engines, to reach the shores of Crete by nightfall. As night closed in the men on board the caiques could only just make out the tips of the mountains of

Crete on the distant horizon. The wind had dropped during the afternoon, which left the German flotilla stranded, thirty miles adrift from their destination. As the gloom turned to darkness, the mountain troops began to realise their impending peril. Throughout daylight hours they enjoyed the protection of the Luftwaffe, but during the night British warships dominated the waters surrounding Crete.

Cunningham had been kept well informed about the whereabouts of the convoy through signals intelligence, and he used this information to direct his cruiser squadrons. As had happened at Cape Matapan, a reconnaissance aircraft was sent out from Egypt to sight the convoy. It was hoped that the Germans would attribute the interception of their flotilla to the sighting by the pilot rather than to a security breach. After the war, both Churchill and Cunningham maintained the deception when describing the operation in their memoirs.

At 22.30 the cruiser *Dido* detected the first convoy using radar, and Glennie sent a sighting report back to Alexandria. Captain McCall, from the flagship *Dido*, gave the order 'on searchlights!' which revealed the *Lupo*, a light destroyer flying the Italian ensign. The Italian cruiser was struck twice by the *Dido* before she was hit by an eighteen-inch shell from the *Ajax*. The shell pierced her hull and left many dead and wounded. Despite being badly damaged, the *Lupo* managed to escape and British destroyers made easy work of the remaining light craft.

For the troops on the caiques the brief battle was a terrifying experience. With only planks of wood to protect them against British warships, many hauled down their sails in an effort to make them less conspicuous. White beams from the twenty-inch searchlights cut through the night air probing the darkness, drawing closer to the German flotilla with every sweep of the water. The mountain troops waited in a silence that was only broken by the lapping of the water. A rifleman from the mountain troops described the searchlights as 'fingers of death. Sharp cut against the darkness they grope blindly here and there over the water.'[3] The spotlight touched on the mast of one of the vessels, but then carried on. Minutes past and the men in the caiques began to wonder if they had escaped. Then there was a whisper of 'warships' and suddenly a searchlight illuminated the caique. As the spotlight reached them, the German soldiers immediately stood up from their hiding place and started waving handkerchiefs and white towels in an effort to surrender. The captain of the *Dido* gave the order to fire, despite some reported protests from his crew. (The bombing of a hospital ship in Greece from which the *Dido* had rescued survivors may have been fresh in his mind.) Under the captain's orders the *Dido*'s light arms were turned on the caiques and the whole area was lit up with criss-crossed tracer and pom-pom fire.

Oswald Jahnke of the mountain troops described the scene on the caiques: 'shells began to explode . . . we could see our boys jumping into the sea. Our ship was illuminated by the fire.' Jahnke was ordered to put his lifejacket on and to remove his boots. 'Our officer called "Good luck boys!" and ordered our first rank to jump into the sea.'[4] Lieutenant Walter Henglein described how his caique attempted to surrender: 'We unfurled a white towel at the stern and . . . signalled with white handkerchiefs. The English must have seen . . . watching through binoculars.' The caique was struck by a number of shells wounding twenty men. They attempted to take the wounded below deck but they were 'hit by a 7.5-cm shell that destroyed the infirmary room and everything in it'.[5] Rifleman Wittmann, from the mountain troops, recalled jumping into the black waters as the first salvoes crashed into the caique, 'like a tempest, sending showers of wood and debris about our ears'.[6] Corporal Karl Grimm reported that a British cruiser had passed repeatedly through the wreckage and fired on the men in the water; the man next to Grimm was hit in the head with a machine-gun bullet and sank without trace. Others were dragged under the water by the suction of the propellers.

Glennie reported that his men had gone about their duty with: 'zest and energy'.[7] He went on to mention that he had sympathy for the Greek crews who manned the caiques and who were 'obviously pressed men, standing on deck waving white flags . . . it was distasteful having to destroy them in company with their callous masters'.[8] The battle at sea was every bit as intense as the battle on land. Glennie was in no position to accept surrender or take prisoners. An Australian crew member from HMAS *Perth* commented on the machine-gunning of Germans in the water: 'War is inhuman and when a man has seen his comrades killed before his eyes he is apt to let instinct overcome reason.'[9] Both Churchill's and Cunningham's accounts stated that German losses exceeded 4,000 dead; the first reports from the German Twelfth Army stated that nearly all the men had perished and calculated a figure of 2,331 dead, although the final report by the Twelfth Army stated that thirteen officers and 311 other ranks had been lost. Many of the men who jumped into the sea were kept afloat by their lifejackets in the relatively warm water. Despite being badly damaged, the Italian escort *Lupo* returned to the scene to pick up German survivors from the water. As day broke German seaplanes appeared to rescue those in the water who had survived the night.

The following day King led Force C inside the ring of Axis air bases searching for the second convoy. The Luftwaffe attacks began at 07.00. Three hours later, a lone caique was sighted. As HMAS *Perth* approached, the Germans had run up a white flag and lowered the swastika, signalling that they were about to surrender. Lifeboats were lowered but only a fraction of the soldiers entered them. J Nelson of HMAS *Perth* recalled that the number of men evacuating the vessel was 'comparatively small . . . we opened fire with pom-poms'. Nelson likened it to 'pouring water on an ants' nest'. Germans flung themselves in the water from all directions.

Nelson then noticed a German clinging to the side 'of the forward mast riggings'. A second shell hit and 'after the smoke had cleared he had disappeared'.[10]

The main flotilla was sighted by King at 10.00. The Italian escort, the *Sagittario,* had laid down a smoke screen allowing the remainder of the convoy to disperse and flee among the various creeks and inlets. The *Sagittario* fired torpedoes in the direction of the cruisers *Perth* and *Naiad* before being hit several times and withdrawing. Force C had been under heavy air attack throughout the morning; the concussions of repeated near misses and the rattle of anti-aircraft fire dazed those on board the vessels. After running low on anti-aircraft ammunition, King halted the pursuit of the second convoy. Cunningham was critical of King's decision, stating that the safest place was probably among the flotilla of caiques where the Luftwaffe was reluctant to intervene for fear of killing their own men. Churchill was of the opinion that King's decision had spared the lives of 5,000 German soldiers. However, King had completed his objective and engaged the second convoy, which had dispersed and fled, marking the end for the seaborne invasion. If King had pursued the convoy deeper into the Axis ring of airfields, he would have subjected his squadron to a longer ordeal at the hands of Luftwaffe. It was not certain that the Luftwaffe would refrain from bombing, regardless of what was below them; also the convoy had dispersed and King's squadron were unlikely to find them.

Despite King's prudence, his squadron suffered aerial bombardment. When dawn broke on 22 May, King's group could not hide from enemy reconnaissance planes as they advanced towards the Kithera Channel. The Luftwaffe quickly swarmed over Force C and mounted an attack that lasted for nearly three and a half hours. King's flagship, *Naiad*, had suffered damage from no fewer than thirty-six near misses, and was reduced to a speed of sixteen knots. The *Carlisle* was also damaged in the bombardment. The German pilots attacked King's squadron with a total disregard for anti-aircraft fire. German bombers intentionally approached their target with the sun behind them. Looking into the sun, gunners could at best only hope to hit their target.

As Force C headed towards Rawling's main battle group at the entrance to the Aegean, German aircraft turned their attention to the destruction of the battleships *Warspite* and *Valiant*. The *Warspite* was hit on the starboard side, putting her anti-aircraft guns out of action and causing fires below deck. Charles Maddon, the executive officer of the *Warspite*, described the scene: 'cries of burned and wounded men could be heard...men were thrown in all directions amongst piles of iron work.' After reporting to the bridge, Maddon noted that the 'calm blue afternoon seemed unreal after the dark and smelly carnage below'.[11] Bellowing huge plumes of smoke and without half of her anti-aircraft guns, the *Warspite* was in a vulnerable position. An order was given to all ships to put up an 'umbrella barrage' to protect her.

As the two squadrons came together, King assumed command over the joint force. At this point King made another controversial decision after he spotted a lone caique near the island of Antikithera. Despite being pursued by nearly 320 aircraft, King abandoned his cautious approach and ordered the destroyer *Greyhound* to break from the cover of the main fleet and engage the caique. After destroying the German vessel, the *Greyhound* was singled out by the Luftwaffe, as she returned to the relative safety of the fleet. She was hit three times, once fatally, penetrating the aft deck and exploding in the aft magazine. The *Greyhound* exploded with terrific force; men on the nearby *Valiant* were thrown off their feet and injured by the strength of the blast. She sank within minutes. Forty survivors from the *Greyhound* wallowed in a huge pool of oil that lay across the surface of the sea. As the *Kandahar* and *Kingston* endeavoured to save the survivors, German aircraft strafed and bombed those in the water. Many men burnt to death as the large pool of oil was set alight by an incendiary bomb. The Luftwaffe meticulously followed their orders to destroy the Mediterranean Fleet, and they did not refrain from attacking vessels that were temporarily engaged in rescuing survivors, or from machine-gunning men in lifeboats, such is the brutality of war. A young seaman who was a survivor from the *Greyhound* found himself in a lifeboat with nineteen other men; as a German plane approached he dived into the water to avoid the bullets; as he came to the surface he saw that every man in the boat had been killed.

With the *Kandahar* and *Kingston* under attack, the anti-aircraft cruisers *Fiji* and *Gloucester* were sent by King to assist. The *Gloucester* and *Fiji* were in a difficult position as they had expended over three quarters of their anti-aircraft ammunition. When King was eventually informed of the vulnerability of the two vessels, they were immediately withdrawn. Fatally, the British Fleet was split into three groups. Two vessels were sent to search for the survivors from the *Greyhound*, and the *Gloucester* and *Fiji* were at full speed trying to catch up with the battle fleet and practically defenceless. The *Gloucester* was subjected to an air attack for an hour and a half; during the attack she was hit three times, twisting her super-structure out of all recognition. The *Gloucester* received crippling damage; she was ablaze and reduced to just twelve knots. It was agreed that the *Fiji* could not risk further damage and, after throwing life rafts overboard, she left the *Gloucester* to her fate. The *Gloucester* was never seen again.

After the war Cunningham was critical of the dispersal of Force C. He described King's decision as a 'disregard of a golden rule . . . never to detach ships for any particular tasks'. Cunningham maintained that: 'The fleet should remain concentrated and move in formation to wherever any rescue or other work had to be done.'[12] In his memoirs, Cunningham praised the crew of HMS *Gloucester*: 'She had endured all things, and no ship worked harder or had more risky tasks.' The *Gloucester* was previously considered to have led a charmed life: 'She had been hit by more bombs than any other vessel, and had always come up smiling.'[13] Cunningham had promised to go on board and talk to the men on her return to Alexandria but they never returned. The body of the *Gloucester*'s captain was washed ashore to the west of Mersa Matruh four weeks later. The *Gloucester* was originally thought to have sunk without any survivors; however, almost 500 men were saved by Italian destroyers or German seaplanes and became prisoners of war.

The *Fiji* managed to survive no fewer than twenty separate air attacks before she was hit alongside. The bomb blew a hole in the cruiser's bottom and she came to a standstill with her engine room flooded. After being hit by a further three bombs, she capsized and sank; over 500 of her crew were left in the water clinging to life rafts. They spent several hours in the water before the *Kingston* and *Kandahar* arrived out of the gloom to pick up survivors who were hauled aboard through scramble nets. In all, 523 of the *Fiji*'s crew were rescued out of 780.

The main battle group was still under attack as these events took place. Two bombs hit the *Valiant* (on which Lieutenant Prince Philip of Greece was serving). Such a large concentration of ships provided an excellent target for the Luftwaffe and swarms of fighters and bombers circled overhead. The German airfields at Eleusis (Greece) were likened to a bees' nest, as a constant flow of planes came in to refuel and then took off again. General Richthofen of VIII Fliegerkorps was lifted by the success of the Luftwaffe and pressed for a new attempt to land seaborne convoys in Crete. Student and Admiral Schüster viewed the landings as a disaster and refused Richthofen's request.

Throughout the course of the day, the Mediterranean Fleet suffered badly. In just three days, two cruisers and four destroyers were sunk and two cruisers, four destroyers and a battleship were damaged. Cunningham stated: 'We cannot afford another such experience and retain sea control in Eastern Mediterranean.'[14] During the evenings Cunningham would wait in his office in Alexandria 'dreading the sound of the telephone bell which was usually the harbinger of more bad news'.[15] As Cunningham received news of the Mediterranean Fleet he was in a sombre mood. He believed that the decision to detach the *Greyhound* from the cover of the main fleet was the catalyst for the losses. For Longmore's successor, Air Chief Marshal Tedder, it was no surprise. Tedder had stated previously to Cunningham that his fleet could not survive in waters surrounded by enemy airbases without sufficient air cover.

On the night of 22 May the destroyers *Kashmir*, *Kelly* and *Kipling* were deployed under Lord Mountbatten to search for survivors from the *Fiji* and patrol Canea Bay. At 07.55 the next morning the *Kelly* and the *Kashmir* were sunk. John Blackie, who was on board the *Kashmir*, recalled that the actions during the night included intercepting caiques and firing salvoes towards German positions at Maleme. Blackie stated that they were due to be on their way to Egypt by daylight but: 'These short actions resulted in us not being clear of Crete by daylight. Soon after sunrise, we were spotted by 24 Stuka dive bombers. One after another, the Stukas peeled off from their formation and dived, some almost vertically, upon the *Kelly* and *Kashmir*. In spite of weaving at full speed, both ships were hit. The *Kelly*, heeling on a full-speed turn, rolled over, exposing her underside and trapping a high proportion of her ship's company. *Kashmir* was hit abreast the funnel and blown in half, sinking in a few minutes. While in the water and quite defenceless, the survivors were subjected to quite unforgivable machine-gun attacks. This so enraged Able Seaman Ian (Dusty) Rhodes . . . that he swam back to the after part of the *Kashmir*, which had not yet sunk, manned one of the Oerlikon guns and engaged the bombers.' The dive-bombers quickly turned their attention towards Rhodes. '[But] his great bravery was rewarded by his shooting down one of the bombers . . . The oily salt-water cheer that went up as the plane hit the sea . . . must have given many enough hope to survive the ordeal.'[16] After the guns were submerged underwater, Rhodes calmly swam back to his colleagues; after the war he was awarded the Conspicuous Gallantry Medal.

As they waited in the water Blackie and his shipmates could hardly believe their luck as they spotted the mast of the *Kipling* appear on the horizon. As the *Kipling* started to head towards the men clinging to the hull of *Kelly*, she clipped the wreck and tore a gash in her side. Blackie described the damage. 'Some compartments were flooded, weakening the bulkheads, which limited her speed to twenty knots and restricted her to altering course in one direction only . . . [also] she trailed an oil slick that was visible from the air.'[17] Under repeated air attack the *Kipling* stayed on the scene to rescue survivors. After an exhausting swim to the scramble nets of the *Kipling* Blackie recalled his relief at getting on board. 'I do not know how I reached the deck, only that a navy cup was thrust into my hands with the instruction: "Drink this lad, Nelson's proud of you!" I swear the cup was half full and of course it was neat navy rum!' Blackie described the journey to Alexandria. 'The next few hours were ones of miracles, horror, courage, sacrifice and supreme seamanship. Limited in speed and steerage, *Kipling* survived 83 bombs aimed at her. On many occasions she was enveloped in cascades of water from near misses, but the gun crews fought on although soaking wet and eyes near closed with salt and cordite smoke. I watched in near disbelief as the black shapes of bombs fell around, some so close that I felt that I could catch one. The bombers screamed as they dived, the bombs whistled, and as they exploded it sounded as though the side of the ship was being whacked with a giant drumstick. The ship lifted and lurched, throwing around those able to move and hastening the passing of the dying. Then there would be an almost uncanny quietness as the enemy aircraft left to refuel and rearm. Soon it would start all over again with a lookout reporting: "Aircraft in sight, Red 160 degrees, Sir." This time it must be the end, we all thought. But instead, the time came when we were left alone.' Blackie spent the night sleeping on the deck abreast the funnel. He recalled: 'I awoke to find that the man I had slept next to was dead. I had wondered why my flippant question: "Quiet isn't it?" was unanswered . . . We spent much of the morning burying the dead the traditional way: the body was tied in a hammock with a practice shell at the feet, placed on a mess deck table, covered with the White Ensign and tipped over the stern into the sea to the plaintive call of the bosun's pipe and with the shipmates at attention.'[18] When she eventually reached the sanctuary of Alexandria, she was so short of fuel that her engines stopped fifty miles short outside the harbour, and she had to be towed in by tugs. The whole Mediterranean Fleet had been listening to the feat of the *Kipling* and marvelled at her escape. Historian Ian Stewart stated that the commander of the *Kipling* had forgotten the: '"golden rule." For this 279 survivors, including [Lord] Mountbatten, had cause to be thankful.'[19]

After the smashing of the 5th Destroyer Flotilla, Cunningham had literally no ships that were 100 percent serviceable. On the morning of 23 May he decided to recall his ships to Alexandria. Cunningham's decision was spurred by a calligraphic error. Rawlings stated that his battleships had plenty of short-range anti-aircraft ammunition, but 'plenty' was mistakenly transcribed as 'empty'. It is widely believed that this mistake may have inadvertently saved the Mediterranean Fleet from further heavy losses. Force C returned to Egypt to refuel on the night of 22 May. Cunningham was assured by signals intelligence that no further attempts would be made to land German troops in Crete.

On 23 May Cunningham received a note from the Admiralty stating that it was 'vitally important to prevent seaborne expeditions reaching the Island in the next day or two, even if this resulted in further losses to the fleet'.[20] Cunningham replied that the withdrawal of the fleet was necessary to refuel and restock ammunition, adding that his fleet was operating 400 miles from its base. Cunningham described the operations in Crete as 'nothing short of a trial of strength between the Mediterranean Fleet and the German Air Force'. He wrote: 'I am afraid that in the coastal area we have to admit defeat.' Cunningham maintained that his losses were too great to justify further operations around Crete. He cited the enemy command of the air with the clear Mediterranean weather was: 'too great odds for us to take on.' Cunningham's stark reply finished: 'This is a melancholy conclusion, but it must be faced.'[21]

When Churchill's Private Secretary, John Colville, mentioned his regret at the loss of so many ships, Churchill snapped: 'what do you think we build ships for?' Churchill concluded: 'the loss of half the Mediterranean Fleet would be worth while in order to save Crete.'[22] The Chiefs of Staff intervened in the argument between Alexandria and London and stated to Cunningham that unless 'more drastic action were taken', then the enemy would be able to reinforce the island considerably. They also stated that the fleet would be forced to operate during the day if enemy movement was detected on the Cretan north coast 'though considerable losses might be expected'.[23] Clearly tired of the long-range criticism from London, which had previously dogged the likes of Wavell and Longmore, Cunningham's reply was swift and brutally frank. He highlighted the losses in the previous three days and stated that it was not 'the fear of sustaining losses, but the need to avoid losses which will cripple the fleet without any commensurate advantage'.[24]

As Cunningham completed these messages to London, he learned that the aircraft carrier *Illustrious* had been damaged, resulting in a thirty-foot hole in the starboard bow. The *Illustrious* had been caught by bombers in an operation against Axis airfields at Karpathos; the *Nubian* acting as an escort cruiser was also badly damaged. The next day the battleship *Barham* was attacked by fifteen bombers and also badly damaged. These attacks served to strengthen Cunningham's argument but further damaged the morale of the fleet.

On 23 May the *Glenroy* made its way to Crete with an infantry battalion, escorted by the anti-aircraft cruiser *Coventry*. After he realised that the *Glenroy* was due to arrive off Crete in broad daylight, Cunningham sent an order for the ship to turn back. The Admiralty then sent a direct instruction countermanding Cunningham's order. The overrule from London bore all the hallmarks of Churchill's influence; he had previously sent Wavell a message stating the vital importance of saving Crete for the security of Egypt, and that 'great risks must be accepted to ensure success'.[25] Cunningham reaffirmed his order within the hour, and was incensed at the interference from London. Cunningham summarised the incident after the war, stating: 'The less said about this unjustifiable interference by those ignorant of the situation the better.'[26] A second attempt to land the troops on the island on 26 May failed when the *Glenroy* was attacked by the Luftwaffe and set on fire; Cunningham eventually recalled her yet again to Alexandria. A troop of commandos under Colonel Laycock were landed successfully on the island during the night of 24/25 May, but only in time to cover the defenders' retreat across the mountains.

The navy had fulfilled its obligation to the army and Cunningham was worried about the Mediterranean Fleet being subjected to the onslaught from the Luftwaffe. The navy claimed that no transport had reached the island, which was not strictly true, as a small convoy had got there carrying two tanks at Kastelli Kissamos. But by the time the tanks arrived the battle for the island was already decided.

The naval battle proved that a battle fleet could not survive within range of an enemy air base. It was apparent that anti-aircraft fire alone could not sustain the British Fleet. Cunningham wrote after the war: 'Why the authorities at home apparently could not see the danger of our situation in the Mediterranean without adequate air support passed my comprehension.'[27] Air support was desperately lacking, but the nearest operational RAF airbase was 400 miles away. The US military attaché wrote: 'It was the first engagement of a first-rate fleet without air support with a first-rate air power.' The conclusion: 'a complete undeniable air victory.' It was noted that Crete was not to be considered as an exceptional case in that 'similar losses can be inflicted on any navy ... without adequate fighter support [that] ventures within range of land-based dive bombers'.[28]

The seaborne invasion had been thwarted, but the Luftwaffe had ultimately won the battle for the sea. General Halder noted in his diary on 28 May: 'The English have uncontested control of the sea; we have uncontested control of the air.'[29] It was not enough to command the seas; one must also command the air above. During 22 May the Luftwaffe clearly asserted the importance of airpower in modern warfare. The VIII Fliegerkorps under Richthofen had inflicted crippling damage on the Mediterranean Fleet at sea and helped to turn the land battle against the defenders.

The decisions taken on land were such that the prevention of a seaborne landing was largely insignificant in determining the course of the battle. During the nights of 21 and 22 May, men of the Royal Navy died to preserve the opportunity for Freyberg and his commanders to rip the heart out of the German invasion by taking the fight to those paratroops based around Maleme airfield. The sacrifices of the Mediterranean Fleet were largely in vain as the opportunity to isolate the German forces were squandered by those in command.

NOTES

1   Cunningham, A, *A Sailor's Odyssey*, London: Hutchinson, 1951, p. 364.
2   Stewart, Ian, *The Struggle for Crete 20 May–1 June*, London: OUP, p. 88.
3   Ibid, p. 280.
4   MacDonald, Callum, *The Lost Battle – Crete 1941*, London: Macmillan, p. 239.
5   Ibid, p. 240.
6   Stewart, op. cit., p. 280.
7   Clark, Alan, *The Fall of Crete*, London: Cassell, 1962, p. 113.
8   MacDonald, op. cit., p. 241.
9   Ibid.
10 Ibid, p. 243.
11 Ibid, p. 247.
12 Cunningham, op. cit., p. 373.

13 Ibid, p. 371.
14 Churchill, Winston, *The Second World War*, Vol. III, London: Cassell, 1950, p. 260.
15 Cunningham, op. cit., p. 390.
16 Hutching, Megan (ed.), *A Unique Sort of Battle. New Zealanders Remember Crete*, Auckland: HarperCollins, 2001, p. 109.
17 Ibid.
18 Ibid, p. 110.
19 Stewart, op. cit., p. 285.
20 Cunningham, op. cit., p. 374.
21 Churchill, op. cit, p.260.
22 Ibid., p. 259.
23 MacDonald, op. cit., p. 252.
24 Clark, op. cit., p. 120.
25 Churchill, op. cit., p. 260.
26 Ibid.
27 Cunningham, op. cit., p. 375.
28 MacDonald, op. cit., p. 254.
29 Stewart, op. cit., p. 259.

CHAPTER XII

The Battle for Galatas

Had the battle for Maleme followed the same pattern of events as at Retimo and Heraklion, Student's invasion would have ended in an unmitigated failure. At Retimo, Colonel Campbell and Major Sandover utilised the merit of immediate counter-attacking. The Australians constantly harassed German positions and attacked intelligently throughout the night. From the German commanders' perspective, the relentless counter-attacks created the illusion that Retimo was heavily fortified; in reality the Germans had outnumbered the defenders.

At Retimo Colonel Campbell deduced that possession of Hill A was vital to retaining control of the airfield. Having lost Hill A on the opening day, Campbell had relentlessly attacked to regain the position on the hill, and on the fifth attempt he was successful. Campbell had visited the foot of Hill A personally to organise the assault. Captain Moriarty took control of the Australian 2/1 Battalion to lead the counter-attack. During the morning the defenders saw a German aircraft mistakenly dropping bombs among the parachutists on the hill, killing sixteen of their number. Heartened by the misguided air attack, Moriarty led his group in a determined counter-offensive up the slopes of Hill A. As Moriarty's men poured over the crest of the hill, the Germans fled down the slopes towards the road, leaving their dead and fifty-nine prisoners. The survivors from Major Kroh's 1st Battalion took refuge in an olive oil factory at Stavromenos.

Campbell had not only regained the hill, but also two tanks that were lost in operations the night before. Meanwhile at the foot of Hill B Colonel Sturm's detachment were forced to surrender to the Australians. Sturm did not make a good prisoner; clearly frustrated at his capture he swore continuously in German. Throughout the rest of the day the enemy to the west were content with consolidating their position around Perivolia and did not make a further attempt on Hill B. Campbell had succeeded in splitting the enemy into two sections and isolating the German assault.

This was the spirit in which the battle should have been fought around Maleme; the same unyielding persistence should have been employed to retain control of the airfield, which proved to be the centrepiece of the battle. It must be noted that the air attacks at Heraklion were far lighter than those experienced at Maleme. But Campbell's tactics of mobile and rapid counter-attacking had rendered the Luftwaffe impotent, as they did not have definitive opposing lines and could not distinguish between friend and foe.

An assault on the olive oil factory was planned for 22 May. The Australians suffered a heavy blow when Captain Moriarty fell to a sniper's bullet while carrying out a reconnaissance mission for the assault. With the loss of Moriarty, Campbell personally mounted the attack against the olive oil factory and 200 men from 5th Greek Battalion were brought in to assist. When the attack was mounted the Greeks failed to move and the Australians assaulted the factory alone. The attack soon became pinned down by heavy fire from the paratroops and Campbell's men were forced to shelter below a bank short of the factory. Campbell ordered his men to remain in cover until darkness fell when they were able to withdraw in relative safety.

During the afternoon of 23 May around fifty German aircraft attacked the 2/11 Battalion causing thirty-nine casualties. Later that evening the 3rd Battalion under Captain Wiedemann attempted to attack Australian lines. An Australian private described stopping the German advance: 'Our forward troops stood up and shot them down like rabbits.'[1] Privates Johnson and Symmons had been wounded in the early afternoon but persisted in operating their Bren gun until the Germans were pushed back; Symmons died of his injuries later that evening. Australian troops laid out captured signals requesting the bombing of the village of Perivolia where Captain Wiedemann's men were hiding. Stukas duly obliged at 17.00. In the midst of the bombing the Germans fell back to St George's Church, a 'huge structure of granite blocks surrounded by a stone wall'.[2] The church was positioned on high ground, which provided the perfect vantage point for observing fresh attacks on Perivolia, and directing fire against the advancing Australians. At this point a stalemate ensued as it had at the olive oil factory. But it served to tie up defending troops while the fate of the island was decided at Maleme.

On 25 May Campbell launched an attack against the factory with a tank backed up by 75mm gun support. Captain Embrey and his group stormed the factory and they successfully took it with the capture of eighty-two prisoners. Inside the factory only German wounded could be found; all the able bodied troops had escaped, including Major Kroh. It proved impossible to clear the Germans from their positions among the houses and gardens; the Cretan police had attacked without success. Campbell had captured 500 Germans who were imprisoned in a cage south of Hill D. On the following day the church was taken after the Australians reduced the building to rubble with two captured anti-tank guns. With the aid of recaptured I tanks an attempt was made to capture Perivolia village and in heavy fighting, in which the tanks were damaged by German anti-tank weapons, Sandover's men were forced back. Sandover decided to halt his counter-attack to prevent further waste of life.

At Retimo, as at Maleme, the ground was strewn with German dead. As he made his way back to company headquarters one night, Lew Lind noted that around 400 German bodies lay in front of Australian positions. 'The bodies had swollen to nearly double their size and had literally burst from their uniforms.' Lind recalled that wherever he stepped he 'seemed to stand on spongy, nauseating flesh . . . I felt as though I had lived through a nightmare'.[3] On 21 May a truce was called at Retimo to gather the wounded. A joint hospital was established near the village of Adhele with Australian and German doctors working side by side and sharing medical supplies. Operations were often carried out without anaesthetic, and many died due to lack of medical supplies. Squadron Leader Howell described the conditions: 'There was no room to walk between bodies on the floor . . . Men were bleeding and being sick over each other.' Due to the poor quality of the water it was drunk mixed with Samos wine, and soon 'everyone became intoxicated . . . In the morning they came and carried out the dead.'[4]

In the eastern sector of Heraklion the condition of the paratroops grew even more desperate on the second day. On the evening of 22 May Bräuer was forced to withdraw his men to Ames Ridge two miles south-east of the airfield. Within the defenders' perimeter lay the bodies of 950 Germans, added to 300 German dead within the Greek sector. A further 200 German corpses lay in the surrounding hills. The German troops capable of fighting could not have exceeded 600 out of over 2,000 men dropped on Heraklion. The British and Australian troops had suffered around fifty casualties.

The surviving paratroopers were short of ammunition and food. Colonel Bräuer's men at Heraklion were suffering from thirst and dysentery caused by drinking water from irrigation ditches. Bräuer, who was later captured in Libya, described the condition of his men to the east of the airfield in Heraklion: 'we were at our wits' end. I had eighty men left of my eight hundred, no food, little ammunition.'[5] Many Germans lost their lives in the search for water, shot dead by snipers. As at Retimo an agreement was made under which the dead could be buried and casualties evacuated. A Greek commander fighting in the west of Heraklion reported to Brigadier Chappel that the Germans had resorted to using Cretan women and children as a screen. Chappel responded immediately and sent a message threatening the execution of all his prisoners if the Germans continued the practice, which they promptly stopped.

On the outskirts of Heraklion, Cretan guerrillas were wiping out whole companies of German troops. The Black Watch steadfastly defended the high ground around Heraklion with artillery and mortar support. The York and Lancs guarded the area south of the town, but were running low on small arms ammunition; Captain Rabbidge stated that his troops were reduced to using RAF 303 tracer and incendiary rounds. The Cretan Minister of Justice, who was watching the York and Lancs battle from afar, noticed a soldier of 'the White and Red Rose stop for a moment to put a rose in his buttonhole before running on'.[6]

After the heavy losses inflicted on the enemy during the first day, Chappel seemed content with securing his perimeter, although Bräuer's men never posed a serious threat to the airfield. Freyberg ordered the forces between Heraklion and Retimo to make contact with each other, and he was confident that they would do so. But Chappel did not realise the importance of clearing his area towards Retimo and sat on his victory at Heraklion. For the surviving Germans at Heraklion the situation bore little resemblance to what they were led to believe would be an easy victory. They had been reduced to foraging for food and were desperate for water in the stifling heat. It was almost impossible to wash and many of the men were suffering from diarrhoea; the wounded lay tormented with pain and had little hope for respite. German paratroops knew that the defenders were relatively unscathed by the events and believed that they would soon advance to rout them.

However, Chappel did little to exploit German despondency. He did not launch any attacks at night, which the Germans had feared most. After darkness set in, the shooting ceased. Chappel explained that 'by a tacit and mute understanding no firing took place at night for it would have inconvenienced both sides equally'.[7] Chappel stated that during the night his men liked to stretch their legs; also, casualties were evacuated, and rations and ammunition were distributed. During the next four days Chappel's large force at Heraklion stood idle. The Germans made no aggressive moves until the outcome of the battle for Maleme was beyond doubt. Only the Luftwaffe were active, making at least two raids a day on Heraklion, which reduced the town to rubble. The destruction of Heraklion was retribution for the ferocious resistance demonstrated by the Cretans.

For the Cretans this was not a foreign battlefield and they were in no mood for compassion or sentiment; they annihilated their enemy wherever they found them. John Pendlebury, who had reached legendary status among local Cretans, was heavily involved in the street fighting around Heraklion. Despite being a senior SOE officer, Pendlebury had little warning of the German invasion. When the attack started, he was visiting friends in the Hotel Knossos and was anxious to reach his band of partisans. At dawn on the second day of the battle, Pendlebury left Heraklion and headed for Mount Ida in a car driven by a Cretan guerrilla, Georgios Drosoulake. Just outside the city at Kaminia their car was ambushed by a German patrol. In the ensuing fight Pendlebury killed three of the enemy before being seriously injured in the back and chest; his driver, Drosoulake, was killed outright. Some local Cretans carried Pendlebury to a house where he was nursed by Drosoulake's wife and her sister. Three days had passed when a truck full of German troops arrived. Mrs Drosoulake was boiling some water for her patient when she heard her sister begin to scream. The Germans had raced upstairs and barred the door. Raised voices were heard before a burst of Tommy-gun fire and Pendlebury was executed where he lay. Such was the legend of this man on the island that the Germans still searched for him long after he was dead. Eventually they returned to dig up his body and identified him by his glass eye.

During the night of 26 May Chappel asked Freyberg if he should attack, but the outcome of the battle had already been decided. CREFORCE headquarters seemed preoccupied with the battle in their immediate vicinity, and did not consider the option of destroying enemy forces between Heraklion and Retimo. Lack of wireless communication proved critical. Unaware of the events at Maleme, the garrisons at Retimo and Heraklion believed that all they had to do was to hang on to their positions and the German invasion would die. In the absence of any clear instructions, Brigadier Chappel stayed strictly within the confines of the orders given to him at the beginning of the battle. Chappel did not offer a decisive blow against the Germans, but he stayed loyal to his objective, to deny the airfield and harbour to the enemy. He had no means of knowing that the enemy had expended the last of their airborne reserves and the invasion flotillas were defeated.

Chappel has been criticised for not crushing his severely depleted enemy at Heraklion, although this argument overlooks the fact that his men lacked ammunition for a major encounter. Some believed he should have cleared his area before moving on to Retimo and eventually advancing to the aid of the New Zealand Division at Maleme. However, if Chappel had hoped to reinforce Retimo and thereby sweep towards Suda and Maleme, he would have needed to send relief to Retimo by the second day. If the disaster at Maleme was to be averted then Chappel needed to break the Germans west of Heraklion town on the first or second day. At this stage it was unclear how many paratroopers would arrive and a sea landing was also expected, so it was understandable that Chappel remained concentrated on securing the airfield and harbour. With hindsight we can deduce that it was feasible to push through to Retimo, but it would have taken an extremely daring man to attempt it without knowing all the facts. Captain Fleming wrote: 'Our intelligence and communication with Freyberg was nil.'[8]

Having secured Maleme as a secure supply line of troops, Ringel felt he could wait to further augment his forces before taking any offensive action. The 1st and 2nd Battalions of 95th Mountain Artillery Regiment landed in Crete, with the 95th Anti-tank Battalion with twenty 50-mm anti-tank guns and the 55th Motorcycle Battalion. The constant stream of reinforcements and supplies was a great boost to German morale. However, Ringel's prudence could have worked against his men as the Chiefs of Staff in Germany required the Luftwaffe for the attack on Russia and they expected the majority of the aircraft to be withdrawn from Crete in preparation for BARBAROSSA no later than 25 May. It was perhaps no coincidence that by 25 May, Ringel believed that his troops were strong enough to break the line at Galatas in a decisive action. However, Ringel was not able to concentrate all his strength against the New Zealanders on the front line. The Mountain Pioneer Battalion, under Major Schätte, was engaged in fighting with the 8th Greek Regiment at Kisamos Kastelli.

As Major Schätte's group patrolled the area surrounding Kastelli, they came across some unburied corpses of Mürbe's detachment from the initial landings. According to reports from the 5th Mountain Division, the bodies showed signs that atrocities had taken place. Some appeared to have been repeatedly stabbed and eyes had been gouged out. This discovery provoked harsh new measures to be imposed by the Germans, which meant that any civilian carrying a weapon would be shot. For every attack on German troops, ten hostages would be shot and the surrounding villages burned to the ground.

On 24 May Stukas began bombing Kastelli, hitting the prison where the German captives had been incarcerated for their own safety. The newly freed prisoners made directly for Major Bedding's headquarters, taking him and his Second Lieutenant Baigent prisoner. A rescue attempt by Lieutenants Campbell and Yorke was driven off and Campbell was killed in the process. The Germans were now advancing in great strength from the east, supported by a number of anti-tank guns. After the bombing of Kastelli had begun, many of the Greek garrison were drawn back into the town over concern for their families. The Greeks had expended much of their ammunition and over 200 were killed in futile charges against their enemy. By midday the Germans had fought their way into the centre of Kastelli town and proclaimed its capture.

Many Greeks carried on the fight with organised resistance at the western end of the harbour. Augmented with weapons taken from Mürbe's men, the Greeks were able to hold out in houses until 27 May, by which time Major Schätte's men had systematically destroyed every house with anti-tank guns. The few surviving Greeks fled the town into the hills. The final stand by the Greeks at Kastelli infuriated the Germans, who vented their anger by selecting over 200 inhabitants to be shot in the square for the alleged mutilation of Mürbe's men. A boy of 14 was among those executed. These reprisals were all the more deplorable as the New

Zealand advisor to the Greeks, Major Bedding, and the surviving paratroops from Mürbe's detachment, had assured Schätte that the Greeks had fought honourably.

Although both sides were guilty of committing atrocities, German claims were overstated and clearly meant for propaganda purposes. Colonel Bräuer discussed the issue of atrocities with Dr Wenner of the German Criminal Police. Wenner was sceptical about the claims of mutilation. Bräuer stated after the war that the 'unbelievable heat' during the 'battle and the large number of ravens on Crete were responsible for the rapid decomposition of the corpses'.[9] Many of Mürbe's men fell to primitive weapons such as axes or clubs; in 'legitimate' fighting, these weapons inflicted wounds that some felt were consistent with atrocities. The weapons used accounted for slashing injuries to head, neck and chest areas and the loss of eyes were due to decomposition and various scavenging animals. German troops assumed that because their men had not died from bullet wounds, their injuries were caused after capture.

A subsequent judicial investigation by the Germans, carried out by Judge Rudel, revealed six to eight cases of mutilation in Kastelli, two or three in Retimo, and fifteen elsewhere. All these cases were attributed to 'fanatical' civilians. Judge Rudel emphasised the way in which British and New Zealand troops sought to protect German prisoners from the local population wherever possible, 'even going so far as to fire on the mobs'.[10] Despite Judge Rudel's findings, a campaign was started by Nazi propaganda accusing local Cretans and Commonwealth troops of committing atrocities against German soldiers. Such allegations were a useful tool to justify retribution by the German army, who were determined to punish the population of Crete for fighting a partisan war. The British were particularly sensitive about the German propaganda campaign as they were worried about the political effect in the United States. The British authorities were keen to understate the fighting role of the civilian population on Crete as they had failed to form a home guard. Without recognised markings, the Cretan partisans had no protection under the Geneva Convention and many were executed as a result. Failure to utilise the Cretans as an organised fighting unit was undoubtedly a humanitarian mistake, but many have regarded it also as a tactical error. The counter-attacks by local Cretans at Kastelli, Retimo and Pink Hill proved that the Greeks were able fighters if given direction. If Freyberg had paid more credence to men such as Pendlebury and Forrester, a local militia could have assumed a greater responsibility and influence in the battle.

As Schätte secured Kastelli to the west, Ringel was preparing to advance into Prison Valley. Colonel Ramcke followed up the retreat of the 5th Brigade on 23 May, advancing along the coast towards Platanias. Hargest's 5th Brigade, who had withdrawn from the east of Maleme the previous evening, had not long established themselves in their new position at Platanias, when artillery shells from the 95th Mountain Artillery Regiment started to land among their lines. Outbreaks of fierce fighting between infantry occurred around the Platanias bridge and along the coastal road. During the afternoon, RAF bombers were spotted on their way to bomb Maleme airfield. The sight of the bombers briefly raised the morale of the 5th Brigade, but the raid did little damage to the Germans at Maleme. Later in the afternoon it was clear that the 2nd Battalion from the 85th Mountain Division were succeeding in their attempt to outflank New Zealand positions to cut them off from Galatas. Hargest and Puttick had foreseen the danger and were primed to pull the 5th Brigade back farther beyond Galatas and Daratsos. By the early hours of next morning, Hargest's exhausted men had completed the withdrawal behind the Galatas ridge near the General Hospital. The wounded were carried on improvised stretchers made from doors and ladders, or two rifles and battledress. The Germans were quick to follow, but were forced back on numerous occasions by the unconventional tactics of the Maoris, who with alarming bravery would turn suddenly and charge with bayonets fixed sending the paratroops sprawling in disarray. A battalion of the 85th Mountain Regiment attempted to encircle the retreating New Zealanders on the right flank. Fierce resistance from the 8th Greek Regiment and Cretan irregulars halted the mountain troops, led by Major Treck. The intervention from the Greeks and Cretans prevented the encirclement and destruction of the New Zealand Division.

Freyberg's mood was pessimistic, his forces were steadily depleted and there was no viable way of reinforcing them. Freyberg wrote in his report that the enemy bombing was so accurate that it was only 'a question of time before our now shaken troops must be driven out of the positions they occupied'. Without artillery, transport and tools Freyberg believed 'there were two alternatives, defeat in the field and capture, or withdrawal'.[11] In contrast to Freyberg's mood, the Chief of Staff sent an optimistic message to Wavell and Cunningham on 24 May stating that: 'If we stick it out [the] enemy's effort may peter out.'[12] Churchill, typically attempting to inspire the impossible, presumably instigated the message.

On 24 May there was little action at Prison Valley. However, in nearby Canea, the Luftwaffe decided to demonstrate their awesome power. German aircraft launched a savage bombardment against Canea to dishearten the population, and break up communication and supply lines for the front at Galatas. In ten-minute intervals waves of Stukas attacked the town; lone fighters would peel off from the main group to machine-gun down alleyways; others would intermittently rake the nearby woods with fire. Birds flew from every direction in bewilderment and the bomb blasts created huge dust clouds, which rose high above the town. The attack lasted for over four hours. Sergeant Charles recalled after the attack:

'I felt sick . . . to think of all the innocent people being indiscriminately slaughtered.'[13] Other eyewitnesses likened the bombing of Canea to the 'end of the world'.[14] At one stage there were approximately fifty aircraft in the sky. Roy Farran noted: 'The way they came over in ceaseless squadrons to bomb that helpless town was quite merciless.'[15] Women and children took refuge in cellars, as the bombs tore through Canea. In the midst of the bombing, Geoffrey Cox recalled a solitary drunk Australian deserter, wandering in the street oblivious to the chaos that was happening around him. As bombs whistled through the air, the Australian nonchalantly scavenged for wine and bread from the debris. His indifference to the attack raised spirits, as did his bounty, which he shared with the inhabitants of the cellar. The whole of Canea was ablaze; red and yellow flames writhed and twisted high into the sky. The villagers stood in stunned silence as they watched their homes burn; some men were in tears; others violently cursed the Germans. For some Cretans, Canea was the only town that they had ever known. On the evening of 24 May Freyberg moved his headquarters to Suda Point. As he passed through Canea, he saw the dying embers of what was left of the town; masonry filled the street with broken carts, household items and clothing. Among the debris there were corpses caked in white dust. Canea was reduced to a heap of rubble. Throughout the smashed streets, dust and smoke lay like a thick fog across the roads; the grey mass was broken only by the dull flickering flames of the burning wreckage.

On the morning of 25 May General Student landed in Maleme. He had previously been refused permission to leave Athens until victory was guaranteed. Goering had sent him to Crete now to ensure that the Luftwaffe was credited with the victory over the army. Although Student was in Crete, he had no control over operational orders and his adversary Ringel remained in command. Student decorated some of his men, but the moment was tarnished by the reality of what had happened. As he travelled through the Maleme area, Student saw at first hand the terrible cost of the initial invasion. He passed many wooden crosses around the airfield that marked the graves of his young paratroopers. According to von der Heydte, Student appeared to have aged; his creation had been half destroyed and lay in ruins. Von der Heydte recalled that the 'price of victory had . . . proved too much for him'.[16] In Berlin the invasion of Crete was eventually announced on the radio; this was a sign that they were assured of victory. It was stated in the 6th Mountain Division War Diary: 'The situation appeared to be sufficiently under control to allow information on the fighting to be issued from now on.'[17]

German confidence was well justified, as the defences around Prison Valley and Galatas were poor. Trenches were badly dug with inadequate barbed wire defences, which were ineffectual against mortar and air attacks. The New Zealanders had little artillery support, but they had six

Vickers guns in position. The battered New Zealanders of Petrol Company, who had few weapons, and virtually no ammunition, defended Pink Hill. The New Zealand Divisional Cavalry under Major John Russell reinforced the line. The 19th New Zealand Battalion held the Canea–Alikianos road, with the Maoris to their left, and two of Vasey's Australian battalions at the base of the valley. The second Greek Regiment was based on the southern heights past Perivolia. There were not enough troops to occupy Ruin Hill, which was a good strategic position that looked out towards Red Hill to the north, and Wheat Hill to the east. The 18th New Zealand Battalion covered the right flank on the coast. The medical officer of the Composite Battalion recalled that morale among the men was suffering; he noticed an increasing number of 'slightly wounded men being brought in by three or four friends in no hurry to go back'.[18] With this in mind, and a German attack imminent, Kippenberger made a personal tour of inspection. He soon came to the conclusion that the Composite Battalion was in no condition to face the 'heavy attacks that must come soon'.[19] Kippenberger noted: 'I was only too clear that the unit had little fighting value left.'[20] Subsequently, the 4th Brigade took responsibility for the areas previously occupied by the Composite Battalion.

During 24 May the men at Galatas enjoyed a brief respite from air attack as the Luftwaffe concentrated on the destruction of Canea. The stench of the town's burnt-out buildings was carried on a gentle wind. The morning had been relatively cool, the sky was overcast, and a faint mist was in the air. As the afternoon wore on, the sun broke through the clouds and turned the sky red; as the light faded, the New Zealanders could see enemy flares in the west. Trepidation filled the air; Kippenberger and his men knew that the Germans were stronger than before and they must hold the line at Galatas if the island was to be saved. As morning broke on 25 May, German aircraft massed above the heads of the New Zealanders at Galatas. The battle around Prison Valley opened with a tremendous bombardment on New Zealand positions from the air, with mortar and artillery fire. One company recorded up to six rounds a minute falling on their position; as the bombs hit, the red earth was thrown violently into the cobalt sky. The explosions created swirling clouds of fine red dust that choked the defenders. During the afternoon the bombardment was concentrated on Galatas itself. The ferocity of the explosions deafened those on the ground and left them senseless. Corporal James Rattenbury from the 19th Battalion stated: 'I was buried to shoulder height in a slit trench with two others by a bomb explosion on HQ. I struggled out; one other person was completely buried and one was killed. Whilst trying to get the buried chap out, I dug a pick into his head. He was unconscious and was sent to 6 Field Ambulance towards Suda Bay. My hearing was affected, but otherwise I was ok.'[21]

After the bombardment, the 100th Mountain Rifle Regiment, under

Colonel Utz, attacked the heights of Galatas; they were supported by Ramcke's troops. Heidrich's battle weary soldiers were to act as reserve. The infantry attack began with the crackle of small arms fire that grew into a thunderous clatter punctuated by the crunch of mortar bombs. The medley of drivers and artillery personnel from Russell's Divisional Cavalry sniped effectively as the German infantry advanced. The green figures were cut down as they moved from the twisted shadows of olive trees to the sun drenched luminous patches of open ground. All around, branches and leaves fell as bullets cut through the thick olive groves. During the midday heat, many of the mountain troops found themselves trapped in a stifling oven of sun-baked rocks. As the afternoon progressed, and the shadows lengthened, the mountain troops began to make progress. John Russell's men, south of Galatas, were heavily attacked, but the 18th Battalion's line, farther up the coast, was the first to break. Lieutenant-Colonel Gray found his position at Ruin Hill under great pressure and was forced back. The mountain troops were quick to exploit the first sign of weakness among the New Zealanders and promptly seized Ruin Hill, which overlooked the positions around the Galatas heights. Simultaneously, Ramcke's group was making good progress south of the coastal road on the right flank of Ruin Hill. Gray led a small party including a padre, cooks and clerks, to halt the infiltration from Ramcke's men. But the superior weapons of the Germans forced Gray's party back, with only twelve of their number left intact. Captain Basset had visited the front to see the 18th Battalion's predicament for himself. He noted that the sky was swarming with German aircraft; dive-bombers 'made the ground a continuous earthquake'. What Basset thought would be a relatively simple task turned into a 'nightmare race dodging falling branches.' As Basset headed towards the right flank of Gray's position he found himself in a 'hive of grey-green figures'.[22]

By 19.00 there were only a few survivors of two companies, desperately holding Wheat Hill from the enemy who were closing in around them. John Russell's men south of Galatas were also hard pressed; it was reported that 200 wounded filled the regimental aid post and the trucks were 'taking them down to the Advanced Dressing Station in loads like butchers' meat'.[23] To the north, the 18th Battalion had suffered 100 troops killed, and there was a stream of walking wounded fleeing their positions. From the commanding vantage point of Ruin Hill, the Germans were able to rain continuous mortar and artillery fire down onto New Zealand positions at Wheat Hill. After Kippenberger had refused two requests to withdraw, D Company were quickly overrun and surrendered. As the German attack became concentrated on Galatas, Kippenberger went to the thick of the action. On his way to the front he discovered a hollow covered with undergrowth that housed 'a party of women and children huddled together like little birds. They looked at me silently, with black, terrified eyes.'[24]

The Germans soon tore through the defences on Wheat Hill and the defensive front began to crack. New Zealand troops from the 18th Battalion and Composite Battalion began to retreat en masse towards Galatas town. The seriously wounded were left behind to fall into German hands. Men scurried back with fear in their eyes screaming: 'Back, Back! ... They're coming through in thousands. Back for your lives.'[25] As the walking wounded stumbled towards Galatas, the retreat was verging on disarray. Lieutenant-Colonel Gray was one of the last to return, 'looking twenty years older than three hours before'.[26] Kippenberger was trying desperately to rally his troops and screamed at the top of his voice: 'Stand for New Zealand!'[27]

Kippenberger proceeded to plug the gaps in the line with elements of the 4th and 5th Brigades. The defences in Galatas itself held firm. A group of Australian artillery appeared at an opportune moment with four Italian seventy-five-millimetre guns. The artillery fire scattered German concentrations that were building among the houses and gardens on the northern outskirts of Galatas. Eventually Cemetery Hill fell and German troops surrounded Pink Hill. The Petrol Company, an improvised collection of fitters and drivers, under Captain Rowe, resisted the cream of Hitler's infantry. Two platoons from the 19th Battalion were sent to assist the defence of the hill. Rowe's men were subjected to intense fire and plunging raids from dive-bombers. Rowe waited until the last minute before deciding that his men could endure no more and they were withdrawn to Galatas. Despite fighting a retreat, the New Zealanders' discipline in holding their fire to the last moment roused respect from Ringel. 'Never before [the fighting in Crete] had we run up against men who would stand and shoot and stay and fight it out.'[28] A German officer recalled a New Zealander who 'pulled two egg-shaped hand grenades.' The first exploded prematurely taking off his left hand, but he succeeded in throwing the 'second one to the feet of the Germans only three paces away'.[29]

Kippenberger was still desperately trying to rally his troops when swarms of Germans began to appear on the horizon, and he was also informed that the right flank was in serious danger of collapse. Kippenberger's efforts were in vain and he was forced to retreat through Galatas and re-form a new line at Daratsos. Not all of the defenders retreated; John Russell's men risked being cut off south of Galatas. German troops from the 2nd Battalion poured into Galatas. Kippenberger decided that 'it was no use trying to patch the line anymore, obviously we must hit or everything would crumble away'.[30] He decided that an immediate counter-attack was needed to save Russell's men and gain respite from the German onslaught. The counter-attacking force consisted of two companies from the New Zealand 23rd Battalion, who were 'tired, but fit to fight and resolute'.[31]

Kippenberger addressed his troops with his pipe in his mouth; he informed them that if the counter-attack was not successful the whole front would collapse. At this point Roy Farran's light tanks arrived. Farran described Kippenberger, 'walking up and down steadying everyone'.[32] Kippenberger welcomed their arrival and asked Farran to drive into Galatas town to assess the situation. Meanwhile the troops fixed bayonets and waited. Sandy Thomas from the 23rd Battalion described his fear mounting; his throat was dry and stomach frozen. He recalled the mood in his platoon: 'Everyone looked tense and grim and I wondered if they were feeling as afraid as I.' As Thomas glanced around the platoon, he recalled: 'It occurred to me suddenly that this was going to be the biggest moment of my life.'[33]

Farran's battered machines rumbled up the road towards Galatas, spraying machine-gun fire as they went. On reaching the centre of the village square, the second tank was hit by an anti-tank rifle wounding the driver and second commander. The two tanks returned to Kippenberger; Farran disconcertingly reported over the noise of the engine: 'The place is stiff with Jerries.'[34] Kippenberger asked Farran to return into the village, but this time leading the infantry. The injured crew from the second tank were taken out and replacements were found to drive the tank. Farran took them down the road for some basic instructions.

As they set out, Thomas looked skywards towards 'the twinkling stars and prayed fervently for guidance'.[35] A whistle was blown and orders were barked as the line of 200 men started to advance grimly. Stragglers who had fled less than an hour earlier, returned to their ranks for the counter-attack; even the walking wounded requested to join the group. The mercurial Captain Michael Forrester had also taken his place among the ranks of the 23rd Battalion; typically he was without a helmet and carrying only a rifle and bayonet. Forrester recalled that the Maoris began 'their haka war-chant and everyone took it up. The noise was incredible.'[36] Thomas wrote: 'One felt one's blood rising swiftly above the fear and uncertainty until only inexplicable exhilaration, quite beyond description, remained.'[37] With that they ran up the hill, with white houses either side of them, unable to keep pace with the tanks.

As the group disappeared from view, Kippenberger described a sudden outbreak of noise: 'scores of automatics and rifles being fired at once, the crunch of grenades, screams and yells – the uproar swelled and sank, swelled again to a terrifying crescendo.'[38] Gray heard what he described as a 'wild-beast noise of yelling charging men as the 23rd swept up the road'.[39] Fire came from everywhere, behind walls, through windows and rooftops. Belated mortar bombs fell harmlessly behind the attackers, who were already among their enemy. The Germans had been caught unawares and many of them were still inside the houses. Hand-to-hand fighting ensued in the streets; bayonets were used on both sides; in some cases men fought with their bare fists. In one instance, a large German seized a New Zealander by the throat and used him as a human shield. The soldier was released when the German fell to a blow from the butt of another New Zealander's rifle, who had crept up behind him. The German's victim, a company cook, picked himself up and joined the attack once again. Women and children fled their homes that once again became a battlefield. As the tanks burst into the village for a second time, the Germans were taken by surprise. They had repelled the first assault so successfully that they thought the fighting was over for the night. Farran's tank circled around shooting at the doorways of houses. His tank was hit by fire from all angles. In the distance Farran could see German distress flares going up into the sky and shortly afterwards mortar fire rained in on the square. Farran's tank was suddenly hit by a blinding flash and his gunner dropped from the turret groaning in pain. Farran had also been hit and he slumped with his gunner to the bottom of the turret, as the Germans shot holes out the tank with anti-tank rifles. Farran was hit twice more, before pushing his gunner out of the turret and escaping to the cover of a stone wall. Farran lay badly wounded 'in the infernal din',[40] and he prayed for the arrival of the New Zealand infantry.

As Sandy Thomas and his men advanced, they saw the driver of the second tank hurtling towards them. A frantic face appeared from the turret of the tank and screamed that the area was crawling with Germans and his lead tank had been destroyed. He demanded that Thomas clear the road of his men and let him through. Thomas ordered him to turn the tank around, before thrusting the point of his pistol against the driver's head through a square opening in the front of the tank. The driver quickly protested: 'I'll do anything I'm ordered – it's the bastard above who needs the pistol.'[41] As the tank began to turn and move off, the hysterical man in the turret leapt from the tank and made off down the road screaming. Thomas raised his revolver and took aim, but could not bring himself to shoot. Suddenly 'a shot rang out and the screams ceased. A private soldier with a smoking rifle looked grimly around his friends.' Nothing was said as the party moved onwards. Thomas reflected after the battle: 'When one man breaks, he affects the man who is wavering, and in no time a strong company can become a rabble.'[42]

As the New Zealanders surged into the town, Thomas recalled 'screams and shouts showed desperate panic in front of us and I suddenly knew that we had caught them ill-prepared',[43] although Thomas noted: 'Had our charge been delayed even minutes the position could easily have been reversed.' Grenades were thrown from the windows of the houses and brilliant tracer bullets ricocheted all around. As Thomas's men engaged their enemy, bayonets entered chests and throats 'with the same horrible sound, the same hesitant ease as when we used them on the straw packed dummies at Burnham'. The charge by the New Zealanders was a success:

'The Hun seemed in full flight . . . they swarmed wildly, falling over one another – there was little fire against us now.' As he turned to face more of the enemy, Thomas remembered the 'sound of the tinkle and rattle of a grenade', as it fell behind him. Thomas shot an assailant who plunged towards him, before being struck by 'something like a sledge-hammer'[44] on the thigh. At the moment a bullet smashed into his thigh, the grenade exploded, peppering Thomas with shrapnel up his back. Everything went black and Thomas felt himself struggling to regain self control; the cracking of fire overhead and shrieks receded into the background as he lay in the road. When Thomas regained consciousness, he could hear a distinctly English voice. Farran lay a few yards away from Thomas and was shouting: 'Come on New Zealand! Clean 'em out New Zealand!'[45] Thomas had been hit with an explosive bullet that had turned his thigh into a 'warm mangled mess'.[46] A fellow wounded soldier dragged Thomas into a ditch, which offered some protection.

By midnight the re-capture of Galatas was complete. The New Zealanders had restored the line at a heavy cost during the street fighting and they suffered terrible casualties. After the attack, Kippenberger described his state as 'more tired than ever before in my life, or since', as he fumbled in the dark to find Inglis's command post which was a 'tarpaulin-covered hole in the ground'.[47] Kippenberger informed Inglis that he required at least two fresh battalions to restore the right flank and hold onto the gains at Galatas. Inglis accepted that with the right flank exposed, Galatas was indefensible; he therefore reluctantly decided to withdraw the men to a shortened defensive line beyond Karatsos. Dittmer of the 28th (Maori) Battalion offered to counter-attack again, but there seemed no option but to fall back. Both Freyberg and Puttick were convinced that a stand-up fight to the finish would have been suicidal in the face of German air supremacy. To avoid unnecessary loss of life, Kippenberger's men were ordered to withdraw for a second time. In the midst of the battle it was difficult for Freyberg to comprehend that the enemy pressure might fade. A German officer noted: 'We were both amazed and relieved that the counter-attack after clearing the town of Galatas advanced no further.'[48] Freyberg was unaware that the enemy would withdraw their crushing airpower and divert their supplies for their forthcoming offensive against Russia.

Kippenberger's men re-formed a line at Daratsos; Russell's survivors and those stranded at Pink Hill disengaged to join the line. In Galatas town, the seriously injured were left behind, including Sandy Thomas and Roy Farran. As the men retreated Galatas fell into silence; only the groans of the wounded could now be heard in the narrow streets. The silence was abruptly broken as German mortar shells began to fall on the town once again. The women of the village braved the shells to bring the injured water. A 12-year-old girl emerged from the broken masonry to tend to the wounded; she covered them with rugs and offered them sweet goat's milk. Ian Stewart wrote that all had retreated apart from Sergeant Hulme who had learnt during the day that the enemy had killed his brother and he was seeking vengeance. Hulme dressed in a German uniform, looted from a dead parachutist, and walked alone among German lines, with a sniper's hood pulled over his face. He could expect no mercy if he was caught. German reports on the battle for Galatas made reference to New Zealand troops using German uniform; it seemed that they were justified. During the night Hulme managed to kill three German troops who ventured from their lines to scavenge for food.

During the battle for Galatas the New Zealanders had illustrated what could be achieved with a determined counter-attack. If the men of the 23rd had been unleashed on the paratroopers at Maleme on the first night, the Germans would have been defeated. An attack on the second night by the 21st and 23rd Battalions could have made the breakthrough to the Tavronitis. One notable factor from the conflict in Crete was that the commanders, with the exception of Inglis and Kippenberger, consistently underrated the fighting power of their men, although Dr Stephanides was concerned that he was increasingly treating soldiers with no apparent injuries. Many were suffering the effects of nervous exhaustion. Stephanides described the moment after one of the men he was treating dropped a mug: 'we all threw ourselves flat on our faces on the floor, including the man who dropped the mug!'[49] Everyone laughed afterwards, but Stephanides detected that it was not a hearty laugh.

Churchill wrote to Freyberg: 'Your glorious defence commands admiration . . . We know enemy [sic] is hard pressed. All aid in our power is being sent.' To Wavell he sent: 'Victory in Crete essential at this turning point in the war. Keep hurling in all aid you can.'[50] On 26 May Freyberg decided that the battle was lost. He cabled Wavell: 'in my opinion the limit of endurance has been reached by the troops under my command here at Suda Bay.' He continued: ' No matter what decision is taken by the Commanders-in-Chief from a military point of view our position here is hopeless.'[51] Freyberg believed that the island was lost long before he officially reported to Wavell. On the evening of 24 May Freyberg wrote in his report: 'The enemy bombing was accurate and it was only a matter of time before our now shaken troops must be driven out of positions they occupied.'[52] After reading what was effectively Freyberg's request for authorisation to evacuate the island, Wavell replied that if Freyberg were to hold on the 'effect of the whole position in the Middle East would be all the greater'. He also stated that the commandos of Layforce, under Colonel Laycock, would be landed on the night of 26 May. With these reinforcements Freyberg might be able 'to push the enemy back or at least relieve the sectors in greatest danger.'[53] Wavell suggested that Freyberg join with troops at Retimo and prevent further enemy incursions from the east. Later that afternoon Freyberg began discussing the possible with-drawal to Sfakia. Freyberg could not officially set the evacuation in motion, as he had not received official permission from Wavell. Freyberg stated that the Commander-in-Chief and his staff would not say 'stand and fight it out, nor would they contemplate evacuation'.[54] Freyberg noted that 'once the word "withdrawal" is used no more fighting takes place',[55] although preparations for the evacuations were made, and food dumps were established for the journey to Sfakia. Freyberg requested that eighty tons of meat and biscuits be landed at Suda, therefore it was imperative that he should 'keep Suda and prevent it from being under fire on the night of the 26th'.[56] It was decided that a line must be maintained west of the Kladiso river. The line was to be held by the New Zealanders of 5th Brigade, and the 19th Australian Brigade, under Brigadier Vasey. The 2nd Greeks in the hills to the south supported them on the left flank. Behind the line was Force Reserve, which consisted of 1,200 men from the 1st Welch Regiment, the Rangers and the Northumberland Hussars. That night, two destroyers, *Hero* and *Nizam*, appeared with the mine layer *Abdiel* at Suda Pier with vital supplies. These ships also carried two battalions of 400 commandos under Colonel Laycock. As the commandos arrived they were told to jettison their heavy equipment and radios, thus ruling them out of any offensive role.

NOTES

1   Stewart, Ian, *The Struggle for Crete 20 May–1 June*, London: OUP, 1991, p. 363.
2   Clark, Alan, *The Fall of Crete*, London: Cassell, 1962, p. 90.
3   MacDonald, Callum, *The Lost Battle – Crete 1941*, London: Macmillan, 1993, p. 216.
4   Ibid, p. 215.
5   Stewart, op. cit., p. 370.
6   Ibid, p. 317.
7   Ibid, p. 367.
8   Ibid, p. 368.
9   Bräuer statement, WO311/372/PRO, 15 February 1946, XC131897.
10   Clark, op. cit., p 84.
11   Davin, D, *Official History of New Zealand in the Second World War*, Wellington: 1953, p. 354.
12   Churchill, Winston, *The Second World War*, Vol. III, London: Cassell, 1950, p. 260.
13   Stewart, op. cit., p. 372.
14   Beevor, Anthony, *Crete – The Battle and the Resistance*, London: John Murray, 1991, p.186.
15   Farran, Roy, *Winged Dagger*, London: Cassell, 1948, p. 93.
16   MacDonald, op. cit., p. 264.
17   Stewart, op. cit., p. 377.
18   Clark, op. cit., p. 147.
19   Ibid.

20   Ibid, p. 148.
21   Hutching, Megan (ed.), *A Unique Sort of Battle. New Zealanders Remember Crete*, Auckland: HarperCollins, 2001, p. 128.
22   Stewart, op. cit., p. 384.
23   Ibid, p. 385.
24   Beevor, op. cit., p. 187.
25   Thomas, W B, *Dare to be Free*, Alan Wingate, 1951, p. 26.
26   Stewart, op. cit., p. 387.
27   Ibid.
28   Clark, op. cit., p. 149.
29   Ibid, p. 153.
30   Ibid, p. 154.
31   Beevor, op. cit., p. 188.
32   Ibid.
33   Thomas, op. cit., p. 28.
34   MacDonald, op. cit., p. 265.
35   Thomas, op. cit., p. 28.
36   Beevor, op. cit., p. 189.
37   Thomas, op. cit., p. 29.
38   Beevor, op. cit., p. 189.
39   Davin, op. cit., p. 313.
40   Farran, op. cit., p. 100.
41   Thomas, op. cit., p. 29.
42   Ibid, p. 30.
43   Clark, op. cit., p. 156.
44   Thomas, op. cit., p. 31.
45   Farran, op. cit., p. 100.
46   Thomas, op. cit., p. 31.
47   Beevor, op. cit., p. 191.
48   Clark, op. cit., p. 157.
49   MacDonald, op. cit., p. 267.
50   Clark, op. cit., p. 163.
51   Ibid, p. 164.
52   Davin, op. cit., p. 294.
53   Ibid, p. 365.
54   Stewart, op. cit., p. 401.
55   Freyberg, Bernard, comments on the battle for Crete, 31 October 1949, CAB 106/701.
56   Ibid.

CHAPTER XIII

Evacuation

The new line west of the Kladiso river held largely thanks to a misguided raid by the Luftwaffe, who strafed and bombed a battalion of the 85th Mountain Regiment for forty-five minutes. The raid demoralised the German troops who had been advancing towards Perivolia where the 2nd Greek Regiment was in the process of disintegration. Two Australian battalions, the 2/8th and 2/7th, bolstered the line, blocking the end of Prison Valley. To the north were three reduced New Zealand battalions from 5th Brigade who formed a line in front of Canea. On 26 May Freyberg handed control of the retreating forces over to General Weston, having lost confidence in Puttick's judgement. Puttick stressed to Freyberg that the Australians holding the newly formed line in the south were under extreme pressure, and that he was considering a further withdrawal. New Zealanders of 5th Brigade were weary after a week of fighting and it was rumoured that in the south the 2nd Greeks were about to break. Freyberg retorted that it was imperative that the new line be held at all costs and vetoed a general retreat. A further withdrawal would have brought the Germans within a mile of the docks and thus endanger the landing of Laycock's commandos and vital supplies. Freyberg went on to say that Force Reserve would relieve the New Zealanders of 5th Brigade and informed Weston of the orders he had given to Brigadier Inglis: 'I advised him to put in the Force Reserve to stabilize the line and relieve the NZ Division that night.'[1] Puttick's Australian battalions under Brigadier Vasey were ordered to stand firm.

Brigadier Inglis was originally appointed to command Force Reserve. However, Inglis presumed from a short conversation with Weston that 'he intended to use these troops himself and not through me'.[2] Therefore, Inglis believed that Force Reserve were no longer his responsibility, and did nothing to prevent the sequence of events that led to their needless sacrifice. The leadership of Force Reserve was the subject of much controversy. The troops of Force Reserve had remained idle during the key battles for the island and many felt that they should have at least been used to support the counter-attack at Galatas.

During the afternoon Brigadier Vasey reported that he was concerned

231

about enemy forces penetrating his left flank and described his situation as 'dangerous'. When Weston was informed, he insisted that the Australians would have to hold on for a further day. Although the line was under extreme pressure it had not broken. Reports of troops falling back did not come from the forward battalions and the main line remained intact. The German 5th Mountain Battalion noted on 26 May that they were meeting fierce resistance throughout the country in various methods of warfare, including snipers and machine-gun nests. German movement on the left flank had drained Vasey of his confidence and he contacted Weston at 18.00 and informed him that it was impossible for his men to retain their position. Vasey requested that his troops be withdrawn in conjunction with the New Zealand Division to a shorter line east of Suda Bay. Weston stated that he was unable to give an immediate decision, but he would discuss Vasey's concerns with General Freyberg. At 21.30 Weston informed Freyberg of Vasey's request to withdraw. Freyberg reaffirmed that Force Reserve were to relieve the New Zealand Division and insisted that Vasey's troops hold the southern part of the line. Freyberg recalled: 'I at once sat down and wrote an order that the Australians were to continue to hold their line.'[3]

Crucially Weston failed to send a dispatch rider to inform Vasey or Puttick of Freyberg's decision. Puttick and Hargest were increasingly frustrated by the lack of direct orders coming from Freyberg and found it difficult to communicate with Weston, who appeared to be suffering from acute fatigue. Puttick was convinced of the necessity of an immediate withdrawal. He stated: 'the enemy movement round Vasey's left flank . . . would cut the line of retreat at the head of Suda Bay.'[4] Also, senior commanders had difficulty in locating General Weston's headquarters, which were situated in a peasant's house around the 42nd Street area. This was a sunken track running south from Suda towards Canea. The 42nd Field Squadron, Royal Engineers, gave 42nd Street its name when they were based there before the invasion. Without clear instructions from Freyberg or Weston, Puttick took a unilateral decision. At 22.30 his patience ran out and he overruled Freyberg's order for the Australians to stand firm, and ordered both Vasey and Hargest to withdraw their troops to 42nd Street under cover of darkness. According to the Official New Zealand War Historian, Puttick took 'full responsibility for counter-manding General Freyberg's order'.[5] He telephoned Vasey and Hargest personally to authorise the withdrawal. Puttick's decision probably saved the Australian troops from being outflanked and cut off the following day, but crucially neither Puttick nor Inglis had informed Force Reserve of the withdrawal.

After a meeting with Freyberg that evening, Weston ordered Force Reserve to march to the front and replace 5th Brigade, unaware that the Australians on their left flank had withdrawn. Weston was finally informed of Puttick's decision at 01.00. Half an hour later, Weston sent out some dispatch riders to belatedly recall Force Reserve without avail. Force Reserve were allowed to march to their deaths or capture without knowing that the line was fatally compromised by the retreat of the Australians on their left flank. Force Reserve had suffered only slight casualties throughout the battle; they had fought a series of small encounters on the outskirts of Canea, and had only vague information about the battles at Maleme and Galatas. Lieutenant Duncan, who was to lead Force Reserve, had spent the evening at Weston's headquarters trying to establish the fate of his troops. He recalled: 'Weston would not alter his wish to hold the front line.' Duncan pointed out that if he 'sent Force Reserve forward he would never see them again'.[6] Force Reserve moved forward shortly after midnight. As they passed through Canea, they were enveloped in the stench of death and an eerie silence. The only movement came from flames that flickered softly among the debris. As Force Reserve progressed there was a growing sense of solitude; they encountered neither friend nor foe, only the unburied dead were there to greet them, as they took up their positions among the olive groves. By 02.30 they had reoccupied the old positions of 5th Brigade along the line west of the Klasido river.

The first encounter took place in the early hours of the morning. One of Sergeant Creighton's soldiers asked him if he could stretch his legs and walked off into the olive grove and did not return. Shortly after, two Cretan children came running out of the woods; one had been shot in the back. Creighton and his men grabbed their weapons and headed towards the olive grove; they had walked about fifty yards when they spotted a German officer 'immaculately dressed, with beautiful polished helmet and boots'.[7] Creighton took aim and shot him through the chest and the German officer fell dead. This incident was the catalyst for a series of skirmishes that broke out across the line.

Five German Regiments were poised to attack Suda: Ramcke's group along the coastal road, the 100th Mountain Regiment under Utz, the 3rd Parachute Regiment, the 141st Mountain Regiment and the 85th Mountain Regiment under Krakau. The Germans were unaware that 5th Brigade and the 19th Australian Brigade had withdrawn to 42nd Street, leaving Force Reserve hopelessly isolated. During the initial skirmishes, Utz reported that he had lost contact with the enemy in the south, a clear indication that Vasey's men had withdrawn. Ringel immediately ordered Utz to push forward towards Suda Bay and cut off the enemy's retreat.

The line at the Kladiso river was a mile and a half long, and was held by 1,200 troops of Force Reserve who were expected to repel an assault from 4,500 well-equipped Germans, who had already begun to exploit the open left flank vacated by Vasey's men. At 08.30 Ringel launched a general attack backed by machine guns and mortars. Duncan quickly realised that the German attack was making unopposed progress in the south and was attempting to encircle his men. From the beginning of the fighting, Duncan's men had tried to contact Weston's headquarters without success. A series of runners were killed as they ran across open ground trying to send messages back to Weston. Duncan stated that he received no message to withdraw and commented: 'I would have been off like a "scalded cat" if I had.' Duncan confirmed: 'I was quite aware how precarious our position was.'[8] Fire rained on Duncan's troops from all sides. From his command post, Duncan could hear the destruction of his forces; the ominous rattle of German Spandaus and the thud of mortars gradually consumed the sound of single rifle shots and Bren fire. Under tremendous pressure, Duncan was forced to withdraw B and D Companies on the left flank.

Eventually runners were able to communicate Duncan's orders and the troops began to run for their lives. Groups of men from B and D Companies splashed through the shallow water of the Kladiso with the grey figures of their German pursuers emerging closely behind them east of the river. Intermittently the troops would halt their retreat to fire at the enemy before stumbling on. After an hour, the retreating troops reached a clearing through the olive trees where they saw a line of riflemen before them. Their first reaction was that the enemy had encircled them before they realised that the line was made up of troops clad in khaki uniform. The retreating troops of Force Reserve had reached the defensive line formed at 42nd Street.

As the Germans pushed forward in pursuit of Force Reserve, they ran into the new positions of the 5th New Zealand Brigade and the Australians, in front of 42nd Street. Groups of hungry and exhausted Maoris rested in the sun when suddenly there was a series of explosions around their position, followed by a rattle of small arms fire, which clipped the leaves off nearby trees. Their reaction was immediate, bayonets were fixed, magazines filled and safety catches released. Captain Rangi Royal issued final instructions to B Company, brandishing a bamboo walking pole in one hand and a pistol in the other. The Maoris of 5th Brigade led a frantic counter-attack by the point of the bayonet. At this point the Germans were just 200 yards away from 42nd Street and the appearance of the yelling Maoris through the olive groves sent them immediately to ground and they opened up heavy defensive fire. The stationary German positions were quickly enveloped on the flanks by the surging Maori charge. Some were seen firing captured Spandau from the hip, while a comrade ran along side carrying the ammunition belts. Sapper Douglas Chitty recalled: 'The order was given to fix bayonets and then a Maori officer jumped up on the embankment waving his stick and shouting, "charge!" We all rushed back into the olives – the Maoris yelling war cries – and soon had the Germans fleeing before us. I did not bayonet anyone but may have shot someone – it was all so confused.' After getting separated from the main group, Chitty came across a German medic attending to three German wounded: 'he greeted me in quite a friendly fashion and offered me a glass of wine, which I readily accepted. One of the Germans had been bayoneted in the thigh and his leg had swollen to elephant size. They didn't seem to worry about me, even though I had a rifle. I tried to make conversation with the medic fellow, but we had no common language. Then he gave me some ointment to put on some open wounds I had on my legs and with that I continued on back to 42nd Street.'[9]

When the fighting abated, over 300 Germans lay dead. Private Finlay described the scene: 'The German bodies were strewn everywhere, bayoneted to death. There were bales of sandbags stacked in a woolstore, which the Germans had tried to hide between. [It] was like a slaughter-house. There were bayoneted Germans everywhere. The dead were carrying Hudson chocolates, plus American cigarettes (no doubt from the deserted stores in Greece). The enemy were slaughtered in rows wherever they went to ground and turned to face the rampaging Maori warriors.'[10] The casualties were so severe that the Germans claimed that atrocities had taken place. The Germans were themselves guilty of atrocities that day. It was reported that Germans executed wounded members of the Welch Regiment who had surrendered at the Kladiso river; other captives were made to stand along the front and draw fire from their own side.

The counter-attack at 42nd Street had succeeded in halting the German advance in the south and allowed around 400 men from Force Reserve to escape encirclement through the hills of Suda and the streets of Canea. As the Germans pushed forward at what remained of Force Reserve, Kurt Meyer, from the 100th Mountain Regiment, noted that nearly fifty enemy troops remained to defend the Kladiso bridge with grenades and bayonets. When the battle was over Meyer recalled just 'four men, pale and shattered, [were] taken as prisoners'. Some 200 of the Welch Regiment and the remnants of the Rangers and Northumberland Hussars were involved in a fighting retreat through the streets of Canea. From 42nd Street, Hargest observed their last stand as they were driven through the town to a hill where they were annihilated. Hargest commented on Force Reserve's destruction: 'Whoever sent them should have been shot.'[11] On the hill only an isolated Bren gun section were able to hold out until the following morning. Captured New Zealanders witnessed the Bren gun team operating relentlessly throughout the day. As they ran short of ammunition, a member of the team casually emerged from the gun pit and walked around the hillside in full view of the Germans, who were only 100 yards away. He entered a nearby gun pit and reappeared with some Bren ammunition, before walking through a barrage of bullets at the same leisurely pace for a second time. As the Bren gun opened up again, the

New Zealanders gave a cheer, having been inspired by what they had just witnessed.

It was not until midday that Ringel ascertained that the defenders intended to abandon the Canea and Suda areas. Throughout the morning Ringel expected to clash with the bulk of the enemy force at Canea. The war diary of the 5th Mountain Division noted that they had encountered elite forces around the Canea area. The Germans quickly established a roadblock outside Canea and Ringel's trap was sprung. Ringel's plan of encircling the defenders was complete, but they had only managed to capture remnants of Force Reserve. The defeat of Force Reserve wasted 1,000 of the fittest troops remaining in Crete. Once again the chain of command in Crete was in a shambles; Puttick blamed Weston, Weston blamed Puttick for countermanding Freyberg's orders, and Freyberg blamed Inglis for failing to command Force Reserve. However, the withdrawal of the Australians had bolstered the line at 42nd Street that successfully held and counter-attacked against the German advance.

As von der Heydte entered the streets of Canea he recalled that they were 'strewn with debris ... [and] ... here and there a fire still smouldered'.[12] In the deserted streets, rats ran for cover among the rubble and gutted houses. A pungent smell of olive oil and wine from smashed vats and casks mixed with the stench of decomposing flesh. On reaching the town square, German troops were reunited with their injured comrades who had been left behind in makeshift hospitals by retreating British soldiers. The mayor of Canea met with Captain von der Heydte to offer the formal surrender of the town, ensuring that no further casualties were lost. At first, the mayor did not believe that von der Heydte was the leader of a conquering army such was his bedraggled appearance. By evening the swastika flew over the harbour.

The last stand by the troops at 42nd Street gave Freyberg some respite, but he was still awaiting authorisation from Wavell for a general retreat. Lacking any order from Wavell, Freyberg instructed Colonel Laycock that his commandos were to provide a rearguard with the three remaining *I* tanks. On the afternoon of 27 May Freyberg sent a personal message to Wavell stating that his men could not continue to function without adequate air support and he dismissed Wavell's plan of rallying troops at Retimo as out of the question. Freyberg also stated his intention to withdraw all troops in the Maleme, Suda and Canea areas to the beaches of Sfakia, a small fishing village on the south coast. Wavell was caught between pressure from Freyberg to withdraw from Crete and Churchill's repeated exhortations to 'hurl in reinforcements' to save the island. Realising that Crete was lost, Wavell made a unilateral decision as he replied to the Prime Minister that there was 'no possibility of hurling in reinforcements'. He then formally requested permission to authorise the evacuation of the island. Wavell waited ten hours for a reply from the War

Office until Churchill finally accepted the fate of his forces in Crete. Churchill announced to the War Cabinet: 'all prospect of winning the battle in Crete now appeared to have gone.'[13] Wavell described 27 May as his 'worst day of the war'. During 27 May Rommel had captured the Halfaya Pass in North Africa, Rashid Ali and his followers held Baghdad in Iraq and Churchill had overruled Wavell's decision not to intervene in Syria. To make matters worse Churchill issued Wavell with a blunt warning that he faced dismissal from his position. The sequence of adverse events that befell Wavell on 27 May was testament to how much pressure he was under. Wavell was required to direct operations in a number of theatres, which inevitably brought his downfall.

That evening CREFORCE headquarters withdrew southwards by car and truck over the mountains towards Sfakia. Rumours of a general retreat and evacuation were rife among the defenders of Crete. As Freyberg predicted, the defenders began hurrying along the roads in disorder; the retreat represented a rout rather than a close run battle. Nearly every yard men passed discarded equipment including various arms, gas masks, kit bags, grenades and burst open suitcases. Freyberg stated: 'people had taken a flying start in any available transport they could steal and which they later left abandoned.' Freyberg concluded: 'Never shall I forget the disorganization and almost complete lack of control of the masses.'[14] Leading the withdrawal were the troops from Suda who had been involved in little fighting on the island and had spent the two weeks awaiting transfer to Egypt.

At Suda, Laycock's commandos and two companies of Maoris, under Captain Rangi Royal, acted as a rearguard along the Canea–Retimo road to allow the remnants of 5th Brigade to withdraw to the south. Laycock argued that his men did not have heavy weapons and were not capable of holding the position, but the order stood. West of Suda only the dead and seriously wounded remained, many lying semi-conscious in ditches or in olive groves, dying of thirst as their wounds turned gangrenous. On 28 May Royal's men came under attack from elements from Lieutenant-Colonel Wittmann's motorcycle detachment. German accounts stated that the fighting was fierce and costly – 'every tree had to be fought for'.[15] Under heavy mortar and machine-gun fire, Rangi was able to hold on until late morning. In the afternoon Laycock's commandos came under attack, and the battalion soon became scattered due to lack of cover or entrenching tools. As the Germans began to infiltrate the flanks of the rearguard, they retreated into the hills carrying their wounded.

With the Suda front broken, Ringel was free to pursue the retreating lines of British and Commonwealth troops across the mountains. However, the Mountain Troops advanced cautiously after the fierce Greek resistance they had experienced at Alikianou. While the Germans were dithering over their next move, Freyberg's men were making their way up the mountain road to safety. As had happened previously in Greece, secret papers were burned and preparations were made to move the men to the south coast. Kit was booby-trapped with grenades, vehicles were sabotaged and explosive charges were placed in fuel dumps timed to go off the following morning. By 28 May the bulk of the forces elsewhere in Crete had disengaged and were making their way down to Sfakia. Crucially, Ringel disregarded information from prisoners of war, which suggested that Freyberg's force would attempt to escape through the tiny fishing village of Sfakia. Instead Ringel persisted in his original plan to relieve the men at Retimo and Heraklion, rather than advancing on the road to Sfakia.

Heraklion had suffered badly from the intensive bombing of the Luftwaffe who had attacked the town for three days as a reprisal for their defeat there. According to Captain Tomlinson, in Heraklion there was 'one large stench of decomposing dead, debris from destroyed dwelling places, roads were wet and running from burst water pipes.' The corpses had attracted the attention of emaciated stray dogs. 'There was a stench of sulphur, smouldering fire and pollution of broken sewers. Conditions were set for a major epidemic.'[16] The hospital at Knossos, which had previously been respected by the Germans, was now heavily mortared and machine-gunned. The hospital was virtually surrounded and there was little hope of bringing the wounded away. The Germans claimed that it was being used as an observation post. Closer to the truth was the fact that the Germans were frustrated by the delaying battles that hindered their progress.

Chappel was told in a cable from the Middle East that warships would arrive in Heraklion at midnight to evacuate his troops. The ships would be able to take a maximum of 4,000 troops, which meant that there would be scarcely enough room for the British and Commonwealth troops, not to mention the Greeks and Cretans. As night fell the defending battalions began to make their way towards the harbour. A member of the Black Watch noted that pity was felt for the Cretan people who had fought beside them so valiantly and now were 'being abandoned, on tiptoe at midnight, and without warning, to the vengeful enemy'.[17] On 28 May the white-haired Satanas, clad in Cretan dress, appeared in Heraklion to meet Brigadier Chappel. Satanas said to Chappel: 'My son' placing his hand on Chappel's shoulder 'We know you are going away tonight. Never mind! You will come back when the right time comes.' Chappel endeavoured to gather as many weapons as possible to hand over to the guerrillas as Satanas had vowed 'to carry on the fight.'[18] The Cretan guerrillas had heard of the evacuation, but unfortunately the Greek army had not. Nevertheless, it was decided in Alexandria that there was not enough room for the Greeks to embark on the evacuation warships.

The evacuation from Heraklion represented the most dangerous phase of the withdrawal from the island, as it involved negotiating the waters of the Kaso Strait that were dominated by the Luftwaffe. Cunningham entrusted the retreat at Heraklion to Rear Admiral Rawlings and Force B. The evacuation force comprised the cruisers *Orion*, *Ajax* and *Dido* and six destroyers: *Hotspur*, *Decoy*, *Kimberley*, *Hereward*, *Jackal* and *Imperial*. Rawlings' force left Alexandria on 28 May at 06.00. By late afternoon the Luftwaffe attacked south of the Kaso Straits, damaging the *Ajax*, which was sent back without completing the passage to Heraklion. The remainder of the fleet was unscathed and arrived off the port in Heraklion at 23.00.

On 29 May 3,486 men were evacuated from Heraklion. While cruisers lay outside the harbour, the destroyers went in to the main jetty and acted as lighters, ferrying the troops to the cruisers before taking their own complements. Brigadier Chappel's force was embarked in this manner, including all the Australian and British troops (apart from the seriously wounded cut off outside the perimeter at Knossos). At 03.20 the evacuation ships sailed, with the Germans unaware that the withdrawal was underway. Cunningham was keen not to risk his fleet against the Luftwaffe. He recalled: 'We were not really in a favourable condition to evacuate some twenty-two thousand soldiers ... in the face of the Luftwaffe.'[19] The navy were once again without their own air support due to the damage sustained by the aircraft carrier HMS *Formidable*. Despite his reservations, Cunningham admitted that there was no option but to support the army.

Although the initial evacuation had gone smoothly, HMS *Imperial*'s steering gear failed after an hour at sea and the *Hotspur* turned around to come to her aid. A mixture of Black Watch and Australian troops were taken off the *Imperial* and boarded the *Hotspur*. The troops from the *Imperial* had to jump from one ship to another as the *Hotspur* came alongside. All were taken on board safely apart from a group of inebriated Australians who could not be roused. As the *Hotspur* pulled away she fired torpedoes into the *Imperial*, leaving her to sink with the Australians on board.

At 06.00 the first of the Luftwaffe appeared to begin an attack that would last for over eight hours. As the inevitable bombs fell, the evacuation vessels rose out of the water as they accelerated, weaving left and right. The commander of each vessel watched the bombs fall from around 500 feet, when he would direct the vessel accordingly and generally avoided being hit. At the same time a deafening array of anti-aircraft fire was pumped into the air, and multiple pom-pom and four-barrelled machine guns mounted on each side of the ship created a barrage of fire. Corporal Johnstone, who was on one of the destroyers, recalled that a bomb fell towards a gunner firing a pom-pom: 'I glanced at the sailor ... I didn't see the slightest emotion in his face, [despite the fact that] the bomb only missed by about three feet.'[20]

At 06.25 the destroyer *Hereward*, carrying a load of 450 men was hit amidships, Rawlings had no choice but to leave her; previous experience had proved that vessels caught outside the umbrella barrage created by the main battle group were vulnerable. The survivors who littered the water were machine-gunned by a Stuka until an Italian Red Cross seaplane brought them under protection. The majority of the crew from the *Hereward* were rescued by a combination of Italian seaplanes and torpedo-boats. 'The Italian Navy had not forgotten the help given to their own survivors after the battle of Matapan.'[21]

Worse was to follow for Rawlings' squadron that morning. The *Orion*, the most over-crowded of ships carrying over 1,000 soldiers, received two direct hits. Two bombs penetrated three levels of the deck causing devastation among those aboard. The troops on the crowded decks were showered in deadly shrapnel; 260 men were killed and 280 wounded. The men in confined spaces below decks suffered horrific casualties. *Orion* bore the marks of her ordeal as she came into harbour at Alexandria; she was described as a 'terrible sight and the messdeck a ghastly shambles'.[22] The *Dido* was also hit twice, the explosion destroyed the guns which flew upwards and fell smoking into the sea. But she was still able to operate. As many as 103 out of 240 members of the Black Watch were killed by the blast, or drowned in the water that was pumped in an attempt to prevent the fire spreading to the magazine. That evening a soldier from the Black Watch, lit up by a searchlight, played a lament from the bridge. When the vessels finally reached Alexandria on 29 May, the garrison at Heraklion had lost over one fifth of their number. It was a tragedy that the men who had fought so bravely and won their battle at Heraklion had suffered so badly in the evacuation. For the defenders, Heraklion was the most satisfactory of the three major engagements on the island. Those at Heraklion had effectively defeated their enemy on the first day, and had vigorously defended their positions for the remaining eight days against increasing numbers.

On receiving official confirmation of the withdrawal, Freyberg immediately attempted to contact Campbell at Retimo, to order his men to retreat across the mountains to the south coast. Attempts to drop the message and supplies from the air had failed, as there were no ground flares to signal to friendly aircraft. Landing craft arrived with supplies from Suda but no word came of the evacuation. Campbell decided that he could not contemplate leaving his position without officially receiving word, although he was interested to hear from a BBC broadcast that 'the situation in Crete is extremely precarious'.[23] Campbell accepted that he could not break the German hold on the coastal road; instead he insisted on continuing the defence of the airfield as ordered. On 29 May a Greek officer warned Campbell that the British were evacuating the island and that Ringel's men had entered Retimo from the west with motor-cycle troops. Wittmann's motor-cycle detachment waited through the night for the arrival of two tanks that had landed the previous day in Kastelli. Reinforced with tanks Wittmann advanced on to Retimo. Campbell's infantry initially opened fire but the battle was short-lived. Australian soldiers on the beach signalled seawards in the hope that Royal Navy ships were in the area. Germans could be heard in the distance shouting: 'The game's up, Aussies!'[24]

Rather than risk the slaughter of his men, Campbell decided that he would surrender intact; the Germans had also threatened reprisals against the people of Crete if Campbell's resistance continued. With no hope of reaching Sfakia and German reinforcements linking up with those already at Perivolia, Campbell was forced to surrender. He sent a message to Major Sandover: 'I am going to capitulate. I advise you to do the same. Destroy all weapons you possibly can.'[25] Accompanied by his two commanders, he walked forward with a white towel tied to a stick and gave his surrender. Campbell became a prisoner of war while his colleague, Major Sandover, escaped to the hills along with thirteen officers and thirty-nine troops. Sandover and his men lived in the Cretan wilderness for several months before escaping to Egypt by submarine. Sandover received a message from a Cretan man who had helped him: 'Major, my greatest wish is that you will take a glass of wine in my house the day we are free. That is all I wish to live for.'[26] As Campbell's men surrendered, Lew Lind described the solemn moment as the captured men walked through the battlefields. The ground was 'thickly spread with corpses'. Lind noted a paratrooper 'hanging from the telephone wires. Half his head had been blown off.'[27] During a conversation with Campbell, a German major enquired why 'kindred nations should fight?' Campbell tactfully replied that the fight must continue to a conclusion: 'God's iron plough, war, must tear up man's earth before the seed of the future can grow.'[28] Ten days' fighting at Retimo were rendered useless as the battles elsewhere on the island had failed. Despite lacking anti-aircraft guns and being short of ammunition, the men at Retimo repulsed the airborne landing and killed approximately 700 of the enemy. Of the 1,000 troops that formed the garrison at Retimo, 160 were killed in action, 140 had escaped to the hills, heading for the south coast, and 700 were taken prisoner.

Eventually Ringel ordered his troops to capture the village of Stilos, located six miles from Suda Bay and on the road through the mountains to Sfakia. The defence of the main retreating column was reserved for the commandos of Layforce. The commanders of Layforce, Colonel Laycock and Evelyn Waugh, found it impossible to obtain clear instructions from senior commanders. As Laycock and Waugh sought clarification of their orders, Brigadier Major Freddie Graham organised the commandos into two battalions of 400 men. As he prepared his men, Graham noticed the hordes of retreating troops trudging past. Graham was appalled at the roads that were filled with straggling troops 'shambling along in desperate haste. Dirty, weary and hungry – a rabble, one could call them nothing else.'[29] Charles Stewart from Layforce wrote of the retreating troops: 'discipline seemed to have left them . . . they had sore feet through sweat and marching, the skin peeling off their shoulders.'[30]

On 27 May Hargest's men reached the village of Stilos. Here the men could regroup for the remainder of their journey across the White Mountains; a barn was set up for a dressing station for the wounded. New Zealander Colonel Thwigg described the sight of countless men lying wounded. 'It was like the scene of the wounded at Atlanta in *Gone with the Wind*.' Cox agreed it was indeed 'life imitating art with a vengeance'.[31] Kippenberger commented that the signs of the pressure of war were beginning to show. He noticed one of his officers 'walking very fast with odd automaton-like steps and quivering incessantly'.[32] Herbert Longbottom recalled reaching the village of Stilos: 'parched with thirst, drinking deep from the cool water of the village well, and filling our water bottles, which gave us the energy to move on. From there it was a seemingly endless climb up into the mountains with the Germans always in close pursuit. On the way up, Tom and I searched an abandoned jeep and found a full bottle of gin, which we promptly used to wash our tired feet. This helped to harden the skin, which was very fortuitous, because shortly after the sole of my right boot came off, which didn't make it any easier to walk!'[33]

After resting for a while the exhausted troops spotted the German 85th Mountain Regiment advancing towards them. Although exhausted, the New Zealanders soon rose to the challenge. They advanced behind a stone wall within twenty yards of their enemy and rained fire on the Mountain Troops from above. In a brief, but highly successful action, Sergeant Hulme won the Victoria Cross. If the Germans had arrived twenty-four hours earlier, they would have destroyed the helpless retreating hordes. The majority of those at Stilos did not know that their freedom was due to the anonymous Greeks and Cretans who had fought tirelessly at Alikianou and delayed the German advance. The Greeks who fought so magnificently at Alikianou had succeeded in holding their positions against Krakau's 85th Mountain Regiment, for long enough to keep the prospect of saving British and Commonwealth troops from capture alive. Krakau's men advanced with extreme caution and had only reached the hills south of Perivolia; it was this hesitancy that allowed Freyberg's forces to escape encirclement. If Krakau had reached Stilos before 28 May, his forces could have blocked the road leading to the mountains and Sfakia. The Greeks had sacrificed themselves for the sake of their comrades; they were cut off without hope of supply or knowledge of other events on the island.

On 28 May Dr Theodore Stephanides described the men as they withdrew to Sfakia: 'many of them would crack an occasional joke or sit down at the side of the road for a quiet cigarette.' Stephanides was not aware that the retreat was the first stage of a complete evacuation. 'I thought that we were retiring to another defensive position . . . owing to a temporary reverse.'[34] Stephanides found it hard to comprehend the gravity of the situation. He wrote that it 'seemed somehow more like a crowd leaving a football match and finding the trains were not running'.[35] As he trekked across the mountains he met an old Cretan man on a pony who explained to him that he was going down to the coast to kill Germans. Stephanides noticed that he was carrying an ancient rifle and suggested that the old man should choose a weapon from the discarded piles at the side of the road. The old man agreed this was a good idea and went into the village to spread the word.

Captain Peter McIntyre, New Zealand's Official War Artist, recalled: 'Single file the endless line climbed up and up.'[36] Men lay asleep in the road while others stepped over them. The soldiers who attempted to sleep during the day were denied rest by the incessant bombing. As night fell they made their way through the mountains. Second Lieutenant Peter Wildey described the march over the mountains: 'Everybody was exhausted . . . you couldn't move by day too much because . . . planes would just pounce on you and shoot you up . . . The first place we headed for was the Askifou Plain. It's way high up. It was very cold up there. I was with Major and his batman [who] was very, very tired. We were staggering along and [he] said, "Look, sir, I can't go any further. I've just got to have a sleep." He got on a pile of rocks . . . like it was a feather mattress . . . General Freyberg came through at one stage in a battered old car, sort of urging us on.'[37] The retreating soldiers left a littered path of debris including abandoned vehicles, gasmasks, kit bags, mess tins, photographs, cartridge boxes and rifles. The pale blue light of the stars lit the dusty road that was strewn with exhausted retreating troops. Either side of the road was the dim glow of the tips of cigarettes that brightened and dimmed as men smoked. The dark silhouette of the jagged wall of mountains loomed high against the sky as the men got nearer. Black shapes of trudging men could be seen as far as the eye could see in front and behind. There was barely a word spoken between the retreating soldiers; they plodded on in silence, with the exception of a scuffed boot on the road or a clink of a rifle butt against a water bottle. In the darkness an eerie orange flame flickered from the wreck of an Australian transport intermittently revealing the twisted forms of olive trees.

As Theodore Stephanides and his comrades progressed towards the mountains, a German plane appeared and dropped a flare, lighting up the road, rooftops and olive trees. All the men scattered to the roadside to take cover. Stephanides described the troops retreating in 'perfect order' until 'thirty or forty planes swept unexpectedly out of the skies . . . swooped and roared in our direction'.[38] Stephanides and his comrades quickly took refuge in a disused lime kiln. Each blast shook the ground above them and showered them with chunks of earth that rattled against their steel helmets. Although they were below ground level, the blasts were so strong 'that it felt like a thump in the solar plexus . . . Time seemed to be petrified.' After what seemed like hours, the attack abated and men began to emerge dazed from their shelter. Nearby houses were on fire and there were a 'number of huge craters on and around the road and one smashed truck with its driver lying dead beneath it'. [39] Soon all the men appeared from their hiding places and the retreat continued as before.

Air attacks continued to be a source of antagonism for the troops, although they were now less frequent. On one occasion when the Luftwaffe threatened, an Australian was heard screaming: 'if anybody moves, I'll shoot them!'[40] Similarly, as Kippenberger used a torch to read a map, he provoked threats and curses from fellow soldiers; one man got to his feet and kicked the torch from his hands. Kippenberger immediately rose and grabbed the man by the throat, nearly throttling him. He then proceeded to warn the others that if anyone objected to him using a torch again, he would shoot. Roy Coates from the 18th Battalion recalled an air attack as he retreated across the mountains. 'We'd crossed through the grapevines . . . when we heard the planes, so everyone dropped to the ground . . . somebody said to keep moving, because they'd frozen . . . things would have been all right if they had not moved . . . all hell let loose. I was flat on my stomach looking upwards . . . Bill Somerville, who was next to me, tried to get a slightly better view; he lifted his head a bit more, and I just started to say, "Pull your head in," and he suddenly slumped against me. I half turned around and it had just ripped his throat right open. He was dead. I didn't think you could die so quickly . . . There were others injured and killed . . . Many [of the wounded] were just left. They couldn't do anything. If you were in retreat, you couldn't say, "Hang on, I'll just pick this chap up." There's nothing you can do, and it's vital that the able bodied people do get away.'[41]

Daylight gave faces to the retreating men, many of them walking wounded with bloody bandages and missing limbs. During the daytime, men slept in the boulder-scattered countryside, crouching in primitive shelters; many went without food and water. Norm Delaney noted the desperation of some of his colleagues: 'We were a bit short of water. I remember seeing [two] English bloke[s] . . . they found a truck, and turned a tap on underneath and the engine water came out of it. The silly idiots drank it. Some one yelled out to them, "Hey! There's anti-freeze in those trucks." They took no notice. Next thing, we hear them moaning and rolling around.'[42] Passing trucks threw up huge clouds of dust that choked those at the roadside as they rested. Occasionally a lorry would pass 'jammed with wounded, with bandaged men clinging to every corner of it – and a few who looked shamefully fit also grabbing a ride'.[43] There were cases of troops attempting to disguise themselves as injured men by administering false field dressings so they could get off the island with the wounded on the first night.

Local Cretan farmers were extremely tolerant and forgiving of the thousands of passing troops who drank their wells dry and stole eggs and livestock. Soldiers would scramble for vantage points around wells where they could relieve their parched mouths, filling steel helmets, water bottles or webbing equipment. Geoffrey Cox recalled that he joined a queue for twenty minutes before he was able to lower his water bottle. 'It was brackish water, with a brown stain but we drank it thankfully.' Cox recalled a queue for a place at the well was hundreds long until a plane appeared sending men for cover among the rocks. When the plane had passed, the queue formed again and many men who had lost their place 'sat brokenly on rocks nearby, too exhausted even to argue with those now ahead of them'.[44]

As the troops retreated up the mountain the landscape changed notably. The ground became rockier and olive groves were replaced by pine and gorse trees. From the slopes above, a sweet scent of flowering jasmine and lavender emanated. This was hard terrain for troops who were malnourished and whose boots were falling to pieces. Many replaced worn socks with field dressings. Once the men had reached the summit of the steep olive and pine clad slopes of the White Mountains, they were amazed by what they saw. Suddenly before them was a lush green patchwork of fields with beautiful trees and white-washed houses dotted in between a circle of hills. This was the Askifou Plain, a fertile flat piece of ground of meadows, orchards, small tilled fields and tumbling streams and in a bowl. Past the Askifou plain was the Imbros Gorge, a ravine of great beauty and strong scent of wild thyme and pine. This sight immediately lifted the men's spirits.

'Across the plain, the khaki columns crept like ants making thin wavering lines in the distance.' They quenched their choking thirst with long draughts of clean cool water from a well in the plain. Captain Peter McIntyre described the cold water as 'giving wonderful relief to raging thirsts. You gurgled it down, letting it spill over and run down your chest.'[45] Men washed and set down to sleep in the long grass of a nearby orchard. Dubbed the 'saucer', the Askifou Plain was described as too idyllic for war, but war had found it and one noticeable sign was the wreck of a dilapidated tractor that the Luftwaffe had taken the time to destroy. McIntyre noted that this secluded valley would have previously seen little of life passing. With the arrival of the defeated British and Commonwealth troops, the plain was privy to a significant moment in history, witnessing the British Empire fighting for survival. The valley was now subjected to 'dive-bombers and the hurtling trucks and heard the rattle of machine-guns. Civilization had caught up with it.'[46]

By night the troops had vacated the idyllic scenery of the Askifou Plain and were marching down the mountain where the cliff fell away to sheer drops. The sea could be seen in the distance; only a precipitous decline along a goat track stood between them and freedom. The failure to build a road connecting to the port was angrily felt. The senses of the retreating men were dulled and thinking was confused. 'Tempers flared up out of tiredness.' Captain McIntyre recalled: 'I remember threatening to swipe Mick [an Irishman called Barry Michael] for brushing against me.' Nerves were tattered and the men had scant food during their retreat; their rifles left raw marks on their shoulders. But the instinct to survive seemed to override all else: 'Your feet seemed to move mechanically. Your whole body ached.' The darkness brought the longing for sleep. As McIntyre forced himself on he could feel his senses begin to fade, 'I could hear the feet tramping inside my head, but could feel nothing.'[47] McIntyre and his comrades eventually reached the coast and took refuge in a cave waiting for their evacuation.

Lance Corporal Herbert Longbottom described his exhaustion as he staggered closer to Sfakia: 'When I found it difficult to put one foot in front of the other, the words of the Psalmist came into my mind: "I will lift my eyes to the hills. From whence comes my help? My help comes from the Lord." Soon after I had collapsed on the road in complete exhaustion, but help from the Lord came very quickly in the form of the boot of my friend Tom kicking me in the ribs and forcing me to get up and go! Finally we made it to the top of the track at Imvros, and thankfully made our way down to the shelter of some caves high above the harbour at Sfakia.'[48] After about an hour's sleep, Geoffrey Cox and his men decided to carry on their journey. About a mile from Sfakia, Cox was met by a tense looking officer with his hand on his revolver. He told Cox that only formed units would be allowed into Sfakia and certainly no individuals during daylight hours. The officer went as far as to threaten to arrest Cox as a deserter. After Cox had explained that he was attached to Freyberg's headquarters, the officer sent him in the direction of Wadi. Eventually Cox found a truck and drove it to Imvros, a village at the southern exit from the Askifou Plain. There he met Brigadier Vasey, a tall Australian with a nasal voice: 'his conversation liberally sprinkled with "bloody"'. After showing Cox Germans advancing through a pair of binoculars he said: 'Tell your General we can hold the bastards for at least twenty-four hours.' Cox managed to reach Freyberg and Puttick that night. On meeting Cox, Puttick said: 'We did our best. We did all we could.' As night fell calls could be heard from those unable to keep up with their comrades. The wounded could be heard shouting: 'Christ, where's the beach, where's the beach?' as they staggered towards the shore. [49]

As Peter Wildey eventually reached Sfakia he noticed a commotion. He soon realised that German troops were coming through a deep ravine below them. 'This was serious, so we opened up on them with the Tommy gun. It was a bit out of range to be very effective, but you could shoot down on them all right.' After a brief engagement, Wildey went to find the headquarters. 'I went in, and Brigadier Hargest was in there, looking absolutely haggard and exhausted. I told him the situation and he said, "You go back up there and make sure everybody keeps them pinned down . . . leave it to me. I'll do something about it." Which he did, because later on I could see a platoon of troops moving on either side of the ravine . . . encircling where these Germans were.'[50] The platoon was led by Charlie Upham. One of his men was held by the ankles over the brow of a hill to fire a Bren gun, with great effect; at the end of the fighting thirty-nine Germans lay dead.

The remnants of the troops on Crete reached the Askifou Plain on 29 May, and the evacuation began the following night. Freyberg had set up a new headquarters in a cave near the bottom of the Imbros Gorge. Weston had organised a rearguard blocking the road at the northern approaches to the plain. In the afternoon the Australians and Royal Marines at Komitades established a new blocking position. Freyberg and the remaining staff were taken off the island in flying boats. Freyberg had stayed in Greece to the last to make sure that his men had been evacuated safely. In Crete, it was essential that he returned to Egypt because he was ULTRA indoctrinated, and also there was nothing to be gained from giving the enemy an unnecessary propaganda coup by allowing senior officers to be captured.

After the damage suffered during the evacuation at Heraklion, the Commander-in-Chief of staff was concerned over the loss of ships from the Mediterranean Fleet. The prospect of sustaining further losses through the evacuation of troops from Crete was in their opinion inconceivable. The Commander-in-Chief of staff advised Cunningham that the evacuation of troops from Crete should be abandoned. Further losses to the Mediterranean Fleet would leave Britain extremely vulnerable in the region. After some contemplation Cunningham replied: 'Gentlemen, it will take three years to build a new warship; it takes three hundred to build a tradition. The evacuation will continue.'[51] During the first two nights nearly 8,000 men were taken off. On the third night most of 5th Brigade were taken off. The troops on the beach had expected a sustained air attack but instead they found that the skies were empty. The 27 May was the last day of heavy air attack as the VIII Air Corps were withdrawn to prepare for BARBAROSSA. On 29 May the largest evacuation took place; over 6,000 men were embarked on the troopship HMS *Glengyle*, and the cruisers *Perth*, *Calcutta* and *Coventry*. A New Zealand officer described a welcome sound of 'Navy voices in cultured Dartmouth accents', shouting in the darkness 'Come on, Come on! Get a move on! Get a move on!'[52] Among those embarked on the *Perth* were Theodore Stephanides and Michael Forrester. The *Perth* was attacked on 30 May, and Michael Forrester formed the opinion that it was much better on land than it was at sea.

The combat units remained intact but the stragglers hindered their progress, desperate to reach the sea. Streams of them had broken prematurely from their positions; the word had got out that the evacuation would take place from the port of Sfakia on the south coast. A New Zealand soldier recalled that on the way down to the beach 'you kept your hand on the man in front of you, so that stragglers could not break in between you'.[53] There was a register of the troops that was read out if any extra men were in the line, then they were simply cut off. The system was designed to save the fighting troops first. However, the system discriminated against gunners and service troops who had fought as hard as the infantry. The New Zealanders had formed a cordon ensuring that fighting troops were taken off the island first. Private Noel Morris from 18th Battalion recalled that he was ordered to form 'a cordon around the beach, with fixed bayonets, and allow through only those units that were under command. There were a few ugly incidents when individual soldiers endeavoured to break the cordon.'[54] Private Ted Martin-Smith formed part of the cordon: 'We were there with fixed bayonets, our battalion, all the way around – not to keep the Germans out, to keep our own blokes out. It was a hurtful thing that, standing there. People did try and break the line. But that's how Crete ended up, and it's something that sticks in my throat.'[55] Kippenberger described the scene as he passed through the men waiting on the beach. 'Some begged and implored, most simply watched stonily, so that we felt bitterly ashamed.'[56]

As darkness fell the destroyers *Napier, Nizam, Kelvin* and *Kandahar* arrived off Sfakia. It was hoped that they had brought much needed rations; unfortunately the majority of the supplies consisted of matches and flour. The destroyers lay offshore for around five hours and were able to embark around 1,000 men. Once on board the ships, men were handed hot cups of cocoa and bully beef sandwiches. The troops found it hard to contain their gratitude and slapped sailors on the back and shook their hands enthusiastically. The evacuated troops welcomed the discipline and order of life at sea, in contrast to the chaos and filth of the retreat. In a raid on the *Napier*, Kippenberger was below deck shaving when a bomb exploded alongside, damaging the engine. Kippenberger recalled 'a stunning concussion . . . everything loose in the cabin crashed all ways, and I found myself sitting on the floor in darkness.'[57] The *Napier* lay dead in the water before they were able to get moving again, but the Luftwaffe did not renew their attack and she crawled to Alexandria on one engine.

On 30 May Cunningham had informed the Admiralty that he was to halt the evacuation to prevent further losses to the Mediterranean Fleet. Cunningham was left with the unenviable task of carrying out the dark reckoning that weighed the losses in crew and shipping against the lives of the men trapped on Crete. He came to the conclusion that a flotilla of vessels under Admiral King would make the final voyage to Crete. On the island Weston and Hargest had been organising their rearguard defences for the evacuation that night. Wavell had sent a message stating that Admiral King's ships would be the last to evacuate the island; any troops remaining after they were filled would be left behind. Weston was shocked by the news and stated in his reply that he was expecting to hold the beachhead for a further three nights and that the 9,000 men remaining on the island had 'every hope' of escaping during the night of 1 June. In London Churchill received the news with predictable dismay. He immediately telephoned the Vice-Chief of Naval Staff and protested. Subsequently, Cunningham came under pressure from the Admiralty, but he stood by his decision. In his dispatch regarding operations in Crete, Cunningham wrote: 'It is not easy to convey how heavy was the strain that men and ships sustained.' The Mediterranean Fleet had suffered almost 2,000 killed in actions around Crete, without the consolation of being able to inflict losses on the enemy. The role of a seaman in the fleet around Crete was essentially one of endurance. Cunningham concluded: 'I felt that the stage had been reached when no more could be asked of officers and men.'[58] The evidence illustrates that Cunningham was not being melodramatic; several of the crew had shown signs that some were finding the strain intolerable. In some instances men had jumped overboard rather than leave Alexandria.

Weston's priority was to embark the Australians who had formed the rearguard for the other troops to escape, and after them would be Laycock's commandos, with the stragglers last. On 30 May Freyberg told Laycock: 'You were the last to come so you will be the last to go.'[59] This effectively meant that Laycock, as the senior officer remaining on Crete, would be forced to capitulate to the Germans the following day. Laycock managed to persuade Weston that his men should be evacuated despite being the last to arrive on Crete and seeing least of the fighting. There is no question of cowardice on Laycock's or Waugh's part; their courage was unquestionable; Beevor stated that Waugh had demonstrated a virtual death wish, although he was terrified of being captured. Laycock had argued that commandos were not suitable for fighting a rearguard action. Yet they had been given the task as they were the only fresh troops available on the island, and this was a poor excuse for disregarding orders.

General Weston dictated the surrender in the form of a short operational instruction. He stated: 'Well gentlemen, there are one million drachmae in that suitcase, there's a bottle of gin in the corner, goodbye and good luck.' Weston flew off the island by flying boat. Graham from

Layforce was left staring at 'the miserable little piece of paper'.[60] Laycock and Waugh soon arrived at Sfakia and ordered Layforce personnel down to the beach to join the queue for landing craft.

At 23.20 a powerful convoy of ships arrived at Sfakia, the troopship *Glengyle*, the cruisers *Phoebe* and *Perth*, with the destroyers *Jarvis*, *Janus* and *Hasty*. The beach was swarming with stragglers desperate for a chance to escape. Word had got out that this was to be their last chance. Some 3,710 troops embarked on King's ships and they set sail at 03.00 on 1 June. As the ships approached Alexandria, the *Coventry* and *Calcutta* were sent out to give them added anti-aircraft protection. Just after 09.00 they were attacked and the *Calcutta* was sunk. King's convoy however reached Alexandria unscathed.

Over 6,500 men were left frustrated on the shores of Crete. A far higher proportion of officers than troops had got safely off the island. Jack Hamson, a prisoner of war in Crete, noted that one of the 'worst episodes' in Crete was the 'notion that superior officers were specially valuable, that there was an obligation upon them to save themselves.' Hamson highlighted that the naval tradition was more admirable, which dictated that 'the commander is the last person to be saved out of the catastrophe', although Hamson noted: 'There were some honourable exceptions, much too conspicuous in their rarity.' Hamson described the evacuation as a 'damnable and disgraceful scramble for priority, a claim to the privilege of escape based on rank and seniority'.[61] This included the members of Layforce. Waugh of Layforce claimed that officers had acted disgracefully in Crete, many taking places in motor transports and leaving the wounded to walk. Laycock himself stated: 'I attribute the fact that so many were left behind to bad beach organisation.'[62] But perhaps the worst injustice was the denial of escape to the remainder of the Greek army who continued to fight in the mountains rather than surrender.

Among those left on the beach included a section of Vasey's troops who formed the rearguard and were blocked on their way down from the upper plateau by hordes of stragglers, unaware that the men of Layforce had slipped past them. These men were from the 2/7th Australian Battalion under Colonel Walker, only sixteen of whom had managed to embark. As the sun rose Walker's men reported that disorganised men on the beach were flying white flags and asked for permission to shoot them, but Walker refused; he knew that surrender was their only option. Men were advised to display as much white cloth as possible. Most wandered off in search of food; a group of Australians slaughtered a donkey and began to roast it on a fire.

Everywhere was still and quiet; many did not know that the last chance of evacuation was gone. On hearing the news that the evacuation had ended, men collapsed with despair; others cursed in anger. Walker had met Colonel Colvin and had established that he was senior to him;

therefore the dubious responsibility of surrendering lay with Walker. Walker trudged his way up to the top of the pass and made his formal surrender to an Austrian. After the surrender had taken place, German planes strafed the Australians' position, killing two men and wounding many others. Three Germans who tried to stop the attack by waving at the planes were also killed.

During the evacuation the Mediterranean Fleet had once again suffered great losses. Three cruisers and six destroyers were sunk, and two battleships, a cruiser, two destroyers and an aircraft carrier damaged. Cunningham observed that such losses would normally occur during a major naval encounter in which the enemy would normally expect to incur greater losses. It was estimated by the US military attaché that seventy-five percent of the battle fleet's effectiveness was lost in Crete. The RAF had suffered the loss of forty-seven aircraft.

NOTES

1   Stewart, Ian, *The Struggle for Crete 20 May–1 June*, London: OUP, 1991, p.406.
2   MacDonald, Callum, *The Lost Battle – Crete 1941*, London: Macmillan, 1993, p. 271.
3   Stewart, op. cit., p. 407.
4   Ibid, p. 411.
5   Ibid.
6   Ibid, p. 414.
7   Ibid, p. 416.
8   Ibid, p. 425.
9   Hutching, Megan (ed.), *A Unique Sort of Battle. New Zealanders Remember Crete*, Auckland: HarperCollins, 2001, p. 128.
10 Ibid, p. 129.
11 Stewart, op. cit., p. 421.
12 MacDonald, op. cit., p. 274.
13 Churchill, Winston, *The Second World War*, Vol. III, London: Cassell, 1950, p. 262.
14 Clark, Alan, *The Fall of Crete*, London: Cassell, 1962, p. 170.
15 MacDonald, op. cit., p. 264.
16 Clark, op. cit., p. 173.
17 Stewart, op. cit., p. 447.
18 Beevor, Antony, *Crete – The Battle and the Resistance*, London: John Murray, 1991, p. 207.
19 Cunningham, A, *A Sailor's Odyssey*, London: Hutchinson, 1951, p. 380.
20 Stewart, op. cit., p. 449.
21 Ibid.
22 Cunningham, op. cit., p. 384.
23 MacDonald, op. cit., p. 276.
24 Long, Gavin, *Australian War History: Greece, Crete and Syria*, Canberra, 1953, p. 274.
25 MacDonald, op. cit., p. 277.
26 Beevor, op. cit., p. 212.
27 MacDonald, op. cit., p. 280.

28   Long, op. cit., p. 274.
29   Beevor, op. cit., p. 200.
30   Ibid, p. 206.
31   Cox, Geoffrey, *A Tale of Two Battles*, London: William Kimber, 1987, p. 96.
32   Beevor, op. cit., p. 205.
33   Hutching, op. cit., p. 129.
34   Stephanides, Theodore, *Climax in Crete*, London: Faber & Faber, 1946, pp. 113–20.
35   Ibid, p. 122.
36   Buckey, Christopher, *Greece and Crete 1941*, London, HMSO, 1952, p. 271.
37   Hutching, op. cit., p. 124.
38   Stephanides, op. cit., pp. 113–20.
39   Ibid.
40   Beevor, op. cit., p. 205.
41   Hutching, op. cit., p. 70.
42   Delaney, N, interviewed by Megan Hutching, 30 November 2000, Tape One, Side B, Alexander Turnbull Library, National Library of New Zealand.
43   Cox, op. cit., p. 97.
44   Ibid.
45   Buckley, op. cit., p. 271.
46   Ibid.
47   Ibid, p. 272.
48   Hutching, op. cit., p. 150.
49   Cox, op. cit., pp. 103–5.
50   Hutching, op. cit., p. 150.
51   Beevor, op. cit., p. 217.
52   Ibid.
53   MacDonald, op. cit., p. 288.
54   Hutching, op. cit., p. 163.
55   Ibid, p. 186.
56   Beevor, op. cit., p. 216.
57   MacDonald, op. cit., p. 290.
58   Stewart, op. cit., p. 465.
59   Beevor, op. cit., p. 219.
60   Ibid, p. 220.
61   Ibid, p. 218.
62   Laycock, PRO DEFE 2/699.

Epilogue

For the men stranded on the island the trek across the mountains had been in vain. Norm Delaney of 27 Battalion was one of those who did not make it to Sfakia. He was on his descent from the mountains when he was told: 'Well, you can all surrender now, because there are no more boats going.'[1] The prisoners of war faced yet another long haul across the mountains to their holding camp, which was based on the site of the 7th General Hospital. In total the Germans had taken 11,835 British and Commonwealth troops captive. Conditions in the prison camps were awful; food and water was scarce and the lack of sanitation meant that dysentery was rife. There were no proper latrines and many of the dead still filled nearby olive groves and ditches, which attracted swarms of flies and caused an unbearable stench. German firing squads added to the dead bodies by regularly executing groups of Cretans in the vicinity. Rations consisted of three biscuits and a little porridge, which later improved to local beans with a little bully beef. Under these conditions approximately fifty troops died of malnutrition and sickness, although the condition of the men was helped a little by the fact that they could keep themselves clean in the sea.

The German guards wandered through the camps on the look-out for gold rings and watches, which they would swap for cigarettes or food. Prison camp conditions were poor due to the German captors' apathy; many of the guards preferred to sunbathe than pay to attention to their captives. The lethargy of the German guards at least gave the Commonwealth prisoners some respite to search for food. Colin Burn from 18 Battalion noted that 'The wire netting wasn't that effective', so the prisoners would escape during the night and search for food. On one occasion a guard who spoke good English remarked to Burn and his colleagues: '"Your friends have plenty of grapes this morning." [Burn replied] " What do you mean, plenty of grapes? You don't give us any bloody grapes." [The guard] said, " My comrade and I were on duty last night, and we were sitting underneath a tree just back from the road, and we counted sixty who went through the fence. But you can't go anywhere, very few of you will ever escape. About the same number came back in . . . so we're not worried." He thought it was amusing.'[2]

The Germans sent out burial and working parties, which buried the dead and set about menial tasks such as repairing roads. Prisoners tried to avoid these at all costs, burying the dead was a very unpleasant task, as the bodies were black and bloated after being baked in the sun. By the end of the summer, the majority of the prisoners were transferred via Greece through to permanent camps in Poland. However, around 800 men were retained in Crete to work for the Germans clearing the wreckage at Maleme airfield, which was a clear breach of the Geneva Convention. Burn reflected: 'Looking back, when you think about what happens today, they should have had psychologists or someone to counsel us . . . There were a lot of chaps who came back who were very sick. [I would] wake up in a bit of a cold sweat and perhaps be back in a work party or somewhere, but not very often. I soon threw it off. A lot of it's in your mental attitude, because there's no doubt about it, chaps were going mad in the POW camps . . . POW life taught you to be more tolerant towards other people . . . You had to be . . . otherwise you'd have never survived.'[3]

The seriously wounded men were flown to Athens for treatment in military hospitals. Sandy Thomas, who was injured at Galatas, was flown to Athens, and despite the gangrenous nature of his wound, his leg was saved. As Roy Farran lay on a stretcher, debilitated with a gangrenous knee waiting for his flight to Athens, he witnessed the nature of the relationship between the Germans and Italians. Farran recalled how the recently liberated Italians took great pleasure in taunting the wounded British; one Italian had approached Farran and spat in his face. A German sentry who had witnessed the incident proceeded to 'give the Italian one of the most severe beatings I have ever seen administered in the whole of my life'.[4]

On 28 May the Cretan guerrilla Satanas received news that a large Italian force had landed in the east of the island. Mussolini had waited until the result of a German victory was beyond doubt before he had committed his troops to the fray. In one last attempt to claim a victory, the Duce boasted that his troops had burst their way through heavy resistance to join their German allies at Heraklion on 30 May. In fact the Italians had faced no resistance and their presence made no difference to the outcome of the battle. The Germans controlled the main area of Crete in the west in conjunction with an Italian contingent of the Siena Division to the east. The arrival of Italian troops on the island heightened tension between the Axis partners. On one occasion an Italian threw a grenade among a group of Germans, killing one and wounding two others. The Italian authorities arrested the offender briefly but then released him, to the fury of the Germans.

Not all of the remnants of Freyberg's army accepted their fate as prisoners of war; many of those on the beach ran into the hills before the surrender had been issued. Also troops who were captured endeavoured to escape from their prison compounds. Over 300 men were rescued from the island by submarine in the following year. Initially life on the run was pleasant in the Mediterranean summer, but as the winter drew in men were exposed in the mountains, food became harder to come by and clothes turned to rags. Norm Delaney, who escaped from a prison camp in the Canea area, recalled that they survived largely on food and charity from the locals: 'If they didn't [give food], there was a good reason – there were Germans about and they were afraid, or they'd been instructed by their husbands: don't feed anyone. But their husbands would probably give us something. We'd shift on because you got too well known in an area and it was bad for the Greeks. If they were caught helping us, they would have been shot or imprisoned. However, they did feed us and gave us clothes and shelter. How [could we] repay them for their kindness and bravery?'[5] Many of the fugitives lived with Cretan families at great risk; Germans executed entire families for harbouring fugitives. Another escapee, Terance Moore, noted: 'The Cretans risked their lives for us, plus their families'; you name it, we owe our lives to them.'[6]

German firing squads were formed by the paratroops before the arrival of the Nazis' trained executioners, the infamous SS. Terance Moore befriended a German guard after being captured at Sfakia. The guard advised Moore that he was to be transported to the fatherland. 'He told me that . . . Hitler Youth were taking us over, and to be careful. It was then that I decided to escape.'[7] Others did not contemplate escaping, as they were aware of the consequences for the Cretan families who harboured fugitives. Gestapo and SS squads that appeared on the island carried out raids to expose villages that harboured escapees. The Cretans continued to pay a high cost for their continued resistance against the occupation of their homeland. The arrival of the SS saw the systematic torture and killing of hundreds of Cretans. During the entire German occupation 3,474 Cretans were killed by Nazi firing squads. After the war the British Prime Minister expressed his gratitude to Cretan civilians whom he referred to as 'those unknown friends'. The name of 'Churchill' became a talisman of hope to the prisoners of war and civilians alike in occupied countries throughout Europe.

From the moment of the arrival of the German troops they found that they could not hide from the Cretans. Danger lurked in various places behind olive trees, rocks and houses. In the homes of local Cretans pictures of their forefathers with pistols and daggers hanging from their belts, served to remind Germans and Cretans alike that men of the Cretan tradition should bear arms. During the years preceding Crete, the Germans had not experienced such fanatical hostility against them; as the Wehrmacht tore through Europe they had experienced only cowed submission. In the face of such resistance, the Germans inevitably began to vent their anger.

255

On 23 May the 5th Mountain Division issued a notice to their troops: 'The murder of a German airman on 22 May has proved that the Greek population . . . is taking part in the fighting.' Orders were given that any Cretan caught with a firearm was to be shot immediately. The notice continued in an ominous tone that would soon become familiar throughout Europe. 'Hostages are to be taken from the villages. [The villagers] are to be informed that 10 Greeks will die for every German.'[8] Goering endorsed the brutal methods employed by the Nazis, who advocated the severest retribution including the total destruction of villages and in some instances the execution of all Cretan males in the village. The majority of the Cretans found guilty of crimes against the Germans did not face a military tribunal. Student also appeared to support the harsh methods employed, stating that legal formalities were not required 'to judge beasts and assassins'.[9]

A New Zealand sergeant described a typical trial, after he was caught with a Cretan who was arranging for him to be evacuated by submarine. 'We were locked in a cell, but each morning the guard took us down to the sea for a swim, gave us something to eat, then took us back to the cell. Then came the day of the interrogation. [The] Greek was taken first and, as they were taking him past us, he made signs not to say he was feeding us . . . He hardly got out the door when there was a shot. We did not see it, but knew what had happened. Our guard made signs they would not shoot us . . . Eventually it was our turn to go down into the room, one at a time. There were two long tables . . . [and] twelve judges in all, we had to go up to the centre where they would shout at us in different languages.'[10] The judges repeatedly threatened the captives saying that they would be charged as spies and shot. However, eventually, the men were taken from the interrogation rooms through the execution area and finally returned to their prison camp in Canea.

On 3 June the Germans sought savage retribution for a group of sixteen mountain troops who were ambushed and killed by Cretan partisans in Paleochora. The nearby town of Kandanos was sectioned off, and all the inhabitants of the village were killed, including domestic animals. This reprisal had claimed the lives of around 180 villagers, the majority of whom were elderly. The village itself was burned to the ground and it was reported that a woman of 84 was thrown alive into her burning house. After this act of savagery, the Germans erected a sign in Greek and German explaining that the action was taken in retaliation for the murder of German troops in the area on 23 May. The bottom of the sign read: 'Kandanos was destroyed on 3-6-41. It will never be rebuilt.'[11]

Two days before the destruction of Kandanos, two German soldiers were found dead near the village of Kondomari in the Maleme area. The next morning four trucks full of paratroops arrived at the scene, led by Lieutenant Trebes. Trebes lined the occupants of the village up in the square and gave them an hour to denounce those responsible for the killings. After the time had elapsed the Germans released the women and children and a group of twenty-one men were taken as hostages. The men were led to the bottom of a hill at the edge of Kondomari and ordered to sit beside the road. As the afternoon wore on the atmosphere became more relaxed and the hostages were even given chocolate and cigarettes by their captors. Some of the hostages had fallen asleep in the midday sun. Suddenly another German truck appeared; a group of paratroops jumped out and fired on the hostages without warning. With this, the onlooking women and children began to throw rocks and scream; as if ashamed of the act they had just perpetrated, the Germans left the scene abruptly without checking the bodies. One man was left alive and later recovered from his injuries. The harsh methods employed by the Germans failed to intimidate the villagers of Kondomari and the village endeavoured to be a source of defiance to the Germans.

The brutal methods employed by the Germans were largely counter-productive and they continued to have security problems throughout the island. George Psychoundakis, who assisted Allied commandos and guerrilla groups, noted in his book *The Cretan Runner*, that on a daily basis: 'we learnt of new burnings and shootings and fear grew inside us but also strengthened the hatred in our souls.' Psychoundakis eloquently wrote: 'Whole villages . . . churches and their schools . . . were burnt and blown up; yet they talked of a New Order. What a monstrosity!' The unjust reprisals perpetrated by the Germans for their fallen brothers, instead of coercing the Cretans into loving them, 'bred hate inside them and armed their spirits with the sharp weapons of future vengeance and liberation'.[12]

Hitler was increasingly worried about the guerrilla activity in Greece, Yugoslavia and Crete. On 29 December 1941 he wrote to Mussolini stressing the importance of destroying 'every nucleus of insurrection or else we run the risk of having to fight a subsidiary war in the Balkans'.[13] At a conference in Hitler's headquarters on 24 September 1943, Field Marshal von Weichs and Admiral Dönitz advocated the evacuation of the island, but the Führer refused to relinquish his hold on Crete. Fears of a British attack through the Balkans became almost an obsession with Hitler. Every month that passed, he felt a growing anxiety about the security of his southern flank and the oil wells at Plöesti. British Special Forces were involved in operations in and around the island to reaffirm Hitler's fears and ensure that he tied down valuable resources securing his prize. A typical operation took place in the spring of 1942 when the Cretan airfields were being used to reinforce German troops in Africa. News of the reinforcements attracted attention from the SAS and SBS who attacked airfields at Heraklion, Maleme and Kastelli. At Kastelli the sabotage operations destroyed five aircraft and over 200 tons of aviation fuel. At Heraklion twenty-one Ju-52s were destroyed. In total the raids had accounted for twenty-six German aircraft and ten German soldiers killed. However, the operation was not without cost to the local population; the following day the Germans executed hostages as a reprisal for the raids.

The resistance on Crete was continued by groups of guerrillas led by British and Commonwealth soldiers. Many of the members of the newly formed Special Operations Executive team appeared on the island to breath life into the insurgence. These men instinctively rejected the conventional military lifestyle and had volunteered for special operations to satisfy a curiosity for adventure and the unpredictable. The lives of the resistance fighters inevitably attracted the attention of writers who have romanticised the role of the outlaw in Crete. In reality, life in the mountains was hard, living rough in caves and stone huts. The wrong cave presented many problems; a large cave would prove too cold, and a small cave would suffocate the occupants with smoke. Food often consisted of what they could scavenge, which meant acorns and chestnuts with long mountain grass soaked in olive oil, or snails collected after rainfall. Occasionally shepherds could provide them with dairy products or rough cuts of meat and offal to roast as kebabs on an open fire. British officers began to learn that to offer to pay for food in the mountains was considered an insult. The Cretan shepherd regarded the mountains as his home and therefore they were his guests. The shepherds often acted as guides through the mountains and were able to deftly hop from rock to rock with the dexterity of a mountain goat. Periodically the shepherds stopped and stood upright on a rock to wait for the rest of their party, watching with amusement as the foreign members of the group stumbled on behind, cursing as they went, twisting ankles and scuffing knees. Whatever hardships the guerrillas had to endure, they were never short of homegrown tobacco or locally brewed raki, which was drunk out of large empty cigarette or salmon tins. Commonwealth troops were often involved in drinking contests with their Cretan counterparts. New Zealander, Sergeant Perkins, was said to have consumed a mammoth three and a half tins of *tsikoudia*, a potent local raki.

British and Cretan humour shared the same sense of the ridiculous which bridged the differences of culture and eased tension during the difficult times. Patrick (Paddy) Leigh Fermor, a member of the Special Operations Executive, had taught George Psychoundakis just one phrase in English: 'I steal grapes every day,'[14] which he made him repeat again and again, much to everyone's amusement. Psychoundakis could pronounce the phrase so well that after he said it, nobody could believe he could speak no other English. The British found constant entertainment in the Cretan capacity for boasting, despite the fact that nobody had doubted their courage, which they had proved without question in fighting against the paratroopers. Theodore Stephanides captured the roguish character of the Cretan guerrilla when he described a meeting with a Cretan during the

258

First World War. The Cretan had proudly professed that he was a brigand; when asked to define the difference between a brigand and a thief the Cretan replied that a common thief in finding a wallet on the floor would simply take it. A brigand would hand it back to the owner before taking it from him face to face.

During the battle for Crete, the guerrilla movement had suffered a couple of major blows; the legendary Pendlebury was dead and Satanas was seriously ill with cancer, soon to die in Heraklion. Despite the loss of Pendlebury and Satanas, new leaders began to emerge. One of the most remarkable guerrilla leaders was Sergeant Dudley Perkins, known to the British as 'Kiwi' and to the Cretans as 'Vasili'. Perkins had escaped the island from a prison camp at Galatas only to return to Crete to lead a very effective guerrilla force. Perkins landed near Koustoyérako in July 1943, where he formed a band of guerrillas around 120 strong. Perkins arranged drops of supplies and arms from Allied planes with which he proceeded to augment his group.

After a series of skirmishes and ambushes, the fighting culminated in a battle at Akhlada on 18 October. Perkins and his men attacked a patrol of nineteen Germans and three Italians near some stone huts in Akhlada, a small plain in the mountains above Koustoyérako. As the German patrol came under fire they immediately sought refuge in the huts. While his men trained their guns on the entrances of the stone huts, Perkins slipped from hut to hut rolling a grenade into each as he went. Ten Germans were killed outright and the remainder of the patrol taken prisoner. Perkins was wounded in the attack; a bullet had struck him in the neck and travelled down his back, where it lodged in his shoulder blade. The survivors were unable to be taken prisoner and sent to Egypt, as the Germans would seal off the area shortly after the attack. Perkins' band drew lots to determine who would be the one to eliminate them. The unwanted task fell to Antoni Paterakis who tied the prisoners in a line and took them to a pothole in a place named Tafkos. Not being a natural executioner, Paterakis concentrated his mind on the ruthless efficiency shown by the Germans as they dispatched his fellow Cretans. The intention was to shoot the prisoners and then roll the bodies down the hole without a trace. However, the first German shot staggered backwards and fell into the hole dragging his comrades who were bound to him one by one into the abyss. The hole was over a hundred feet deep, but some of the Germans survived the drop. Paterakis, determined to finish them off, lowered himself down into the pothole on parachute tapes, but they broke and Paterakis also fell. Still alive, albeit debilitated with an injured back, Paterakis was trapped with the surviving Germans. One of the Germans whispered to him: 'And now, Greco, we will die together.'[15]

Despite being injured, Perkins reaffirmed his hero status with the Cretan people by insisting that his colleagues lower him down to finish the job. After being lowered down, Perkins dispatched the remaining Germans and retrieved Paterakis by strapping him to his own injured back. From that moment Perkins was known as the 'unforgettable Vasili'. Paterakis survived his wounds and was evacuated to Cairo for treatment. A Cretan butcher traced the bullet down Perkins' back and removed it with a large Cretan knife. Perkins continued to organise Cretan resistance, during which time he was promoted to the rank of staff sergeant. Perkins' guerrilla activities were cut short at the end of February when his group fell into a German ambush. Perkins, who was in the lead, died instantly; a Cretan colleague was also killed, while two others were wounded and escaped by hurling themselves off a steep cliff. Despite being badly wounded, the remaining Cretan was able to hold off the fifty-strong German patrol for three hours until he was able to escape under the cover of darkness. The Germans buried Perkins' body outside their barracks at Lakkoi. Local Cretans claimed that Perkins had killed 'over 100 Germans single-handed during the occupation ... the last gallant Kiwi killed in Crete. This man is honoured by all Cretans.'[16]

Following military reverses at El Alamein and Stalingrad, German confidence plummeted and many feared an invasion of Greece and Crete by the Allies. Ammunition stocks were increased and the island was reinforced with tanks and motor transport, at a time when the Russian front was in desperate need of them. Bräuer succeeded General Andrae as German commander on Crete. Bräuer was the most humane German commander to take command in Crete, although he made it clear that he would not tolerate resistance activities against his men, or local collaboration with the British. General Bräuer stated: 'We will in the event of an invasion defend Crete to the last man and the last round.'[17] Bräuer's rhetoric did little to raise German spirits. He was keen to play down rumours of atrocities and also endeavoured to impress upon his men the mentality behind the Cretan resistance against German occupation. A British officer wrote of the Germans: 'They know the Cretans hate them.' The Cretans 'are living for the moment to dig up their rifles and say it with bullets'. At the same time he noted that the 'Germans are hurt and puzzled at not being loved, and are constantly asking why?'[18] Psychoundakis wrote: 'They [the Germans] reached to our very bowels.' Psychoundakis described the Germans as 'utter barbarians', who had 'provoked a storm in the soul of a race like the hiss of a poisonous snake about to strike'.[19]

British officer Paddy Leigh Fermor, known to the Cretans as 'Michali', had proved himself an integral part of guerrilla operations in Crete and was keen to capitalise on the vulnerability of German morale. He prepared propaganda literature to play upon the feelings of isolation of the occupying Germans. Leigh Fermor devised an ingenious method of circulating the literature, which was to stamp the paper with swastika insignia along with a message in Greek to return immediately to German soldiers. This ensured that the intended audience would read the messages and at the same time would make the Germans look foolish. A sample of Leigh Fermor's leaflets described the Germans as 'infinitely worse than the Turks . . . You have proved yourself savages, and as such you will be treated. But not yet.' The literature played heavily on German nervousness and paranoia. 'Unseen watchers dog your footsteps. When you eat and when you drink, when you wake and when you sleep.' The leaflet concluded with a menacing threat. 'The long Cretan knife makes no sound when it strikes between the shoulder blades . . . The hour of vengeance is drawing near.'[20]

General Müller succeeded Bräuer as the commander of Crete and proved himself the most hated general of all. He made himself a reputation for extreme brutality and introduced a regime of aggressive patrolling to quash the Cretan resistance in the mountains, but the Germans feared going into the mountains more than the resistance fighters feared their patrols. One Cretan described the moment as he tried the door to deliver some washing water to a German lieutenant billeted in his village. He found the German inside upright in his bed: 'clutching his submachine gun, his eyes popping out of his head.'[21]

As for Germany's Axis partners, the overthrow of Mussolini in July 1943 had effectively ended their significance on Crete. The Duce's downfall prompted jubilation in Italian barracks, black shirts were destroyed and his portrait taken down. General Carta was a friend of the Italian royal family and was not a fascist; his administration on the eastern part of Crete had been humane. When word of the Italian armistice reached the Italian troops, they reacted as if the war was over and drank themselves into oblivion in the naïve hope that they would be allowed to go home. General Müller offered the Italian troops three options: to continue to fight under German command thus showing their allegiance to Mussolini's puppet government; or they could perform non-combatant duties for the Germans on the island. If the first two options were refused they would be imprisoned. The Italians were warned that anyone who sold or destroyed his weapon would be shot. General Carta considered resistance against the Germans but quickly came to the conclusion that it would be futile without a British landing. Carta circulated Müller's order stating that it was 'essential to follow the orders of the German command with a sense of realism'.[22] Tragically, those Italians who refused to work were embarked in a ship which was promptly sunk by an Allied submarine. Paddy Leigh Fermor arranged for Carta's escape to Egypt and on 23 September they were both taken off the island by a Royal Navy motor launch.

Leigh Fermor returned to the island by parachute on 4 February 1944. He had devised a plan to abduct General Müller, who was responsible for much of the cruelty carried out by German forces on the island. Leigh

Fermor's intention was to achieve a significant yet bloodless coup against the Germans that could not justify cruel reprisals against Cretan civilians. The abduction of Müller was designed to halt his reign of tyranny and create a priceless opportunity to reaffirm German fallibility. However, Müller was replaced by General Kreipe before Leigh Fermor could implement his plan. Leigh Fermor's colleague, Captain Bill Moss, noted: 'we supposed that one general was as good a catch as any other.'[23] General Kreipe was their new target, and what followed was an extremely embarrassing episode for the Germans and a propaganda coup for the resistance fighters.

Originally, Leigh Fermor wanted to abduct the general in his villa, but the security proved too strong. After an inspection of Kreipe's villa, they saw the general drive past in his car. In an act of audacious bravado the men waved at Kreipe; as if frozen with astonishment the general reciprocated and waved back. This gave Leigh Fermor the idea of abducting Kreipe in his own car. For three consecutive days, Leigh Fermor and his men stood in wait for Kreipe's car, taking Benzedrine tablets to keep them alert. Leigh Fermor and Bill Moss waited by the road clad in German uniform. When the car arrived, they stepped into the road and Leigh Fermor saluted, before shining a torch on the general and asking for his papers. As the driver began to protest, they wrenched the doors of the car open, Moss coshed the driver and Leigh Fermor handcuffed the general. Captain Moss took the wheel of the car and they drove off towards Heraklion. They proceeded to drive past German sentries, taking advantage of the Germans' automatic respect for authority. Leigh Fermor put his head out of the window and shouted to the German guards to acknowledge the passing of the general. 'The sentry leapt to attention with a bang of his heels and the car was speedily lost in the dark.'[24]

Moss and two Cretans escorted the general across Mount Ida. Meanwhile, Leigh Fermor had taken the car as close as possible to the coast and made footprints in the sand to suggest that they had escaped to sea. Leigh Fermor snapped the pendants off the car for souvenirs and left a note on the windscreen, explaining that the abduction was a legitimate operation initiated from Cairo and therefore no reprisals against the local population could be justified. They also scattered empty tins of English brand cigarettes. Leigh Fermor's attempted deception appeared to have failed as the Germans were out in force searching around Mount Ida for the general. Despite Leigh Fermor's strict instructions for a bloodless operation, his Cretan colleagues had taken the driver to a secluded spot and killed him. They allowed the driver a final look at a picture of his family by dimmed torchlight before his throat was cut.

At dawn Leigh Fermor's group were reunited at Anoyia. The guerrillas constantly moved Kreipe from cave to cave, meticulously planning their movements to be one step ahead of the Germans. Kreipe became increasingly disconsolate; he seemed preoccupied with the loss of his Knight's Cross that had gone missing during the initial struggle. On 7 May the Special Boat Squadron notified Leigh Fermor that a torpedo-boat would be sent to pick up General Kreipe. The torpedo-boat arrived on 14 May to evacuate the general and his escort, and so ended Leigh Fermor's operation that had astounded the world. During his time with the band of guerrillas, Kreipe had witnessed such a large number of armed men, who fearlessly guided him across the island that he mentioned to Leigh Fermor: 'I am beginning to wonder who is occupying the island – us or the English.'[25]

Leigh Fermor had an enforced six months' absence from Crete after leaving the island with General Kreipe. He spent most of the six months in hospital with a paralysing rheumatic fever brought on by living in the harsh conditions of the mountains. For his leadership role in the Kreipe abduction, he was awarded the Distinguished Service Order, which was pinned to his pyjama jacket while he was in hospital. After fully recovering, Leigh Fermor returned to Crete; George Psychoundakis described his return to the island as 'high-spirited'. As Psychoundakis approached a table filled with British officers and Cretans singing and drinking, Leigh Fermor handed him a glass of rum. Psychoundakis protested: 'Mr Michali. It's midday, I haven't eaten anything today, and if I drink that I'll be drunk.' Leigh Fermor replied: 'my child, what is drink meant for? You can't rub it into your scalp or clean your gun with it.' Leigh Fermor added: 'You drink it . . . to make you happy and ready to dance and sing and to forget all your worries.' He concluded: 'in fact, to get drunk, as you say. That's just what it's meant for.' In the company of hardened drinkers of the SOE, who had dubbed their mess in Cairo 'Hangover Hall', Psychoundakis proceeded to gulp down numerous glasses and discovered his severe lack of tolerance for the potent liquor. As the world began to rotate, Psychoundakis began to make his way down towards the centre of the village, whereupon his friend, Manoli Gyparis, seized him as he was threatening to shoot a passing donkey in the head with his pistol. Luckily for the innocent creature, Psychoundakis had already emptied his pistol by randomly firing in the direction of Gyparis, who was able to take cover behind a rock. After the incident Psychoundakis wrote that Leigh Fermor had returned to many 'of his friends in Crete, whom he loved as they did him, there was plenty of reason to drink and celebrate'.[26]

In late August, approximately four months after the general's abduction, German troops embarked on the most serious wave of reprisals against villages in the Amari valley. Many were looted and burnt to the ground. All the males who were found in the area were shot. After the destruction of the villages, the Germans dropped leaflets stating that they had been destroyed as they had harboured the general and his captors.

The Kreipe abduction was criticised for causing unnecessary suffering for the Cretan population, but it seems unlikely that the destruction of the Amari villages was connected with the abduction. The delay of nearly four months between the abduction and so-called German reprisals makes the connection improbable. It is more likely that the Germans had used the abduction of Kreipe as an excuse to launch what was essentially a pre-emptive strike, against possible Cretan insurgence at Amari, in preparation for withdrawing their forces west from Heraklion. George Psychoundakis stated that the Germans were 'making ready to evacuate the whole of Crete'. The Germans were determined to launch the campaign of terror against the villages as a precautionary measure against bands of guerrillas and the 'Cretan people in general [who] might fall upon them as they withdrew to avenge all the evil they had suffered'.[27]

When the Germans withdrew from Greece in 1944, the garrison on Crete were left isolated and effectively abandoned to their fate. Young Cretans were determined to prove themselves before the war ended. In Halepa, a young shepherd was reported to have shot dead a German officer and stolen his ceremonial dagger as a trophy. In Canea an incident occurred when two Cretan boys attempted to wrestle a Luger from a German officer. During the struggle the German officer was shot and killed. Ironically the officer was a German doctor who was popular among the local community for treating Cretan patients.

Local Cretan forces besieged German troops until May 1945, when Admiral Dönitz ordered the surrender of the island. Ugly scenes erupted in Crete with angry Cretans seeking to take revenge on German troops and their collaborators. With Crete's long history of occupation and revolt, the island's inhabitants have developed an instinctive loathing of traitors. German collaborators could expect only the most unforgiving vengeance. A German conspirator caught by Cretan guerrillas begged for the opportunity to commit suicide as he stood before the edge of a cliff. The guerrillas granted his wish, but not before breaking his legs with heavy rocks some way from the cliff face, forcing him to drag his broken body an agonising distance before he plummeted to his death. In a court in Heraklion, five German informants were tried for betraying members of the Cretan resistance. When only two out of the five prisoners received death sentences, the court was stormed by armed Cretans who dragged the prisoners into the prosecutor's office, before hacking them to death and disposing of the bodies through a window onto a raucous crowd below.

The biggest problem that faced the British now was to prevent vengeful Cretans from attacking the Germans who were concentrated on the west of the island. The German troops remained in possession of some awesome firepower and were deeply fearful of the Cretan population, which constituted an explosive concoction if neglected. Freyberg's intelligence officer, David Hunt, devised a solution to the problem by moving the Germans farther west to the Akrotiri peninsula, where they were guarded by a line of British troops formed across the neck of land. Hunt had witnessed German gliders land at Akrotiri four years previously, and the symmetry was not lost on him. Hunt described the end of the Nazi occupation as 'an agreeable example of the wheel turning full circle'.[28]

For the people of Crete the end of occupation did not signal a release from their suffering. Crete was drawn into the civil war on the mainland and many of the resistance fighters were soon drafted into the Greek army. The civil war in Crete culminated in the defeat of the ELAS in 1948.

Student stated after the battle that 'Crete was the grave of German parachutists'.[29] Between 20 May and 2 June 3,986 Germans were killed and 2,594 wounded in Crete; nearly half of this total were casualties on the first day. Some 1,653 of the casualties were paratroopers, 'the flower' of the Third Reich. The loss of a third of Student's fleet, 350 aircraft and including 151 Ju-52 transports, had serious implications for the Nazi war effort. The losses incurred by the German airborne units had rendered the landing on Malta impossible; Hitler turned down Student's proposed operation stating that it would 'cost too many losses. He thought the German airborne troops were too weak for the operation.'[30] Later, when Student received the Iron Cross and Knights Cross at Hitler's head-quarters, congratulations were offered before Hitler reaffirmed his position: 'Of course, you know General, we shall never do another airborne operation.' Hitler continued: 'Crete proved that the days of the parachute troops are over.' The Führer noted that the parachute arm relied entirely on surprise. He concluded: 'In the meantime the surprise factor has exhausted itself.'[31] The irony was that Student was to command the defence of the Arnhem front in the autumn of 1944 when Anglo–American troops attempted an airborne landing with equally disastrous results.

The cost of gaining Crete might have been worthwhile if the strategic plan for attacking British interests in the Mediterranean had been carried out. The airfields on Crete, which had been so fiercely fought over, were used only briefly to send supplies across the Mediterranean to Rommel in 1942. As BARBAROSSA opened in June 1941, Crete became a backwater for German strategy. Hitler had always viewed the significance of the island as a diversion for the invasion of Russia. Goebbels deliberately leaked a rumour to a German paper that the operation in Crete had been a rehearsal for the invasion of England. He then proceeded to recall the entire issue to ensure the maximum coverage by foreign journalists, and a further rumour was spread that the Führer was furious at Goebbels' indiscretion. Goebbels noted in his diary: 'The high command is very pleased by the success of my article. It helps them very considerably.'[32]

The article had caused a stir throughout the world, but it did not fool the British authorities who were kept well informed of the forthcoming Russian offensive through ULTRA decrypts.

Most of Student's paratroopers were sent to Russia as ground troops where an even greater tragedy would unfold. Historians who believed that the fatal delay to BARBAROSSA (leading to the German defeat at Stalingrad) was directly related to the battle of Crete have subsequently reassessed Crete's significance. It is now widely accepted that the delay to BARBAROSSA was caused by adverse weather conditions. BARBAROSSA could not have started on 15 May because Polish and Russian river valleys were still flooded, and partly impassable due to exceptionally heavy rainfall. Beevor maintained that if Crete did have an effect on the Russian campaign, 'it was that German production of transport aircraft never caught up in time for the Stalingrad airlift'.[33] Also, if Crete had not been defended, Student's forces would not have sustained their heavy losses and Germans airborne forces would have been able to move on to Cyprus and Malta. Churchill noted: 'Upwards of five thousand of his bravest men were killed, and the whole structure of this organisation was irretrievably broken.'[34] If the British had been victorious in Crete, they could have drawn resources away from Hitler's Russia campaign by using long-range British fighters to threaten the Plöesti airfields.

Churchill took some comfort from the fact that the enemy had paid dearly for their victory in Crete, but he took the defeat as a personal blow. The succession of defeats in Greece and Crete had an adverse effect on the British public. In a poll taken in October 1941 only 44% described themselves as 'satisfied with the government's conduct of war' against 58% before the Cretan campaign.[35] British and Commonwealth troops suffered 1,742 dead and 1,737 wounded; a further 800 troops were killed, wounded or captured after embarking from Heraklion. Wavell was particularly affected by the fate of his old battalion, the Black Watch, in the evacuation from Heraklion. Sir Miles Lampson wrote of Wavell's disposition: 'I don't think I have ever seen our Archie quite so gloomy.'[36] Freyberg was equally disconsolate; on his return from Crete he learned that his stepson had been killed in the desert. After the battle of Crete, Freyberg met Wavell and his wife. Lady Wavell described her husband's distress; she told Freyberg that in previous battles', 'he could always sleep, but during . . . the Crete campaign he had walked the floor and was unable to rest'.[37]

British prestige had suffered yet another setback. One of Churchill's main objectives was to appeal to American public opinion. David Eccles wrote: 'The reaction of the U.S. to our naval losses round Crete, and of the *Hood* has been very bad.'[38] John Colville, the Prime Minister's private secretary, noted in his diary that Churchill had maintained that no error of judgement had been made in the intervention in Crete. The New

Zealand Prime Minister, Peter Fraser, commented on Churchill's decision to commit Commonwealth troops to the Greek campaign: 'I still think that the decision was right.' Fraser also stated that he was surprised to learn that Freyberg had never considered 'the operation a feasible one, though I pointed out to him his telegrams to us conveyed a contrary impression'.[39] Despite Fraser's positive rhetoric, among the Australian and New Zealand governments there was a growing determination never to let ANZAC forces be dragged into a hopeless conflict by the British again. Fraser later reported to his government that in no case 'must we again allow our . . . troops to be exposed . . . to meet a highly mechanised attack armed solely with their rifles and courage'.[40]

On 13 June 1941 Brigadier Inglis visited Downing Street for a conference with the Prime Minister. Churchill described his talks with Inglis as a 'shocking account' of the preparation of troops in Crete. Subsequently, Churchill wrote to General Ismay of the Chiefs of Staff Committee: 'I am far from reassured about the tactical conduct of the defence by General Freyberg', although Churchill qualified this statement by saying 'full allowance must be made for the many deficiencies'[surrounding Crete]. He stated that there was: 'no counter-attack of any kind in the Western sector until more than 36 hours after the airborne descent had begun.' He also noted that there 'was no attempt to obstruct the Maleme airfield: although General Freyberg knew he would have no air [support] in the battle.' The defence of Crete was made up of 'static defence positions, instead of the rapid extirpation at all costs of the airborne landing parties'.[41] The Prime Minister concluded by highlighting the need for a detailed inquiry into the defence of Crete.

Inglis' 'disloyalty' haunted Freyberg for the rest of his days, especially as his openly candid criticisms of Freyberg were published. Hargest was also vocal in his criticism of his general, and made his feelings known to the New Zealand Prime Minister before Freyberg could put forward his case. Hargest's criticism was somewhat hypocritical as he was probably one of the most culpable of Freyberg's commanders. It was Hargest who failed to utilise his reserves to assist Andrew at Maleme airfield on the first day. During the battle, apart from misreading the ULTRA signal regarding the seaborne invasion, the most serious errors of judgement were made by Freyberg's subordinates. One of Freyberg's most admirable qualities was that he refused to apportion blame to others. Freyberg typically stated: 'It was certainly not the fault of the troops. [They were] not beaten by ordinary conditions, but by the great aerial concentration against us.'[42] Paul Freyberg described his father as being in the 'Prime Ministerial doghouse' and for twelve months there was no communication between them. The silence was only broken a year later when Freyberg was wounded at Minqar Qaim, whereupon Churchill sent an affectionate telegram to him, and any apparent rift was mended. When

267

Churchill was writing his third volume of his history of the Second World War *The Grand Alliance*, he was in contact with Freyberg and the general took the opportunity to enlighten Churchill on aspects of the battle that he had not appreciated.

From a soldier's perspective, New Zealander Lance Corporal Allan Robinson defended his general: 'If there was anyone to blame, I'd say it was Churchill for putting us in this invidious position. We didn't have enough equipment, we couldn't get any reinforcements, our supply line was very long, we couldn't get many supplies in, whereas the Germans, they had the air force, they had everything. It was the conditions. We had very little ammunition. We couldn't have done any more than we did. We were ill-prepared against a superior force. This was the first action that the New Zealand Division as a whole had been in, and we were given an awful hammering all right. The planes, the Stukas, they put the fear of God into you when they're bombing you.'[43] The absence of the RAF was a feature of Crete that stirred strong emotions among those who suffered under the Luftwaffe. Ill-feeling between the RAF and the Army was heightened after the battle of Crete, and airmen and soldiers fought in the bars and streets of Alexandria. Peter Wilkinson of the SOE wrote: 'Everyone was pouring shit all over each other.'[44] Ronald Fletcher from 19 Battalion stated after the war: 'Churchill's idea of holding the German advance was a pipe dream. Unless we got some air support our position was precarious.'[45]

In a speech to the Commons on 10 June 1941, Churchill stated that the 'decision to fight for Crete was taken with the full knowledge that air support would be at a minimum'.[46] Churchill believed that the advantage of ULTRA negated German air supremacy. Sir Harry Hinsley has claimed that ULTRA provided 'all the information required to destroy the German attack on Crete'. Freyberg's command seemed to be blighted by security measures and poor judgement. Hinsley also believes that cryptographers at Bletchley Park 'felt very strongly' that their product 'had not been used properly in Crete.'[47] Churchill declared: 'at no moment in the war was our intelligence more truly and more precisely informed.'[48] All speculation surrounding ULTRA is difficult to assess as the only men who knew the truth died before the security surrounding ULTRA was lifted in 1974.

Major F M Hanson asked for permission to crater the airfield at Maleme but he was denied. Hanson wrote; 'I still feel that a major mistake was made in not making the [Maleme] aerodrome unsuitable for landing planes.' Private Patira Edwards, of the 28 (Maori Battalion), agreed: 'I still think they could have made the aerodrome useless. That's what they should have done if they'd dug big holes on the airport, it would have stopped [the Germans] from coming in and landing.'[49] There was little doubt that the Germans would continue to crash land their transports regardless of the status of the airfields. But it must be said that an operational airfield at Maleme could only be of use to the Germans and was integral to Student's gamble to gain control of the island. The Chiefs of Staff perceived Crete as an opportunity to take the fight to the German war machine: 'nobody had felt that the destruction of the airfields really mattered much.'[50] Freyberg stated that the War Cabinet had taken the decision not to mine the airfields. Paul Freyberg maintains that his father had been prevented from taking any remedial action against German landing plans, presumably due to ULTRA security precautions.

An inter-service committee met in June; significantly it comprised relatively junior officers who were not privy to ULTRA, therefore the inquiry produced largely inaccurate conclusions. The inquiry was critical of Wavell's neglect of the island and the apparent lethargy of the RAF in developing the airfields. Wavell reacted angrily to criticism and demanded the withdrawal of the report. Questions were also raised about the judgement of Freyberg in placing troops beyond the Tavronitis river bed as requested by Puttick, which had been prevented by the security restrictions surrounding ULTRA. Freyberg declared after the war that he regretted the decision not to move the troops. He used a quote from Field Service Regulations that stated: 'It is rarely possible to recover in battle from a faulty deployment.'[51] A second copy of the inter-service committee report was given to commander Laycock who set about revising the document to avoid a breach of the security surrounding ULTRA. The inquiry omitted many of the operational misjudgements made when the battle had started and concentrated on the preparation for the island's defences.

Wavell's biographers have made much of the fact that he had a shortage of equipment. Connell stated: 'Any amount of planning any amount of drive could not have replaced the men who were training or fighting elsewhere.' Or more significantly: 'the guns, the transport and the equipment which did not exist.'[52] Wavell maintained after the battle that 'practically all able bodied men on the island were serving in the Greek forces in Albania'. In his account of the battle for Crete Stewart commented: 'Crete became first a minor garrison area, after that a dumping ground, and at last a battlefield',[53] although he noted that 400,000 patriotic Cretans were willing to fight and their energies could have been utilised without detracting from resources in other theatres. Wavell had taken much of the blame for the predicament of the defences in Crete, but in fact the situation was born from the political decisions surrounding Greece, that stretched inadequate military resources to breaking point. The confusion of counsels that surrounded intervention in Greece served to draw attention from the island of Crete, which was perceived by many as the one realistic prize that could be taken from the Greek expedition.

Churchill admitted in his memoirs that the blame for the preparation of the island would have to be shared between London and Cairo, although he attempted to shift the onus by condemning Wavell. 'The story of Suda

Bay is sad.' Churchill noted: 'how far short was the action taken by Middle East Command of what was ordered and what we all desired!' The Prime Minister did briefly acknowledge Wavell's difficult position by stating that to appreciate the 'limitations of human action, it must be remembered how much was going on in every direction at the same time'. But Churchill was vehement in his criticism and concluded that it 'remains astonishing to me that we failed to make Suda Bay the amphibious citadel of which Crete was the fortress'.[54] Churchill's condemnation of the preparation for the island's defences was obviously directed at Wavell. However, it could be argued that the battle for Crete was lost by tactical errors on the ground for which Wavell had no responsibility. Von der Heydte stated at the end of the first day: 'We came very close to losing ... no paratrooper who fought here, believed up to the fifth day that we would win.'[55]

For the scholars who have studied Crete there remains one central line of inquiry. Why did those in command fail to mount a successful counter-attack at Maleme during the initial period of the battle when the Germans were weak? The line that Andrew fell back on at Maleme was certainly stronger than the precarious position of his various units scattered on the edge of the airfield, but it was denial of the airfields that would ultimately win the battle for Crete, not the static resistance of holding a defensive line. The parachute troops were virtually expended; only by securing the runway could the Germans seriously hope to reinforce their men. Hargest and Puttick were both men of proven bravery and military prowess, but both reacted with a sluggishness that fatally damaged the chances of a successful counter-attack. Andrew had made his decision to withdraw under duress of heavy bombardment; holed up in a slit trench he was partly occupied with his immediate safety with bombs falling around his position. Andrew's decision revealed an uncharacteristic pessimism. In hindsight it is relatively easy for historians to assess military tactics in the 'cold light of day'. It is worth noting the effect of what is often referred to as the 'fog of war'; it is a well versed but significant maxim. Prolonged bombing sapped nervous energy, which induced exhaustion and inhibited rational thinking.

Cox stated that in no other battle during the war 'did one side not only have such complete air supremacy, but was also able to exploit that supremacy so effectively'.[56] Crete was significant in that it proved that an unopposed air force working in close proximity with infantry could paralyse an opponent. Freyberg stated in his report that the Germans' absolute air superiority forced his men to counter-attack during the night, only for the gains to be 'bombed off again as soon as it was daylight'.[57] At Retimo and Heraklion the nature of the close quarters fighting had rendered German air power largely ineffectual, but by 22 May at Maleme, the lines were clearly drawn. From this date the air attacks increased significantly and succeeded in pushing the defenders away from the vital airfield.

The complete domination of the skies by German aircraft was unprecedented and was beyond that which any British or Dominion troops had experienced before; it was a feature that made Crete truly unique. Crete represented the way in which future wars would be fought, with domination of the sky a prerequisite for success. The emergence of airpower was facilitated by the outstanding success of the British attack against the Italian fleet at Taranto in November 1940. The airborne attack inspired one of the most controversial and destructive attacks of the Second World War. Admiral Isoroku Yamamoto of the Japanese navy studied the devastating British attack at Taranto and used it as a blueprint for his own daring attack. Yamamoto observed that the destruction of the Italian fleet was achieved with antiquated biplanes and endeavoured to convince sceptics using Taranto as an example. Yamamoto proceeded to mastermind a plan on a greater scale, using modern aircraft and highly trained aviators, to destroy the US Pacific Fleet in a long-range pre-emptive attack at their main base in Pearl Harbor.

At the end of the war Freyberg was at a dinner party in London, with Admiral Cunningham, Peter Fraser and the Marshal of the Royal Air Force Lord Tedder. After the women had left the table the men remained. Cunningham turned to Freyberg: 'and said fiercely to Freyberg, "I was glad when you lost Crete." "So was I," said Tedder.'[58] The rest of the evening was spent discussing the impossible situation that would have resulted from Crete being successfully held. Paradoxically the Allies used Germany's obligation of occupying Crete to create pressure on Hitler. In 1942 the Joint Planning Staff embarked on a policy to turn the whole of the Mediterranean into a 'heavy liability to Germany', thus compelling the Axis powers 'to lock up increasing forces for the holding down of Italy as well as the defence of all threatened points'.[59]

The guarantee given by Chamberlain and fulfilled by Churchill in Greece came at a time when Britain stood alone and her resources were stretched to breaking point. Britain was desperately in need of allies and therefore compelled by politics and diplomacy to involve herself in Greece and subsequently Crete. During late 1943 Hitler's position mirrored that which Churchill faced in 1940. Hitler's forces were heavily committed and in need of allies; they were at war with both the United States and Russia. Despite the advice of Field Marshal von Weichs and Admiral Dönitz in September 1943, Hitler refused to give up Crete. In a tone reminiscent of Churchill during the inception of the Greek campaign, Hitler replied that he could not: 'order the proposed evacuation of the islands on account of the political repercussions that would necessarily follow'. Hitler stated that the attitude of Germany's allies in the south-west and also Turkey 'is determined exclusively by their confidence in our strength. To abandon the island would create the most adverse unfavourable impression.'[60]

The battle for Crete has an enduring fascination because it came at the lowest point in British fortunes in the Second World War. Britain and the Dominions stood alone, in the face of imminent disaster; neither Russia nor the United States had entered the war. Churchill described the battle as a 'confused, disheartening, and vain struggle.' Less than a month after Crete, Germany had attacked Russia and within six months Japan had bombed Pearl Harbor, and Germany had declared war on the United States of America. American influences saw to it that the focus was drawn away from the Balkans and concentrated on Italy. The Prime Minister concluded that the troops who defended Crete 'may feel that they played a definite part in an event which brought us far-reaching relief at a hinging moment'.[61]

Bert Dyson, a lieutenant from the 4th Field Regiment, when asked why he remembered Crete so well, stated: 'it was such a shocking, violent battle fought virtually with our hands behind our backs. We were young and you couldn't possibly forget it you just couldn't.'[62] Private Denis Sampson from the 6th Field Ambulance concurred: 'I think [Crete] was one of the most intense fighting, concentrated fighting experiences. The intensity of it and the compactness of the situation made a stronger mark on people, I think, than otherwise would have happened.'[63] Allan Robinson stated: '[When I got back to New Zealand] I used to have some nightmares, some yelling and screaming sensations. I couldn't sleep, and I just used to have dreams. I know Mum used to tell me she'd come in, "What's wrong, son? You've been shouting." But I don't have any now, it's all out of my system now . . . I enjoy the company of the fellows who came back from Crete now, because we were a special gang . . . we had some good times, we had some good laughs, we had some bad times – terribly bad times, but that's the story of it. I have no regrets about going there, none whatsoever.'[64] Private Jack Christiansen of the 19th Battalion stated simply that: 'It was a waste of time and lives.'[65] Second Lieutenant Peter Wildey recalled: 'It was the fiercest battle in the war that any of us experienced. Inside a week, we had close on 600 killed, and about 2,000 wounded – every ninth man was killed, and every second man was wounded. It was absolute wholesale slaughter. Both sides were firing at very close quarters, as hard as they could go. That's why we remember it so much. We were a bit bitter that they didn't create a medal for us. The only ones that gave us a medal were the Greeks. We got instruction [from the government] – the Greek medal was not to be worn with the British medals. I say "Blow them!" I put it first. If they told me to take it off, I'd take the others off, because it means more to me than all the rest. '[66] Freyberg's personal assistant, John White, stated that Freyberg was angry with Churchill 'for not sending a message of congratulations for the defence'.[67]

Despite being wounded, yet again, during the battle at El Alamein,

Freyberg went on to serve in North Africa and Italy until the end of the war. He continued to gain the respect of his fellow generals and those under his command remained loyal. Later in the war, Hargest made a spectacular escape from an Italian prisoner of war camp, only to be killed in Normandy. Both Sandy Thomas and Roy Farran recovered from their wounds to escape from their prison camps and play an effective part in the fighting in Europe; Captain Forrester also survived to rejoin his regiment. Kippenberger proceeded to command the New Zealand Division at Monte Cassino until he had both of his feet blown off by a mine. Captain Campbell of 22nd Company and Brigadier Burrows, who was involved in fighting around Maleme, both went on to command brigades by the end of 1945. Major Sandover, who led an Australian battalion at Retimo, also progressed to command a division after escaping from the island. Sandover's senior commander at Retimo, Colonel Campbell, was not as fortunate; he was taken prisoner on the island and remained in German captivity for the next four years; when he was released he was promoted to major-general. Lieutenant Charles Upham was awarded the Victoria Cross for displaying: 'Outstanding leadership, tactical skill and utter indifference to danger.'[68] Upham had excelled in the close quarters fighting around Crete, despite being wounded several times and suffering from acute dysentery. Among his feats, Upham had carried a wounded man to safety on 22 May when his company was forced to withdraw, and on 30 May Upham had repelled an attack at Sfakia, killing twenty-two Germans at close range. On 14 July 1942 Upham received a Bar to his Victoria Cross for gallantry in the Western Desert where he was severely wounded and taken prisoner. Upham was one of only three men to receive a Bar to their Victoria Cross. Paddy Leigh Fermor left Crete on 23 December 1944, just in time to enjoy a final extraordinary Christmas party at Cairo; somebody had crumbled Benzedrine tablets in the stuffing of the turkey to give the party longevity. At the end of the war, Leigh Fermor set off on a journey that he had longed to undertake, to Kalimpong and the Tibetan border. When he returned to England, Leigh Fermor joined a group of fellow SOE members who formed SAARF – Special Allied Airborne Reconnaissance Force.

In 1946 Greece called for the return of German generals for war trials. The first Germans to return were the notoriously brutal Müller, and General Bräuer who was least accountable. Both were sentenced to death. Paddy Leigh Fermor attended the trials with some Greek friends. At the end of the trial, Leigh Fermor's colleagues arranged for him to meet the German generals. When Leigh Femor was introduced to Müller as the man who orchestrated the kidnap of General Kreipe, the German general commented: 'You would not have captured me so easily!'[69] Both Bräuer and Müller were hanged on 20 May 1947, on the sixth anniversary of the beginning of the Battle of Crete. Few protested about the fate of Müller, but Bräuer's execution provoked international disapproval that saved other more culpable generals from his fate. After his capture by the British, Student was charged with a series of war crimes that had been perpetrated by his forces during the Battle of Crete. Student was found guilty of employing British prisoners of war in prohibited work at Maleme aerodrome, and the unlawful killing of prisoners who refused to work. German troops under Student's command were also found guilty of the killing of prisoners from the 3rd Welch Regiment at Galatas. Student was sentenced to five years' imprisonment from which he was released early on medical grounds.

Student admitted in 1952: 'the Battle of Crete carries bitter memories.' Of his own performance Student stated: 'I miscalculated when I suggested this attack, which resulted in the loss of so many valuable parachutists.'[70] Over 5,000 German soldiers who fought in Crete received the Iron Cross. Military historian Liddell-Hart wrote: 'It was one of the most astonishing and boldest feats of the war.' German paratrooper Martin Pöppel wrote: 'But what help are such assessments for our brave comrades who rest there, and whose crosses continue to rebuke us, and to warn?'[71] In 1974 the Germans established a war cemetery on Hill 107 above Maleme. Around Hill 107 a memorial plaque reads: 'In this graveyard rest 4,465 German dead . . . 1941–1945 . . . 3,352 . . . died during the battle of Crete between 20 May and 1 June 1941. Their deaths should always make it our duty to preserve peace amongst nations.'[72] The large black eagle that forms the Parachute Memorial stands against the hillside near Galatas. Unlike other occupied people in Europe the Cretans did not destroy Nazi memorials; they preferred to leave them intact as a symbol to remind future generations.

The British, New Zealand and Australian dead lie in the Commonwealth War Cemetery on the shores of Suda Bay. Crete remains an enduring memory for those who fought there, and each year on 20 May veterans from Australia, New Zealand and the United Kingdom attend Galatas for a memorial service. Now Maleme runway is overgrown with scrub and bushes and Hill 107 is covered with trees. Scars from the battle have largely healed, although bullet holes still mark the bridge over the Tavronitis. The rubble has been cleared from Canea and a resurgent bustle of people has returned to the streets and market places. The strategic position of Crete in the middle of the Mediterranean means that Cretans have endured numerous invaders throughout their existence. The German occupation is a fragment of the infinite history that makes up the fabric of the island. Many of the landmarks of the battle now lie among tourist hotels and beach developments and it appears the island is under an invasion of a different sort as a popular holiday destination.

NOTES

1   Delaney, N, interviewed by Megan Hutching, 30 November 2000, Tape One, Side B, Alexander Turnbull Library, National Library of New Zealand.
2   Hutching, Megan (ed.), *A Unique Sort of Battle. New Zealanders Remember Crete*, Auckland: HarperCollins, 2001, p. 198.
3   Ibid, p. 201.
4   Farran, Roy, *Winged Dagger*, London: Cassell, 1948, p. 10.
5   Delaney, N, interviewed by Megan Hutching, 8 March 2001, Tape Three, Side A.
6   Hutching, op. cit., p. 202.
7   Ibid.
8   Stewart, Ian, *The Struggle for Crete 20 May–1 June*, London: OUP, 1991, p. 316.
9   MacDonald, Callum, *The Lost Battle – Crete 1941*, London: Macmillan, 1993, p. 258.
10 Hutching, op. cit., p. 215.
11 Memorial in the main square at Kandanos.
12 Psychoundakis, George, *The Cretan Runner*, London: John Murray, 1955, pp. 45–9.
13 Ridgway, M B, 'The German campaigns in the Balkans', Department for the Army Pamphlet 20-260, Spring 1941, AG 385 (28 AUG 53), Department of the Army, Washington DC, 17 November 1953.
14 Psychoundakis, op. cit., p. 110.
15 Beevor, Antony, *Crete – The Battle and the Resistance*, London: John Murray, 1991, p. 297.
16 Clark, Alan, *The Fall of Crete*, London: Cassell, 1962, p. 203.
17 Beevor, op. cit., p. 271.
18 Ibid.
19 Psychoundakis, op. cit., p. 45.
20 Beevor, op. cit., p. 274.
21 Ibid, p. 272.
22 Ibid, p. 291.
23 Ibid, p. 303.
24 Psychoundakis, op. cit., p. 265.
25 Ibid, p. 271.
26 Ibid, pp. 303–4.
27 Ibid, p. 286.
28 MacDonald, op. cit., p. 303.
29 Freyberg, Paul, *Bernard Freyberg VC – Soldier of Two Nations*, London: Hodder & Stoughton, 1991, p. 331.
30 Ibid, p. 332.
31 Beevor, op. cit., p. 229.
32 MacDonald, op. cit., p. 302.
33 Beevor, op. cit., p. 230.
34 Churchill, Winston, *The Second World War*, Vol. III, London: Cassell, 1950, p. 268.
35 *News Chronicle*, 23 October 1941.
36 Beevor, op. cit., p. 228.
37 Freyberg, op. cit., p. 313.
38 Beevor, op. cit., p. 228.
39 Freyberg, op. cit., p. 326.
40 MacDonald, op. cit., p. 298.
41 Churchill, Winston, PRO PREM Papers 3/109, 14 June 1941.

42   Stewart, op. cit., p. 453.
43   Hutching, op. cit., p. 161.
44   Beevor, op. cit., p. 228.
45   Hutching, op. cit., p. 251.
46   Freyberg, op. cit., pp. 335–6.
47   Hinsley, Harry, 'The Influence of ULTRA in the Second World War', address to Security Group Seminar, 19 October 1993.
48   Churchill, op. cit., p. 240.
49   Hutching, op. cit., pp. 169–70.
50   Stewart, op. cit., p.135.
51   Freyberg, op. cit., p. 278.
52   Connell, J, *Wavell: Scholar and Soldier*, London: Cassell, 1964, p. 449.
53   Stewart, op. cit., p. 36.
54   Churchill, Winston, *The Second World War*, Vol. II, London: Cassell, 1949, pp. 485–6.
55   MacDonald, op. cit., p. 186.
56   Cox, Geoffrey, *A Tale of Two Battles*, London: William Kimber, 1987, p. 109.
57   Stewart, op. cit., p. 333.
58   Freyberg, op. cit., p. 335.
59   Howard, M, *History of the Second World War: Grand Strategy*, Vol. IV, *August 1942–September 1943*, London: HMSO, 1972, p. 226.
60   Stewart, op. cit., p. 486.
61   Churchill, Vol. III, p. 268.
62   Hutching, op. cit., p. 57.
63   Ibid, p. 139.
64   Ibid, p. 161.
65   Ibid, p. 250.
66   Peter Wildey, interviewed by Megan Hutching, 9 November 2000, Tape Two, Side B, Alexander Turnbull Library, National Library of New Zealand.
67   Sir John White, interviewed by Jock Phillips, 25 January 2001, Tape Two, Side A.
68   *London Gazette*, 26 September 1945.
69   Beevor, op. cit., p. 342.
70   MacDonald, op. cit., p. 301.
71   Pöppel, M, *Heaven and Hell: The Diary of a German Paratrooper*, Staplehurst: Spellmount, 1988, p. 68.
72   Plaque at Maleme War Cemetery.

APPENDIX I

'Ten Commandments of the Parachutist'

1. You are the chosen ones of the German army. You will seek combat and train yourselves to endure any manner of test. To you the battle shall be fulfilment.
2. Cultivate true comradeship, for by the aid of your comrades you will conquer or die.
3. Beware of talking. Be not corruptible. Men act while women chatter. Chatter may bring you to the grave.
4. Be calm and prudent, strong and resolute. Valour and the enthusiasm of an offensive spirit will cause you to prevail in the attack.
5. The most precious thing in the presence of the foe is ammunition. He who shoots uselessly, merely to comfort himself, is a man of straw who merits not the title of parachutist.
6. Never surrender. To you death or victory must be a point of honour.
7. You can triumph only if your weapons are good. See to it that you submit yourself to this law – first my weapons then myself.
8. You must grasp the full purpose of every enterprise, so that if your leader be killed you can fulfil it.
9. Against an open foe fight with chivalry, but to a guerrilla extend no quarter.
10. Keep your eyes wide open. Tune yourself to the topmost pitch. Be as nimble as a greyhound, as tough as leather, as hard as Krupp steel, and so you shall be the German warrior incarnate.

The British and German Order of Battle for Crete

British Order of Battle

CREFORCE HQ

1st Battalion Welch Regiment	Major General Freyberg VC
	Colonel Stewart

Maleme and Galatas

2nd New Zealand Brigade	Major General Puttick
3rd Hussars	Lieutenant Colonel Gentry
4th New Zealand Brigade	Brigadier Inglis
18th New Zealand Battalion	
19th New Zealand Battalion	
1st Troop RA	
5th New Zealand Brigade	Brigadier Hargest
7th Royal Tank Regiment	
21st New Zealand Battalion	
22nd New Zealand Battalion	
23rd New Zealand Battalion	
28th (Maori) Battalion	
1st Greek Regiment	
10th New Zealand Brigade	Colonel Kippenberger
New Zealand Divisional Cavalry	
New Zealand Composite Battalion	
6th Greek Regiment	
8th Greek Regiment	
20th New Zealand Battalion	

Suda

Mobile Naval Base Defence	Major General Weston
Organisation	Lieutenant Colonel Wills
	Captain Morse RN
15th Coastal Defence Regiment	

Anti aircraft and searchlight batteries
Marine Composite Battalion
1st Battalion Rangers
Northumberland Hussars
106th Royal Horse Artillery
16th Australian Infantry Brigade Composite Battalion
17th Australian Infantry Brigade Composite Battalion
'Royal Perivolians' Composite Battalion
2nd Greek Regiment

Georgioupolis
HQ 19th Australian Infantry Brigade   Brigadier Vasey
2/7th Australian Infantry Battalion
2/8th Australian Infantry Battalion

Retimo
2/1st Australian Infantry Battalion
2/11th Australian Infantry Battalion
7th Royal Tank Regiment
4th Greek Regiment
Cretan Gendarmerie

Heraklion
HQ 14th Infantry Brigade   Brigadier Chappel
2nd Battalion Black Watch
2nd Battalion York and Lancaster Regiment
2nd Battalion Leicesters
2/4th Australian Infantry Battalion
7th Medium Regiment Royal Artillery
7th Royal Tank Regiment
3rd Hussars
3rd Greek Regiment
7th Greek Regiment

Timbaki
2nd Battalion Argyll and Sutherland
7th Royal Tank Regiment

Strength
The total strength of Allied troops numbered 42,460, half of which were properly formed infantry. The Suda area had the lowest proportion of armed soldiers, 3,000 out of 15,000. The total also included 3,000 Cretan irregulars.

Losses

Killed and Missing	1,751
Wounded	1,738
Prisoners of War	12,254
Royal Navy	1,828 killed and 183 wounded
Cruisers sunk	*Gloucester, Fiji, Calcutta*
Destroyers sunk	*Juno, Greyhound, Kelly, Kashmir, Imperial, Hereward*
Capital ships damaged	*Warspite, Barham, Valiant, Formidable*
Cruisers damaged	*Ajax, Naiad, Perth, Orion, Dido, Carlisle*
Destroyers damaged	*Kelvin, Nubian, Napier, Ilex, Havoc, Kingston, Nizam*

German Order of Battle

IV Air Fleet	General Löhr

VIII Air Corps   General Freiherr von Richthofen
120 Dornier 17s based at Tatoi
40 Heinkel 111s based at Eleusis
80 Junkers 88s based at Eleusis
150 Junkers 87b Stukas based at Mycenae, Molaoï

XI Air Corps	General Student
	Brigadier Schlemm
	Colonel von Trettner
	Major Reinhardt
Storm Regiment HQ	Brigadier Meindl
	Major Braun
I Battalion	Major Koch
II Battalion	Major Stentzler
III Battalion	Major Scherber
IV Battalion	Captain Gericke
7th Parachute Regiment HQ	Major General Süssmann
	Major Count von Uxküll
Parachute Engineer Battalion	Major Liebach
1st Parachute Regiment	Colonel Bräuer

	Captain Rau
	Captain Count von der Schulenburg
I Battalion	Major Walther
II Battalion	Captain Burckhardt
III Battalion	Major Karl-Lothar Schulz

2nd Parachute Regiment

	Colonel Sturm
	Major Schulz
	Captain Paul
I Battalion	Major Kroh
II Battalion	Captain Schirmer
III Battalion	Captain Wiedemann

3rd Parachute Regiment

	Colonel Heidrich
	Lieutenant Heckel
I Battalion	Captain Freiherr von der Heydte
II Battalion	Major Derpa
III Battalion	Major Heilmann

5th Mountain Division

	Major General Ringel
	Major Haidlen
	Captain Ferchl

95th Mountain Regiment

Mountain Artillery	Lieutenant Colonel Wittmann
Pioneers	Major Schätte
Reconnaissance	Major Count Castell zu Castell

85th Mountain Regiment

	Colonel Krakau
I Battalion	Major Treck
II Battalion	Major Esch
III Battalion	Major Fett

100th Mountain Regiment

	Colonel Utz
I Battalion	Major Schrank
II Battalion	Major Friedmann
III Battalion	Major Ehal

141st Mountain Regiment

	Colonel Jais

Strength

Landed by parachute and glider

Maleme	1,860
Ayia valley and Canea	2,460
Retimo	1,380
Heraklion	2,360

Landed by troop-carrier

Maleme	13,980
Total	22,040

Losses

Killed and missing

Paratroops	3,094
Mountain troops	580
Aircrew	312
Wounded	2,594

Bibliography

Primary Sources

Britain

Hinsley, H, 'The Influence of ULTRA in the Second World War', Address to Security Group Seminar, 19 October 1993

Public Record Office – Kew, London

War Cabinet Files (CAB)

CAB 44/120 The plan for assistance to Greece
CAB 69/2 Defence Committee Operations
CAB 79/23 Chiefs of Staff
CAB 106/511 Greece's campaign against the Axis, Oct. 1940–May 1941
CAB 106/382 The Defence of Retimo – Brigadier Campbell
CAB 106/701 Freyberg's Comments on military history of Greece and Crete

Prime Minister's Office Files (PREM)

PREM 1/323 Mediterranean
PREM 3/2 Policy in Greece and Yugoslavia
PREM 3/109 Crete Nov. 1940/Sept. 1942
PREM 3/308 Importance of Crete

War Office Files (WO)

WO 201/2 Despatch of forces in defence of Greek islands
WO 201/12 Greek and Crete forces in November 1940 and February 1941
WO 201/16 Greece appreciation 27 military conversations
WO 201/121 German Airborne Attack on Crete
WO 201/113 Greece and Crete policy moves May 1941

WO 208/4650 German Atrocities
WO 252/1201 Crete – Strategic assessment of the island
WO 287/164 Notes on the fighting in Crete
WO311/372 Charges against German War Criminals
WO87911/297/49 C-in-C Middle East to War Office, 7 July 1940

New Zealand

Alexander Turnbull National Library of New Zealand – Audio Tape
  Interviews
Peter Wildey interviewed by Megan Hutching, 9 November 2000
Delaney, N, interviewed by Megan Hutching, 30 November 2000 and
8 March 2001
Sir John White interviewed by Jock Phillips, 25 January 2001

United States

Ridgway, M B, 'The German campaigns in the Balkans', Department for the
  Army Pamphlet 20–260, Spring 1941, AG 385 (28 AUG 53),
  Department of the Army, Washington DC, 17 November 1953
Documents on German Foreign Policy, series D, vol. X, Washington DC,
  1957

Secondary Sources
Ansel, W, Hitler and the Middle Sea, Durham NC, 1972
Archer, L, Balkan Journal: An Unofficial Observer in Greece, New York: 1944
'Athenian', The Greek Miracle, London, 1942
Barnett, C (ed.), Hitler's Generals, London: Weidenfeld & Nicolson, 1989
Beevor, A, Crete: The Battle and the Resistance, London: John Murray, 1991
Buckley, C, Greece and Crete 1941, London: HMSO, 1952
Burdick, C and Jacobsen, H A (eds), The Halder War Diaries 1939–1942,
  London, 1988
Butler, J R M, History of the Second World War – Grand Strategy Vol.II,
  London: HMSO, 1950
Carlton, D, Anthony Eden, London: Allen Lane, 1972
Cervi, M, The Hollow Legions. Mussolini's Blunder in Greece 1940–41,
  London: Chatto & Windus, 1972
Churchill, W, The Second World War, Vols I/II/III, London: Cassell,
  1948–50
Clark, A, The Fall of Crete, London: Cassell, 1962
Collier, B, A Short History of the Second World War, London: Collins,
  1967
Connell, J, Wavell Scholar and Soldier to June 1941, London: Cassell, 1964
Cox, G, A Tale of Two Battles, London: William Kimber, 1987

Creveld Van, M, *Hitler's Strategy 1940–1941 The Balkan Clue*, London: CUP, 1973

Cunningham, A, *A Sailor's Odyssey*, London: Hutchinson, 1951

Davin, D M, *Official History of New Zealand, 1939–1945 Crete*, Wellington: 1953

De Guingand, F, *Operation Victory*, London: Hodder & Stoughton, 1947

Farran, R, *Winged Dagger*, London: Cassell, 1948

Flower, D, and Reeves, J (eds), *The War 1939–1945*, London: Cassell, 1960

Foot, M R D, *European Resistance to Nazism*, New York: McGraw Hill, 1977

Freyberg, P, *Bernard Freyberg VC – Soldier of Two Nations*, London: Hodder & Stoughton, 1991

Gerolymatos, A, *Guerilla Warfare and Espionage in Greece 1940–1944*, New York: Pella, 1992

Gilbert, M, *Winston Churchill Vol. VI – Finest Hour 1939–1941*, London: William Heinemann, 1983

Gilbert, M, *Road to Victory – Winston Churchill 1941–1945*, London: William Heinemann, 1986

Harvey, J, *The Diplomatic Diaries of Oliver Hardy*, London: Collins, 1970

Hinsley, H F, *British Intelligence in the Second World War Vol. I*, London: HMSO, 1979

Liddell-Hart, B, *Liddell-Hart's Short History of the Second World War*, London: Cassell, 1970

Long, G, *Australian War History: Greece, Crete and Syria*, Canberra, 1953

Hammerton, J, *The Second Great War*, Vol. 4, London: Waverly, 1950

Howard, M, *History of the Second World War: Grand Strategy*, Vol. IV, *August 1942–September 1943*, London: HMSO, 1972

Howard, M, *The Continental Commitment – The Dilemma of British Defence Policy in the Era of Two World Wars*, Harmondsworth: Penguin, 1972

Hutching, M (ed.), *A Unique Sort of Battle. New Zealanders Remember Crete*, Auckland: HarperCollins, 2001

Ireland, B, *The War in the Mediterranean 1940–1943*, London: Sterling, 1993

James, R R, *Anthony Eden*, London: Weidenfeld & Nicolson, 1986

Johnson, A J, *The Making of a Statesman*, Westport: Coreen Wood Press, 1955

Keegan, J (ed.), *Churchill's Generals*, London: Weidenfeld & Nicolson, 1991

Kiriakopoulos, G C, *Ten Days to Destiny: The Battle for Crete*, New York, 1985

Kitchen, M, *A World in Flames*, London: Longman, 1990

Lawlor, S, *Churchill and the Politics of War 1940–1941*, London: CUP, 1994

Lee, S J, *European Dictatorships 1918–1945*, London: Routledge, 1987

Lukacs, J, *The Duel*, Yale University Press, 2001

Macdonald, C, *The Lost Battle – 1941*, London: Macmillan, 1993

Medlicott, W, *British Foreign Policy since Versailles 1919–1963*, London: Methuen, 1968

Middlemiss, K, *Diplomacy of Illusion – The British Government and Germany 1937–1939*, London: Weidenfeld & Nicolson, 1972

Muggeridge, M, (ed.), *Ciano's Diary 1939–1943*, London, 1947

Neillands, R, *The Desert Rats – 7th Armoured Division 1940–1945*, London: Weidenfeld & Nicolson, 1991

Papagos, A, *The Battle for Greece*, Athens: Alpha Editions, 1949

Pelling, H, *Winston Churchill*, London: Macmillan, 1974

Pöppel, M, *Heaven and Hell: The Diary of a German Paratrooper*, Staplehurst: Spellmount, 1988

Psychoundakis, George, *The Cretan Runner*, London: John Murray, 1955

Robson, M, *Italy, Liberalism and Fascism 1870–1945*, London: Hodder & Stoughton, 1992,

Rhodes-James, R, *Anthony Eden*, London: Weidenfeld & Nicolson, 1986

Sherwood, R E, *The White House Papers of Harry Hopkins VI 1939–1942*, London: Eyre & Spottiswoode, 1948

Simpson, T, *The Battle for Crete*, London: Hodder & Stoughton, 1981

Smart, N, *The National Government 1931–40*, London: Macmillan, 1999

Smurthwaite, D, *Touch and Go, The Battle for Crete 1941*, London: National Army Museum, 1991

Somerville, C, *Our War. How the British Commonwealth Fought the Second World War*, London: Weidenfeld & Nicolson, 1998

Stephanides, T, *Climax in Crete*, London: Faber & Faber, 1946

Stewart, I, *The Struggle for Crete 20 May–1 June*, London: OUP, 1991

Stokesbury, J, *A Short History of World War Two*, London: William Morrow & Co, 1981

Taylor, A J P, *English History 1914–1945*, London: OUP, 1965

Thomas, W B, *Dare to be Free*, Allan Wingate, 1951

Tsoucalis, C, *The Greek Tragedy*, London: 1969

Verney, G, *The Desert Rats – The 7th Armoured Division in World War Two*, London: Greenhall, 1954

Wilmot, C, *The Struggle for Europe*, Wordsworth, 1997 edn

Wiskeman, E, *The Rome–Berlin Axis*, London: OUP, 1949

Young, P, *A Short History of the Second World War 1939–1945*, London: Triling & Co, 1968

Index